# What the Ballad Knows

# The New Cultural History of Music

SERIES EDITOR  Jane F. Fulcher
SERIES BOARD  Celia Applegate
Philip Bohlman
Kate van Orden
Michael P. Steinberg

*Staging the French Revolution:*
*Cultural Politics and the Paris Opera, 1789-1794*
Mark Darlow

*Music, Piety, and Propaganda:*
*The Soundscapes of Counter-Reformation Bavaria*
Alexander J. Fisher

*The Politics of Appropriation:*
*German Romantic Music and the Ancient Greek Legacy*
Jason Geary

*Defining Deutschtum:*
*Political Ideology, German Identity, and Music-Critical Discourse in Liberal Vienna*
David Brodbeck

*Materialities:*
*Books, Readers, and the Chanson in Sixteenth-Century Europe*
Kate van Orden

*Singing the Resurrection:*
*Body, Community, and Belief in Reformation Europe*
Erin Lambert

*Electronic Inspirations:*
*Technologies of the Cold War Musical Avant-Garde*
Jennifer Iverson

*Musical Solidarities:*
*Political Action and Music in Late Twentieth-Century Poland*
Andrea F. Bohlman

*Cultivated by Hand:*
*Amateur Musicians in the Early American Republic*
Glenda Goodman

*Sounding Feminine:*
*Women's Voices in British Musical Culture, 1780–1850*
David Kennerley

*Socialist Laments:*
*Musical Mourning in the German Democratic Republic*
Martha Sprigge

*What the Ballad Knows:*
*The Ballad Genre, Memory Culture, and German Nationalism*
Adrian Daub

# What the Ballad Knows

*The Ballad Genre, Memory Culture, and German Nationalism*

ADRIAN DAUB

Oxford University Press is a department of the University of Oxford. It furthers
the University's objective of excellence in research, scholarship, and education
by publishing worldwide. Oxford is a registered trade mark of Oxford University
Press in the UK and certain other countries.

Published in the United States of America by Oxford University Press
198 Madison Avenue, New York, NY 10016, United States of America.

© Oxford University Press 2022

All rights reserved. No part of this publication may be reproduced, stored in
a retrieval system, or transmitted, in any form or by any means, without the
prior permission in writing of Oxford University Press, or as expressly permitted
by law, by license, or under terms agreed with the appropriate reproduction
rights organization. Inquiries concerning reproduction outside the scope of the
above should be sent to the Rights Department, Oxford University Press, at the
address above.

You must not circulate this work in any other form
and you must impose this same condition on any acquirer.

Library of Congress Cataloging-in-Publication Data
Names: Daub, Adrian, author.
Title: What the ballad knows : the ballad genre, memory culture,
and German nationalism / Adrian Daub.
Description: New York, NY : Oxford University Press, [2022] |
Series: New cultural history of music series | Includes bibliographical references and index.
Identifiers: LCCN 2022000225 | ISBN 9780190885496 (hardback) |
ISBN 9780190885519 (epub)
Subjects: LCSH: Ballads, German—History and criticism. |
National characteristics, German, in literature. | LCGFT: Literary criticism.
Classification: LCC PT581.B3 D38 2022 | DDC 831.009—dc23/eng/20220113
LC record available at https://lccn.loc.gov/2022000225

DOI: 10.1093/oso/9780190885496.001.0001

9 8 7 6 5 4 3 2 1

Printed by Integrated Books International, United States of America

CONTENTS

*Acknowledgments* vii

Introduction: What the Ballad Knows  1

1. The Ballad's Years of Travel: The *Musenalmanach* for 1798, Orality, and the Ballad Form  44

2. The Ballad, the Voice, and the Echoes of War  73

3. Balladic Consciousness: The Ballad on the Opera Stage  104

4. Memorizing Ballads: Pedagogy, Tradition, and the Open Secret  130

5. The Ballad and the Family  154

6. The Ballad and Its Narratives  183

7. The Ballad, the Public, and Gendered Community  211

8. The Ballad and the Sea: Regionalism, Mourning, and the Modern National Imaginary  234

Epilogue: The Ballad as Record  263

*Index*  271

ACKNOWLEDGMENTS

This book has occupied me for the better part of a decade. In the summer of 2012 I was on a train to Dresden when I found myself without a book to read. Unbidden, the ballad "Das Grab im Busento" came to my mind, and I realized I had never thought about the theme of hiddenness in the poem, and about the fact that hidden in plain sight in its midst was a clearly homoerotic portrait of a beautiful youth. A few months earlier, during a conversation with several colleagues—in my mind's eye, Sepp Gumbrecht, Karl-Heinz Bohrer, and Sigrid Weigel are among them, but after all this time I cannot swear to it—we realized we all knew the poem by heart. And now I realized that I'd kept the words safe ever since encountering them in a little Ravensburger volume on the *Völkerwanderung* (Migration Period) as a boy of maybe nine or ten. I'd brought them on my own *Wanderungen*, had grown attached to them as I'd grown more attached to words in general. And had never asked what the poem was actually about. This book originated in that moment—I resolved to take seriously both what was going on under the surface in these poems, and to respect that they were to a considerable extent surface. A pleasure to remember, a pleasure to hear, a pleasure to have move through your mouth. That they were a morsel of childhood and home.

So many have helped the project along in the decade since. Lea Pao's brilliant work on information and poetry was a constant inspiration. Ilinca Iurascu's and Lauren Shizuko Stone's work on German realism and gender helped me hone my sense for forms of poetry I knew well as a reader, but had rarely taught or studied. Denise Gigante and the students of our co-taught graduate seminar allowed me to try out some ideas that would wind up germinal for this book. Colleagues from a wide range of disciplines at the Clayman Institute for Gender Research have enabled and sharpened my thinking. Tom Grey and David Levin helped me think through *The Flying*

*Dutchman* and about Wagner's relationship to popular culture. Alex Rehding and Naomi Waltham-Smith helped me clarify my thinking about music and the category of popularity. Michael Taylor read through drafts of the final manuscript, and Christina Misaki Nikitin read over the final version. I want to thank Norm Hirschy for his calm and thoughtful stewardship of the manuscript, and the brilliant reviewers who spurred me to try to make this book better and better.

Chapter 4 previously appeared as "Platen's Retreat" in *The German Quarterly*, and portions of Chapter 5 were previously published as "The Ballad and Its Families" in *Colloquia Germanica*. This book was supported by a grant from the American Musicological Society, which allowed me to give the topic the level of detail I feel it deserves. My research was supported by the Michelle R. Clayman Institute for Gender Research; by the Division of Literatures, Languages, and Cultures; and by the Stanford Humanities Center. I want to thank all these publications and institutions for their assistance.

I would like to dedicate this book to a great many people up and down my family tree: To my grandmother who was an inexhaustible fount of literary parodies, to the point that I still encounter poems and realize that she'd taught me some foul-mouthed persiflage of them decades ago. To my mother and father who still hold on to works memorized a long time ago—from my father's Latin recitations owed entirely, it seems, to the consequences of truancy in Latin class to my mother's Shakespeare fondly remembered from her one magical year as a fourteen-year-old in the United States. And to my daughter to whom I recited "Das Grab im Busento" on her third night on this earth.

# | Introduction

*What the Ballad Knows*

The Sporthalle in Cologne is not the sort of place one would think has a role to play in the history of poetry. Before it was torn down in 1999, it was a typical postwar construction in brown brick, steel, and concrete, functional rather than aesthetic. During the forty-one years it was open, it hosted indoor biking events, boxing matches, concerts by Led Zeppelin, Johnny Cash, and Frank Zappa, and was a favorite convention hall for the Social Democratic Party (SPD). On November 13, 1976, the arena was packed for a single man with an acoustic guitar, who seemed nervous and underprepared, plucking at his strings and talking over his own lyrics. That man was Wolf Biermann.

Biermann, born in Hamburg in 1936, had moved to the communist German Democratic Republic (GDR) in 1953, had worked as a directorial assistant at Brecht's Berliner Ensemble, and had worked with the composer Hanns Eisler. In essays, poetry, and songs published and performed largely in West Germany, Biermann was heavily critical of the GDR, and especially its ruling party, the Socialist Unity Party (SED). As a consequence, he was banned from performing publicly in 1965. His first album, *Chausseestraße 131*, was recorded on a simple tape recorder in Biermann's apartment at the eponymous address, and then smuggled to the West for pressing. The resulting low-fi do-it-yourself aesthetic (the rumble of the trolley line number 12 crossing the Oranienburger Tor below is clearly audible on the album) meshed well with the yearning for authenticity characteristic of the emerging counterculture on the other side of the wall.

In 1976, Biermann received permission to travel to West Germany for a series of concerts, the first of which was to take place in the Sporthalle. It was filmed in its entirety and also broadcast live via WDR public radio (whose reach was largely the center-west of West Germany). In the TV broadcast of the evening, Biermann is visibly nervous, but also seems to deliberately accentuate the amateurism of his performance. He doesn't always nail the fingering, he corrects himself and comments on his own performance as it goes on. The singer, who had performed and recorded in his own kitchen in East Berlin for over ten years seemed intent on bringing that improvisational aesthetic onto the stage before thousands. Or rather, as he put it later in his reflections on that night, he performed "on stage and before the TV cameras as though I were privately with seven people in my room in the Chausseestraße."[1] He points out that this actually reversed his usual setup: "in the Chausseestraße visitors would often tell me: Man, you're singing as though there were thousands of listeners in a hall here."[2] He had previously brought the great public into his private setting; now he made a private setting public.

Biermann's visible nervousness throughout the evening, and the crowd's acceptance of it, suggest that both had a sense of what was coming. As an encore he performed the "Ballad of the Prussian Icarus." The Prussian Icarus, he sang, had wings of heavy wrought iron; the barbed wire girded around his body had begun to seep into his way of thinking, and so he sat there and could not do what Icarus is supposed to do—soar, dare, be free. In the first stanza, the Prussian Icarus is identified as the Prussian eagle who indeed to this day rises from the wrought-iron handrails of the Weidendammer Bridge overlooking the Tränenpalast, the "palace of tears," then an infamous border checkpoint between East and West. In the second stanza, Biermann seems to suggest that the GDR itself is the Prussian Icarus, its bold visions for a better future weighed down by political repression and the barbed wire all around—the state that wanted to be nothing like Prussia had turned into exactly the ironclad oppressor it once set out to displace.[3]

In the final stanza, Biermann then identifies himself as the Prussian Icarus—as an unhappy citizen of a country that he is nevertheless unable or unwilling to leave. "I'll stay until I fall because / that hated bird has deadly claws / and drags me over the edge," Biermann sang, and when he sang it in Cologne on November 13, 1976, the utterance turned performative. Whether he knew it at the time or not, the act of singing about "the hated bird" would constitute the moment that the bird indeed dug its claws into him. And while the German phrase "over the edge" ("über den Rand") may

---

1 Wolf Biermann, *Preußischer Ikarus: Lieder, Balladen, Gedichte, Prosa* (Cologne: Kiepenheuer & Witsch, 1978), 109: "auf der Bühne und vor den Fernsehkameras als wärest du privat mit sieben Leuten in der Chausseestraße in deinem Zimmer."

2 Biermann, *Preußischer Ikarus*, 109: "In der Chausseestraße sagten oft Besucher: Mensch! Du singst, als ob wir hier ein paar Tausend in einem Saal sind."

3 Biermann, *Preußischer Ikarus*, 103.

simply refer to the Spree River under the Weidendammer Bridge, in context it seems clear that he envisions precisely what ended up happening: a forced rather than chosen emigration, a step across the Iron Curtain that Biermann, a convinced communist and fierce critic of Western imperialism, would never have taken by himself.

Even though he refused to condemn the GDR as much as his West German audience might have liked during the Cologne concert, songs like the "Ballad of the Prussian Icarus" were the last straw for the SED back home. News came that Biermann was to be stripped of his citizenship on November 16, whereupon the WDR ran a slightly edited video of the concert on November 17, and on November 19 the main German public TV station ARD aired the footage from the concert in its entirety. This was significant because unlike the regional WDR, the ARD could actually be received (albeit illegally) on television sets in the GDR. By being thrown out of his country, Biermann for the first time had found a way of actually reaching his fellow citizens there.

*Der Spiegel* once called the concert in the Cologne Sporthalle "the most important German-German TV event prior to the fall of the Berlin Wall."[4] The "Ballad of the Prussian Icarus," it has seemed to many since, was the first rumbling of the discontent that would eventually sweep away the East German state. But perhaps the "Ballad of the Prussian Icarus" mattered not only as a political harbinger. Perhaps it also mattered as a ballad.

For in a strange way, Biermann lived out an old fantasy concerning the ballad. Here was Biermann, singing both as an everyman and a highly specific narrator. He was getting himself kicked out of his homeland by singing this specific ballad—it's hard to imagine the identity of the singer mattering more. And yet, he appeared on stage with a dressed-down casualness that seemed to indicate that he was really no different from any of the thousands in his audience. He was not the star of the evening, but instead spoke and sang for millions who could have said or sung similar things. His decision to designate his song a "ballad" suggested as much.

But above all, Biermann's performances were remarkable for their mode of dissemination—and that mode of dissemination constituted an important part of their legend. How these songs came to their listeners was as interesting a tale as what they were actually saying. These songs made political points simply by existing, by circulating, and by moving through a population in a particular way—by catching on, by being suppressed, by being understood and misunderstood. It is no accident that songs like this would be drawn to the ballad genre. The explosiveness of the direct, democratic

---

[4] Claus Christian Malzahn, "Die Odyssee des Preußischen Ikarus," *Der Spiegel*, November 4, 2006.

relationship between singer and audience had long been one of the hallmarks of ballad aesthetics and the main political promise it held for its promoters.

> In the GDR . . . the direct censorship in a paradoxical way brought about something like a communist distribution of forbidden poems: they went from hand to hand, were typed up, photographed. The songs multiplied in a geometric row via taped copies and went right from one person to the next.[5]

Biermann's description captures something Susan Stewart has described as "distressed genre."[6] His songs carried the stamp of long circulation, even though that stamp was to some extent owed to artifice. Stewart applied the moniker to the ballads collected by British antiquarians like Thomas Percy (1729–1811) and Joseph Ritson (1752–1803) in the late eighteenth century. Biermann here describes something analogous for dissident ballads circa 1976. In both cases, the distressedness of the ballad is not offered as an aesthetic good in itself: rather the distressedness testifies to a "communist distribution" of poetry, the fact that it has passed through "the people" and carries their concerns and their thinking in its very sound: "The ever-louder murmuring [*Rauschen*] of the bad copy lends the songs a sound which at Chausseestraße always sounded to me like the murmuring of the large crowd of people, through which the song had passed from tape recorder to tape recorder. And I sometimes thought: yes, this sounds better, sounds more political than the flawless hi-fi sound of a record."[7]

Biermann was singing truth to power, and his politics were as sincere as they were straightforward: here was a singer punished simply for singing. And yet, while the personal stakes of the evening couldn't have been higher for the performer, what were the stakes for the audience? Although the performance was stubbornly small-bore and intimate, Biermann's concert was nevertheless a media spectacle—people were watching a singer sing his life away on national television. And while Biermann would leave the performance in an as-yet unknowable direction, his audience, largely young middle-class West Germans, would drive home to suburban homes in Bonn, Aachen, or Dormagen with a secure and satisfied sense that they'd watched history

---

5 Biermann, *Preußischer Ikarus*, 113: "In der DDR, dort bewirkt die direkte Zensur auf eine vertrackte Weise so etwas wie eine kommunistische Verteilung der verbotenen Gedichte: sie gehen von Hand zu Hand, werden abgetippt, photographiert. Die Lieder vervielfältigen sich in geometrischer Reihe durch Tonbandkopien und schön direkt von einem Menschen zum andern."

6 Susan Stewart, "Notes on Distressed Genres," chap. 3 in *Crimes of Writing* (Oxford: Oxford University Press, 1991), 78f.

7 Biermann, *Preußischer Ikarus*, 113.

being performed for them in a way that would in no way touch or alter their own lives.

In other words, then, Biermann's performance of "The Ballad of the Prussian Icarus" was two things at once: a flashback to a long-lost (and possibly mythical) mode of embedding oral poetry into social and political life; and a thoroughly modern media event, foreshadowing, as *Der Spiegel* correctly noted, the iconic television images around the fall of the Berlin Wall. Neither of these two dimensions eclipses the other—neither Biermann's authenticity nor its canny medial exploitation constitutes the truth of the matter. The evening of November 13, 1976, suspends the ballad between the personal and the political, the long line of tradition and the disruptions of the modern, the universal and the individual. And if it spoke about German nationhood, it did so in a deeply ambivalent and contradictory way. In this respect, "The Ballad of the Prussian Icarus" was a classic, albeit late, representative of the form.

Biermann also hewed to a particular dual temporality of the ballad. As it emerged into literary history in the eighteenth century, and as it became a mainstay of the canon in the nineteenth century, the ballad lived off two separate but coequal positionings. On the one hand, the popularity of reciting, repeating, and reading a ballad lived off the fantasy that the reciter or reader was tapping into, and in some sense reconstituting, an earlier, a premodern, an oral mode of relating to poetry and to the community. It made the modern reader feel like a bard of ancient times. All the while, of course, the appeal of such a revival depended on how disjunct the premodern world evoked by balladic orality felt. Even though oral poetry persisted in nineteenth-century Germany, even though there were plenty of murder ballads still making the rounds, the literary ballads circulating in schoolbooks and magazines implicitly positioned the oral modes they aped as irretrievably lost. The ballad genre attained its greatest successes while mourning its loss of primacy.

## The Fates of the Ballad

This book is based on the observation that "the ballad" always seems to be far from the ballad. In a recent book on the ballad, Ulrich Gaier deliberately declined to say what the ballad "is," and instead centers what was, at different times, called a ballad.[8] This is surely the right approach, as the ballad boom that took hold in Germany and that runs from the 1780s well into the 1970s represented as much an expansion in fact as it was one in nomenclature. The

---

8 Ulrich Gaier, *Ballade und Romanze: Poetik und Geschichte* (Würzburg: Königshausen & Neumann, 2019), 11.

poems usually thought of as ballads were not uniformly published as such. Some were called *Romanzen*, *Legenden*, or any of many other monikers. Only rarely were these distinctions meant to indicate important differences, and as the poems began to circulate—via periodicals, anthologies, song settings, and the like—the designations became additionally fluid. "Der Gott und die Bajadere" ("The God and the Bayadere"), one of Goethe's poems of the so-called ballad year of 1797, was designated an "Indian legend," but soon appeared in anthologies as a ballad, while its first song setting designated it a *Romanze*.

Once we emphasize, like Gaier, what is called a ballad over some stable definition thereof, we find ourselves quickly carried beyond the bounds of literature. Ballads constitute a genre that lives in translation—in the concert hall, in a pop concert, at the beginning of a movie, or one that can be played wordlessly on a piano.[9] It seems to have its essence in just how widely it can be shared. A poem like Schiller's "Ritter Toggenburg" (1797) was set to music by Johann Friedrich Reichardt, Johann Rudolf Zumsteeg, Franz Schubert, and Johann Vesque von Püttlingen, and popularized in English by Thomas Carlyle, Thomas Hardy, and Edward Bulwer-Lytton. There existed an operetta by Franz Mögele based on "Toggenburg," and a *Lustspiel* (never performed) on themes suggested by the poem by Michael Beer.[10] The poem inspired a symphony by Wendelin Weißheimer (discussed in more detail in Chapter 7), and a raft of paintings, etchings, and broadsheets. The Residenz in Weimar boasts a fresco based on "Toggenburg," and the Kunsthalle in Karlsruhe holds sketches for a (never realized) triptych inspired by the poem. In its peregrinations, the poem itself changed little, but what could be done with it culturally at any given moment was itself astonishingly broad. "Toggenburg" intersected with Victorian medievalism, Nazarene neoclassical art, with a burgeoning *Lied*-culture, with popular entertainments and emerging art music. In between, it made appearances in schoolbooks and case studies by Sigmund Freud, in the Westerns of Karl May, and in Leopold von Sacher-Masoch's *Venus in Furs*.[11]

As in the case of Biermann's "Ballad of the Prussian Icarus," sharing was the point: the fantasy that governed the response to Biermann's ballad, both among those who applauded him and among those who expatriated him, was a fantasy of commonality. Specifically of a commonality that cut both ways: hearing it meant agreeing with it, and singing it meant giving voice to a shared sense or knowledge. Ballads were a literature in common,

---

9 James Parakilas, *Ballads without Words* (New York: Amadeus Press, 1992).

10 See Michael Beer, "Der neue Toggenburg," in *Sämtliche Werke* (Leipzig: Brockhaus, 1835), 775f.

11 Leopold von Sacher-Masoch, *Venus im Pelz*, in Hieronymus Lorn, *Ein adeliges Fräulein* (Berlin: Globus, 1910), 18.

written in a language understood to be common language, taken to be circulating among the common people. They came to constitute a canon people could refer to as a shared resource (ballads were frequently anthologized in a *Hausschatz*, a "house treasure"). These poems seem too simple, too transparent, too self-explicating to require a touch of the hermeneut.

Ballads were poetry one lived with. One read them, of course—in anthologies, in almanacs, on the first or last page in a popular magazine. But one did not just read them. One heard them, saw them illustrated, heard them sung, encountered them as program music. Of course, as Biermann's example makes clear, commonness holds countless ambiguities and traps. But literary studies have to some extent accepted this fiction of the common, which has tended to put ballads at the margins of the high literary canon. While ballad revivals swept much of Europe in the late eighteenth century—from the antiquarianism of the British Isles to the first stirrings of *costumbrismo* in the Iberian peninsula—the questions and stakes around this "in common" posed themselves differently in different national contexts. In Germany, they appeared on a cultural scene obsessed with questions of common German cultural heritage, but quickly became swept up with a prospective nationalism that envisioned a German nation for the future. They appeared in a cultural scene where literature was beginning to develop a new sense of self-confidence, an outsized sense of its own political ramifications. They also appeared in a context in which the boundaries of the nation were still being negotiated, inevitably by drawing on and projecting onto what supposedly lay beyond it.[12] The ballad thus was not—and could not be—just nostalgic. Johann Gottfried Herder called song the "ewiger Erb- und Lustgesang," meaning a song motivated by heredity and tradition on one hand, and sheer life force on the other. Its sounds were, as Gottfried August Bürger (1747–1794) noted, "living breath [*Odem*], which blows across all human hearts and senses."[13] Although the ballads collected in Herder's *Stimmen der Völker in Liedern* (1807) would together constitute the beginnings of a ballad canon, they seemed to belong to life more than to literature. In his first edition of the book (1778/9), Herder had presented them as *Volkslieder* (folk songs): even though many of them had identifiable authors and were of recent vintage, they were supposed to matter to their audience as a shared possession of the *Volk*.

Ballads emerged into a public sphere where several arts were expanding their sense of their own political and cultural ramifications—from the theater reforms of the late eighteenth century, to the print revolution in music

---

12 Ottmar Ette, *Mobile Prussia: Views Beyond the National* (Stuttgart: Metzler, 2021).

13 Gottfried August Bürger, "Herzensausguß über Volkspoesie," in *Sturm und Drang: Dichtungen und theoretische Texte in zwei Bänden*, ed. Heinz Nicolai (Munich: Winkler, 1971), 2:1654.

publishing—and were dealing with radically expanded audiences. And since the ballad came to Germany allied with an ideology of organicism, it did not, indeed could not, emerge as simply as a literary phenomenon. It was a musical, philosophical, graphic, performed genre—and the literary poetics of the ballad are as important to its phenomenal spread in Germany as they are misleading when considered apart from development in musical aesthetics. These texts have come to be more at home in the concert hall, the school textbook, or the illustrated edition for young readers than in a literary seminar. Rather than literature that takes possession of us, ballads seemed, especially in Germany, like objects of which one could take rather unproblematic possession: you read the poem once and you had understood it; you memorized it and found you could recite it still decades later; it was safely under your belt, even if you never returned to it. Ballads are literature one can live with; literature one doesn't have to actually read to know. Most visual representations of ballad plots in nineteenth-century Germany are made for the market and are marked as illustrations. Some cases, such as Carl Wilhelm von Heideck's 1818 drawing of Bürger's ballad "Lenore" (Fig. I.1), are almost cartoonish. The cultural framing of these poems tended to underplay their seriousness, or seemed to heighten their appeal to consumers rather than "serious" readers. They are part of the individual's cultural inheritance—not as a prized heirloom, but as a trinket one is surprised to learn one has held on to.

When the ballad came to the attention of aestheticians, poets, and musical theorists in late eighteenth century Germany, they agreed on two seemingly contradictory points: The ballad had long circulated among the common people in Germany. And the ballad was a recent invention modeled on ballad revivals in the English-speaking world. Even by the early nineteenth century, histories of literary criticism largely agreed that the British import had come first, that, in other words, the German literary world took note of folk ballads only after it began being interested in literary ballads. It is interesting that even in moments of supreme mystification, the ballad theorists of the Romantic generation generally acknowledged this somewhat counterintuitive provenance.

As the poet and editor Ignaz Hub put it in the foreword to his anthology *Deutschlands Balladen- und Romanzendichter* (1845), the important theoretical interventions on behalf of the ballad, above all by Bodmer and Herder, and the important formal innovations, above all by Gleim and Bürger, all happened under the impression of influences from the British Isles, and to a lesser extent of French translations of medieval Provençal lyrics. "The epic songs mostly from the fifteenth and sixteenth centuries, which then widely shared in common, those true branches of the old Germanic tree of poets . . ., were little known during Bürger's lifetime."[14] While the "then" (*damals*) is a

---

14 Ignaz Hub, *Deutschlands Balladen- und Romanzendichter von G. A. Bürger bis auf die neueste Zeit* (Karlsruhe: Creuzbauer, 1860), vi.

FIG. I.I Carl Wilhelm von Heideck (1788–1861), "Lenore" from "Twelve Drawings on Bürger's Poetry" (1818).

bit ambiguous, Hub's implication seems to be that these old German ballads were in fact circulating when Bürger wrote his ballads, but there was no attempt to harness them within the new literary form. The attempts to collect genuinely popular material in a systematic fashion came later, with the Romantic generation—with collections like Achim von Arnim and Clemens Brentano's *Des Knaben Wunderhorn* (1805–1808), or Johann Gustav Gottlieb Büsching and Friedrich Heinrich von der Hagen's *Sammlung deutscher Volkslieder* (1807).

This staggered adaptation and the fact that the ballad was, somewhat paradoxically, understood as a native import, had, as Chapter 1 will explore in more detail, ramifications for what the ballad was taken to know and how it was taken to know it. The first theoretical treatises to deal seriously with the ballad form in Germany were written by Bürger and Herder in the 1770s, and even they treated the ballad as one aspect of oral popular culture among many. On the other hand, the actual ballads that preoccupied the British theorists had entered into circulation in Germany quite a bit earlier—albeit through translation and import. Walter Falk has suggested a tripartite definition of the art ballad: it "unites the epic and lyric aspects" that earlier popular balladry had kept separate; it "is traditioned in a fixed, written form"; and "it is intended for an educated literary public."[15] When Bodmer and Herder were writing, this was the only way in which balladry circulated in the German public sphere—and it was usually balladry from outside Germany.

Falk positions Johann Wilhelm Ludwig Gleim as the first author of art ballads in Germany. Although inspired by the medieval Provençal ballads, Gleim ultimately drew on the form and the plots found in the works of the baroque Spanish poet Luis de Góngora (1561–1627) and François Augustin Paradis de Moncrif (1687–1770). At the same time, Gleim's romances drew on far less high-literary forebears—their laborious titles and ripped-from-the-headlines plots were indebted to the murder ballads of German popular culture—a deliberate challenge to the high-minded rationalism and classicism that held sway in aesthetics at the time. If we choose to locate the origins of the form among the first canonic authors to write ballads of their own rather than adapt them, then it emerged in the generation that grew up in the shadow of, and positioned itself in opposition to, Johann Christoph Gottsched (1700–1766) and his classicist and rationalist poetics. Gottsched's *Versuch einer critischen Dichtkunst* (1730) was notable for the horror it expressed at corruptions of classical form. Gottsched insisted, primarily in the field of theater, on establishing an autonomous sphere of poetic art that was to be distinct from popular forms. And Gottsched inveighed against simplistic meters and against rhyme as corruptions of more elevated poetic form.[16] The ballad violated all of these precepts, and it is perhaps for that reason that Gottsched's critics, Bodmer and Gleim among them, were initially drawn to the genre.[17]

But this is only half the story. Gottsched and his allies did not experiment with writing ballads. But at the same time, they were instrumental in shaping the initial reception of the British ballad boom in German-speaking

---

15 Walter Falk, "Die Anfänge der deutschen Kunstballade," *Deutsche Vierteljahresschrift für Literatur und Geistesgeschichte* 44 (December 1970): 675.

16 Johann Christoph Gottsched, *Versuch einer critischen Dichtkunst* (Leipzig: Breitkopf, 1730).

17 Falk, "Die Anfänge der deutschen Kunstballade," 679.

lands. Johann Christoph's wife, Luise Adelgunde Gottsched, translated "The Ballad of Chevy Chase" sometime between 1739 and 1743 as part of her translation of the great organ of Enlightenment commonsense philosophy, Joseph Addison's *Spectator*. "Chevy Chase" gained its popularity in England as part of the systematic recovery of popular orality, which culminated in Percy's *Reliques of Ancient English Poetry* (1765). It arrived in Germany as an itinerant curio, as part of a learned literary network looking to educate bourgeois households, rather than as a family heirloom of the *Volk*. And, most important, it didn't really arrive as an specimen of the ballad genre at all: in introducing the poem, Luise Gottsched rendered the word "ballad" as *Tanzlied*, or dance-song.[18]

When Friedrich Gottlieb Klopstock wrote a version of "Chevy Chase" in 1749, he likewise did not use the word *Ballade*. But he already pointed to the curious entwinement of oral tradition and literary remediation that would become constitutive for the ballad phenomenon. His "War Song, in Imitation of the Old Song of the Chevy Chase" ("Kriegslied, zur Nachahmung des alten Liedes von der Chevy Chase-Jagd") comes with an author's note explaining that "this song will be known to readers of *The Spectator*, which in the seventieth issue of the first volume explains in detail the natural beauty of the text." In order to remind his readers, Klopstock even quotes a few lines—in Luise Adelgunde Gottsched's translation.[19] The poem deeply influenced poetry in the second half of the eighteenth century. It introduced what came to be called the "Chevy-Chase-Strophe" (ABAB, with four and three stresses respectively). It became popularly associated with non-classical topics. Gleim's *Preussische Kriegslieder* (1758) are entirely in the meter and are balladic in nature. Through the Göttingen *Hainbund*, a group of Storm-and-Stress poets, the meter also entered nature poetry. Just as consequential for the ballad is the way Gleim and others deployed the meter in their "Anacreontic" lyric poetry, which emphasized a light, ironic, slightly humorous tone.

The ballad thus emerged in Germany somewhere in between classicist aesthetics and an anti-classicist reaction, somewhere in between a uniquely German set of aesthetic concerns and ones understood to be international, maybe even a foreign import. Importantly, what may present in hindsight as two starkly contradictory origin stories for the ballad form were not experienced as such at the time. For all the outsize claims made for ballad and romance by the theorists of *Sturm und Drang* and by the Romantic generation, they never owned the ballad to the extent that hindsight might suggest. In Germany, the temporality of the ballad seemed to function differently than in England. The equation that held, as David Buchan has put it,

---

18 Karl Nessler, *Geschichte der Ballade Chevy Chase* (Berlin: Mayer & Müller, 1911), 177.

19 Helmut Pape, *Klopstock: Die "Sprache des Herzens" neu entdeckt* (Berlin: Lang, 1998), 226.

"that which was 'folk' was assumed to be 'old' "[20] was not as thorough in the German-speaking world as it tended to be on the British Isles. The ancestral oral culture that the ballad compilers of the British Isles simply cataloged, many a German analog seemed to understand as still in existence, perhaps even only on the verge of becoming realized. That meant that the ballad initially contended with culture as it actually was, not just with an idealized retroprojection of it.

The Swiss philologist Johann Jacob Bodmer (1698–1783) was among the first to seize on the ballads of the British Isles to stake a somewhat counterintuitive claim for them as a source of authenticity for an authentically German art. Much like Shakespeare's plays and Gothic architecture, the ballad, although similarly hailing from outside of Germany's borders, furnished German critics of Enlightenment aesthetics with a supposedly homegrown antithesis to "rule aesthetics" in the mode of Gottsched. The ballad was particularly useful in this effort because it both lacked the portable rules of classical meter and the massive scale of the ancient epic. As Bodmer put it, "ballads are on a small scale what the romances are on a large one." For him, then, ballads were resolutely medieval, they were remnants of a past poetic practice. And they were deliberately minor forms. This wandering, unmoored capaciousness would continue to draw German thinkers to the ancient ballad for the remainder of the eighteenth century.

At the same time, the description Bodmer provided in the preface to his second volume of *Old English and Old Swabian Ballads* (*Altenglische und altschwäbische Balladen*) clearly spoke to discourses around directness and simplicity of expression that guided artworks by Bodmer's own contemporaries. Ballads, he wrote, lacked the "psychological plan" of the epic, or its narrative economy. "But they make up for this lack with the simplicity [*Einfalt*] of their form, with the openness of their heart, with the trueness of their feelings."[21] Compared to the careful, rational calibration of classicist aesthetics, ballads seemed to come from a more impulsive, more authentic place. And in terms of their interaction with its audience, they reversed the polarity of classicism: classicist aesthetics had to be taught, they had rules, they relied on objective measure; but those rules were often offered to ensure universal translatability and appeal. Not everyone could sculpt a classical statue—but anyone was meant to be able to see why it was beautiful. The ballad became

---

20 David Buchan, "Talerole Analysis and Child's Supernatural Ballads," in *The Ballad and Oral Literature*, ed. Joseph Harris (Cambridge, MA: Harvard University Press, 1991), 60.

21 Johann Jacob Bodmer, *Altenglische und Altschwäbische Balladen* (Zürich: Füeßly, 1781), 2:1.

one of the emblems of the opposite configuration: almost anyone could compose a ballad, but while it spoke directly to its audience that audience was emphatically not everyone.

More than any other text, Johann Gottfried Herder's anthology *Stimmen der Völker* buoyed the fortunes of the ballad form in the German-speaking world, even though the word "ballad" is used sparingly throughout. The texts Herder gathered here were drawn from Scottish ballads and Nordic sagas, they came from Greenland and Madagascar, and they were drawn as much from known, identifiable poets as from ethnographic reports. Herder identified them as "popular songs" (*Volkslieder*), independent of their literary merits or origins in written literature, independent of whether they were ever sung or not, and independent of whether they had identifiable authors. As we shall see in Chapter 1, while the ballad scandals of the British Isles were about precise questions of status and provenance, the ballad boom in Germany from the first relied on creative imprecision. In introducing the songs, Herder made clear why he felt he didn't need to be precise: these songs were a sideshow. "The collector of these songs never had either the time nor the ambition to become the German Percy," he cautioned. "The pieces found within were either brought to him by a stroke of good fortune, or found along the way while searching for other things."[22] The ballad was defined by what it was not: not the epic, not Shakespeare, not the source of a national literature. The reason these ballads mattered anyway, as Herder wrote in another essay, was that they came even more directly from the everyday life of the *Volk* than the knightly romance or the courtly epic. They were small, representative, ultimately unremarkable parts of the "primordial soup" of oral tradition, and precisely because they were unremarkable they were more authentic.

> Whosoever would concern himself with the raw populace [*Volk*], with its primordial soup of fairy tales, prejudices, songs, and rough language: what a barbarian would he have to be! He would come to dirty up our classical, syllable-counting literature, like a night owl amid the beautiful, colorful, singing plumage![23]

Ballads—like fairy tales, like songs, like proverbs—were a far more direct, far less self-conscious expression of a certain kind of popular culture. In *Von deutscher Art und Kunst*, the text that constituted in important respects the poetics for the *Stimmen der Völker*, Herder explained why they were worth taking seriously as literature. But taking song seriously in Herder's framing

---

22 Johann Gottfried Herder, *Stimmen der Völker in Liedern* (Tübingen: Cotta, 1846), 54.

23 Johann Gottfried Herder, "Ähnlichkeit der mittlern englischen und deutschen Dichtkunst," in *Stimmen der Völker in Liedern*, 47.

was about something other than learned literary hermeneutics—it was a matter of intuition. In fact, the kind of literature collected in the *Stimmen* was fundamentally debased by being collected in writing. "The more distant the people is from artificial, scientific thinking, language and writing, the less its songs have to be made for paper and verses made of dead letters."[24] The categories that shaped the sound of the ballad were different from those of written poetry: the "mysterious force that that these songs possess," Herder says, depends on "the lyrical, the lively and the dance-like of song, on the lively presence of the images, on the connectedness, even necessity of the content, the emotions."[25]

When Bürger, himself the author of "Lenore" (1773), one of the early German ballads to find international success, wrote his defense of oral poetry, he likewise turned to emotion to justify its appeal: his essay, first published in the *Deutsches Museum* in 1776, was entitled "Herzensausguß über Volkspoesie"—here, appreciating the poetry of the people was a matter of pouring out your heart, not showing off your knowledge or your ability to work in a particular tradition. And, more emphatically than even Herder, Bürger suggested that forms like the ballad returned poetry to a more original, less alienated state—a state in which the divisions that had characterized above all classicist aesthetics melted away. Throughout the nineteenth century, this promise never seemed to flag: in 1890, the *völkisch* critic Julius Langbehn would claim for Goethe's balladry that, unlike in his classicist works, "his style does not grow from the outside in, but inside out."[26] No matter what levels of self-reflectiveness, irony, or citationality art ballads engaged in, many analysts compulsively understood them in terms of organic unity. Bürger was chiefly thinking about the division between the epic and the lyric in poetry, but what made interventions like his so powerful was that it was not difficult to espy behind that particular division many others: between art and life, between form and content, between understanding and intuition, between artist and audience. "Through popularity [*Popularität*]," Bürger proposed, "poetry shall be again what it once was, shall be what God made it, and as what he laid it in the souls of the elect."[27] Like Herder after him, Bürger regarded popular poetry as a part of everyday life, and he made perhaps clearer than Herder that this entailed that poetry be inserted into a varied, and at times contradictory, range of contexts. Bürger listened "in the

---

24 Ibid.

25 Johann Gottfried Herder, *Von deutscher Art und Kunst*, in *Sturm und Drang* (Munich: Winkler, 1971), I:262.

26 Julius Langbehn, *Rembrandt als Erzieher* (Leipzig: Hirschfeld, 1891), 31: "hier wächst sein Stil von innen nach außen, nicht von außen nach innen."

27 Bürger, "Herzensausguß über Volkspoesie," 2:1652.

light of dusk to the magic sound of ballads and popular song [*Gassenhauer*], under the linden trees of the village, in the spinning rooms."[28] Rather than some numinous "spirit" of the people, Bürger embedded popular poetry in the pursuit of everyday life. Notice, for instance, that his *Volk* lives in small villages and in urban environments (the metaphor of *Gassenhauer* drawing on a distinctly urban imaginary[29]), and both in spaces coded as stereotypically male (the field of labor and of battle) and stereotypically female (the spinning room as a locus of information exchange).

From the first, then, German theorizations of the ballad combined claims about literary history with claims that, to the modern ear, sound anthropological. For all the mystifications entailed in the ballad revivals, the thinkers involved in establishing the importance of the form were asking trenchant questions about oral culture, about information, about community. When in August 1814, Goethe visited the celebrations of the feast day of St. Rochus in the town of Bingen in the Rhine valley, he did so not as a folklorist looking to celebrate specific customs, but as a researcher of popular culture. The text he wrote about it, observers have noted, seems to anticipate some of the techniques deployed in the field of anthropology in the twentieth century.[30] One of his persistent fascinations in the essay concerned the way local oral traditions informed the ritual: "Here," Goethe remarks, "one came to know the true essence of the legend when it wanders from mouth to mouth, from ear to ear." The legends around St. Rochus traveled almost universally among the townsfolk, but they changed and distended in the traveling. At the same time, its travel democratized rather than bastardized the legend: "There were no contradictions in it, but an infinity of differences."[31]

---

28 Bürger, "Herzensausguß über Volkspoesie," 2:1654.

29 In modern German, "Gasse" is a distinctly urban alleyway. While the eighteenth century also spoke of "Gassen" as narrow paths in rural settings (perhaps most famous the "hohle Gasse" in Küsnacht, still used in Schiller's *Wilhelm Tell* [1804]), the *Gassenhauer* was understood to derive from similar terms across the European languages that each drew on words for urban roadways: Adelung's *Grammatisch-kritisches Wörterbuch der hochdeutschen Mundart* (1796) mentions, among others, the Danish *gadevise* (a melody of the alleyway), the French *vaudeville* or *villanelle* (which both contain the word *ville*), and Spanish passacaglia (originally passa-calla) (Adelung, *Grammatisch-kritisches Wörterbuch der hochdeutschen Mundart* [Leipzig, 1796], 2:427).

30 Michael Saman, "Towards Goethean Anthropology: From Nature and Art to Human Society," *Goethe Yearbook* 27 (2020), 137–163. [forthcoming]

31 Johann Wolfgang Goethe, "Sankt-Rochus-Fest zu Bingen am 16. August 1814," in *Goethe Werke* (Berliner Ausgabe) (Berlin: Aufbau, 1960), 15:511: "Hier lernte man das eigentliche Wesen der Sage kennen wenn sie von Mund zu Mund, von Ohr zu Ohr wandelt."

By the time the novelist and critic Willibald Alexis wrote "Ueber Balladenpoesie"[32] ("On Ballad Poesy," 1824), his considerations drew on different observations of orality altogether, but retained an anthropological lens. These observations were made possible by European colonialism. Adelbert von Chamisso (1781–1838) was himself the author of several famous ballads, but he was also an active natural scientist and explorer. From 1815 to 1818, Chamisso participated in a circumnavigation of the globe by a Russian expedition. While his focus during his travels was the natural environment, the poet also returned with many observations of the native populations he encountered, including on their relationship to poetry. Alexis's essay drew on these observations and positioned balladry as a descendant of the rhythmic ritualized speech by which, Chamisso claimed, Pacific Islanders navigated their social lives: like these formulae, ballads were "hereditary sayings" (*erbliche Sprüche*). A bit of history-writing and information-relay inhered in them, even as they became more lyricized and autonomous from everyday life.[33] In all these constructions, the ballad functioned as a piece of *Volksgeist*, of the spirit of the people and an age: the ballad knows things, and one must treat it as both more and as less than literature to use them correctly. Hans-Robert Jauß once pointed out that the distance between the "foreign horizon of a text" and the "horizon of the present-day interpreter" became visible as a problem only once both "the concept of 'Spirit' inherited from German Idealism and the ideal of exactitude of positivism" had faded, since they "appeared to vouch for an immediate access" to the past.[34] In the conception of history implied by the ballad genre, neither *Geist* nor positivism truly ever went away.

Bürger's appeal to emotion, intuition, and popularity had its critics. Friedrich Schiller, for instance, worried that Bürger intervened too little in transmuting the feelings of everyday life into those of poetry.[35] "Mr. B.," he wrote, "all too often *mixes* himself with the folk to whom he ought to simply descend, and instead of pulling the folk up to his level, he all too often enjoys making himself common with them."[36] But Bürger's friend and student August Wilhelm Schlegel remarked in a posthumous essay that the demand for the "popular" for Bürger never meant "simplistic." For one

---

32 Willibald Alexis, "Ueber Balladenpoesie," *Hermes oder kritisches Jahrbuch der Literatur* 21, no. 1 (1824): 1–113.

33 Alexis, "Ueber Balladenpoesie," 11.

34 Hans-Robert Jauß, *Ästhetische Erfahrung und literarische Hermeneutik* (Frankfurt: Suhrkamp, 1997), 657.

35 Hans Richard Brittnacher, "Die Austreibung des Populären—Schillers Bürger-Kritik," *Goethe Yearbook* 25 (2018): 103.

36 Friedrich Schiller, "Über Bürgers Gedichte," in *Theoretische Schriften* (Sämtliche Werke 5) (Munich: Hanser, 1962), 5:976.

thing, writing poetry in a popular mode still meant writing poetry. But more important, "the desire to understand everything, meaning to grasp everything by means of the intellect, is surely a fairly unpopular desire."[37] This captured an emergent problem of the nineteenth century: the *Volk*, and popularity, were themselves complicated. The ballad mimed one sort of broad appeal and factually possessed another—part of the form's portability likely rested simply on the fact that a ballad did not project one identifiable horizon of expectation, or, as it began its travels across media, one "generic contract."[38]

In Schlegel's generation, enthusiasm for the ballad form's instinctive effects went beyond a simple aversion to the rule-bound poetics of Enlightenment classicism. The ballad was soon part of the Romantic project of a New Mythology.[39] In a later essay explicating one of his ballads, Goethe would posit a kind of balladic egg, which one should seek to "incubate" ("nur bebrüten") in order to properly bring it to life.[40] Treating the ballad correctly meant absorbing it, to treat it as an organ rather than an object. Understanding the ballad meant relying on one's native enthusiasms as a guide rather than the external application of one's judgment. Just as one need not interpret a myth to grasp its meaning, so is a ballad too vulnerable a thing to be forcibly cracked open. One could, of course, crack it open, and in fact it was an easy thing to do. But doing so meant destroying the ballad functioning as a ballad, as myth. Like the naïve in Schiller's essay on "Naïve and Sentimental Poetry," the ballad was often positioned as a look back into childhood—of a people and of an individual. In observing the balladry of Scotland, Dr. Johnson had observed that "diction, merely vocal, is always in its childhood."[41] Willibald Alexis thought the ballad belonged "to the childhood of a people,"[42] and in the literary historian Josef Bayer's words in the 1860s, balladry has "a breath of early days, a fresh, energetic sense of morning, the state of the people as of yet untouched by reflection."[43] At the same time, whether it was the individual or their community that was in this

---

37 August Wilhelm Schlegel, "Bürger," in *Vermischte und kritische Schriften* (Leipzig: Weidmann, 1846), VII:78.

38 Fredric Jameson, *The Political Unconscious* (Ithaca, NY: Cornell University Press, 2015).

39 Friedrich Schlegel, "Rede über Mythologie und symbolische Anschauung," in *Gesammelte Werke* (Vienna: Klang, 1846), 5:197.

40 Johann Wolfgang von Goethe, *Goethe's poetische und prosaische Werke in zwei Bänden*, ed. Friedrich Wilhelm Riemer and Johann Peter Eckermann (Stuttgart: Cotta, 1832), 1:432.

41 Cited in Paula McDowell, *The Invention of the Oral: Print Commerce and Fugitive Voices in Eighteenth-Century Britain* (Chicago: University of Chicago Press, 2017), 278.

42 Alexis, "Ueber Balladenpoesie," 11.

43 Josef Bayer, *Von Gottsched bis Schiller: Vorträge über die classische Zeit des deutschen Drama* (Prague: Mercy, 1869), 12.

manner "untouched by reflection" was regarded as an important distinction. Bürger criticized that his contemporaries regarded the ballad as "the poetical ABC."[44] In fact, ballad poetics frequently exhibited a strange mix of egalitarianism and elitism: anyone could grasp the meaning of a ballad, but educated readers were especially wont to miss that meaning. And not understanding the ballad could itself constitute a judgment on the person failing to understand: they were insufficiently authentic, insufficiently in tune with the spirit of the people. The ballad always included two things: an outstretched hand inviting the reader in and a built-in invitation to be misunderstood.

Ballad writers, composers, and illustrators made use of this duality in various ways. Hans Blumenberg once posited that "the discovery of the capacity for creativity is part of the self-articulation of modern consciousness"[45]—in balladry, as in fairy tales, modern consciousness got to imagine itself as uncreative, as purely receptive of an ancestral past. The ballad was cannily constructed to be a found object. It was a fabricated memory on which the imagined communities of the emergent European nation-states could rely. This receptivity of course also contained the possibility of misreception—as Benedict Anderson put it, "the 'nation' was an invention on which it was impossible to secure a patent."[46] The terms of reception were always themselves contested. Because it presented in black and white print what was supposed to be lived practice, the ballad risked always already misreceiving the past. Bürger claimed in the 1770s that, in the ballad, epic and lyric are one and the same—compacted, as in Goethe's later proposal, not so much by primitiveness as by use.[47] The best teacher of how to bring together "the lyric and the epic-lyric style of poetry," he argued, was simply to overhear ballads and romances wafting on the evening air.[48]

The ballad was located resolutely on the other side of any mechanism by which poetry constituted itself as an art medium in the late eighteenth and nineteenth centuries: in an age when the lyric won out over the narrative, it was on the narrative side; in an age when poetry was supposed to transport something other than information, the ballad seemed to be uncomfortably close to an information delivery system; in an age where lyricization supposedly moved poetry out of the public realm and into some sort of interiority, the ballad remained public in its address. When it came to the autonomy of art, the art ballad was caught in a dialectic: on the one hand,

---

44 Bürger, "Herzensausguß über Volkspoesie," 2:1654.

45 Hans Blumenberg, *The Legitimacy of the Modern Age* (Cambridge, MA: MIT Press, 1985), 107.

46 Benedict Anderson, *Imagined Communities: Reflections on the Origin and Spread of Nationalism* (London: Verso, 2016), 67.

47 Goethe, *Goethe's poetische und prosaische Werke*, 1:432.

48 Bürger, "Herzensausguß über Volkspoesie," 2:1654.

so many of the early ballads and romances of Goethe and Schiller, such as "Der Zauberlehrling" or "Die Kraniche des Ibycus," are poems about art and artist figures; on the other, if its topics seemed to position these poems as forerunners of *l'art pour l'art*, the form itself reflected—at least to many of Goethe's and Schiller's contemporaries—a stage of the development of poetry where it had a definite, non-aesthetic function in society.

To be sure, none of these difficulties in locating the ballad prevented the form from being accorded a certain dignity, or led to its being regarded as unartistic—far from it. But the ballad extended uncomfortably into domains of which poetry was otherwise eager to divest itself. At a moment when literature began to undergo a series of enclosure movement, the ballad remained stubbornly itinerant. There are few outright defenses of the ballad from the nineteenth century, because no defense was needed. Few actively disparaged the ballad; they simply placed it far away from whatever was most vital in literature and poetry. In the eighteenth century, the ballad had become scandalous only when it revealed itself a modern simulacrum pretending at being ancient.[49] In nineteenth-century Germany it was absolutely unscandalous—literature that accommodated itself so well into everyday life that it was easy for it to disappear from view altogether. That seems at once like an appropriate and a cruel fate for poems that traced for themselves a lineage from emphatically popular, frequently oral, forms. Just as, once upon a time, murder ballads circulated throughout marketplaces and taverns, so the modern ballad cycles through textbooks, anthologies, and song settings belonging to everyone and no one. It was unclear to whom it belonged, and even to which art it belonged. As poets from Bürger via Schiller to Uhland articulated the poetics of this fashionably unfashionable genre, composers, illustrators, playwrights, pedagogues, and political agitators staked their claim to it.

The great modernizer of the form, at least in the conventional telling of the ballad's history, is Heinrich Heine (1797–1756). Heine critiqued German literature's fixation on the past and reoriented it toward the demands of the present. The ballad almost by necessity came in for criticism in this project. But Heine restricted his critique almost entirely to the generation of his immediate predecessors and teachers. In *Die romantische Schule* (*The Romantic School*, 1836) and elsewhere, he can be quite scathing when describing the ballad as backward-looking and conservative, but he aims those barbs not at the originators of the form, at Bürger, Goethe, or Schiller, but rather at his teacher August Wilhelm Schlegel and Schlegel's fellow Romantics. His charge returns to the question of *Geist*, but shifts its emphasis: the problem was not that Schlegel did not understand the *Geist* of the Middle Ages, rather

---

49 Maureen McLane, "Mediating Antiquarians in Britain, 1760–1830," in *This Is Enlightenment*, ed. Clifford Siskin and William Warner (Chicago: University of Chicago Press, 2010), 257.

that he did not understand the *Geist* of his own time. "Herr Schlegel managed to praise to the rabble that poetry in which the past lies in its coffin [*eingesargt*], at the expense of poetry in which our present lives and breathes."[50] Similarly, Heine compares Ludwig Uhland's balladry to "a knightly steed" that "was ever ready to trot back into the past, but grew recalcitrant the moment when it was driven forward, towards modern life." As a result, Heine notes approvingly, Uhland was forced to abandon poetry altogether in favor of politics. The horse has been retired, "and has all possible virtues now, and just the single defect: that it is dead."[51] Heine did not fault the ballad for failing to go with the time—his own ballads and romances, which are dotted throughout his poetic work from the earliest success, the *Buch der Lieder* (1827) all the way to his posthumous poems, are mostly in a Romantic mode. They follow their great antecedents in yearning for a lost world of plenitude, uncharacterized by alienation, atomization, and mediation. But they acknowledge that the world into which they are published is the opposite of that world, yes, that the very yearning may simply be a product of bourgeois modernity, the alienated subject, the consumer.

When it came to that generation of poets that first brought the ballad to the masses (Bürger, Goethe, Schiller), Heine imputed greater nuance to their generation than to Schlegel's. If anything, he seemed to regard them as allies against the historicism of the Romantic generation. As Gottfried Weißert suggested, Heine's modern rejection of historicism and heroism in his ballads actually distinguishes his work more from the balladry of the early nineteenth century than that of the late eighteenth.[52] When Schlegel "wants to disparage the poet Bürger," Heine wrote, "he sets Bürger's ballads side by side with those Old English ballads collected by Percy, and proceeds to show how [Percy's] are simpler, more antique [*altertümlicher*], and therefore more poetic."[53] Whether or not this was entirely fair to Schlegel (it almost certainly wasn't), it is clear that Heine thought that the mission of Bürger's ballads had never been one of mere emulation, that side-by-side comparisons with folk ballads were never reflective of his intention, and that simplicity and naïveté may never have been his sole objective. Heine will make appearances in nearly every chapter of this book for a very simple reason: Heine was essentially correct to think that he was not modernizing a hide-bound form, but instead removing the phony cobwebs the previous generation had laboriously draped over it. What Heine and his generation excavated in the ballad—its ironies, its attention to changing notions of publicness, the way

---

50 Heinrich Heine, *Die romantische Schule*, in *Werke und Briefe in zehn Bänden* (Berlin and Weimar: Aufbau, 1972), 68.
51 Heine, *Die romantische Schule*, 146.
52 Gottfried Weißert, *Ballade* (Stuttgart: Metzler, 1993), 103.
53 Heine, *Die romantische Schule*, 68.

it dialogued not just with ancient orality but mainly with distinctly modern forms of media—had been present in the form since at least Goethe and Schiller.[54] The ballad was never just a literary text, and therefore able to traverse and to demarcate a rapidly evolving landscape of interlocking media. Heine's generation—Anette von Droste Hülshoff and August von Platen, but also Richard Wagner and Robert Schumann—exploited this mobility to the fullest. But they did not invent it. While the sub-genres of the ballad largely shadowed other literary genres in their logics—the gothic tale, say, or the historical novel, the verse epic, and later even the faits-divers—, this intermedial path was uniquely the ballad's.

For this reason, the history of poetics gives at best an incomplete picture of the status of the ballad. Theories like Bürger's and Uhland's shaped how a certain readership encountered these texts, but it is the argument of this book that the ballad, by dint of its mobility, was also theorized in much more pragmatic ways. Adapting a ballad, setting it to music, illustrating it, anthologizing it, dramatizing it, incorporating it into larger works: all these things make some assumptions, or even establish, exactly what a ballad is, how it works, and why it matters. Klopstock's impact was not confined to the literary realm, but came to involve a variety of media. We shall see in Chapter 2 how the poet promoted the public recitation of his poetry, making it a linchpin in a late eighteenth-century boom in sounding out poetry and prose to one another, first in private settings, and increasingly in paid public fora as well. But Klopstock also provided the impetus to renewed interest to poetry staged to (or increasingly sung to) music. Schiller's early poetic efforts, undertaken while he was a student at the Karlsschule in Stuttgart, were highly influenced by Klopstock. But so was the work of another student, the musician and composer Johann Rudolph Zumsteeg. While Schiller had taken to reading and declaiming Klopstock's poetry, Zumsteeg decided, inspired by Georg Benda's melodramatic works, to set Klopstock's poems to music.[55] "Setting" [*Vertonen*] in the 1770s meant writing an accompaniment to which a poem like "Friedensfeyer"[56] could be half-sung, half-recited; by the time Zumsteeg began setting his erstwhile schoolmate's ballads to music, "setting" meant turning a ballad into a *Lied*.

While ballads were, both in the aesthetic treatises of the time and in the broader discourse, presented as relics of a bygone age, lost, unmoored,

---

54 Winfried Freund, *Die deutsche Ballade: Theorie, Analysen, Didaktik* (Stuttgart: Schöningh, 1978), 93.

55 Katherine Hambridge and Jonathan Hicks, "The Melodramatic Moment," in *The Melodramatic Moment: Music and Theatrical Culture, 1790–1820* (Chicago: Chicago University Press, 2018), 8.

56 Ludwig Landshoff, *Johann Rudolf Zumsteeg (1760–1802)* (diss., LMU Munich, 1900), 34.

vanishing, the fact was that in this pragmatic sense ballads were omnipresent. Between the 1730s, when Mrs. Gottsched didn't seem to understand what exactly a ballad even was, and the 1830s that saw Chopin's highly abstract piano *Ballades* become wide critical successes, the word "ballad" began to insert itself into the lifeworld of the German middle classes at an impressive pace. For an index of a disappearing world, the ballad seemed to be thriving. And the ballad was "popular," though not quite in the way that Bürger had supposed. Throughout the nineteenth century, there existed a tension between two senses of popularity, with each making reference to a different understanding of "the people." "The people" could mean an authentic, original, unalienated, and monolithic populace—hearty peasants rooted in the soil, tradition, and the language. This was the discourse of *Volkstümlichkeit*—of rootedness in folk ways.[57] Or it could mean the emerging urban or industrial mass[58]—driven by a desire for mindless distraction, beholden to the ever-accelerating whims of fashion, and, as the century wore on, frequently gendered as female and racially othered.[59] In 1888, the sociologist Ferdinand Tönnies would find the formulation "community" (*Gemeinschaft*) and "society" (*Gesellschaft*) for these two forms of common life—and the circulation of songs would be one of the ways he distinguished the two.[60] The "popular" dimension that Bürger and Uhland felt balladry had lost concerned the first sense of "the people"; that it was interlacing itself with unprecedented efficiency with the second sense of "the people" was for them a sign of just how far the form had fallen. But not all advocates of the ballad thought this way. And many who consumed, shared, and adapted ballads in those years were entirely unencumbered by these worries.

This is where the intermedial nature of the German ballad comes to matter: because while many arts—literature, the performing arts, instrumental and vocal music, opera—negotiated the tension between these two senses of popularity, they each negotiated it in a different way. The retrospective, antiquarian impulse that drove the Romantic generation to emulate the ballad-collectors—the impulse that yielded the Grimms' fairy tales as much as *Des Knaben Wunderhorn*—of course partook of this first sense and was often tinged with profound cultural pessimism.[61] At the same time that Uhland, Alexis, and others could claim that the ballad was disappearing among "the people," the fact was that everyday Germans were coming into

---

57 Matthew Gelbart, *The Invention of "Folk Music" and "Art Music": Emerging Categories from Ossian to Wagner* (Cambridge: Cambridge University Press, 2009).
58 See Leo Löwenthal, *Literatur und Massenkultur* (Frankfurt: Suhrkamp, 1990), 28f.
59 See Barbara Kosta, *Willing Seduction* (New York: Berghahn, 2012), 28.
60 Ferdinand Tönnies, *Community and Civil Society* (Cambridge: Cambridge University Press, 2001), 167.
61 Miriam Noa, *Volkstümlichkeit und Nationbuilding* (Münster: Waxmann, 2013), 164.

contact with more and more aesthetic objects that billed themselves as ballads. They just were encountering them in different and new ways: in a bourgeois household they might enjoy them as recited by the children during a soirée, in more proletarian ones they might sing them in their local choral society or be made to memorize them by the local schoolmaster. Somehow this kind of popularity wasn't the "right" kind of popularity to the Romantic nationalists, the kinds of communities it gathered weren't the "right" kind of communities to the Herderian communalists. But they shaped the path the ballad cut across the German nineteenth century, and they even shaped how its relationship to the nation was understood and lived.

While the ballad entered literature with a halo of ephemerality and fugitivity characteristic of oral culture, its ephemerality was always a pretense, one that left in its wake a slew of objects and records. "Writing moves words from the sound world to a world of visual space," Walter Ong argued, "but print locks words into position in this space."[62] The mobility of the printed, literary ballad soon resembled that of its imagined oral precursors, but it was part of its appeal that this secondary circulation somehow nevertheless constituted a loss: the ballad now circulated as a reified text rather than living tradition. It was explicit in traveling through the widening circuits of an expanding landscape of publishing (including music publishing); it participated in the expansion of certain institutions like the *Musikverein* and the opera; it partook of the dawning mass age through schoolbooks and exercises meant to inculcate the canon in an ever-widening circle of grammar school students. The ballad was such a natural traveler because it was positioned as national "German art." But the many arenas which it traversed—visual art, music, publishing, etc.—stood each in a very different relationship to the construct of "Germany" and to whatever was supposed to lie outside of it.

By the time the ballad began to insert itself into German literary life in the 1780s, the ballad was no longer a purely literary phenomenon. The boom in the musical presentation of poetry began in the 1770s, and by 1788 the success of Bürger's "Lenore" also extended into this emerging realm: Friedrich Ludwig Aemilius Kunzen's setting of the ballad alternated sung and narrated portions.[63] The emergence of the literary ballad thus coincided with the emergence of a whole host of aesthetic practices that all extended, in their own way, claims about literature: the practice of *Vertonung*, the development of public declamation, the emergence of the *Lied*. Theories of what a ballad was were not limited to poets explaining their craft: they appeared in books on public declamation, in reviews of recently published music, in discussions

---

62 Walter Ong, *Orality and Literacy* (London: Routledge, 2003), 119.
63 Ulrich Kühn, *Sprech-Ton-Kunst* (Tübingen: Niemeyer, 2001), 146.

of musical soirées, in school curricula, and in opera libretti. Theorization of the ballad was broad-based and diffuse, and it proceeded apace with the pragmatics of the ballad—what different constituencies sought to do with this most itinerant of forms.

The genre's sudden hypervisibility once again seemed to make the ballad communal property, and not the province of the philologist. While ballads circulated in a great many contexts in nineteenth-century Germany, their preferred and privileged extra-literary medium of circulation was surely music. That is to say, music functioned as a medium for commonality and community that seemed somehow connected to the kind of community the old tales recited by bards around campfires were supposed to have called into being. And it is also to say that music generally circulated more in the nineteenth century than it had previously, and that the ballad traveled on a wave created by a burgeoning publishing industry, an expanding musical-pedagogical complex, wider availability of musical instruments, and rapid urbanization. But urbanization and an expanded publishing industry were of course not unique to Germany—the cultural reception, filtered through residual Romanticism and burgeoning nationalism, played a key role.

In nineteenth-century Germany, the ballad setting was more than an adaptation. Rather than a secondary remediation, or at worst a cash-in, it was frequently fêted as a coequal creation: "Is there a single ballad poet," wrote Max Runze in 1888, "whose works, insofar as they contained any deeper poetic meaning, did not shape themselves under [Carl] Loewe's masterful creative hand [*schaffender Meisterhand*] into new, delightful forms of life?"[64] For a composer who set poems by many of the titans of German literature, this is a fairly large claim to make. For Runze, and for many others like him, the musical ballad was a new creation, just as lively and just as urgent as the circumstances that gave rise to the original poem. Of course, there were other voices that treated the composer as a mere adapter. But such assessments were often shadowed by the sense that, if they did their work correctly, the ballad composer could be a second creator.

And music was indeed seen as the preferred medium for such second creation. As the Young Hegelian Ernst Theodor Echtermeyer (1805–1844) wrote in the *Hallesche Jahrbücher* in 1839, "the ballad wants to be heard rather than read, and requires, in order to unfold its full effect, musical accompaniment."[65] The poet Wilhelm Müller (1794–1827), whose poetry is remembered today mostly for having been set to music by Franz Schubert, in a letter describes song settings as suitable substitutes for other forms of public sounding out: "My poems, which are with few exceptions ill-suited

---

64 Max Runze, *Loewe Redivivus* (Berlin: Duncker, 1888), 94.

65 Ernst Theodor Echtermeyer, "Unsere Balladen- und Romanzenpoesie," *Hallesche Jahrbücher* 97 (April 23, 1839): 771.

for public declamation, would be leading only a half-life, a paper life, black on white, until music breathes life into them, or at least wakes in them what was sleeping within."[66] The ballad revivals across different European nations at the end of the eighteenth century drew to varying degrees on the ballad's musicality. But in Germany there emerged, at the same time, an ideology of music that treated music as a more profound level of signification than language was capable of. At times, this understanding rendered the ballad's musicalness—the way in which it seemed to recall music and call forth music, the way it was music and begged to be accompanied by music— a wholesale resurrection of its primary orality. The critic Wolfgang Menzel in 1838 wrote of "Die Lore-Ley" (1824), perhaps the most folkloristic of Heine's poems, that, despite the poet's populist inclinations, "the song is, for all its seeming simplicity, far too sophisticated, too clearly a product of art, to ever become a true *Volkslied*." But, he added, Silcher's famous setting of it "sounds entirely folk-like."[67] What, at least to Menzel's ears, Heine tried at and failed in words—the seeming paradox of inventing something that emerged organically from the common people—music could achieve. Listening to a ballad setting was a legitimate continuation of the hearsay by which it had initially constituted itself.

This supposition was more than just pure ideology. When "Der Erlkönig" was first presented to English readers, it was as an ancient German folk tale. The irony is that while the story was not then, thanks to the ubiquity of Goethe's poem and Schubert's setting it quickly became something of the sort: a cultural shibboleth deeply anchored in collective consciousness in Germany. Many observers (most recently Christopher Gibbs[68]) have pointed to the fact that this anchoring owes more of a debt to Schubert's setting of Goethe's poem than to Goethe's poem itself. Certain details that are almost invariably considered part of the tale—the father driving his horse through a desolate landscape full of worry for his sick child—are nowhere suggested in Goethe's text. They are however implicit in Schubert's rendering of it: whereas Carl Loewe's setting slowly escalates the tension (something Goethe himself felt was far closer to his intention), Schubert opens with the song's iconic hammering triplets. Schubert's rider is terrified long before his child begins to have visions of the Erl King and his daughters.

At stake in this shift are questions of temporality, of narrative and agency. Schubert's setting is, as Johann Vesque von Püttlingen observed in 1858, closer to a *Lied*; it is drenched in one particular mood and maintains it

---

66 Wilhelm Müller to Bernhard Joseph Klein, December 15, 1822; cited in Reinhart Meyer-Kalkus, *Geschichte der literarischen Vortragskunst* (Stuttgart: Metzler, 2020), 78.

67 Cited in Bernd Kortländer, *Heinrich Heine* (Stuttgart: Reclam, 2003), 91.

68 Christopher H. Gibbs, "'Komm geh' mit mir': Schubert's Uncanny Erlkönig," *Nineteenth Century Music* 19, no. 2 (1995): 116.

throughout, whereas the literary source dramatizes a gradually mounting dread.[69] The generic difference comes with a whole range of attendant questions: what, for instance, is the moral of the story of "Der Erlkönig"? Schubert's father seems doomed to lose his son with the first repetition of the uncanny and iconic arpeggio—his blindness to the world his son describes is entirely about whether he will ever know why his son dies. Loewe's version of the same figure may be making a fateful decision in ignoring his son's pleas. Different ways of accentuating and triangulating the hybrid genre of the ballad thus encapsulated different readings of what exactly the ballad genre meant to say—about fate, about free will, about feeling, about knowledge, about the individual and the collective.

The *Lied* would dominate nineteenth-century German composition far more than it ever did the eighteenth. It also, as Kira Thurman has shown, became a powerful stand-in for German nationhood, and for a specific imaginary national body. While its mobility marked it out for export and adoption by other groups—Thurman in particular points to the long tradition of African American singers using this form to "participate in a transatlantic and white high culture to which they had historically been denied access"[70]—such mobility was also always policed and curtailed. There were right and wrong people to sing a *Lied*, right and wrong bodies to sound out their psychological depths. The emergence of the modern *Lied* had its origins in developments in aesthetics that changed both how music and how literature were understood. Herder had insisted on the musicality of language, on its connection with the pre-rational mind, on its direct connection with an authentic self.[71] While these ideas would indeed come to define the astonishing cross-pollination of an emerging literary canon and an emerging Romantic musical language in the generation of Schubert and Loewe, it is important to note that ballad-settings predated the heyday of the *Lied* by about a generation. Composers did not turn to ballads as a sub-form of the *Lied*; rather, the ballad setting became a locus where a newly ascendant music publishing industry was able to articulate its relationship to an emerging literary and didactic canon. It began in direct dialogue with the eventually canonic authors, and was undertaken by a largely forgotten generation of composers—Johann Friedrich Reichardt (1752–1814), Johann Rudolf Zumsteeg (1760–1802), and Carl Friedrich Zelter (1758–1832).

---

69 Johann Vesque von Püttlingen, "Über den Erlkönig von Schubert," *Monatsschrift für Theater und Musik* 4 (1858): 585.

70 Kira Thurman, "The German Lied and the Songs of Black Folk," *Journal of the American Musicological Association* 67, no. 2 (2014): 567.

71 Jane K. Brown, "In the Beginning Was Poetry," in *The Cambridge Companion to the Lied*, ed. James Parsons (Cambridge: Cambridge University Press, 2004), 20.

The ballad-setting attained broad currency and immense popularity among the first generation of composers to have grown up with literary ballads: Franz Schubert was born in the "ballad year" of 1797, Carl Loewe a year earlier in 1796, and Robert Schumann in 1810. While it became central to *Lied*-aesthetics, the ballad-setting did not sit easily with the prevailing trends and preoccupations of the 1820s and 1830s.[72] Romantic writers had clearly positioned balladry as akin to mythology, but in some sense the ballad's investments in mythology were too partial, too opportunistic: "We do not have a mythology," Friedrich Schlegel had declared, and in a way ballads didn't have one either, in the sense that they ground up whatever mythology seemed ready at hand.[73] In musical Romanticism this arbitrariness became a problem of form. As Ruth O. Bingham has pointed out, the ballad's peripatetic topics, their narrative and affective self-containment, stood in a deeply ambivalent relationship to the song cycle, which strove for overarching musical forms and thematic links.[74] Benedict Taylor has pointed to Romantic music's fascination with non-linear, non-teleological time and, as a consequence, with cyclical forms.[75] David Ferris has argued that by grouping and arranging individual *Lieder*, the composers of the Romantic generation explored a "sense of incompleteness and potentiality."[76]

The ballad, neatly packaged and narratively self-contained, streamlined in its drive toward a clean denouement, seemed to partake of none of this. When ballads occurred in groups, it was a matter of marketing, not of theme. This integrated the ballad into the circuit of the music market, with all of the arbitrariness, modishness, and caprice that could imply. The ballad was, or easily could become, a commodity. In Theodor Fontane's *Effi Briest* (1895), the concert singer Marietta Tripelli is asked to sing a ballad and her hosts hand her "a half dozen booklets of notes, which his friend rifled through in quick succession." Tripelli is unimpressed as Fontane traces how she makes her choice: Goethe, it turns out, is too old as a text: "'Erl King,' bah, humbug!" Loewe is too old as a composer: "And here are Loewe's ballads, not the latest either." Certain stories themselves seem to repetitive: "'The Bells of Speyer'... oh, the eternal ding dong." Others offend good taste: "The scenery

---

72 Nancy F. Garf, "Lieder Cycle," in *Encyclopedia of the Romantic Era, 1760–1850*, Vol. 2, ed. Christopher John Murray (New York: Fitzroy Dearborn, 2004), 682.

73 Schlegel, "Rede über Mythologie und Symbolische Anschauung," 5:197.

74 Ruth O. Bingham, "The Early Nineteenth-Century Song Cycle," in *The Cambridge Companion to the Lied*, ed. James Parsons (Cambridge: Cambridge University Press, 2004), 117.

75 Benedict Taylor, *Mendelssohn, Time and Memory: The Romantic Conception of Cyclic Form* (Cambridge: Cambridge University Press, 2011), 23.

76 David Ferris, *Schumann's Eichendorff Liederkreis and the Genre of the Romantic Cycle* (New York: Oxford University Press, 2000), 65.

chewing [*Kulissenreißerei*] is tasteless and stale." Finally she decides on one of the oldest texts in the bunch: "Oh, but here 'Sir Olaf,' that works."[77] It's hard to say for certain how often scenes like these played out in nineteenth-century Germany. But perhaps Fontane's point is simply that, by its various modes of circulation, the ballad made itself susceptible to assessment according to considerations of fashion and consumption.

Other composers were intent on moving the ballad in the exact opposite direction, or to have the ballad move their music in the opposite direction: away from the market and toward the sphere of autonomous art. When Wagner positioned the ballad as a "mythico-poetical creation of the folk," when Runze claimed Loewe's ballads as an ancestor to Wagner's works,[78] when Max Kalbeck argued that the ballad settings were really "folk-like total works of art en miniature [*volkstümliche Gesamtkunstwerke im Kleinen*],"[79] but above all when composers sought to meld the traditionally miniaturized ballad form with counterintuitively monumental genres—music drama, opera, oratorio—they all sought to resist the ballad's assimilation into the logic of market and bourgeois home. When the ballad entered symphonic space and attained monumental proportions—for instance, in tone poems or in a symphony like Joachim Raff's Symphony op. 177 (based on Bürger's "Lenore"), the ballad was melded with cyclic form after all.[80] As German opera gravitated toward through-composed forms and away from number opera, the ballad functioned both as an emblem of organic form and as an unwelcome remainder of the episodic, the self-contained, the self-limiting in popular song. And when German orchestral music, in particular in the New German School, began looking beyond the sonata form, the ballad furnished them with a powerful guiding image—all the while giving their efforts something a little comical, as pithy, playful thirty-line poems somewhat incongruously yielded forty-minute symphonic poems.

Whether it was musical or literary, a form of the *Lied* or an anthologized art ballad, ballads frequently did not have the dignity and authenticity that German nationalists in particular were wont to accord the village commons—balladry often had a whiff of the book market, of consumerism, of a use object imbibed and discarded. For all of Herder's celebrations of oral culture, the physical object he offered his contemporaries was precisely a collection "made for paper and verses made of dead letters." The ballad is not Wolf Biermann seated in his apartment on Chausseestraße 131 singing into a tape recorder—it is Wolf Biermann seated under the flood lights in the Cologne Sporthalle,

---

77 Theodor Fontane, *Effi Briest*, in *Romane und Erzählungen* (Leipzig and Berlin: Aufbau, 1973), 7:96–97.

78 Runze, *Loewe Redivivus*, 112.

79 Max Kalbeck, *Johannes Brahms* (Berlin: Deutsche Brahmsgesellschaft, 1915), 4:138.

80 Taylor, *Mendelssohn, Time and Memory*, 15.

in a complicated pas-de-deux with modernity, politics, and history. For more nationalistic and conservative critics, this represented a profound fall of the vaunted ballad tradition. When he presented his *Meister-Balladen* in 1900, the conservative poet Börries von Münchhausen argued that "the ballad has been pushed too far into the background, a powerful form of poetry resplendent in many colors," that it "has either been lost altogether or has gotten off track in the worst ways."[81] The "real" ballad, for Münchhausen, was frankly medievalist, emphasized oral presentation, was deeply serious and profoundly anti-modern. It was "monumental, where lyric poetry is a miniature and a mosaic."[82]

Few today would agree with this assessment—we have gotten more attuned to the notes of irony and self-awareness that suffuse the most famous and most successful exemplars of the form from Gleim to Bertolt Brecht. However, even though Münchhausen's emphasis on a "lost" art of balladry in the midst of an unprecedented remediation and proliferation may strike us as absurd, in one central respect the critical treatment of the ballad today implicitly agrees with him: granted, they ended up in the collective memory, in our schoolbooks, in Disney movies, but this is something that happened to them along the way, not something that somehow defines the genre. Surely they were written to emulate the oral forms of old, not to animate the oral forms of modernity? This book questions that assumption. It does not attempt to detect the undertows that connect a poem by Goethe or Schiller back in time to the *Moritaten* of the eighteenth-century market square, but instead wonders about the gravitational pull of the ballad as experienced in the latter half of the nineteenth century, when every child knew "Das Grab im Busento" by heart, when Paul Dukas set "Der Zauberlehrling" to music, when for every ballad one could name a student could roar out a well-known parody. A gravitational pull that ultimately emanated from a place like the Sporthalle.

During the period under discussion in this book, the ballad canon comprised poems that were more frequently anthologized than analyzed. Wolfgang Kayser, in his 1936 book *Geschichte der deutschen Ballade*, which reflects to a troubling extent the Nazi years' influence on how the ballad canon was understood, makes explicit how the supposed straightforwardness of the ballad and its utility for a German national project mutually implied each other. For Kayser, in balladry "a world opens up that echoes with the thunder of hooves of storming mares." He also claims for the ballad a kind of instinctual understanding that makes analysis superfluous, a *post*

---

81 Börries von Münchhausen, "Vorwort," in *Göttinger Musenalmanach für 1901* (Göttingen: Horstmann, 1901), x–xi.

82 Börries von Münchhausen, "Zur Ästhetik meiner Balladen," *Deutsche Monatsschrift für das gesamte Leben der Gegenwart*, Vol. 11 (Berlin: Duncker, 1907), 332.

*festum* exercise parasitical to its living, breathing practice: "this is no accidental window into a world; we no longer feel a poet who speaks but are pulled along into the world of the insecure, the fateful. We recognize these segments of a world as belonging to ourselves and as binding."[83] Only by being naïve and receptive, only by letting the ballad work on what is already latent within us, Kaiser thinks, do we manage to understand it. And not much is required to understand it beyond this kind of attunement.

Such balladic naïveté is uncomfortably bound up with national history. But as Biermann's Cologne concert suggests: perhaps balladic innocence was of a different register all along? Biermann's pose of the simple singer just sitting down before 10,000 strangers to perform what came to his heart was just that—a pose. His performance was a calculated challenge to a totalitarian system, his naïveté one formal strategy at his disposal. If balladic innocence, and balladic adolescence, are suspect after the abuses to which they were put, by and under the Nazis, what about balladic craftiness? What if we allowed this quality, rather than Kayser's lordly shouts and flashing steel, to guide the story of the ballad? As Karl Riha pointed out in a 1965 book, it is another distinguishing feature of the German art ballad that it has a continued history in modernism.[84] Riha traces a lineage of modern ballad writing from Frank Wedekind via Georg Heym, Kurt Tucholsky, Erich Kästner, Joachim Ringelnatz, and above all Bertolt Brecht, all the way to writers like Günter Grass and Gerhard Rühm. Riha felt compelled to trace this second coming of the *Kunstballade* because the ballad was largely understood to have disappeared with the onset of modernism—relegated to the ham-fisted efforts of folkish poets with unsavory Nazi ties like Münchhausen, or as an object of parody for snarky modernists. Riha not only pointed out that the ballad had a second, far more ironized, far more critical, afterlife; but he also pointed out that, when examined in the right light, this modernist balladry really didn't look all that different from the classic efforts of Bürger, Goethe, Schiller, Uhland, Heine, Droste-Hülshoff, and Fontane.

This was less about residual fealty on the part of the iconoclastic balladeers of the early twentieth century and more about the fact that the classic ballads themselves had been possessed of a pronounced ironic playfulness. Folkish ballad-evangelists of the early twentieth century, such as Münchhausen or Agnes Miegel, had imbued the art ballad with a kind of simple-mindedness and unsubtle monumentality that it never possessed in either the eighteenth or the nineteenth century. And the blood-soaked coldness of Kästner's or Brecht's ballads drew, for their part, on a tradition of spectacularly callous

---

83 Wolfgang Kayser, *Geschichte der deutschen Ballade* (Berlin: Junker und Dünnhaupt, 1936), viii.

84 Karl Riha, *Moritat, Song, Bänkelsang—Die moderne Ballade* (Göttingen: Sachse & Pohl, 1965).

*Moritaten*. Kästner and Brecht were perhaps most overt in training the inherent nostalgia in the form of the ballad onto the oral culture of an urban, perhaps even proletarian, milieu—but they were far from the first. The German ballad always looked backward to the tradition of *Bänkelsang*—a carnivalesque multimedia performance that combined Grand Guignol plots, visual aids, and music. Rather than the lone bard by his campfire, their vanished balladeer was a carnival barker desperately distracting an audience while his associates picked its pockets.

Instead of designating an epistemological and poetological problem, the German ballad tended to occupy a double position—it gestured at orality, but remained resolutely literary; it pretended at folk character, but was equally imbued with a genius aesthetic; it could appear straightforwardly Romantic in its holism and organicism, but just as often deeply ironic in its formal features. The story of the ballad in Germany is not primarily that of poets looking for something auratic and authentic. Instead, German poets discovered the form as a means of reflecting on what happened to aura and authenticity under conditions of modernity.[85]

If Heinrich Heine's generation made explicit the ballad's link to mass culture, mass media, and mass readership that had furnished the backdrop to ballad writing since the start of the century, then this was true for literary authors as much as for the composers who adapted their work. On the musical side, this book shifts the emphasis from Loewe and Schubert, who wrote many of the ballads that have remained canonic, to Schumann, Wagner, and Liszt and their followers—in whose hands the ballad always tended to exceed the decorous bounds of the *Lied*, always seemed to strain toward different, more complicated forms. Rather than striving to reflect a native simplicity of their source material, their balladry responded to the contradictions and fractures that had always already animated the form in Germany. Theirs was also the generation that opened the ballad genre to women: although the 1790s saw an unprecedented efflorescence of writing by women in German-speaking Europe, those women writers largely tended to avoid the ballad (Amalie von Imhoff [1776–1831] being one notable exception). This changed by the mid-nineteenth century, as Annette von Droste-Hülshoff wrote some of the most influential ballads in the German canon.

Insofar as ballads celebrated an original unity of a people and of its poetic canon—and they rarely did—, it was one that they thought no longer accessible to them. But they knew better than to attempt to restore that unity—there was no more gathering around the fairground or fireplace to listen to songs, all there was were memorization exercises at school, mass-market

---

[85] David Atkinson has recently made an analogous claim for certain British ballads: Atkinson, *The Ballad and Its Pasts: Literary Histories and the Play of Memory* (Woodbridge: Boydell & Brewer, 2018).

anthologies with illustrative etchings, and amateur music performances. The German ballad emerged in a concrete and complicated dialogue with German nationalism. Given that creative appropriation was a particularly central feature of German balladry, and given that the ballad was conceived both with a view to a fictional vanished primary orality and a very real secondary orality (by song, by memorization, etc.), the ballad had the distinction of being both freighted with a great significance and of being so omnipresent that it complicated overly straightforward meaning attributed to the form. Germans looked to ballads to tell them about German nationhood in a multitude of ways—but the fact that they did so by singing, memorizing, reciting, staging, orchestrating, instrumentalizing, parodying, and paraphrasing meant that they found strikingly different things there. And it meant that ambitious poets, composers, pedagogues, and visual artists could do interesting, even subversive things, all the while hewing to a seemingly straightforward tradition.

## The Ballad as Memory Culture

The ballad has always been about memory. The *Moritat* that started becoming a popular form of public poetry in the seventeenth century was a medium of communal recall, of information relay.[86] Even though it eschewed overt didacticism, the life lessons the ballads of Goethe and Schiller imparted felt like they were preserving a kind of folk wisdom—often enough to respect one's station, to know one's place, to be content with what one had. And reciting the ballad reinstated, if not the news that, say, a murder ballad had once conveyed, then at least the kind of community that could be called into being by such news. In the case of the musical ballad, as Carl Dahlhaus noted, this influenced the characteristic tone of the ballad: was the musical ballad a formal whole that presupposed some foreknowledge on the part of its listeners, or was it a "discursive" creation that unfolded the story, as it were, for the first time?[87] The ballad was where a nebulous notion of collective (national) memory met very concrete and very modern techniques and questions of individual memory and recall.

As Walter Benjamin put it, "the listener's naïve relationship to the storyteller is controlled by interest in retaining what he is told."[88] The ballad both

---

[86] For a recent study of one such information relay, namely ballads telling stories of crime, punishment, and execution see: Una McIlvenna, *Singing the News of Death: Execution Ballads in Europe, 1500–1900* (Oxford: Oxford University Press, 2022) [forthcoming].

[87] Carl Dahlhaus, *Nineteenth Century Music* (Berkeley: University of California Press, 1989), 105.

[88] Walter Benjamin, "The Storyteller," in *Illuminations* (New York: Schocken, 1968), 97.

fits this mold and does not: ballads are poems recited to an audience meant to retain them; they are received by that audience in order to pass them on. This is the ballad's inherent democracy. But if memory is indeed "the epic faculty par excellence," as Benjamin claims, then memory functions slightly differently in the ballad: part of what makes the ballad so memorable is its portability, the fact that it is short, succinct, centered on memorable poetic devices, a catchy rhythm, striking plots. Balladry was to some extent a discourse of the other—but there was an ambiguity as to what constituted the other. Was it *Geist*, the mythopoetic sense of the common people, a folk tradition? Or was it the lowest common denominator of poetic language, bleated at you by tragedians on summer break, recited in class, learned by heart as punishment, sung during outings?

Starting with Bodmer, Germans had largely understood the ballad as a fragment of the epic. Many of the same factors that made it so memorable were understood as a symptom of the ballad's partiality. It embodied some element of "the course of events," some particular truth about the world to be remembered. The whole to which the individual ballad referred was missing, but under ideal conditions its very democracy and ubiquity made up for this lack: for in their totality the trove of ballads (as the fairy tale, mythology, and others) resurrected the whole. Its popularity, wrote Bürger, "turns poetry back into that state in which God created it and placed it into the souls of the elect."[89]

The ballad was understood to partake of collective memory, but it also projected the fantasy of collective memory forward. In 2000, Jan Assmann took Claude Levi-Strauss's distinction between "cold" and "hot" elements of cultural transmission and pointed to places where ancient cultures appeared to be occupying middle points between maintaining their relationship to the world through memory and using memory to transform themselves toward some kind of altered present or future.[90] The ballad pretended to retain and preserve a cultural heritage and collective memory, while actually creating a new and distinct collective memory, all the while populating it with Germanic kings, knights, and nature spirits. David Atkinson has noted a similar duality in the imaginary provenance of the Anglo-Scottish ballad. The codified understanding under which the ballad became part of the literary canon in the eighteenth and early nineteenth century was the following: the ballad was plucked from oral circulation and brought into written circulation. But in fact, this was always more of a convenient myth than a reality. The divisions between orality and literacy, between folk and

---

89 Bürger, "Herzensausguß über Volkspoesie," 2:1655: "Durch Popularität, mein ich, soll die Poesie das wieder werden, wozu sie Gott erschaffen, und in die Seelen der Auserwählten gelegt hat."

90 Jan Assmann, *Religion und kulturelles Gedächtnis* (Munich: Beck, 2000), 26.

high culture on which it depended, simply had not existed with sufficient clarity to make it anything more than that.[91]

But in the German-speaking world this fantasy of an original orality of the ballad authorized, and indeed provided an ideology for, a new, secondary orality. If anthologies made poetry part of the bourgeois interior, then memorization was one way in which poetry was integrated into lived domesticity.[92] At the same time, the ballad emerged in Germany alongside a wholesale reconceptualization of the way human memory functioned. The kind of memory on which it drew was in the first place an unconcealment of collectively held beliefs, opinions, and superstitions. The ballad drew from an inborn memory and life feeling and brought to light thoughts one recognized, even if one had never thought them like this before. This theoretical understanding influenced how this poetry one could live with was actually lived with. For instance, ballads were frequently used as memory training in Germany—schoolteachers used them to discipline their students; popular recitation sought to instill a shared "high German" pronunciation in their audiences; Freud used them to interrogate the vagaries of memory.

But because the theory of collective memory that subtended their popularity diverged from the mnemonic methods and cognitive architectures of the German Renaissance, memorizing the ballad meant something different.[93] Where the learned men of the Renaissance had relied on individualistic methods of recollection, the ballad was implicated in a memorial program that relied on students' intuition to put them in touch with a kind of collective memory. It claimed, after all, to teach them to remember something that they already knew. The ballad was part of an anti-methodological pedagogy, a pedagogy in spite of itself. In her memoirs, the writer Fanny Lewald (1811–1889) positions her youthful preoccupation with ballads as something of an extracurricular activity. Although Lewald did attend (private) school, which was unusual for a woman even of the upper bourgeoisie of her age, the encounter with ballads seemed to take place outside of the classroom. "I had an incredible memory for words," she recalls, "which however shrank to the exact extent as I developed a memory for facts, a phenomenon that occurs almost as a rule in curious children." When she was ten or eleven, Lewald recalled later, "I knew most of Schiller's and Goethe's ballads by heart." This memorization she recalls as an almost creaturely, intimate, bodily relationship to language: "Rhythm, sound and rhyme were so pleasurable to me that I took them in as though a breath of fresh air."[94]

---

91 David Atkinson, *The Anglo-Scottish Ballad and Its Imaginary Contexts* (Cambridge: Open Book Publishers, 2014), 34–36.

92 Catherine Robson, *Heart Beats: Everyday Life and the Memorized Poem* (Princeton, NJ: Princeton University Press, 2012), 106.

93 Frances A. Yates, *The Art of Memory* (London: Bodley Head, 2013), 356.

94 Fanny Lewald, *Gesammelte Werke* (Berlin: Janke, 1871), I:162–63.

While a literary mind like Lewald's was of course likely to encounter the ballad and its intrinsic demand for memorization as something pleasurable, the ballad was foisted upon others more or less against their will. At the same time, they too were supposed to draw from the ballad more than just a sense for the literary canon, or for literature in general. The Prussian School Laws and Regulations put out periodically by the minister of education in Berlin speak to the way the ballad made it into the classroom. The curricula they include for both *Gymnasien* (university preparatory schools) and *Realschulen* (professional schools) give some sense as to what it was supposed to teach there—familiarizing students with poetry, as noted, was only a minor aspect of this mission. The *Realschule* in Remscheidt in Western Germany introduced ballads in seventh grade: students were to "memorize 8 simple ballads,"[95] and learn how to summarize what they had read. But the ballads were evidently meant to do more: they could introduce students to "the spelling of foreign words," teach them to "repeat a narrative from history or legend" in their own words.

In eighth grade, by contrast, students encountered ballads more on their own terms—again, "8 ballads are learned by heart, mostly Uhland and Schiller." But this time, the ballad becomes a way of exploring versification, rhyme structure, and meter, and furnishes topics for student essays "mostly about history and German heroic poetry." But in Grade 9 the ballad disappears: now we are dealing with the epic, with classical and medieval meters (hexameter, distich, the *Nibelungenstrophe*). Instead of ballads, students now memorize "8 poems, mostly Schiller"—it isn't hard to guess which ones these would have been, and they are unlikely to have been ballads. And Grade 10 is given over to drama—the only two works mentioned by name are *Wilhelm Tell* and *Jungfrau von Orleans* (*The Maid of Orleans*)—and to "more difficult Schiller-poems." The dominance of Schiller and the dominance of the ballad in classrooms seem to have ebbed and flowed in tandem.[96]

Schiller's ballads were probably presented to the students as a kind of national heirloom. However fanciful that notion, these poems of course ended up entwining themselves into the biographies of generations of students. Not uniformly, of course, not predictably. But they were there. In 1933, eighteen-year-old Englishman Patrick Leigh Fermor (1915–2011) undertook a hiking journey across Europe, first traveling up the course of the Rhine, a sojourn that would eventually take him through much of the German-speaking world. The literarily inclined young man found a world structured

---

95 Ludwig Adolf Wiese, ed., *Verordnungen und Gesetze für die höheren Schulen in Preussen* (Berlin: Wiegand und Gieben, 1875), 350.

96 Peter Pabisch, "Glühendes Wort zum Ideal über der versagenden Realität—Zu Schillers Balladen," in *Who Is This Schiller Now?*, ed. Jeffrey L. High, Nicholas Martin, and Norbert Oellers (Rochester, NY: Camden House, 2011), 72–73.

by poetry, more specifically by the poetry of the nineteenth century. At an inn near Heidelberg, the proprietress greets him with "Wer reitet so spät durch Nacht und Wind?"—only in retrospect does Fermor realize the old woman welcomed him with an ironic invocation of the first line of "Der Erlkönig."[97] As he continues his travels and continues to encounter written poetry in oral forms, Fermor comes to reflect on those poems one carries with oneself. There are those poems one was forced to memorize, and beyond that a "private anthology" of literary texts, "both of those automatically absorbed and of poems consciously chosen and memorized as though one were stocking up for a desert island or for a stretch in solitary."[98] Fermor's "private anthology," in his accounting, contains ancient epics, Shakespearean soliloquies, and some standouts of lyric poetry. Unlike the Heidelberg landlady's, it contains no ballads. But perhaps that is the point: the memory anthology of a young man with literary ambitions either didn't include the ballad, or didn't quite count it. A bright young literary man like Fermor probably knew many ballads, but they somehow didn't rate inclusion. One filed them away with the popular tunes one couldn't get out of one's mind, or with folk songs or nursery rhymes learned in childhood. But matters were different with a Heidelberg innkeeper—no Shakespearean soliloquies, only a half-joking invocation of an opening line from a Goethe ballad.

As the welcome Fermor received in Heidelberg suggests, the memorialization (and memorization) of the ballad was not usually about deep structures of feeling; it was frequently about recognition and applicability, both routinely ironized. What Helmuth Lethen identified as a kind of coldness characteristic of the ballads of Brecht and Weill was really true of most of the German art ballad canon.[99] The brutality by which ballad protagonists often get their comeuppance, the way in which the seriousness of their fate is often told in fairly unserious rhyme: all of these speak to a sadistic rather than sympathetic streak. There wasn't a whole lot of incentive in these poems to get personally invested. This coldness was, if anything, exacerbated by the various paths by which the ballad circulated in Germany—familiarity could easily become laced with a soft contempt. There was the philistine contempt of the innkeeper invoking Goethe—the contempt of those who resent the sphere of *Bildung* because it has been forced upon them. And there was the condescension from young men of Fermor's set.

Where the two sides agreed was that the ballad didn't need to be understood, to be penetrated by either intellect or feeling, in order to be

---

97 Patrick Leigh Fermor, *A Time of Gifts* (New York: New York Review Books, 2005), 66.

98 Fermor, *A Time of Gifts*, 83.

99 Helmut Lethen, *Cool Conduct—The Culture of Distance in Weimar Germany* (Berkeley: University of California Press, 2002), 48.

memorized. In the beginning of Thomas Mann's *Buddenbrooks* (1903), little Antonia (Tony) Buddenbrook rushes through the catechism, which she has memorized but not exactly understood. "Once you were moving, she thought, it felt just like racing down 'Jerusalem Hill' on the sled with her brothers in winter: every thought vanished from your mind, and you couldn't stop if you wanted to."[100] The novel positions this facility with memorization, as Catherine Robson has pointed out, to suggest Tony's troubling "ability to internalize her society's commandments."[101] A young man of the upper bourgeoisie like Fermor could think of his "private anthology" as somehow deeply connected to his personhood. For many others, memorization is a concession of one's own subjectivity to convention and societal forces.

In an essay called "Che cos'è la poesia?," Jacques Derrida asks what it means to know literature by heart. He is particularly interested by the moments when "by heart" means that the text "is confided . . . to a certain exteriority of the automaton, to the laws of mnemotechnics, to that liturgy that mimes mechanics on the surface," rather than "pure interiority, independent spontaneity."[102] To recite ballads is to regurgitate all the stories, gossip, useless information that the world and our station within it have crammed down our throats. Speaking with Mikhail Bakhtin, one could think of it as иноязычие, or other-languagedness: a necessary acknowledgment or awareness that what we say has preconditions that lie outside of the world constituted in and through our own language.[103] To have memorized in this context means to have accepted the way in which the world has interpellated you. Balladry promised to tell the individual of a collective unconscious. But there was of course a risk that it was collective in all the wrong ways: a trace not of some ancestral knowledge of spirit, but of the deformations wrought by schoolmasters, mass media, and other assorted social pressures. Stewart notes this as the "antipersonal dimension of distressed genre"—instead of reaching for something deep and individual, it settles for a thinned-out collectivity.[104] Balladry is about recognizing together, but it is frequently about nothing more than recognizing that togetherness.

While working on this book, its author decided to run a brief unscientific survey: he asked roughly 200 volunteers who had all attended school in Germany, and who were between eighteen and sixty-seven years of age, to identify lines from four ballads—two by Goethe, one by Schiller, and one by

100 Thomas Mann, *Buddenbrooks: The Decline of a Family* (New York: Knopf, 1993), 3.
101 Robson, *Heart Beats*, 106.
102 Jacques Derrida, "Che cos'è la poesia?," in *The Lyric Theory Reader*, ed. Virginia Jackson and Yopie Prins (Baltimore: Johns Hopkins University Press, 2014), 289.
103 Mikhail Bakhtin, *The Dialogic Imagination: Four Essays* (Austin: University of Texas Press, 1981).
104 Stewart, "Notes on Distressed Genres," 92.

Fontane, all of which had been popular in schoolbooks at one time or another. Only six of them were able to identify all four texts, but most strikingly, the majority of the respondents could identify exactly one, but not the others—even if there was a broad spread with regard to which one. One respondent gave a clue as to why this might be: they could, they said, still remember exactly how the poem had been presented visually in their school textbook. The vast majority of the respondents had learned *a* ballad in school—but, it seemed, at the exclusion of all the other ballads. Which ballads they remembered seemed to owe everything to questions like: which textbook had their class used? Where had they gone to school, and when? The ballad canon is a substitutive canon—one poem set to music is another not set to music, one poem forced upon students is another not forced upon students—and therefore a centripetal canon that seems to restrict as it develops.

The kind of "private anthology" Fermor imagines is deliberately assembled. Balladry, by contrast, is the dross that clogs the operations of memory, like a song lyric that one is half-horrified, half-embarrassed to realize one has retained even though one had no intention of doing so. Several respondents to the author's survey admitted that they couldn't remember an exact line or title, but remembered the parodic version favored by their parents: "it's 'Die Kraniche des Ibykus,'" one respondent wrote, "or as my father called it 'Die Ibiche des Kranikus.'" The ballad has frequently functioned as an index for the vagaries of memory, either a thing that won't leave the memory, or won't fit in it correctly. In Heine's *Lore-Ley* (1824) a lone skipper finds himself seized by an ancient tale "that won't leave my mind" ("will mir nicht aus dem Sinn") and that ultimately drowns him in the Rhine. Heine's poem has performed that same magic on generations who have recited or sung it. Just as easily as creating a sudden connection, a local argot, the ubiquity of the ballad was capable of delimiting those who belonged from those who didn't. Fermor, a foreigner arriving in Germany at the dawn of the Nazi era, asks, "how was I to know that it was the first line of Goethe's famous *Erlkönig*"— he feels, in the moment, all the more the foreigner.[105] At their worst, like any canon, the German art ballads can be little more than identity politics for those forces already dominant in German society and education—the *almans*, the high German speakers, the *Bildungsbürger*.

But the author's survey brought home that the ballad's inveterate wandering makes it a difficult accessory to an identitarian project as well: far more respondents than could identify any one ballad, could name a parody of a ballad. They remembered the bowdlerization, but not the original, something that felt, to this author, very true to the thing itself. After all, if ballads are poems that enter memory covertly and haphazardly, they

---

105 Fermor, *A Time of Gifts*, 66.

also are never reliably at home there. The writer Sylvia Wright coined the term "Mondegreen" for a line of poetry misheard and misremembered. The coinage drew on a mishearing of a seventeenth-century ballad collected in Percy's *Reliques*—where Percy writes, "And laid him on the green," young Wright had heard "And Lady Mondegreen." And where Fermor's "private anthology" is a gesture of secure possession, a traveler's backpack of memorized text, Wright's misperception of Percy's poetry doesn't so much destabilize the author function as restore an instability that was supposed to be there all along. Percy heard "laid him on the green" centuries ago, and Wright heard "Lady Mondegreen"—but who is to say who is right?[106] And in the end, a parodic bowdlerization like "Die Ibiche des Kranikus" recapitulates precisely the kind of authorless oral transmission that had fascinated the romantics and Herder when it came to the *Volksballade* in the first place: how many of my survey respondents who imputed the joke to their fathers, would have known that the parodic line is documented as early as the 1850s, that it was part of Büchmann's *Geflügelte Worte: Der Citatenschatz des deutschen Volkes* by 1864, that Heinrich Schröder cites it in his study of *Schüttelreim* as "that old schoolboy chestnut [*Pennälercitat*]"[107] in 1905, that it was adduced as an example of metathesis (sound/letter transposition) as a "natural law of language" by the philologist Wilhelm Meyer (1845–1917) in 1908,[108] and that it, in fact, somewhere along the line, gained a bilingual opening line that reshuffles Schiller's "Sieh da, sieh da, Timotheus" into the pseudo-Latin line "Timo, timo, Siehdazius." Many of these lines of transmission, these schoolyard traditions are likely lost to history, and it is not the intention of this book to trace them. What this book does propose is that the heyday of the German ballad has to be understood against the backdrop of this kind of transmission—that the art ballad laid him on the green only with the possibility of Lady Mondegreen already in mind.

## Overview of the Book

The following eight chapters lay out the ballad's curious trajectory within German culture. Chapter 1 ("The Ballad's Years of Travel") focuses on the German ballad's vexed and contradictory relationship to oral culture. Like the English ballad revival, the German art ballad emerged from the antiquarianism of the late eighteenth century—but it emerged a few years later,

---

106 Sylvia Wright, "The Death of Lady Mondegreen," *Harper's* 209 (1954): 48–51.

107 Heinrich Schröder, "Schüttelformen," *Zeitschrift für deutsche Philologie* 37 (1905): 257.

108 Wilhelm Meyer, "Die Metathesis ein Grundgesetz der menschlichen Sprache," *Zeitschrift für den deutschen Unterricht* 22 (1908): 25.

which made all the difference. While the English ballad was encumbered by a host of fraught epistemological questions (How authentic was a poem? What was its relationship to its oral models?[109]), the German ballad was instead characterized by an ironized indifference to such questions—it played with categories like authenticity, originality, and orality, but always found ways to invert or subvert its own antiquarian claims. This chapter uses the *annus mirabilis* of the German *Kunstballade*—the summer and autumn of 1797, during which Goethe and Schiller wrote the ballads for Schiller's 1798 *Musenalmanach*—to show how German balladry came to rely on a different understanding of authenticity. Where the English ballad collectors of the eighteenth century had asked philological questions, Goethe and Schiller tethered the ballad's authenticity to a notion of *Geist*. If it was well invented, a ballad could be authentic.

Chapter 2 ("The Ballad, the Voice, and the Echoes of War") explores the earliest public dimension of ballad performance. Before it entered concert halls and musical soirées as a subgenre of the *Lied* form, the ballad became an important aspect of Germany's vibrant culture of public declamation. During and immediately after the Napoleonic Wars, ballads emerged as a mainstay of the public declamations that became exceedingly popular in the first years of the nineteenth century. As Germany came under French rule and as citizens of the various Germans states were politicized as Germans (which largely meant as speakers of the German language), public sounding-out of language attained a hitherto unknown political dimension. The ballad became part of this movement. At the same time, however, while the interest both in public declamation and in the ballad form were clearly indebted to the spirit of Romanticism, they drew just as much on German Classicism. It was Classicism that had first made public declamation a broadly profitable entertainment, and it was with Classical trappings that most of the poetic recitals of the era plied their trade. There was thus an aesthetic and political doubleness at the heart of this first national instrumentalization of the ballad—one that was to have effects for ballad aesthetics going forward.

Chapter 3 ("Balladic Consciousness") follows the ballad onto a very different kind of stage. The early nineteenth century was the high point of the operatic ballad. Romantic composers like Marschner, Devrient, and Meyerbeer had largely relied on the form as just another operatic number. This was something that Wagner would not permit himself when he composed *Der fliegende Holländer*: for one, he decided to include a ballad that uncannily prefigured the rest of the opera; for another, he suggested that the opera itself was really little more than an extended ballad. The mode of

---

109 Prys Morgan, "The Hunt for the Welsh Past in the Romantic Period," in *The Invention of Tradition*, ed. Eric Hobsbawm and Terence Ranger (Cambridge: Cambridge University Press, 1983), 55.

collective listening, the mode of consciousness and unconsciousness Wagner proposes both in Senta's ballad itself and in his comments on the piece, seems to draw on Heinrich Heine's understanding of the ballad form—as in the subject matter for his opera (which Heine presented as parody and Wagner as tragic drama), Wagner draws on Heine's irony and renders it perfectly serious.

Even the most cursory look into syllabi, textbooks, and teaching plans of nineteenth-century German *Gymnasien* tells us that ballads were among the most frequently memorized poems. Chapter 4 ("Memorizing Ballads") reflects on the impact that this ubiquity within a project of contemporary memorialization had on the writing of ballads. When ordinary Germans knew literature by heart (or simply took themselves to "know" literature), they usually knew ballads. Ballads were understood to help train memory and build certain literary sensibilities—but that did not exhaust their pedagogical value in the eyes of nineteenth-century pedagogy. As this chapter demonstrates, there were far more mysterious teachings. At the same time, ballads were not passive grist for this ideological mill. Instead, they cannily exploited the fact that they would circulate further than any other poetic genre, and that they could, in their very circulation, make visible and audible things that would escape notice in a smaller readership. The chapter focuses on August von Platen's "Das Grab im Busento"; anthologized and memorized at infinitum, it makes its listeners and reciters parties to guarding a secret, a secret that they do not know, but will nevertheless pass on.

The ballads of the *Musenalmanach* and beyond centered on individuals, usually outsiders—destitute treasure-seekers, wandering bards, lost boys in the marshes, sorcerer's apprentices. As Chapter 5 ("The Ballad and the Family") shows, the next generation of ballad writers, Heinrich Heine, Anette von Droste-Hülshoff, and August von Platen (each born within a year of the publication of the *Musenalmanach*), moved the art ballad away from the single episode toward being a "minor epic"—which in turn made it possible to present family relationships within the form. This was more than a shift in content, involving instead a wholesale reconception of how the ballad form preserved and transmitted its content. These poems no longer take the ballad's modes of transmission as an unproblematic given (aping oral modes of tradition)—what families transmit from generation to generation emerges as a problem analogous to what the ballad transmits and how.

Chapter 6 ("The Ballad and Its Narratives") investigates the rapid spread of the musical ballad beyond the established song setting in the 1840s and 1850s. When Chopin premiered his first *Ballade* in France, German reviewers scratched their heads over the phenomenon of a "ballad without words." Within a few years, the idea had little strangeness to it—by mid-century, a new musical genre, the symphonic poem, had emerged and ballads were a frequent quarry for symphonic compositions.

And yet, as sympathetic as the ballad was to programmatic music writing, it also posed challenges for adaptation—after all, the audience's familiarity with the story of, say, "Lenore" or "Der Zauberlehrling" ("The Sorcerer's Apprentice") went well beyond their familiarity with, say, *Don Quixote*. When most of the audience could have not only repeated the story, but repeated the poem a symphonic poem was based on, the temporality of the program ran up against another, equally well defined temporality. This created difficulties for those composers of the New German School that turned to classic *Kunstballaden* for their *sujets*. But it also allowed them to pose fundamental questions about programs, about narrative, and about musical hermeneutics. The chapter considers the instrumental ballads of Frederick Chopin and Clara Schumann, the choral ballads of Robert Schumann and Franz Liszt, and the symphonic ballads of Joachim Raff, and concludes with the wandering ballads of the "Wunderhorn" cycle that wander through the symphonies of Gustav Mahler.

Chapter 7 ("The Ballad, the Public, and Gendered Community") investigates the kinds of audiences ballads brought into existence. Ballads appeared on the scene with an appeal to an imagined community, but in their actual circulation through the parlors, classrooms, cafés, and concert halls of the nineteenth century, they relied on actual publics to make them a reality. Such communities were frequently strongly gendered: choral societies emerged in the wake of the Napoleonic Wars as conduits for nationalism, and they were tightly integrated with a project of national masculinity. At the same time, the boom gave employment to a great many women composers and instrumentalists; and while either writing or conducting a symphony was not an option that was realistically open to women, a set of ballads for a mixed chorus very much was. As a result, the history of the choral ballad was strongly interwoven with a crop of highly talented women composers, who explicitly reflected on how exactly they ought to integrate themselves into a gendered tradition.

At the same time, the gendered tradition began emerging as a problem in other quarters. Starting in the 1830s, a group of Berlin poets, artists, and politicians began jousting in balladry—among their number were several of the great ballad writers of the middle of the nineteenth century, such as Theodor Fontane and Paul Heyse. The group, which called itself Der Tunnel über der Spree (The Tunnel over the Spree River), conducted frequent balladic competitions, which they in turn framed in balladic terms. Their self-descriptions of these events hearkened back to the idea of a "battle of the singers" (*Sängerkrieg*), to the medieval troubadours of Provence and to the Tannhäuser legend. Their emulation of these homosocial singing competitions had one marked difference vis-à-vis these famous forebears: there appear to have been no women present. The ballads collected by the members of the

Tunnel, and frequently made popular afterward, reflect extensively on themes of homosociality and nationhood.

The ballad has an ambiguous relationship to the nation. Its reemergence in the eighteenth century was closely tied to the rise of nationalism, and since the ballad was taken to speak for the people, it allowed that people to constitute itself in the first place. However, while the ballad's audience were indeed increasingly national reading audiences, the ballad often purported to speak for the victims of nation building: for the minstrels of the Scottish Borders, the Jacobite rebels, the colonized, the slave. The ballad, in other words, reframed regionalisms (and regional nostalgia) for a national audience. Chapter 8 ("The Ballad and the Sea") investigates this dialectic of local and universal with respect to Germany's most specific local marker—little of Germany's population lived near the sea or made its living immediately from it. And yet, as the nineteenth century wore on, as Germany unified and decided that it required colonies, a broad swath of political actors needed to convince the German public that the sea was more than a regional concern. One of the literary genres to which they turned in order to make their case was the ballad; and yet the ballad also managed to offer up resistance to their instrumentalization.

# 1 | The Ballad's Years of Travel

*The* Musenalmanach *for 1798, Orality, and the Ballad Form*

By the time Johann Gottfried Herder made him the protagonist of "Erlkönigs Tochter" ("Elf King's Daughter"), Herr Olof had been traversing the craggy landscape of European balladry for centuries: Herder based his 1778 poem on the Danish poem "Elverskud" by Peder Syv from 1695, but there are dozens of earlier variants of the poem from across Scandinavia. In Norway he was Olav Liljekrans, and as Clerk Colvill, Herr Olof haunted the popular ballad of the British Isles. His peregrinations were oddly appropriate for a form that seems to thrive on wandering. While the rediscovery of the forgotten knightly epics was understood as a journey inward, to the mythic heart of the nation, the ballad was usually understood to come from abroad. It was identified with the nation, but also in important respects refused to be identical with it. The poems themselves frequently announced as much in their plots: "Chevy Chase," the first English-language ballad to cause a stir in Germany, is set in the Scottish Borders region and tells the story of a calamitous boundary crossing. As Ulrich Gaier has pointed out, "ballads bring to consciousness that someone puts up a boundary, defends a boundary or crosses one."[1] Specifically, ballads frequently deal with individuals who have trespassed where they should not have. Epic travel is goal-oriented, but the paradigmatic balladic wanderer gets sidetracked, gets stuck, or gets waylaid, often with disastrous consequences. In introducing Schiller's "Die Bürgschaft" in his *Bardenhain*, an 1819 collection of poems for "Germany's well-bred Sons and Daughters," Theodor Heinsius claims that in the realm of the ballad "it is not the strength of free will that rules, as it does in the epic,

---

1 Gaier, *Ballade und Romanze*, 11.

but instead the power of feeling."[2] Odysseus can complete his epic travel because he samples the distractions along his way but does not allow them to fully seduce him.[3] The ballad protagonist is a less disciplined Odysseus. Herder's Herr Olof is supposed to be en route to the safe haven of marriage, but something happens to slow him down—something tempting, something feminine, something supernatural. The boy in Goethe's "Erlkönig," too, is not really doomed until he tears his face from his father's shoulder and leers at Erlking's daughters prancing in the night. Mikhail Bakhtin famously suggested that the chronotope, the way time and space are organized and imbued with meaning in literature, has "intrinsic generic significance."[4] Wandering seems to be the ballad's chronotope. And its penchant for detours contains an entire world picture en miniature. Getting lost in this forest seems to activate old tropes of sin and damnation, which detract from what Dante called the "free and straight" path.[5]

The ballad's relationship to wandering runs deep, but the poems themselves are frequently deeply ambivalent about the kind of wandering discourse they constitute. In one of the most puzzling episodes shared by the different versions of "Erlkönigs Tochter," Herr Olof arrives at his bride's house only to be met by his own mother. She recognizes his deathly pallor and asks him what has happened to him—he tells her the truth: he has been seduced by the spirits of the forest and will now succumb to them. At this point, Herr Olof's mother asks a strange follow-up: what am I supposed to tell your betrothed? ("Was soll ich nun sagen deiner Braut?") Not the truth, surely. Herr Olof responds with a couplet that she repeats almost verbatim to Herr Olof's betrothed the next day ("Sagt ihr, ich sei im Wald zur Stund, / Zu proben da mein Pferd und Hund"). The couplet functions as cover story for what really happened to Herr Olof—and it seems essential that Herr Olof's mother get it just right. Their collusion also seems to overcome a gendered division typical of the epic: while it is of course still Herr Olof who gets to ride, have adventures, and die, oral transmission makes the mother his accomplice. In discussing "the literature of the North" in 1800, Madame de Staël claimed that in Northern climes being the teller of a tale was a form of self-empowerment: Ossianic poetry "gave man a prodigious sense of his own

---

2 Theodor Heinsius, "Die Bürgschaft—Eine Romanze von Fr. V. Schiller," *Der Bardenhain für Deutschlands edle Söhne und Töchter* (Berlin: Dieterici, 1819), 20.

3 Theodor W. Adorno and Max Horkheimer, *The Dialectic of Enlightenment* (Stanford, CA: Stanford University Press, 2002), 49.

4 Mikhail Bakhtin, "Forms of Time and the Chronotope in the Novel," in *The Dialogic Imagination: Four Essays*, ed. Michael Holquist (Austin: University of Texas Press, 1981), 85.

5 Robert Harrison, *Forests: The Shadow of Civilization* (Chicago: University of Chicago Press, 2009), 84.

individual forcefulness and the power of his will."⁶ "Erlkönigs Tochter" is a story about telling stories, and about the powers that telling stories confers.

"Erlkönigs Tochter," presented by Herder as one version of an orally transmitted poem, has at its heart a moment that points to the importance of precise oral transmission. But in the poem this precision is not a matter of fealty, but rather of profound faithlessness: Herr Olof and his mother insist on precise repetition of a specific couplet because it is essentially a lie, a cover story. The couplet that Herr Olof has his mother repeat to his betrothed is meant to conceal from the young woman the supernatural horror of Herr Olof's end. The line thus seems to make a dual point about oral transmission: Firstly, orality is not necessarily a guarantor of authenticity, but just as easily the opposite—of pretense, of distortion, of obfuscation. And secondly, oral language is not so much evocative or descriptive—rather it can crucially misrepresent the world, in particular when it comes to the supernatural element in it. Herr Olof and his mother conspire to dissolve what the son sees in Goethe's "Der Erlkönig" into what the father sees: a crown and train into fog, a song into the rustle of leaves. The poem is a sort of reverse magic formula—it does not conjure, it abjures.

Both the story and the form of "Erlkönigs Tochter" remind readers that they are supposed to imagine the ballad itself as wandering: from mouth to ear, from town to town, from Herr Olof to his mother, and from his mother to his intended. In this context, concerns about the accuracy of transmission have a contradictory role to play—which is likely a reason why, from Syv to Herder, this old oral poem was circulated so early and preferably in writing. This remained generally true for the art ballads that later followed Herder's example, whether they were based on earlier texts or invented out of whole cloth: even though they owed their existence to the pen and the printing press, they yearned for the orality of the campfire and the marketplace. But the reverse was also true: no matter how old the story was that the ballad related, some part of it yearned for the fixity and safe passage afforded by the written word. This duality impacted the German ballad differently than the British. In the British tradition, the antiquarian claims predominated, and they committed the ballad to having been originally oral and a matter of writing only secondarily.⁷ Proximity to an original discourse was a major attraction of the form—and whenever scholars called that proximity into question with respect to one ballad collection or the other, one of the British

---

6 Germaine de Staël, *De la Littérature considérée dans ses rapports avec les institutions sociales* (Paris: Crapelet, 1800), 215; De Staël, "On Literature Considered in Its Relationship to Social Institutions," in *Major Writings of Germaine de Staël* (New York: Columbia University Press, 1987), 174–77.

7 Kenneth McNeil, "Ballads and Borders," in *The Edinburgh Companion to Sir Walter Scott*, ed. Fiona Robertson (Edinburgh: University of Edinburgh Press, 2012), 24.

Isles' many antiquarian scandals of the era erupted. These scandals varied in the nature of the charge, but all of them put pressure on the authenticity of the texts presented by antiquarians from Thomas Percy to George Borrow. In each case, the question was just how far the poems had traveled before they made it into print, and how much of their content had safely survived each of the journeys.

The biggest scandals of the era concerned the purported ancient Scottish epics of Ossian and the ballads collected in Percy's *Reliques* and centered on the question of whether these were truly popular texts or literary artifacts made to resemble popular texts.[8] Were they traditional or invented? In other cases, for instance Joseph Ritson's criticism of Percy's methods (as in the later *Wunderhorn* controversy between Achim von Arnim and Clemens Brentano[9]), the question was whether the editor had gone too far in polishing oral culture for a literary audience.[10] In the case of Borrow, who acknowledged taking his Nordic ballads from books rather than transcribing them from the oral reports, controversy swirled around the question *which* editions Borrow had used—medieval collections closer to the source or modern reimaginings by contemporary Danish poets? As David Duff has recently argued, there were of course many pointed political questions layered on top of these editorial questions: questions of class (whether ballads were courtly or products of the common people, for instance) and questions of territoriality and portability (whether ballads emerged from a specific region, for instance).[11] But these political questions were focalized through editorial issues.

In the mid-1700s, German balladry was comparatively marginal, and its provenance was comparatively undertheorized. This would change quickly with the onset with the aesthetics of *Sturm und Drang*, with the immense popularity of Bürger's ballads, and the collective output of Goethe and Schiller. But the lag would nevertheless shape the art ballad's distinctive characteristics in Germany, especially when it came to its relationship to oral culture. The authors who constitute the canon of *Kunstballaden* in the late eighteenth century reflect the anxieties about the ballad's provenance, its years of travel, its awkward position somewhere between translation, edition, and retelling—but they arrive in each case at a point of indifference about it. As Hannah Berner put it in a recent study, their investments in sounding

---

8 Nick Groom, *The Making of Percy's "Reliques"* (Oxford: Clarendon, 1999), 21.

9 See Oscar Fambach, *Ein Jahrhundert deutscher Literaturkritik, 1750–1850* (Berlin: Akademie, 1963).

10 See E. David Gregory, *Victorian Songhunters: The Recovery and Editing of English Vernacular Ballads and Folk Lyrics, 1820–1883* (Oxford: Scarecrow, 2006), 37.

11 David Duff, *Romanticism and the Uses of Genre* (Oxford: Oxford University Press, 2009), 129.

folk-like and their emphasis on artistry are "complementary."[12] For by the time they got around to concerning themselves with the questions that roiled their English colleagues, concepts like *Geist* held sway in German letters—a subject-object that allowed the ballad to participate dialectically in opposing fields. But, as Ernst Bloch has pointed out, spirit in Hegel's system always appeared as the element of contradiction—spirit is never mere reduplication of what is merely given, it has a great deal of autonomy from the given.[13] Whether in the work of Hegel, Novalis, Friedrich Schlegel, Friedrich Daniel Ernst Schleiermacher, or Wilhelm von Humboldt: the subject-object functioned self-reflexively. Likewise balladry—in particular art balladry—wasn't simply a piece of anthropology, it was art created by recognizable authorial subjectivities for a modern audience to reflect on the conditions of its own naïveté. This distinction, this ironic, and in its self-conception modern, separation from tradition was something a generation of German poets and thinkers came to by way of the works of Ossian.

## Echoes of Ossian

James Macpherson's collected edition of *The Works of Ossian* was published in 1765, and by the end of the decade the work had deeply enraptured Johann Wolfgang von Goethe. The young Goethe translated different portions of the Ossianic poems, including a trilingual version in Gaelic, English, and German. There is some disagreement as to when and in whose translation Goethe first encountered *Fingal* and *Tamora*, but we know he owned a copy of the book when he came to Strasbourg in 1770, where he lent it to Herder. It is quite likely that Goethe read the book earlier, however—when he returned to Frankfurt from Strasbourg in 1771, he seems to have done so without the copy of the book lent to Herder. In his own translations from the Ossianic poems he relied instead on a copy from his father's library.[14]

In *Die Leiden des jungen Werthers* (*The Sorrows of Young Werther*, 1774), the novel that emerged from Goethe's time in Wetzlar, Goethe had his hero say that "Ossian has taken the place of Homer in my heart."[15] Scholars have debated to what extent this statement reflects Goethe's own proclivities around that time, and Goethe himself was careful to walk it back decades later. Speaking to Henry Crabb Robinson in 1829, the aging Goethe

---

12 Hannah Berner, *Inszenierte Volkstümlichkeit in Balladen von 1800 bis 1850* (Heidelberg: Winter, 2020).

13 Ernst Bloch, *Subjekt-Objekt* (Frankfurt: Suhrkamp, 1977), 136.

14 F. J. Lamport, "Goethe, Ossian and Werther," in *From Gaelic to Romantic: Ossianic Translations*, ed. Fiona Stafford and Howard Gaskill (Amsterdam: Rodopi, 1998), 98.

15 Johann Wolfgang von Goethe, *Goethes Werke (HA)* (Munich: Beck, 1981), 6:82.

expressed "contempt" for Ossian and insisted that "no one remarked that while Werther is in his senses he talks about Homer and only after he goes mad is in love with Ossian."[16] Robinson's recollections were published decades later, and even if Goethe said what Robinson reported, there is the possibility that the poet was deliberately misreading his own earlier text. But there is little dispute that Ossian, for Goethe as for Werther, was an intense experience that quickly turned fraught.

In 1775, Samuel Johnson's *A Journey to the Western Islands of Scotland* launched the most concerted assault on Macpherson's editions, though controversy had been raging among the cognoscenti since their publication.[17] Arguing from an empiricist theory of mind and with an eye toward documentary evidence, Johnson contended that *Fingal* and *Temora* could not possibly be the relics of an ancient oral tradition: they were "too long to be remembered," he pointed out, and how then were they supposed to have made it unscathed from the days of Ossian, son of Fingal, down to his supposed editor Macpherson? Johnson did not accuse Macpherson of outright fabrication: portions of the work, he conceded, might well be oral and thus historic; it was the whole that was untrue. "[Macpherson] has doubtless inserted names that circulate in popular stories, and may have translated some wandering ballads, if any can be found."[18] For Johnson, orality—and specifically, balladic orality—was a way of unmasking Ossian as fiction.[19] Oral culture was inherently limited (by the capacities of human memory, by the vagaries of an orally sustained historic record, by the limited purview of those who are forced to rely on oral culture). And what Macpherson asked his readers to believe oral culture could conceivably transmit simply didn't pass the test of common sense.

It is not clear when Goethe learned of Johnson's criticisms, but he had arrived at some sort of skepticism vis-à-vis Ossian on his own by the time he had Werther offer his encomium to the grizzled bard. And by the time he set down to write the novel over the span of just over in month in 1774, he portrays Werther's fascination with Ossian with a good deal of irony. Goethe has his protagonist imagine Ossianic scenes that seem almost comically overwrought. Werther imagines how "from the mountain-tops, mid the roar of torrents their plaintive sounds issuing from deep caverns, and the sorrowful lamentations of a maiden who sighs and expires on the mossy

16 Johann Wolfgang von Goethe, *Goethes Gespräche* (Leipzig: Biedermann, 1909), 1:135.

17 Fiona Stafford, *The Sublime Savage: A Study of James Macpherson and the Poems of Ossian* (Edinburgh: Edinburgh University Press, 1988).

18 Samuel Johnson, *A Journey to the Western Islands of Scotland* (London: Strahan/Cadell, 1785), 274.

19 See Katie Trumpener, *Bardic Nationalism: The Romantic Novel and the British Empire* (Princeton, NJ: Princeton University Press, 1997), 90.

tomb of the warrior by whom she was adored."[20] Compressed in this manner, *topos* compounded upon *topos*, the world of Ossian seems not so much sublime or authentic as it does clichéd. Rather than express his admiration for Ossian, Goethe seems to take stock of a past fascination, and to poke gentle fun at it. He is creating, as F. J. Lamport points out, a "more than semi-autobiographical scapegoat figure."[21] Goethe's protagonist rhapsodizes about the authenticity of the Scottish bard, only to suggest that perhaps that bard was created precisely for such would-be rhapsodes as him. If anything, the imaginary meeting with the "wandelnden grauen Barden" ("the grey-haired wayfaring bard") heightens the suspicion that in Ossian authenticity and Werther's projection are one and the same.[22] Ossian matters as an atmosphere, not as a verifiable text corpus.

James Boswell, Johnson's great friend and hagiographer, broke with Johnson on the question of what exactly would make Ossian authentic. Boswell, who took the same trip as Johnson, came to radically different conclusions about orality and the Ossian question. As Taylor Walle has shown, Boswell de-emphasized the (epic) whole compared to Johnson. Boswell granted that even if Macpherson had undertaken a reconstruction from fragments, it didn't make Ossian in any way inauthentic.[23] But more important, Boswell put more stock in orality and seemed less concerned with extolling the literary constitution of the Enlightened Republic of Letters, believing instead that much could be preserved, recalled, and handed down in a linguistic family through oral culture alone. In his *Journal of a Tour of the Hebrides with Samuel Johnson* (1785), Boswell relates an episode of recitation: "I could not perceive much poetical imagery in the translation. Yet all in our company who understood Erse, seemed charmed with the original. There may, perhaps, be some choice of expression, and some excellence of arrangement, that cannot be shewn in translation."[24] The sheer atmosphere

---

20 J. W. Goethe, *The Sorrows of Young Werther*, trans. R. D. Boylan (Boston: Niccols, 1902), 87: "Ossian hat in meinem Herzen den Homer verdrängt. Welch eine Welt, in die der Herrliche mich führt! Zu wandern über die Heide, umsaust vom Sturmwinde, der in dampfenden Nebeln die Geister der Väter im dämmernden Lichte des Mondes hinführt. Zu hören vom Gebirge her, im Gebrülle des Waldstroms, halb verwehtes Ächzen der Geister aus ihren Höhlen, und die Wehklagen des zu Tode sich jammernden Mädchens, um die vier moosbedeckten, grasbewachsenen Steine des Edelgefallnen, ihres Geliebten." (Goethe, *Goethes Werke*, 6:82.)

21 Lamport, "Goethe, Ossian and Werther," 104.

22 Wolf Gerhard Schmidt, *"Homer des Nordens" und "Mutter der Romantik": James Macphersons Ossian und seine Rezepton in der deutschsprachigen Literatur*. 4 vols. (Berlin: DeGruyter, 2004).

23 Taylor Walle, "James Boswell and the Ossian Question," Stanford University Classics Department Literate Orality and Oral Literacy Colloquium, December 2014.

24 James Boswell, *The Journal of a Tour to the Hebrides with Samuel Johnson* (London: Baldwin, 1786), 325.

created by spoken Erse for Boswell spoke to the authenticity of ancient Scottish poetry, just as much as for Johnson it strongly hinted at the fact that it was fabricated. (As Katie Trumpener has pointed out, Johnson likewise had moments in which Ossian recited in Erse deeply impresses him—it simply didn't convince him.[25])

This suggests that the standard of authenticity was different between the two men. Boswell no longer regarded the Ossian question as black and white: the question wasn't whether every word of what Macpherson had published was authentic; it was whether its spirit was. And even if some of Ossian was a modern reconstitution, the fact that actual speakers of Erse reacted with instinctual approval to its recitation proved that it came from an authentic place. But authentic in what way? For Boswell, the home the individual ballad found in oral social recitation vouched for its authenticity, even if the literary object presented in book form was likely not historic. Goethe does not seem to have read Boswell's book. And yet by different paths he and Herder had left behind their veneration of the Ossianic epics for a more clear-eyed admiration, one that strikingly resembled Boswell's. Their position was widely shared among German literati. As early as 1768, at the height of Ossian mania in Germany, the Enlightenment essayist Helferich Peter Sturz, who had recently passed through England on his *grand tour* of Europe, reported on the controversy, but explained that he trusted Macpherson. Not primarily because Macpherson had shown him "twelve notebooks of the Erse original," but more importantly on the strength of Macpherson's reading from them: "The language sounded melodic enough, but a solemn, guttural lament, like all languages of uneducated peoples."[26] The German Ossian boosters, in other words, largely arrived at their conviction along aesthetic rather than epistemological or philological paths.

While translating the poems from the Gaelic, Goethe and Herder first became suspicious of Macpherson's tendency to smooth over the rugged edges of the original.[27] In December 1775, Edmund de Harold, who had undertaken the second full Ossian translation into German, wrote to Herder that he was "persuaded that Mr. Macpherson is the author not only of the English translation of Ossian Poems, but also of the Celtic originals which he pretended to have discover'd."[28] Although Boswell's book had yet to make the journey to central Europe, Herder's solution was in keeping with Boswell's instinct: he assumed the whole was phony and the parts were genuine, and turned the

---

25 Trumpener, *Bardic Nationalism*, 90.

26 Helferich Peter Sturz, "Briefe eines Reisenden vom Jahre 1768," *Deutsches Museum* 1 (Leipzig: Weygand, 1777): 215: "Die Sprache klang melodisch genug, aber feyerlich klagend und gutteral, wie alle Sprachen ungebildeter Völker."

27 Howard Gaskill, "Herder, Ossian and the Celtic," in *Celticism*, ed. Terence Brown (Amsterdam: Rodopi, 1996), 266.

28 Schmidt, "*'Homer des Nordens' und 'Mutter der Romantik,'*" 4:627.

"Homer of the North" back into "wandering ballads." He included selections of Ossian in the *Volkslieder* (in later editions titled *Stimmen der Völker, The Voices of the Peoples*) in 1778, but he presented them in self-contained narrative pieces, rather than as excerpts that hinted at an epic whole. And in his essay on "Homer und Ossian" from 1795 he suggests that Macpherson's inability to produce originals condemns him, but adds that if "he simply received raw material, and put together with a creative hand what he then presented," then "all the more laudable for him, and all the more instructive for us."[29]

His reasons for remaining credulous of the parts even as he was disabused of the whole were encapsulated in Herder's essay "Über Bild, Dichtung und Fabel" ("On Image, Poetry, and Fable," 1787). Herder's "folk song" editions can strike a modern reader as awfully cavalier in treating their material: Herder habitually presented as a translation of a folk song something that differed in meter, rhyme scheme, enjambment, and even story from the original. "On Image, Poetry, and Fable" explains why he felt licensed to rewrite the songs in such a manner. Herder sought to present the idea "behind" a particular folk song, even if he divested it of its external trappings. We tend to still think of myth the same way, but modernism has moved us away from the idea of looking at poetry with this optic.[30] Herder's argument was that in creating ideas out of sense data, our soul allegorizes "just as much as our language." It turns objects into images according to rules (Herder speaks of "metaschematisieren").[31] And when it comes to expressing "these thought images, which are entirely its work," the soul is once again translating, othering, "alläosieren." Herder's point was to warn against the straightforward citation of certain (usually classical) *topoi*, plots, or metaphors. Since the internally created idea was always different, its expression, even if it turned to similar ideas, should be different. "If your speech or poetry requires such images: express them in your own fashion, however you experience them, however the spirit of your poesy demands it."[32] The kind of fealty the "spirit" of these folk songs demanded, Herder thought, actually committed the translator to changing them in the translation. The editor's duty was not to the words of the original, but the spirit that created the original's overall impression.

This idea of a "spirit" that shines through the particular articulation of a ballad was to remain a fixture in German thinking about the ballad for the next decades. When in 1821 Georg Wilhelm Friedrich Hegel was lecturing

---

29 Ibid., 4:521: "empfing er nur rohen Stof, und sezte mit Schöpferhand zusammen, was er dargestellt hat."

30 Carl Dahlhaus, Aporien der Programmmusik," in *Klassische und romantische Musikästhetik* (Laaber: Laaber, 1988), 365–413.

31 Herder, "Über Bild, Dichtung und Fabel," *Zerstreute Blätter (Dritte Sammlung)* (Gotha: Ettinger, 1787), 96.

32 Ibid., 105.

on aesthetics in Berlin, he sounded in this respect very much like Herder thirty years prior. The great systematician did not accord a particularly exalted place to poetry in his story of art—and the ballad was crucial to why. Poetic language, Hegel proposed, was close to the pinnacle of a progressive and teleological elaboration of the Idea of Art. And this closeness to the pinnacle was itself the problem, for poetry rendered in language something that other, "higher" types of language, above all philosophical reasoning, could much more readily express: "However much poetry thus produces the totality of the beautiful one more time in the Spirit, that spiritual nature at the same time constitutes the great defect of this final province of art."[33] Poetry (and again he emphasized ballads in this regard) was too directly connected to the "Geist": it was intimately connected to the spirit of the people, the spirit of the age—the very thing Boswell and Herder had praised it for. Unfortunately, in doing so poetry came dangerously close to simply spelling out values and cultural perceptions of the world, rather than embodying them sensuously. Why, the philosopher asked, not just write philosophy then?

On the level of content, Hegel placed the ballad at the point where the universal (the "substantial content of a weltanschauung"[34]) is particularized into a dramatic situation—his example was Schiller's Greek-set tale of crime and punishment, "Die Kraniche des Ibycus." For Hegel, Schiller's poem compressed into its 184 lines the totality of Greek thinking about justice and retribution, fate and man's place in the universe. On the level of form, Hegel claimed, the ballad emerged at a moment when epic narration was first formalized—ballads still clung to a *given* topic (rather than just drawing it from the subject's own feelings or response to an outside stimulus, say), but they transfigured it lyrically. Schiller presented a preexisting tale and drew on preexisting customs—but he delved into the psyche of his characters in ways that feel personal. Ballads, Hegel writes, "are more lyrical the more they emphasize that part of the events they report, which corresponds to the inner state of the poet's soul [*inneren Seelenzustande*] as he narrates."[35] Hegel placed the ballad at the midway point between a pure linguistic reproduction of events in the world and the complete lyric retreat into the subjective approach to the world. Given this, it is striking what Hegel did *not* do, namely make a distinction between *Volksballade* and *Kunstballade*. It would have been easy for him to posit the latter as the move away from the mere reproduction of given reality and its transformation by an artist's will. Hegel refused to

---

33 "Wie vollständig deshalb auch die Poesie die ganze Totalität des Schönen noch einmal in geistigster Weise produziert, so macht dennoch die Geistigkeit gerade zugleich den Mangel dieses letzten Kunstgebiets aus" (G. W. F. Hegel, *Vorlesungen über die Ästhetik*, ed. D. H. G. Hotho [Berlin: Duncker & Humblot, 1838], 3:233).
34 Ibid., 3:449.
35 Ibid., 3:449.

do this: for him a murder ballad, as much as a Schiller ballad, persists at the same midpoint between given and self-posited.

In Hegel, too, the spirit of Boswell, rather than of Dr. Johnson, lived on. His example of "Die Kraniche des Ibycus" is instructive: the poem may condense the spirit of an age and the spirit of a people, but neither that age nor that people are the ones of the man who set down the poem in the first place. Hegel didn't grant the existence of the kind of poem as which Macpherson presented the Ossian texts, but perhaps more important, he didn't seem to make a distinction between what Macpherson said Ossian was and what Johnson did: one could capture the atmosphere, the spirit of a people centuries later and from half a world away. "The English possess, primarily from the earlier original epoch of their poetry, many such poems," Hegel allows, "but also in more recent times Bürger, and especially Goethe and Schiller, have developed a mastery in this field."[36] Hegel is clearly aware of the existence of medieval ballads, as well as of German murder ballads. But the idea of making a distinction between them and the product of Goethe's and Schiller's pen, a distinction that made and later ruined Macpherson's reputation, no longer seemed particularly important to Hegel. The modern "mastery" no longer rendered a ballad inauthentic.

There was in Germany a gradual progression from antiquarianism, to its unmasking (or at least problematization), to what we might call "strategic antiquarianism"—the creation of poems meant to look historic but not really designed to fool anyone. This progression constitutes the origin of the German *Kunstballade*. For Dr. Johnson, for Boswell, and for the young Goethe, the question of whether the Ossian poems were truly antiquarian "reliques," or, as Dr. Johnson suspected, simply "wandering ballads" corralled into a fake epic, was a matter of life and death. Proving that Ossian wasn't historic was the same as proving that he wasn't worth reading. Proving even that Ossian was a pastiche consisting of genuinely historic fragments meant that there "was" no Ossian in any relevant sense. It is striking how pointedly Hegel refuses to engage with this question, and striking he never feels the need to explain his refusal. Given that the problem with poetry is its overproximity to the Spirit, which raises the specter of its redundancy, it would seem to matter a great deal whether a ballad really does come from the ambient "spirit" of the people, or whether it is channeled through an individual author's subjectivity and simply dons the garb of folklore. This distinction is

---

36 "Die Engländer besitzen vornehmlich aus der früheren ursprünglichen Epoche ihrer Poesie viele solcher Gedichte, überhaupt liebt die Volkspoesie dergleichen meist unglückliche Geschichten und Kollisionen im Tone der schauerlichen, die Brust mit Angst beengenden, die Stimme erstickenden Empfindung zu erzählen. Doch auch in neuerer Zeit haben sich bei uns Bürger und dann vor allem Goethe und Schiller eine Meisterschaft in diesem Felde erworben." (Ibid., 427/428).

the one that characterizes discussions of the ballads in the British Isles, and it is the one that likewise guided the Ossian controversy in Germany. But by the time Hegel comes to the ballad, he no longer distinguishes between true and invented folklore.

This shift holds true for German thinking about the ballad more generally. Much sooner than British literature, German literature reached a point of indifference between ascribing "genuine" antiquity to ballads and regarding them as modern forms gesturing toward a kind of "distressed" antiquity. And while not all German authors writing about the ballad reach that point for the same reasons as Hegel, most of them seem to have a similar approach: something can come from the spirit of the people and yet be invented by a single member of that group. It need not be antique in order to be genuine. The same is true for the English ballad, of course—Sir Walter Scott didn't expect "The Lay of the Last Minstrel" to be understood as an original border ballad any more than Goethe did "Der Zauberlehrling." But in Britain the ballad took form in the context of antiquarian research characteristic of the late Enlightenment. In Germany, it came of age during the vogue of organicist thinking of *Sturm und Drang*, German Idealism, and nascent Romanticism. It is not accurate to say that the early writers of ballads stopped caring about authenticity and offered up ballads basically as simulacra. Rather, they relied on the altered understanding of authenticity proffered by Boswell: a ballad was authentic even if it did not stem from a genuine antiquarian source; as long as it hewed to a certain *Geist*, it was in a sense true.

Some of this almost certainly had to do with the intermedial nature of the ballad boom, which seemed to dramatize, in the present, the circulation processes that Johnson and Boswell had sought to espy in the Ossian poems' past. In other words: the oral extraction of the ballad was less of an issue for German poets because they understood balladic orality to be a continuing process, and because they understood their texts to be participating in that oral tradition, even if these texts were very much printed and read. Subjective-objective concepts like "spirit" had an inherent ambiguity that to these authors not only expressed where the authenticity of the ballad lay historically, but what could render it authentic in future peregrinations.

On April 7, 1797, at the beginning of the burst of collaborative balladry that would later become known as the *Balladenjahr*, Schiller writes to Goethe that "in presenting the popular character [*Volkscharakter*]" of the commoner, Shakespeare had "a poetic abstraction rather than individuals in mind." "In this," he adds, "he was quite close to the Greeks."[37] Similarly, F. W. J. Schelling reacted to Wolf's *Prolegomena ad Homerum*, by pointing out that if

---

37 Goethe/Schiller, *Der Briefwechsel zwischen Schiller und Goethe* (Munich: Insel, 1984), 1:316.

the person Homer was a fiction he was for that very reason real: "Homer and mythology are one and the same, and Homer was already fully inherent in the first poetry of mythology, he was present as a potentiality."[38] If there were to have been countless "Homerids" rather than one Homer, the epic would have nevertheless preceded its transmission: "[The epics] were already—even if not empirically—present as epic poems, which [the Homerids] recited."[39] It is this idea—quite close to Hegel's treatment of balladry—that stands behind the efflorescence of balladry over the ensuing months: authentic popularity (*Volkscharakter*) is an aesthetic effect of the ballad; one can put it into a poem, even if one has just jotted it down and posted it to a friend. The ballad's historicism is shot through with imaginative work—and not the imaginative work of empathy, but rather the imaginative work of abstraction. In 1820s Berlin, Hegel thus drew on the same sense that had sustained the balladeers in 1790s Jena and Weimar: that connection to the *Geist* was a different matter than actual popular provenance. In speaking to Henry Crabb Robinson about Werther's Ossian mania many years later, Goethe initially replied: "that's partly true," only to then point to the irony of Werther's turn to Ossian. Both this irony and the sentiment of being "partly true" would become guides not only for Goethe's relationship to oral poetry, but to the ballad in particular.

## Ironized Orality

The German *Kunstballade*'s relationship to authenticity, and that meant to orality, to the "wandering ballads" on which it modeled itself, was far less fraught than that of its British cousin. At the same time, the question of orality raised itself far more forcefully the more firmly the ballad became ensconced in a culture of circulation through writing. Nowhere is this more evident than in perhaps the *annus mirabilis* of the German art ballad, the so-called *Balladenjahr*. The poems Goethe and Schiller produced in central ways reflect, and reflect on, the shift in the perception of balladic orality.[40] Goethe had read Friedrich August Wolf's *Prolegomena ad Homerum* in 1795. Wolf had been the first to argue that Homer's epics were in fact oral. After all, Wolf argued, no one reads in the poem, no one sets anything

---

38 Friedrich Wilhelm Joseph Schelling, *Sämmtliche Werke* (Stuttgart: Cotta, 1859), Abth. 1, Bd. 5:416.: "Die Mythologie und Homer sind eins, und Homer lag in der ersten Dichtung der Mythologies chon fertig involviert, gleichsam potentialiter vorhanden."

39 Ibid.: "Es war ein schon—wenn gleich nicht empirisch vorhandenes Gedicht, was sie rezitierten."

40 Erhard Bahr, "Goethe and Oral Poetry," in *Formen und Folgen von Schriftlichkeit und Mündlichkeit*, ed. Ursula Schaefer and Edda Spielmann (Tübingen: Narr, 2001), 169.

down in writing; everyone sings or declaims and listens to singing and declaiming.[41] This makes clear how decisively the terms of the debate had shifted vis-à-vis the Ossian controversy: Dr. Johnson had seen orality as a sign that Ossian's works could not have originally constituted an epic in the vein of Homer; now it turned out orality would have precisely made it so. Wolf's *Prolegomena* moreover proposed that the Homeric corpus was precisely an effect of collecting work in the antiquarian mode: in other words, he portrayed the author of the *Iliad* as a forerunner to Macpherson. The situation was rich in ironies, as seemingly straightforward questions of authenticity and inauthenticity turned out to involve staggered processes of transmission. It was this irony, this play with process, in which the *Balladenjahr* made its home.

At the close of 1796, Schiller wrote to Goethe that "December creeps on and on and you do not come. I fear almost that we will not see each other until '97."[42] Their balladic collaborations were largely pursued across the gulf of such fears and regrets. Schiller was confined to his home and sometimes his bed by illness, while Goethe was consistently detained by the urgent business of being Goethe, and so the two men wrote their ballads as messages in a bottle. While there were visits in the first half of that year, the two of them mostly communicated via letters, usually brought along by visiting friends. These letters touched on current writing projects (Goethe was planning a sequel to *Hermann und Dorothea* and was finishing a draft of *Benvenuto Cellini*; Schiller was mostly preoccupied with *Wallenstein*), but mostly dealt with reflections on genre occasioned by their work. Schiller had begun to study Aristotle's *Poetics* in the spring, and before summer the two men were embroiled in a far-ranging discussion on the relationship between tragedy and comedy, theater and song, high art and popular art. The ballads they wrote seep into their exchanges literally on the margins of discussions of epic poetry and drama, and it is easy to see that these texts partake in Goethe's and Schiller's considerations of both while blending certain features of each.

What Goethe would later refer to as "our ballad studies"[43] seems to have begun in May, but intensified during Goethe's stay in Jena in early June. After that, the letters' postscripts and margins begin to populate with a familiar menagerie of now-canonic ballads. On June 10 and 14, it is "Der Taucher" ("The Diver"); on June 21, Goethe sends his response to "Der Handschuh" ("The Glove"). Before long, ballads were circulating between the two men almost daily. By June 26, Goethe sent Schiller "a counterpart to your 'Kraniche,'"[44] namely "Der Ring des Polykrates" ("The Ring of Polycrates")

41 Bahr, "Goethe and Oral Poetry," 165
42 Goethe/Schiller, *Der Briefwechsel zwischen Schiller und Goethe*, 1:282.
43 Ibid., 1:352: "unser Balladenstudium."
44 Ibid., 1:356.

and by June 27, the addressee already responded with feedback. Increasingly, they involved others in their balladic network. By early August, Schiller had sent some ballads to Herder, in hopes of a reaction and perhaps of spurring the author of "Erlkönigs Tochter" into balladic production of his own. All Herder was able to contribute, however, was to point out that Schiller's "Diver" drew its plot from a fairy tale that Schiller claimed never to have read.

It was clear early on that their products would appear in the next installment of Schiller's *Almanach*. Part of the time pressure, at least for Schiller in his dual role as both contributor and editor, was that some of the poems contained in the *Almanach* were to be set to music. This had been common practice for previous issues: Zelter had set parts of the *Musenalmanach*'s previous issue to music—a selection of his efforts appeared in a slim separate booklet published by Cotta, the same publisher that put out the *Almanach* itself.[45] That selection, however, consisted mostly of straightforwardly lyrical material. Setting ballads to music raised questions that previous collaborations had not. To be sure, the 1798 iteration of the *Musenalmanach* was to contain a large number of non-balladic texts, most famously the "Lied von der Glocke" ("The Song of the Bell"), which the two men clearly accorded pride of place in their efforts to commission song settings for their texts. Nevertheless, when it came to the ballads, the poetological reflections that had shaped the collaboration between the two men quickly came to involve musical considerations.

A majority of the poems written over the course of that summer ended up being set to music, by Johann Rudolf Zumsteeg, Christoph Jacob Zahn, and above all Carl Friedrich Zelter.[46] During that process, the two poets began to articulate on an ad hoc basis what made a successful ballad setting. Schiller passed on "Der Zauberlehrling" ("The Sorcerer's Apprentice") to "his composer in Stuttgart" (meaning Zumsteeg) almost immediately upon receipt, remarking that "I think it would be perfectly suited to an upbeat melody, being in such constant, passionate movement." The primacy of movement and action over psychology thus almost immediately transitioned from a poetological question directly into a compositional one. And it almost immediately came to involve questions of circulation as well: Zelter's settings from the previous year had appeared as an appendix volume at the same publisher, Cotta, which was not traditionally a music publisher. While the technology involved in printing sheet music had improved immeasurably by the 1790s, Cotta's product was in the end a bit ramshackle—sixteen pages containing five compositions, about half of the pages just occupied by text.

---

45 Carl Friedrich Zelter, *Melodieen zum Schillerschen Musenalmanach* (Tübingen: Cotta, 1796).

46 Meredith Lee, "Poetic Intentions and Musical Production: Die erste Walpurgisnacht," *Goethe Yearbook* 12 (2004): 82.

This meant that through-composed song settings, in which the music hewed closely to the drama described in the poem, were largely impossible. Instead, Zelter and his colleagues produced songs that could have appeared in a traditional songbook, with identical strophes that made only minimal efforts to adapt to the plot of the poem. While it certainly made the results of Goethe's and Schiller's efforts look like folk songs, the decision was most likely based on economics entirely. And the decision to write mostly strophic settings inevitably put pressure on the "constant movement" that Schiller so prized in the poems the two men were writing. The path back toward orality for the art ballad was from the first an internally contradictory one.

Schiller and Goethe produced some of the most enduring and famous ballads of the German canon during the summer of 1797. The ballads collected in Schiller's *Musenalmanach auf das Jahr 1798* were written with a readership in mind. Of course, Goethe and Schiller would at times recite the poems for others, or would get others to recite the poems for them—"perhaps," Goethe wrote before setting off for Frankfurt, "one can find along the way good Christian or heathen souls who would like to have such things read to them."[47] But the ballads first made the trip to the other writer's desk, who would reply with notes, and if necessary solicit fact-checking from other learned men in their network of letter-writers. Given that the *Balladenjahr*'s focus on the written word was not entirely a matter of choice or convenience, it is perhaps not surprising that the written word is not treated with much respect in the product of the collaboration. The longing for an original orality—probably as much the conversation the two men could not have in real life as the rhapsodic culture they located in ancient Greece—runs through the ballads produced in this manner. But so does the exact opposite: a distinctly modern distrust of orality. The essay that Goethe and Schiller compiled out of their epistolary reflections, "Epische und dramatische Dichtung" ("Epic and Dramatic Poetry"), proceeds from the assumption that the rhapsodes have vanished under condition of modern artmaking, and that their function has been assumed by the theater instead.[48] It is seductive to think of the joint portrait of the rhapsode that emerges from their essay and letters as a set of self-portraits compiled as the two men began to undertake their "ballad studies." What better way than the ballad to recreate, under modern conditions, an ancient rhapsodic tradition? But Goethe's and Schiller's characterization makes it clear that the balladeer is no latter-day rhapsode: the rhapsode is, we learn, "a wise man, who surveys events in calm collection [*ruhiger Besonnenheit*], his song [*Vortrag*] will aim to calm his listeners, to get them to listen for a longer time and with pleasure;

---

47 Goethe/Schiller, *Der Briefwechsel zwischen Schiller und Goethe*, 1:370.

48 Johann Wolfgang von Goethe, "Ueber epische und dramatische Dichtung," *Goethe's Werke* (Stuttgart: Cotta, 1833), 49:149.

he will aim to disperse interest [into the whole], since he is incapable of balancing an overly lively impression right away." The rhapsode "should not appear . . . in his own poem, it would be best if he were to read behind a curtain, so that one could abstract from all personality and would think one heard only the voice of the Muses as such." Contrast this with the "Mime," who "portrays a particular individual," who hopes that the audience will "feel in unison with the tribulations of his own soul and his own body."[49]

It is hard to make this description of the rhapsode fit with the mounting anguish of the sorcerer's apprentice, or the profound yearning of the titular speaker of "Der Schatzgräber" ("The Treasure Seeker"):

| | |
|---|---|
| Arm am Beutel, krank am Herzen, | Many weary days I suffered, |
| Schleppt' ich meine langen Tage. | Sick of heart and poor of purse; |
| Armuth ist die größte Plage, | Riches are the greatest blessing,— |
| Reichthum ist das höchste Gut! | Poverty the deepest curse! |

This speaker has far more in common with the "Mime," and in fact may represent something of a mixed form between the two. And while Goethe's suggestion that the ballad represents an "ur-egg" (*Urei*) uniting the three poetic arts was still decades in the future, a similar intuition animates these earlier efforts already: in the ballads, some of the constitutive oppositions that were beginning to map out the sphere of the lyric (subjectivity vs. objectivity, reflection vs. narrative) were in a state of indistinction. To pick out just one such opposition, Goethe and Schiller spent much time that spring distinguishing between tragedy and comedy—but "The Treasure-Seeker" mixes the two. The treasure-seeker's potentially tragic flaw leads not to his undoing, but to his learning a lesson—traditionally a trademark of comedic modes.

The main addition to *Faust* that Goethe wrote during the busy summer of 1797 was the "Vorspiel auf dem Theater," a reflection on the many stakeholders who have to come together and bring their competing agendas into momentary congruence to allow for theater. The ballads of that summer persist at the intersection of similarly competing constituencies—reading audiences, listening audiences, singers, reciters, highbrow audiences, lowbrow audiences—and the ballads seem less designed to resolve their competition, as to get them to forget that they are in fact competing. Is the ballad the authentic *Stimme der Völker* (or "the eternal song of inheritance and lust of a people," as Herder had put it in his Ossian essay[50]), or is it a poet's lark

---

49 Goethe, "Ueber epische und dramatische Dichtung," 150.
50 Herder, *Von deutscher Art und Kunst*, 258: "der ewige Erb- und Lustgesang des Volks."

modeled on older popular modes? Does the ballad spring from a spontaneous inspiration, or is it something learned men write when they are out of *Xenien* and decide they don't want to talk about Wallenstein anymore? Does it well up from the individual or the collective psyche? Schiller and Goethe seemed inclined not to answer these questions, but instead to leave the ballad suspended between the two options.

Given the link the reception of Ossian had established between orality and the truthfulness of the ballad, it is not surprising that the ballads of the *Almanach* treat their ambiguous relationship to orality likewise as an ambiguous relationship to truthfulness. Put another way, just as the ballad is never quite at home between oral and literary culture, it likewise belongs in a nebulous half-world between the authentic and the inauthentic. "Die Kraniche des Ibycus" ("The Cranes of Ibycus") even thematizes this in-between state: the trance-like state of the Eumenides may be real or fake, but insofar as it becomes one with the *Geist* of the Greek theater it ends up telling the truth:

| | |
|---|---|
| Und zwischen Trug und Wahrheit schwebet | And now all hearts are heard to beat, |
| Noch zweifelnd jede Brust und bebet, | Fluttering 'twixt truth and dark deceit, |
| Und huldiget der furchtbarn Macht[51] | Awed by the sense of that dread might. |

Goethe and Schiller understood the products of the *Balladenjahr* as standing in between: "Zwischen Trug und Wahrheit," between truth and "dark deceit," between oral circulation and literary exchange, and, not least of all, somewhere between Romanticism and classicism. The medieval subjects and the pervasive Gothicism certainly seemed to ally these ballads with the former; but the emphasis on ancient Greece, on didactic poems with a clear moral, seemed more suited to the latter. More important, the emphasis on traditional form (even if that form wasn't classical) clearly shares the concerns of Weimar classicism. But the emphasis on the quasi-organic processes by which the form has come into existence seems indebted to the ideals of *Sturm und Drang*, or, as Cyrus Hamlin has suggested, "the central tendencies of European Romanticism."[52]

This doubleness is central to the ballad in the German tradition: the ballad form both sustains the fiction of the poem's derivation from oral traditions *and* at the same time punctures that fiction. That puncturing in

---

51 Friedrich Schiller, *Sämtliche Werke* (Munich: Hanser, 1962), 1:350.
52 Cyrus Hamlin, "German Classical Poetry," in *The Literature of Weimar Classicism*, ed. Simon Richter (Rochester, NY: Camden House, 2005), 172.

turn is central to the oral tradition the poem institutes (through memorization, parody, *bon mot*). From the first, Goethe's balladic practice played with orality. On the one hand it aped oral effects, on the other it ironized orality and its dangers. "Der Zauberlehrling" ("The Sorcerer's Apprentice") is one of Goethe's most famous contributions to the *Musenalmanach*, and the one that has probably had the strangest career across media—winding up, after several dizzying turns, in a Disney film of all places. At its most basic the poem tells a story about the pitfalls of oral transmission. The old witch-master has left his hapless understudy alone, and the boy recites a magic formula—not from a book, but from memory:

| | |
|---|---|
| Seine Wort und Werke, | Know his incantation, |
| Merkt ich und den Brauch, | Spell and gestures too; |
| Und mit Geistesstärke | By my mind's creation |
| Thu ich Wunder auch.[53] | Wonders shall I do. |

The problem is: he repeats incorrectly what he has overheard (he forgets an all-deciding word), with humorously disastrous results. Eventually the "Meister" has to step in, and in a thunderous incantation he reclaims for himself the sole right to command the out-of-control broom-army. The apprentice, in other words, treats the magic formula as an oral tradition—one that he can repeat once he has heard it enough times, one that belongs to him as much as to the master, one that is not the property of a single author. But the master signifier turns out to matter more than the apprentice suspected.

The poem thus presents a scene of oral transmission, which is rescued by a "master" and his signification, that is to say by a mode of authorship that brooks no dilution. What the master says goes, and any attempt to repeat what the master says better hew exactly to his wording, or else the consequences could be disastrous. The master's words are not simply words—they are both "customs" or "habits" (*Brauch*—easy enough to pick up, one should assume), as well as "works" (*Werke*). This juxtaposition of, on the one hand, a basically improvisational mode of recitation, which leaves out two syllables ("walle") here or forgets a word there, and which produces only chaos, and, on the other, a mode of faithfully reproducing every word of a "Werk," seems to put the lie to the orality that supposedly vouches for the authenticity of the ballad form.

For it is clear that the kind of "work" that is the master's magic formula goes well beyond the "work-concept" identified by Lydia Goehr. Goehr

---

53 Johann Wolfgang von Goethe, *Goethe: Poetische Werke* (Berliner Ausgabe) (Berlin: Aufbau, 1960), 1:150.

suggests that a work is not one static thing, but comprises rather a set of practices, open-ended, yet not therefore arbitrary.[54] This may well be the work-concept with which the sorcerer's apprentice operates; reality does not bear him out on it, however. The kind of fealty demanded by the magic formula that constitutes the master's work is really that of the written word, of the literary text, the contract, the patent application. Goehr points out that the concept of a "work" toward which one owes a certain degree of fealty is a fairly recent one. Goethe may be pretending to tell a story of the distant past, but the conception of work on which he relies is decidedly prospective. This is true of many of the ballads in the *Musenalmanach*: they happily indulge the kind of "distressed" effects that further the fiction of the ballad as oral poetry. Many of these poems are a pleasure to recite, and especially Schiller's contributions are also quite easy to learn by heart. At the same time, many of them sound a warning about orality; they tell of mishearings or misunderstandings, and insist on the singularity and integrity of the work. Goethe's and Schiller's ballads occupy essentially an impossible middle position—recently invented "work" yet of the folk, celebrations of orality and warnings against it, objects of a tradition which they claim to reflect but which they constitute instead.

Oral transmission and how it relates to truth are central themes of Schiller's "Kraniche des Ibycus." The poem presents the story of a classical minstrel, murdered while traveling to the Isthmus of Corinth. With his dying breath he exhorts a flock of cranes to carry forth the truth about his murder. The Greeks gathered at Corinth despair over the artist's murder and over the fact that, since no one saw the crimes, the murderers can walk among them unmolested. The Eumenides then perform their frenetic ritual, which in fact manages to identify the wrongdoers: the crowd is seized by a kind of rapture, and when the cranes fly overhead, one killer calls out to the other. The crowd, primed by the Eumenides, is able to understand why the cranes so incense the killers, who are then seized.

This is another story all about orality, and as in the case of the "Brauch" that the sorcerer's apprentice fails to understand and replicate correctly, orality is understood by the poem as authenticated by the ethical life of a people—no doubt one reason Hegel was so drawn to the text. Schiller's poem tells an antique story of detection, but its protagonists do not rely on anything as modern as Sherlock Holmes's "Science of Deduction"; it relies on a world of shared meanings, on instinctual understanding, and on voiced orality.

---

54 Lydia Goehr, *The Imaginary Museum of Musical Works: An Essay in the Philosophy of Music* (Oxford: Oxford University Press, 2007).

| | |
|---|---|
| Besinnungsraubend, herzbethörend | In tones that every sense confound, |
| Schallt der Erinnyen Gesang, | The Furies' dismal chorus rings, |
| Er schallt, des Hörers Mark verzehrend, | Curdling each hearer's blood with sound |
| Und duldet nicht der Leier Klang.[55] | That scorns the lyre's majestic strings. |

Vocalized meaning bypasses consciousness straight for the "hearer." It requires no lyre, because it isn't absorbed through one's ears, but through one's marrow. Hearing the Eumenides means recalling having heard them.

Orality is the way in which Ibycus can enlist nature to get justice for a crime only nature witnessed. The fact that the flight of the cranes is readable as a *fatum* in the first place depends on a cooperation between man and nature—"Die Kraniche des Ibycus" presents Greek culture as nature raised to the second power. And what raises it is the living voice, which can call on a flock of cranes to have a meaning, and which can create a state in people that allows them to read that meaning out of same cranes. Orality becomes both the means by which the Eumenides are able to identify the culprits, and the way in which the culprits give themselves away: when one of them sees the cranes and calls out to his compatriot, the people understand immediately what this means. They seize the murderers:

| | |
|---|---|
| ". . . Ergreift ihn, der das Wort gesprochen, | ". . . Hold fast the man who spoke that word, |
| Und ihn, an den's gerichtet war."[56] | And him to whom it was addressed." |

The way the ritual puts the gathered multitudes in a kind of trance that allows them to receive the message that Ibycus has sent them, the way that the knowledge they glean from the cranes of Ibycus is somewhere between an accurate fact and a collective delusion, presents an allegory of the origin of the ballad form. Like the divination of the Eumenides, which flutters "'twixt truth and dark deceit," the ballad hovers between the two poles that had made Macpherson and Johnson such implacable opposites: between verifiable evidence and an evidence derived from the spirit of the people, between an evidentiary and a collective authenticity.

Hegel lauded the way the poem's chorus as bringing together the "substantial" existence of a particular detail with the universality of a broader

---

[55] Schiller, *Sämtliche Werke*, 1:350.
[56] Schiller, *Sämtliche Werke*, 1:351.

ethical framework—"that an individual situation, feeling, representation, etc. is comprehended in its deeper essence and thus itself expressed in a way that partakes of the substance itself."[57] But the antiquarian qualities of the poem were not the result of anything so spontaneous, which Hegel no doubt knew. Goethe and Schiller had done extensive research for the poem. Goethe, for instance, wrote to Carl August Böttiger, the famous classical philologist, on July 16, 1797—that is to say, as the ballad summer was reaching its fever pitch. Goethe inquired about the Greek expression "the cranes of Ibycus," which Schiller hoped to "form" into a ballad ("nun soll aus diesem Stoff eine Ballade gebildet werden"). Likewise, Goethe wrote to Schiller on August 22, 1797, to remind his housebound colleague that the eponymous cranes are migratory birds and would thus fly over the theater in a sedge.

Presenting itself formally as the result of a spontaneous upwelling of Greek spirit, the poem further asks us to understand such instinctual upwelling as the basis of Greek ethical life. But in fact the poem was a work of reconstruction carried out through the very tools of literacy that Johnson had deployed against the Ossian myth: careful research, a skillful combination of sources, and an insight into the inner workings of culture. In drawing out what it presented as the real experience contained in the ancient Greek expression, the ballad actually intended to perform an act of revivification. It was almost an act, not an object, of hermeneutics itself.

## Translating Orality: The *Musenalmanach* in Circulation

In September 1797, with the work on the ballads for the *Musenalmanach* in its final stages, Goethe traveled to Switzerland. Along the way, he stopped by Stuttgart to meet the composer Zumsteeg. The evening involved "verschiedene gute Musik" ("a variety of good music"), Goethe records in his diary, but he is not referring to the ballads Zumsteeg had been setting for him and Schiller.[58] Zumsteeg had set a portion of Ossian in Goethe's translation for piano and voice, and Goethe immediately envisions a theatrical scene:

> In the evening with *Kapellmeister* Zumsteeg, where I heard different excellent pieces of music. He set "Colma" as a cantata in my translation, but only with piano accompaniment; the effect is very good and

---

57 Hegel, *Vorlesungen über die Ästhetik*, 423.
58 On Zumsteeg's interest in Ossian, see James Porter, *Beyond Fingal's Cave: Ossian in the Musical Imagination* (Rochester, NY: University of Rochester Press, 2019), 129.

could possibly arranged for the theater, which is something to think about when I return. If one imagined Fingal and his heroes gathering in a hall, Minona singing, and Ossian accompanying her on his harp, with the piano hidden in the theater, the performance would be certain to have an effect.[59]

The fakery of the scene Goethe imagines here is self-evident: a hidden piano, actors arranged as a pretend audience, and a text whose genuineness Goethe had begun to doubt—but that he still believed would have an "effect" if it were to be performed. The young Goethe had imagined Ossian mystically steeped "in the Spirit of his time." Herder had conjured a detailed scene of reception, where the songs of "an unformed, purely sensual people" resound down the glens, "which have resonated long in the mouth of a paternal tradition."[60] The mature Goethe envisions this "resonance" (*fortsingen*) as a theatrical effect. But even if the scene he envisions for the theater is fictitious, the "effect" he imagines it will have on the audience is not.

In a strange way, the ballads collected in the *Musenalmanach auf das Jahr 1798* were wandering ballads, although of course not in the sense suggested by Dr. Johnson. They were the product of a network of scholars, poets, and composers, and what wandering they'd done they had accomplished by post rather than by bardic retelling. But if they were products of a culture of writing, upon publication they almost immediately entered into a network of decidedly modern circulation. They were recited, adapted, staged, illustrated, sung, of course. But they were also marketed, multiplied, parodied, instrumentalized in ways that both differed from and at times resembled the imaginary of circulation from which they emerged. This was not a secondary development that happened upon these poems from the outside: Schiller had commissioned the illustrations for the *Musenalmanach* well before all the ballads were composed; he had sent several promising entries into the almanac to various composers throughout the summer of 1797. The poems of the *Musenalmanach* evolved alongside their mediatization. They were designed to tell of a primary orality that their authors considered as fictional as that of Ossian; but they were likewise designed to enter into a secondary orality.

---

59 Goethe, *Tagebücher*, WA, III:2, 120: "Abends bey Herrn Capellmeister Zumsteeg, wo ich verschiedne gute Musik hörte. Er hat die Colma, nach meiner Übersetzung, als Cantate, doch nur mit Begleitung des Claviers gesetzt, sie thut sehr gute Wirkung und wird vielleicht auf das Theater zu arrangiren seyn, worüber ich nach meiner Rückkunft denken muß. Wenn man Fingaln und seine Helden sich in der Halle versammeln ließe, Minona, die sänge, und Ossian, der sie auf der Harfe accompagnirte, vorstellte, und das Pianoforte auf dem Theater versteckte, so müßte die Aufführung nicht ohne Effect seyn."

60 Herder, *Von deutscher Art und Kunst*, 258: "eines ungebildeten, sinnlichen Volks, . . . die sich so lange im Munde der väterlichen Tradition haben fortsingen können."

They were not traditional, but they were designed to become traditions in their own right. The ballads Goethe and Schiller wrote over the course of the summer and fall of 1797 tell ironic stories about the dangers and limitations of oral transmission, yet they also allegorize the difficult alchemical process by which fool's gold can be made to yield real gold—by which, in other words, fakery becomes authentic.

This was to become characteristic of the German *Kunstballade*: whatever story the poems told, they also told of the coming-into-being of stories, and their form bore the hope of a future rather than the traces of a past transmission. If form, as Theodor Adorno put it in his *Aesthetic Theory*, is "sedimented content,"[61] then we can read the ballad as tracing this process of sedimentation. It stages, and often spectacularly so, the process by which content becomes form: how this story had to take on this shape in order to survive, to endure and to pass down to its current reader. Perhaps no poem of the *Musenalmanach* is more explicit in presenting the ballad as the process of the purification of the inauthentic than "Der Gott und die Bajadere" ("The God and the Bayadere"). It is a poem entirely about redemption, although of a profoundly unchristian kind. A fallen woman is raised by embracing a god, but what the German literary critic Max Kommerell called her "Liebesdemut" ("loving devotion") is decidedly carnal. Her embrace of the god, in other words, is quite literal.[62] It is in love, Kommerell points out, that her "soulless ministrations" turn into something more.[63] The poem tells of two kinds of coming together, one soulful, one rote, and stages the transition from one to the other. It does so by reflecting on its own ambiguous orality.

Each stanza follows a pattern that Goethe used, although in varied form, throughout the ballads of that year (his Greek vampire tale "Die Braut von Korinth" ["The Bride of Corinth"] is an equally famous example).[64] There is a metric shift toward the end of the stanza, a shift made more abrupt by the fact that there is one line that rhymes with elements of both. The rhyme scheme (ABABCDCDEED) similarly pivots around the fourth line from the bottom. "Der Gott und die Bajadere" is, like "Die Braut von Korinth," a poem of interpenetration and (at times awkward) fusion.

---

61 Theodor W. Adorno, *Aesthetic Theory*, trans. Robert Hullot-Kentor (London: Bloomsbury, 2013), 198.

62 Max Kommerell, "Goethes Indische Balladen," in *Gedanken über Gedichte* (Tübingen: Klostermann, 1985), 370.

63 "Der Gott lehrt sie die Hingabe, sie entfaltet sich an ihm, indem sie so erst die Herrlichkeit der von ihr seelenlos geübten Liebeswerke efährt" (Kommerell, *Gedanken über Gedichte*, 370).

64 Karl Otto Conradi, "Balladen. Experimente mit dem erzählenden Gedicht," in *Goethe: Leben und Werk* (Düsseldorf: Patmos, 2006), 672–73.

Goethe's poems for the *Musenalmanach* frequently recur to established meters that, even at the time, were associated with oral modes. "Die Braut von Korinth," for instance, is kept in what is usually called the Serbian trochee (ABABCCB), after the conventions of the Serbian bards—"Der Schatzgräber" ("The Treasure Hunter") relies on a slightly changed version of the same (ABBCADDC). "Der Gott und die Bajadere" ("The God and the Bayadere") transforms this rhyme scheme, effectively grafting one rhyme scheme (likely based on the Serbian trochee) onto a simple ABBA schema in different meter:

| | |
|---|---|
| Und er fordert Sklavendienste; | And he asks for service menial, |
| Immer heitrer wird sie nur, | And she only strives the more, |
| Und des Mädchens frühe Künste | Nature's impulse now is genial, |
| Werden nach und nach Natur. | Where but art prevailed before. |
| Und so stellet auf die Blüte | As the fruit succeeds the blossom, |
| Bald und bald die Frucht sich ein; | Swells and ripens day by day, |
| Ist Gehorsam im Gemüte, | So, where fills the bosom, |
| Wird nicht fern die Liebe sein. | Love is never far away. |
| Aber, sie wird schärfer und schärfer zu prüfen, | But he, whose vast motive was deeper and higher, |
| Wählet der Kenner der Höhen und Tiefen | Selected more keenly and clearly to try her, |
| Lust und Entsetzen und grimmige Pein.[65] | Love, followed by anguish, and death, and dismay. |

The pivot of each stanza comes at the point of rupture between the two rhyme schemes, between the two meters. We are meant to experience it as rupture. Or, perhaps better, the line that starts with "Aber" seems to venture into altogether uncharted territory, only to repatriate it in the final line—and at times only in the final word—of the stanza. These interspersed lines have sometimes been described as an *envoi*, a feature of medieval ballads that Goethe may have adapted here. But *envois* are short, metrically distinct closing stanzas usually at the end a ballad that provide commentary or a moral. Goethe's lines, however, are absolutely integral to the poem itself, continuing its action while vaulting into an entirely new meter and cadence. In certain stanzas the lines are spoken by a separate speaker, but their status and function change from verse to verse. And the main bulk of the poem, above all through the rhyme in the final line of each stanza, recaptures the anomaly—if this is an *envoi*, it doesn't get to close either stanza or poem.

65 Goethe, *Goethe: Poetische Werke*, 1:160.

It stages a rupture that is then rescinded. Before that final rhyming word, there is something terrifying about these suspended lines that grow like a phantom limb from the compact body of the rhymed couplets. The strange appendage to each stanza is at once quite different from the main strophe (parataxis, different rhyme scheme, etc.) and at the same time full of reminiscences (the "schärfer und schärfer" echoes the "bald und bald," for instance).

This is a process clearly allegorized in the stanza itself: as the Bayadere attends to Shiva, the poem begins to describe a morphological organic process of the type that was something of an obsession for Goethe—"Blüte" (flower) becomes "Frucht" (fruit), "Gehorsam" (obedience) becomes "Liebe" (love), and "Nature's impulse now is genial, / Where but art prevailed before." The stanza tells of a transition and simultaneously stages such a transition on a formal level—but that formal transition isn't nearly so organic, fluid, and effortless. The poem thus stages two different dramas: a complete and total unification, a truly organic process of fusion and evolution metaphorized entirely in natural terms; *and* another unification that proceeds by addition, by prosthesis, profoundly uncanny and very clearly legible as artifice. "The ballad has something mysterious, without being mystical,"[66] Goethe would write later, and here indeed we have both: mystical union and mysterious, uncanny accretion. "Der Gott und die Bajadere" dramatizes both the *telos* of the ballad—perfect original unity—and the *reality* of the ballad—historical processes of, at times awkward, accretion. The relationship of one to the other is frequently marked as uncanny: a horror ballad like "Die Braut von Corinth" ("The Bride of Corinth") stages it as a vampiric, parasitic relationship. The plot of "Der Zauberlehrling" ("The Sorcerer's Apprentice") similarly turns on the tiny but crucial difference in the *telos* of a locution and its execution—the apprentice *wants* to do one thing with words, but his words wind up doing quite another.

All of these poems co-evolved with their song settings, with a view toward some kind of oral reproduction—or at least toward the potential for it. Far from a supplementary aftereffect, the song setting instead helped continue the poem's internal process, helped push it toward orality. By the time Goethe heard Zumsteeg's Ossian setting in Stuttgart, Zelter had already completed his setting of "Der Gott und die Bajadere," sending it to Schiller on August 7, 1797. Zelter's setting represents a reading of Goethe's text: where Schiller explicated his understanding of Goethe's ballads in letters, Zelter set his down in music. While the poets didn't treat Zelter or Zumsteeg as their equals in this creative process, the composers and their readings of the ballads

---

[66] J. W. Goethe, "Ueber die Ballade vom vertriebenen und zurückkehrenden Grafen," in *Goethe's nachgelassene Werke* (Stuttgart: Cotta, 1833), 5:332: "Die Ballade hat etwas Mysterioses, ohne mystisch zu sein."

seem to have influenced how Goethe and Schiller themselves thought about them, and about the ballad genre more generally. In the case of "Der Gott und die Bajadere," Schiller came away impressed with Zelter's work, but reported to Goethe that the central drama of the ballad—the movement toward unification—was largely missing from the song. The musical ballad here comes up against a limitation that would shape its reception throughout the early nineteenth century: its character as *Lied* and its status as a dramatic poem seemed to come into conflict almost by necessity. The relationship between part and whole was centrally different for a dramatic poem than the *Lied* form was able to accommodate. Schiller reports to Goethe that "the ballad's melody does not fit equally well with all the stanzas, but in some, for instance the last one from the end, the chorus works extremely well."[67]

The symmetry of its cadence and meter allowed the ballad to mark identity in difference, allowed the poem to narrate change while remaining song-like in its structure. Instrumental music had a much more difficult time combining these two aspects—strophic structure suggested repetition rather than progression, and it made the dramatic aspects of the balladic text quite difficult to stage, cued as it was to one particular affective pitch. Nothing of course forced composers like Zelter to rely on repeating music for accompanying stanzas that performed vastly different functions in a highly dynamic narrative. Nothing, that is, other than the vagaries of circulation. Goethe and Schiller could cast the creation of their crop of ballads, written with a view to publication and wide circulation in a popular almanac, in academic language and call them "ballad studies." But by the time the poems reached the composers' desk, it seemed, the academic framing had given way to something far more market-driven: what the printer would print, what the subscribers would pay for, and what readers of the almanac might conceivably sit down to play at home. In the Ossian setting Goethe remarked upon, as well as in his setting of "Der Zauberlehrling," Zelter addresses this problem by adding differently accented arpeggios to mark progress in the dramatic action between the stanzas. In a handful of others he adds a coda to mark narrative closure. In yet other settings of the same time (for instance, "Die Braut von Corinth") he keeps the stanzas entirely identical.

The arrangement of "Der Gott und die Bajadere" that Schiller describes here, a setting for harp and unspecified solo singer, opens with an almost baroque-sounding chorale. Zelter's desultory indication that the piece ought to be played "im Romanzenton" (in the tone of a romance) does little to dispel the sense of musical anachronism. Matters are not helped by the fact that, while the concept of a specifically balladic "Romanzenton" in music would indeed emerge over the course of the nineteenth century (designating

---

67 Goethe/Schiller, *Der Briefwechsel zwischen Schiller und Goethe*, 1:374: "Die Melodie der Ballade paßt freilich nicht gleich gut zu allen Strophen, aber bei einigen, wie bei der drittletzten, macht sich der Chor 'wir tragen die Jugend' etc. sehr gut."

FIG. 1.1 Karl Friedrich Zelter (1758–1832), "Der Gott und die Bajadere" for harp, setting of the poem by Goethe.

essentially a slightly more lyrical, less narrative mode of composing *Lieder* based on narrative poems[68]), by 1797 it was still largely a literary term, popularized by Herder and others. Zelter's instructions likely drew from the operatic romance, in particular the *opéra comique* of the era, in which a single or several plucked string instruments accompanied a semi-narrative song. His choice of style was, as Schiller seems to have intuited, likely a matter of expediency, intended to speed and ease the piece's circulation, without making (or caring to make) a particularly convincing thematic or generic fit for Goethe's text.

But this was hardly Zelter's fault. As Schiller's report on the piece indicates, there existed as of yet simply no agreement on which aspects of a romance or ballad (or in the case of "Der Gott und die Bajadere," a "legend") should, or even could, determine the overall gestalt of its musical setting. Franz Schubert set the same music in 1815 (D. 254), and the differences between the two composers' poem to efforts testify to the fact that a generic compact of the ballad setting had in the meantime evolved. Schubert, too, keeps his arrangement strophic, but appends a note that "in these strophes . . . the content of the same should determine the pianos and the fortes." Schubert, too, has the piano frame the poem's trochaic cadence as a chorale of sorts, but, as Lorraine Byrne Bodley has noted, Schubert seems at pains to ironize the religious trappings of this less-than-religious chorale.[69]

---

68 See, for instance, the work of August Reissmann: August Reissmann, *Grundriss der Musikgeschichte* (München: Bruckmann, 1865), 118; and August Reissmann, *Die Hausmusik in ihrer Organisation und kulturgeschichtlichen Bedeutung* (Berlin: Oppenheim, 1884), 213.

69 Lorraine Byrne Bodley, *Schubert's Goethe Settings* (London: Routledge, 2016), 242.

Zelter's earlier setting is deliberately elementary: the chorale's rhythm is measured and simple, the vocal line for tenor or bass is relatively undemanding (Fig. 1.1). Like Schubert's later setting, Zelter endeavors to emulate the strophic structure of Goethe's poem in its one most noticeable formal aspect, namely the pivot from one, fairly established, meter to one that is far more unusual. In 1815, Schubert would simulate this by having the accompaniment and singer enter a syncopated, open-ended lilt, which creates a kind of ironic reply to the far more staid (and in its own way chorale-like) main section of each strophe. Zelter does the same by literally changing his time signature from 4/4 to 6/4—again, his solution seems far more formalistic, far less indebted to a sense of what a ballad is or ought to be like. This is a piece, like the almanac it is meant to accompany, intended to welcome amateurs, to invite reproduction in the home. Its fealty is to the type of object it aims to be part of, not to the kind of text that it draws on.

In Zelter's decision, the two kinds of orality of which the ballad was supposed to partake come into dialogue. On the one hand, the rhapsodic narration of balladry is supposed to contain a dramatic element, is supposed to tell of a development and impart a series of vivid impressions on its audience. For this, it would seem, a purely repetitive *Lied* form is insufficient. But at the same time, Zelter wrote his settings for the same reasons Goethe and Schiller wrote the ballads he set to music: to be anthologized, to be collected, to circulate. And a ballad that stuck to one melody and tempo throughout could fit on one sheet, whereas a dramatic scene like "Colma" could take up twenty times that, which limited its circulation. It is not surprising that Zelter tended to opt for repetition over difference. He likely assumed what Schubert's arrangement would make explicit: what variation would be introduced into "Der Gott und die Bajadere" from stanza to stanza would have to come from the singer, just as in readings of the poem it would come from the reciter. The manner in which Goethe and Schiller came to rely on Zumsteeg, Zelter, and Zahn brought a third figure into their successive stages of remediation: the actor. The ballad could shape the outlines of its reception, but its essence was in the individual sounding out. And it was in this sounding out that the ballad first became entangled with a specifically German national project.

## 2 | The Ballad, the Voice, and the Echoes of War

On April 21, 1813, Johann Wolfgang von Goethe arrived in Dresden from Weimar. He had left to escape the chaos of the Wars of Liberation and was headed for Teplitz in northern Bohemia. Prussia had allied itself with Russia in February, Blücher's troops controlled much of the area, Northern Germany was in open revolt, and Napoleon himself was to arrive in nearby Erfurt only four days later to direct operations. That evening the poet decided to attend a *Declamatorium* by an actor, Christian Gottfried Solbrig (1774–1838), and was altogether horrified. "I have not come across anything quite so hollow, uninspired and tasteless," Goethe remarked in a letter to his wife Christiane Vulpius. Solbrig recited, Goethe reported, "in a most plaintive [*jämmerlich*] tone the most wretched of all the lamentable German songs."[1] Goethe left the performance early.

Goethe registered some relief that the audience—about 300 strong by his estimate—were not particularly receptive to Solbrig and his offerings: "they applauded only once, when [Solbrig] intoned a hooray for Emperor Alexander [of Russia]."[2] But as was the case with many of Goethe's encounters with German patriotism during the Wars of Liberation, his praise of the public is streaked with irony. "Had the poor sucker [*Schlucker*] known his trade,"[3] he remarks, Solbrig would have just intoned some patriotic song and brought down the house. While Goethe was glad that the audience did not fall for Solbrig's sentimental treacle, he remained suspicious that the only times the crowd did get excited was for nationalism at the expense of literary merit.

---

1 J. W. von Goethe, *Goethe-Briefe*, ed. Philipp Stein (Berlin: Elsner, 1905), 6:251.
2 Ibid., 6:251.
3 Ibid., 6:252.

The encounter between poetry and the public in the middle of a patriotic uprising was, to Goethe, clearly a fraught one.

Perhaps more significant than Goethe's discomfort with Solbrig's recitations, and the reactions of their audience, was the poet's coping strategy. Once he returned to his lodgings from the disturbing *Declamatorium*, Goethe decided to write a ballad. "Der Totentanz" (usually translated as "Danse Macabre" or "Dance of Death") is one of his most well-known ballads, and inspired iconic illustrations, as well as several song-settings (including by Zelter, Loewe, and Weißheimer). "Der Totentanz" is a gothic ballad in the vein of "Der Erlkönig," but its grotesquerie has a more pronounced humorous edge. The ballad tells the story of a night watchman at a graveyard who observes the dead rising from their grave to dance, stripping off their clothing and shrouds as they do so. In a moment of characteristic balladic hubris, the watchman steals one such shroud, and as the dead return to their graves, its rightful owner goes on the hunt for the thief. In a panic, the watchman ascends his tower, but the aggrieved skeleton clambers up in pursuit. Just in time, the clock strikes one and the corpse falls apart.

The poem is based on a story Goethe's son August had relayed to the poet. But we can perhaps conjecture about why Goethe would have turned to this material in the middle of an escalating war, or, for that matter, almost immediately after seeing Solbrig's *Declamatorium*. "Der Totentanz" is, after all, about a single man faced with a communal ritual at once ghoulish and preposterous. It is about a dance of death that everyone involved seems to take quite seriously, but that is, seen by the bright light of the full moon, quite risible. But, just as significantly, the preposterousness does not make the ritual any less dangerous—the watchman almost pays for his irreverence with his life. Absurdity and very real violence are uncannily entwined in Goethe's poem, and unlike in some other gothic ballads of Goethe's the awe of the supernatural never wins out over the absurdity of it all. The reason for this has everything to do with voice: "Der Totentanz" is a poem that is particularly funny when spoken out loud. Where in "Der Erlkönig" Goethe's prosody creates uncanny effects of thundering hooves and rustling trees, here the prosody clicks and clacks with all the jangling-bone consonants the German language has to offer (Goethe rhymes "vertrakte" and "Takte," to cite just the most egregious instance). The humor of "Der Totentanz," the ridiculousness of the mass movement the watchman observes, depend on declaiming the poem out loud. "Der Totentanz" manages to celebrate the vocalization of poetry in two, seemingly contradictory ways: vocalization conjures the immediacy of a supernatural menace, but it also, even before the clock strikes one, renders explicit the absurd underside of the menace. In the middle of a pan-European cataclysm, Goethe uses a gothic miniature, a seemingly timeless fable about hubris and humility, to evoke the atmosphere of April 1813, an atmosphere defined by the great war and the swelling passions of nationalism, and to register his at times bemused, at times horrified incomprehension—what Karl Kraus called Goethe's profound "sense of emptiness" when it came to his compatriots' newfound "excited state."[4]

What is perhaps less noticeable is that "Der Totentanz" is about the ballad's ambiguous position vis-à-vis public recitation: while Goethe doesn't mention Solbrig's program containing any ballads, many evenings of this type would have consisted mainly of ballads. In the middle of a great Europe-wide Dance of Death the ballad became not just a way to recollect the distant past, but to fetishize the living voice. The ballad was one way in which a specific mode of public address was practiced and its audience habituated in those all-important years of the 1810s: a mode of public enunciation that trafficked in communal emotions, and in the excluding properties of the national language. In a heightened political climate like that of the spring of 1813, at a time when literature was pressed habitually into the service of a chauvinistic assertion of a German national culture, the ballad's medieval origins and supposedly anti-classicist aesthetics made it a seductive and seemingly straightforward vehicle for a poetic mass politics. And yet, as in the case of "Der Totentanz," the ballad was never quite the straightforward carrier of a national voice that the declaimers seemed to offer it as. The heyday of the ballad's public performance and declamation largely unfolded in an historic environment in which public utterance in the German language was uniquely politicized. It is safe to say that Goethe was leery of linguistic mass politics; it is equally clear that other poets embraced it—but any ballad written during the era had to contend to some extent with a background of pervasive balladic bellowing. Many of them thematized the link explicitly: Ludwig Uhland's 1814 ballad "Des Sängers Fluch" ("The Bard's Curse") places two bards, their voices, and the feelings they evoke in public, in competition with a king's authority. The king kills one of the bards, but the second bard places the titular curse on the king. He will no longer be spoken of; all song and tale about him will fall silent.

By the 1810s, invoking the bard in a ballad had attained a new and different valence in Germany. Uhland's ballad was inspired by several English and Scottish romances collected in Herder's *Stimmen der Völker*—but his treatment of the bard reflected a specifically German bardic politics, one that was more about an anger aimed forward in time than a nostalgia aimed backward. The bard figures in English literature are backward-looking figures of mourning—"last minstrels" who speak for regional differences that are on the brink of extinction, about to be submerged into a homogenized English national and literary identity. In the Scottish Borders, as Katie Trumpener has argued, the bard functions as "the mouthpiece for a whole society,

---

4 Karl Kraus, *Die letzten Tage der Menschheit* (Vienna: Die Fackel, 1920), 174.

articulating its values, chronicling its history, and mourning the inconsolable tragedy of its collapse."[5] The bard's songs came from the past and had to be artificially salvaged into a modern written literature. Their sound was always a past one. Jean Paul, in his *Vorschule der Ästhetik* (*School for Aesthetics*, 1804), says that Ossian "finds future and eternity only in the past."[6] This was indeed what drew German Romantic music, from Felix Mendelssohn to Johannes Brahms, so powerfully toward Scottish themes.[7] But in actual ballad-writing in Germany, this was never quite as true as it was taken to be for Ossian—these poems imagined a future for themselves. And that future often rested on the living language, the live voice. In Germany, retrospection was of course also an inalienable aspect of the ballad revival. Especially in the first decades of the nineteenth century, the ballad's gestures and the practices constituted or imagined around it were not so much about the past but about the present. There was vital interest in keeping ballads circulating orally rather than in and through print. Where Percy's *Reliques*, for instance, endeavored to capture the once-thriving balladic tradition in print at the moment of its extinction, German authors and educators found it politically important to keep the ballad vocal, to keep sounding it out. After all, the nation that it was supposed to be articulating did not yet exist.

Not surprisingly, this sounding-out had an emphatically public dimension: To be sure, both during the Napoleonic Wars and in the Restoration Era that followed, poetry, like music, was frequently a non-public pursuit, and even reading out loud was usually done in the smallest of groups. But public recitation frequently sought to gather a community: in the musical evenings of the early nineteenth century and the Biedermeier period, the now-canonic ballad-settings of Schubert and Loewe were part of the texture of an expanded domesticity. Less well remembered, and now largely extinct, are the *declamatoria* of the kind Goethe attended in Dresden—a mostly German practice that first arose in the late eighteenth century but was well established by Goethe's time. However, given the linguistic politics and the prevailing understanding of declamatory practice, the *Declamatorium* was not just one more means of circulating ballads—instead it created a counter-circulation, constituted different publics. After all, while the German *Lied* was popularizing German balladry by insisting that even an audience that didn't speak German could profit from listening to a song setting, the *Declamatorium* insisted on a linguistic community as its audience. While classical music disseminated German art ballads internationally, declamatory practice did the opposite—it imagined tight bounds to such dissemination.

---

5 Katie Trumpener, *Bardic Nationalism: The Romantic Novel and the British Empire* (Princeton, NJ: Princeton University Press, 1997), 6.

6 Jean Paul, *Werke* (Munich: Hanser, 1963), 86–92.

7 Fiske, "Brahms and Scotland," *Musical Times* 109 (1968): 1106–7.

# Declaiming the Nation

The *Declamatorium* was a public performance, sometimes by established theatrical actors, at others by specialized declamators, that combined dramatic recitation with a few scenic trappings, some melodramatic interludes, and the occasional tableau vivant.[8] It could take place in semi-public settings, but most frequently itinerant orators seem to have demonstrated their craft in the court theaters during the summer off-season. It could even be included as an encore or interlude in a musical or theatrical evening. The practice clearly drew on certain conventions of the German melodrama, but was widely understood to be a new form.[9] And, at least for a time, it was extremely popular: the *Morgenblätter* spoke in 1810 of "a fashion for declaiming [*Deklamir-Mode*]."[10] Declamation-mania carried the fetishism of the speaking voice during the mass death of the Napoleonic Wars well into the postwar era, where it entwined the presentism of the living voice with the irrecoverability of the collectively mourned recent dead. That sense of mourning was not continuous, nor did it assert itself identically in all parts of the German-speaking world. But the overall sense traced in this chapter—that the ballad was a form to be sounded out viva voce, while at the same time often dealing with voices that were mere echoes of the past—can be traced throughout the period, and well into mid-century.

Public recitation was not a secondary means by which pre-existing literature circulated—it influenced, at least for a time, what was considered literature at all, and it shaped, more lastingly, poetic and compositional practice.[11] In March 1809, the composer Johann Friedrich Reichardt (1752–1814), who had set many of Goethe's poems to music, spent time in Vienna and public declamation seems to have been very much on his mind.[12] When, for

---

8 In what follows, I will render the word as *Declamatorium*, which is the spelling we find in the encyclopedias of the age, but Germans were inconsistent with regard to what they called the form. Some used the term "Deklamatorium," some used the plural "Deklamatorien," while others used "Deklamatoria" or "Declamatoria," etc. There was even the usually slightly dismissive "Klamatorium." Since the different renderings do not appear to have tracked with any difference in usage, I have opted to equalize them in the English translations for ease of reading.

9 Ulrich Kuhn, *Sprech-Ton-Kunst: Musikalisches Sprechen und Formen des Melodrams im Schauspiel und Musiktheater (1770–1933)* (Tübingen: Niemeyer, 2001).

10 *Morgenblätter für gebildete Leser* (1810), 4:524.

11 Edward F. Kravitt, "The Influence of Theatrical Declamation upon Composers of the Late Romantic Lied," *Acta Musicologica* 34, no. 1/2 (1962): 18–28.

12 Francien Markx, "Towards a German Romantic Concept of the Ballad: Goethe's 'Johanna Sebus' and Its Musical Interpretations by Zelter and Reichardt," *Goethe Yearbook* 19 (2012): 1–28.

instance, he critiqued a declamation of ballads by Gottfried August Bürger by a "Madame Bürger" (likely no relation), he wrote as someone who had pored over the question of how to render the printed word melodiously and accurately—after all, Reichardt had set many of Bürger's ballads as songs, and had written the then most popular musical version of "Lenore." While he allowed that Madame Bürger acquitted herself with "art and truthfulness" in most respects, he criticized that in certain moments "the wish for a partial expression of the word [*Wortausdruck*] while keeping the tone uniform" stuck out too much.[13] Between the lines, then, Reichardt understood public declamation as a cousin to his own efforts at *Vertonung*, at setting balladry to music: it constitutes a parallel but different project of making the ballad sound in public. Reichardt's own version of "Lenore" was, as was common in ballad settings at the time, a "strophic" setting, meaning that each stanza of the poem was set to an identical accompaniment, rather than modulating the emotional effects of Bürger's escalating drama. It is clear that his criticisms of "partial expression" and "uniform tone" very much cast his adaptive practice and Madame Bürger's side by side. His compositional practice treated declamation as a competing but coequal mode of balladry. And how could he not? He was likely aware that the first setting of Bürger's ballad, a version published by Friedrich Ludwig Aemilius Kunzen in the 1770s, included only a few meager sung portions, and otherwise was scored for a reciter and an instrumental accompanist. Such melodramatic settings were common well into the mid-nineteenth century. Being a good ballad composer thus entailed being a connoisseur of public declamation.

At the same time, for all the similarities he seems to have ascribed to their respective aesthetic projects, Reichardt's audience was of course conceived altogether differently from Madame Bürger's. Composition and declamation may have appealed to similarly well-heeled constituencies, but their imagined audience, the pathways of circulation they meant to activate, differed greatly. German musicians, music theorists, and music publishers were intent on establishing music as an export item, something that could transcend national boundaries. Public declamation, by contrast, sought to activate, and indeed establish, an emphatically German audience. Reichardt had relied on very different strategies: almost immediately after composing his song setting of "Lenore," Reichardt and his publisher had created an edition in English, using a translation by Benjamin Beresford, who specialized in ballad translations for musical audiences, clearly eying an international market.[14]

---

13 Johann Friedrich Reichardt, *Vertraute Briefe geschrieben auf einer Reise nach Wien* (Amsterdam: Kunst- und Industrie-Comptoir, 1810), 82.

14 Walter Salmen, *Johann Friedrich Reichardt: Komponist, Schriftsteller, Kapellmeister und Verwaltungsbeamter der Goethezeit* (Hildesheim: Olms, 2002).

Settings like Reichardt's helped make allegedly "characteristic" German art an item consumable in other languages and countries. Performances like Madame Bürger's, by contrast, served to create an inside and an outside to the German language: they helped equalize the many dialects, regional accents, and frames of reference within the German-speaking lands into one allegedly "common" language within, and defined a space outside of the linguistic community.

Whether in his diaries or in a work like *Die Wahlverwandtschaften* (*Elective Affinities*, 1809): Goethe was anything but alone in portraying the way evenings like Madame Bürger's mixed music and literature as artless and amateurish. Something about *Declamatoria* appeared to his contemporaries ripe for parody and jest. Jean Paul (Johann Paul Friedrich Richter) places in his *Dr. Katzenbergs Badereise* (*Dr. Katzberg's Bathing Voyage*, 1809) an episode set at a public reading (*Declamatorium*). His description of the reciter's "poetic cow-herding" (*dichterische Alpenwirtschaft*), a brilliant shower of "verbal rapids" washing over the audience, in which "the music chimes in (on small motions of his fingers) sometimes above, sometimes below his waterfalls, and everything harmonizes,"[15] is suffused with not-so-subtle ridicule. The *Declamatorium*, Jean Paul's description suggests, is at once a site of scenery-chewing excess and of overly calculated interactions between words and music. Like Reichardt, contemporary writers seemed to project onto the practice many of the anxieties that attached to emerging "serious" theatrical practices. The dramatist August Klingemann dedicated an entire satire (*Posse*) to *Schill, oder das Deklamatorium zu Krähwinkel* (*Schill, or the Declamatorium of Krähwinkel*, 1812). In 1813, the popular Austrian writer Carl Meisl premiered his "mythological caricature" *Orpheus und Euridice, oder So geht es im Olymp zu!* (*Orpheus and Euridice, or This Is How Things Go on Mount Olympus!*, 1813)— in it, Jupiter demands from Orpheus "an entertainment for [my] heart," and bids the other gods guess what kind of entertainment he has in mind. Minerva cheekily suggests a *Declamatorium*: "That would help us sleep. I sleep so little as it is."[16]

Elise Sommer (1761–1836) wrote a poem "To a Friend" and adds the epigraph "After a declamatorium given by him."[17] Like Jean Paul, she likens her friend's elocution to a roaring river, a "Suada" that throws itself "over the cliff loudly into the domestic bay." For much of the poem, it is unclear whether Sommer is making fun of her friend or not. The poem closes on an amorous note, with the "sounding mouth" rather than the friend as the object of

---

15 Jean Paul, *Werke* (München: Hanser, 1959–1963), 6:202.
16 Carl Meisl, *Theatralisches Quodlibet* (Pest: Hartleben, 1820), 79.
17 Elise Sommer, *Gedichte* (Frankfurt a.M.: Herrmannsche Buchhandlung, 1813), 284.

longing—"your sounding mouth sounds on within us."[18] But it opens with the rather brutal line: "Do not be wroth with the immortal ones because they endowed you with little."[19] The rest of the poem works hard to clarify that this "little" is meant to refer to earthly wealth, but in German (as in English with "endow") "verleihen" is not usually a word associated with the actual lending of money. On its face, the poem seems be saying that the declamator may not have much money but does have his overflow of emotions and the oratorical brilliance of his verbal waterfalls. Yet it also has a strong undertow suggesting a different reading: its addressee may not be particularly good at expressing them but should be glad to have such deep, deep feelings.

One reason literary authors had for disliking the practice is one gestured toward by Reinhart Meyer-Kalkus: a sense of being at the declamators' mercy. After all, most listeners would come into contact with an author's text only in the interpretation by a stage actor, and author readings were exceptionally rare at the time (Bürger and his "Lenore" were one notable exception[20]). The public *Declamatoria* were thus inevitably a surrender of authorial control, the public declaimers often careless and slapdash stewards of an author's intent.

The widespread ridicule the form attracted was likely not helped by the fact that "Deklamator" soon doubled as a job description and a criticism of acting that played for the rafters: when Eduard Hanslick recalls his first theatrical experiences in Vienna in his memoirs *Aus meinem Leben (From My Life)*, he criticizes *Burgtheater*-stalwart Heinrich Johann Anschütz (1785–1865) as "too much of a *Deklamator*, if a *Deklamator* of great accomplishment."[21] And in his memoirs, published in 1900, the writer Paul Heyse comments on the premiere of his early play *Die Grafen von der Esche (The Counts von Esche,* 1850) in much the same tones: he complains that Joseph Wagner played the lead as "a mushy *Deklamator*, where I had written a dark, heavy-blooded, irascible hard-head."[22] Behind this dissatisfaction may lurk the fact that declamation relied on a tonality of affects (matching tonal ranges and intensities with certain affects), a kind of emotional alphabet that smacked of the rationalist aesthetics of the eighteenth century (Gottsched had been a champion). Heyse's remark in particular seems to regard an overly declamatory style as the natural enemy of character: you do what the emotion (shared between the

---

18 Sommer, *Gedichte*, 284: "Habe denn Dank für die Stunden! Sie eilten geflügelt vorüber; / Aber Dein tönender Mund tönet noch lieblich uns nach!"

19 Sommer, *Gedichte*, 284: "Zürne nicht mit den Unsterblichen, dass sie Dir wenig verliehen."

20 Reinhart Meyer-Kalkus, *Geschichte der literarischen Vortragskunst* (Stuttgart: Metzler, 2020), 266.

21 Eduard Hanslick, *Aus meinem Leben* (Basel: Bärenreiter, 1987), 76.

22 Paul Heyse, *Jugenderinnerungen und Bekenntnisse* (Stuttgart: Cotta, 1912), I:278.

thespian and his audience) demands, not what the unique individual that you are charged with portraying might sound like. Here, then, the *Declamatorium* melded the aesthetics and preferences of the eighteenth century with those of the incipient nineteenth, mixed classical and Romantic ideologies and aesthetic theories.

The heyday of the *Declamatorium* coincides with the Restoration Era, a period during which it occasioned a great theoretical and critical interest. Reviews and reflections, literary depictions and parodies attest to a robust interest in and widespread popularity of the phenomenon. The idea of buying tickets to have someone recite soliloquies and poetry on stage was novel enough to be remarked upon, but at the same time it was a self-evidently legitimate mode of interacting with literature. By the 1830s, the *Declamatorium* had largely fallen out of fashion and was superseded by other forms of public performance and recitation. Nevertheless, many of the values embodied in the practice survived in amateur settings. Audiences may no longer have bought tickets for an evening of poetry recitation, but they still included such recitations in school events, municipal festivities, family celebrations, and club meetings. Most important, the word *Declamatorium* survived, but now referred to books anthologizing poems to be recited, no longer to public recitation itself. About 900 such anthologies were published between 1840 and 1914.[23]

The *Declamatorium*'s origins thus tied public declamation to the first major wave of German nationalism. And its rise dovetailed with the aesthetics of Romanticism. Many German Romantics, especially those of a more nationalist persuasion, understood "the German people" to be seeking a single voice, and therefore sought to develop public fora in which "the people" could test out that voice. This era furthermore saw the advent of the public lecture in Germany, with its own aesthetics of nationalized orality.[24] Contemporaries saw in the operas of Carl Maria von Weber (himself a friend of *declamatoria*[25]) an attempt to reclaim a German declamatory operatic singing style from Italianate ornamentation.[26] The emerging understanding of medieval song culture, in particular *Minnesang*, emphasized the distinction between literacy and orality. But as Karl Lachmann, one of the fathers of medieval German

---

23 Peter Brang, "Übersetzungsanthologien als Übersetzungsbilder: Hinweis auf den Sonderfall der Deklamatorien," in *International Anthologies of Literature in Translation*, ed. Harald Kittel (Berlin: Schmidt, 1995), 164.

24 Sean Franzel, *Connected by the Ear: The Media, Pedagogy, and the Politics of the Romantic Lecture* (Evanston, IL: Northwestern University Press, 2013).

25 See, e.g.: Max Maria von Weber, *Carl Maria von Weber: Ein Lebensbild* (Leipzig: Ernst Keil, 1866), 3:19.

26 Stephen C. Meyer, *Carl Maria von Weber and the Search for a German Opera* (Bloomington: Indiana University Press, 2003), 8.

philology, made clear in a lecture given in 1833, that distinction was overlaid with another one, between singing (*Singen*) and saying (*Sagen*). German poetry, he posited, had once treated the two as indistinguishable, but as popular and courtly poetry drifted apart, so had singing and sáying.[27] Across several dimensions, then, recitation reinvigorated old juxtapositions while promising a return to a point before they actually became juxtapositions.

For all the ways in which it harmonized with the preoccupations of the Romantic age, however—in particular its interest in the medieval past—the *Declamatorium* was not actually a Romantic institution, nor were its values understood by contemporaries to coincide entirely with those of the Romantic movement. In his *Vorlesungen über Deklamation und Mimik* (1816), the noted declamator and declamation theorist Gustav Anton von Seckendorff claimed that while this type of "rhapsodic declamation" was new to Germany,[28] it had in fact arrived with the popular remediation of the eighteenth-century poetry of Friedrich Gottlieb Klopstock. Seckendorff was correct that Klopstock had actively promoted the public declamation of his works, above all the epic poem *Messias* (1748–1773).[29] As Johannes Birgfeld has shown, "instead of accepting the general trend of readers isolating themselves from each other," Klopstock actively campaigned to promote the practice "of reading literature aloud and in the presence of other literature lovers."[30] As part of this drive toward viva voce recitation, Klopstock himself promoted and organized both communal readings and recitations by the professionals, such as noted actress Sophie Albrecht (1757–1840). Significantly for the fate of the public declamation of ballads, Klopstock's interest in *Lesegesellschaften*, that is, organized communal and public declamation and reading, coincided with a turn away from classical subjects and toward more explicitly "German" themes. But they nevertheless continued to draw on classical forms—Klopstock's programmatic poem "Teone," an "Attempt to Promote the High Art of Declamation" (1767), was an ode. By pointing to this provenance, Seckendorff, speaking when Romantic fetishism of the living voice was at its apex, allied public recitation with an aesthetic that German Romanticism

---

27 Karl Lachmann, "Über Singen und Sagen," in *Kleinere Schriften* (Berlin: Reimer, 1876), 461.

28 Cited in Reinhardt Meyer-Kalkus, *Geschichte der literarischen Vortragskunst* (Stuttgart: Metzler, 2020), 275.

29 Mary Helen Dupree, "From 'Dark Singing' to a Science of the Voice: Gustav Anton von Seckendorff and the Declamatory Concert around 1800," *Deutsche Vierteljahresschrift für Literaturwissenschaft und Geistesgeschichte* 86, no. 3 (2012): 368.

30 Johannes Birgfeld, "Klopstock, the Art of Declamation and the Reading Revolution: An Inquiry into One Author's Remarkable Impact on the Changes and Counter-Changes in Reading Habits between 1750 and 1800," *Journal for Eighteenth Century Studies* 31, no. 1 (2008): 104.

tended to be rather skeptical of. Rather than styling itself as a revival of an ancient German bardic tradition, public declamation arrived in Germany as an aesthetic practice associated with classicism—an association it was to retain throughout the period of its popularity.

A general review of a series of *Declamatoria* in the periodical *Der Aufmerksame* from 1812 highlights that such presentations "generally touch upon the area of sculpture, with a characteristic dusting of Greek or Roman style."[31] Allegorical stylings, laurel wreaths, and togas abounded. When Johann Friedrich Reichardt, during the same 1810 trip that brought him to Madame Bürger's *Declamatorium*, met Seckendorff in Vienna, the composer reported that Seckendorff and his declamation partner expressed a wish, once the war was over, to travel to Italy "to study on the old classical soil the high art of pantomime and attitude according to the greatest masters of antiquity, and to then return fulfilled [*vollendet*] to the Fatherland."[32] In other aspects of German culture during the Napoleonic era, nationalism had a decidedly anti-classicist bend—precisely because classicism was understood as Mediterranean, un-German, foreign. With respect to recitation, even when it came to an anti-classical form like the ballad, this was clearly not the case. Ballads in *Chevy Chase Strophen* mingled easily with iambic hexameters; the subject matter ranged from patriotic themes of the day to the oratory of Cicero.

Nevertheless, public recitation was an area where classicism was never content to return to, match, or imitate the Greeks. Johann Joachim Winckelmann had centered German classicism's program on the idea of an "imitation of the Greek works in painting and sculpture"—in fact, as Peter Szondi argued, Winckelmann's insistence on linking aesthetics to a philosophy of history seemed to argue against any notion of moving beyond imitation.[33] In the sphere of rhetoric, however, from the outset the idea was to outdo the ancients. What gave the modern rhetoricians the boldness to entertain this notion were advances in music theory. In a 1791 essay *Soll die Rede auf immer ein dunkler Gesang bleiben* (*Shall Speaking Forever Remain a Dark Singing*), the educator, philologist, and musical theorist Christian Gotthold Schocher suggested that modern rhetoric might be able to systematize what the ancients had only intuited.[34] After all, Schocher argued, the moderns had clearly exceeded the ancients in their ability to notate and theorize music—why should they not be able to do something analogous in the related field of

---

31 *Der Aufmerksame*, February 29, 1812, n.p.
32 Reichardt, *Vertraute Briefe geschrieben auf einer Reise nach Wien*, 81.
33 Peter Szondi, *Poetik und Geschichtsphilosophie 1* (Frankfurt: Suhrkamp, 1974), 102.
34 Christian Gotthold Schocher, *Soll die Rede auf immer ein dunkler Gesang bleiben* (Leipzig: Reinicke, 1791).

rhetoric?[35] The theory of public oratory combined nostalgic elements of classicism with a profound trust in the modernizing powers of systematicity and scientific inquiry. One reason was surely that the rhetorical arts still needed time to detach themselves from antique antecedents. Another was that Germans had long deliberately de-emphasized these arts. In the late eighteenth century, rhetoric's status in the German-speaking lands was uniquely low. The German Enlightenment had found two nearly opposed reasons for distrusting it: the rationalist High Enlightenment distrusted it for confusing reason with somersaults of language, and the more sensually inclined Late Enlightenment for diverting the directness of expression. Ironically, however, as respect for political rhetoric declined, the demand for public reading of literature went up. This entailed a shift from an audience for political rhetoric to an audience looking for an aesthetic payoff. At the same time, precisely as a consequence of this shift public performances of literature attained a more explicitly political dimension.[36]

## Public Affects

Judith Eisermann points out that in Germany around 1800, recitation came in fairly distinct guises, which varied with respect to how much a reciter was supposed to inhabit what they performed.[37] Some of the distinctions between them concerned externalities, such as whether the declamator wore a rudimentary costume, or whether hand gestures were encouraged or discouraged. Others concerned the degree to which the speaker was meant to identify with what they recited. Most broadly, the difference concerned the relationship between pitch, tonality, and affect. *Vorlesen*, or public reading, somewhat confusingly did not always need to involve the printed word, but it was still modeled on the performance of written text: the performer was supposed to keep their tone level—to narrate rather than embody, miming reading, as it were. *Rezitation*, as Irmgard Weithase puts it, was "semi-text based with a more pronounced affective dimension."[38]

---

35 Dietmar Till, "The Fate of Rhetoric in the 'Long' Eighteenth Century," in *Performing Knowledge, 1750–1850*, ed. Mary Helen Dupree and Sean B. Franzel (Berlin: De Gruyer, 2015), 78.

36 Lorraine Gorrell, *The Nineteenth-Century German Lied* (Pompton Plains, NJ: Amadeus Press, 2005), 113.

37 Judith Eisermann, *Josef Kainz: Zwischen Tradition und Moderne* (Munich: Utz, 2010), 284.

38 Irmgard Weithase, *Geschichte der deutschen Vortragskunst im 19. Jahrhunder* (Leipzig: Böhlau, 1940), 75.

True *Deklamation*, by contrast, was basically scenic acting: the orator moved around the stage, channeled the character in question, emoted, and even used limited props. Yet even such performances were understood as comparatively spare and abstract. In fact, boosters of the practice suggested that it allowed the audience to concentrate on literature in a way that the trappings and effects of traditional drama did not. "In the *Deklamatorien* there was nothing to see," a theater director remarks in the novel *Die Schauspielerin* (*The Actress*) by Friedrich Laun (whose real name was Friedrich August Schulze). "Given that it was far quieter than in a theater, chatter was even more forbidden." And so, the character claims, "it was the least boring thing to actually pay at least some attention to the presentation."[39] Not surprisingly, Richard Wagner, ever anxious about economies of attention in the theater, was in his youth a frequent attendee.[40]

Whereas *Vorlesen* and *Rezitation* were distinguished by their tighter control of affect and flourish, even *Deklamatorien* were judged according to how they marshaled affects, even if they were not supposed to rein them in altogether. They appear to have been highly emotional performances, and between the lines of even the most rapturous reviews one hears a certain amusement over what must have been a penchant for hamming it up. But while a certain affective charge was clearly desired, reviewers were always on the lookout for unfocused histrionics for their own sake. An 1824 report from Hamburg, for instance, offers a critique of a theatrical evening put on by one Herr Stein of Leipzig. His Hamlet, the reviewer thinks, is monotonous and reminds him of a preacher on his pulpit—utterly ill-suited for an "affect role" like the Prince of Denmark. Stein next performed the comedic role of a Prussian Junker coming to Berlin for the first time in August von Kotzebue's comedy *Das Intermezzo*, giving the Junker (who is supposed to be a young man) bent knees throughout. Finally, "he graced us with two *Deklamatoria*, by reciting 'The Diver' and 'The Walk to the Foundry' with musical accompaniment, screaming a lot and pleasing no one." Herr Stein seems to have repeated his performance for several nights, although, as the reviewer notes, "the surest evidence that he did not resonate with the audience is that he played consistently before an empty house."[41]

Another write-up, this one from Munich in 1813, likewise sounds a sour note over the hamminess of the performance, singling out especially the reading of ballads. The review credits the reciter, director of the Munich Schauspielhaus, with great performative zeal, but questions his choice of repertoire: "the selection seems calculated to give the audience proof of his

---

39 Friedrich Laun, *Die Schauspielerin* (Leipzig: Hartmann, 1824), 140.

40 Ernest Newman, *The Life of Richard Wagner* (Cambridge: Cambridge University Press, 1949), 77–87.

41 *Merkur*, October 11, 1824, 492.

strength in presenting such scenes, which require the greatest expenditure of power and fire."[42] The reviewer appeals to the preferences, and indeed the very sensoria of the audience as a corrective against this unremitting intensity. It might have been advisable, he writes, "to be respectful of the minds [*Gemüther*] of the listeners, who may not have entirely enjoyed being shown a long series of images of which each was more high-strung and dread-inducing than the next."[43] What is noticeable and characteristic about reviews such as these is that they fault the likes of Herr Stein for being insufficiently invested in the "affect role" of Hamlet, but overly affective in the concluding *declamatoria*. Overacting appears to have been part and parcel of public declamation, but it appears to have been rather unwelcome precisely when it came to ballads and lyric poetry. Overacting as Hamlet was one thing, overacting from within the national canon, and the ballad canon, was quite another. Public declamation had a political role to play insofar as it taught audiences how to respond to their national language in terms of political emotions.

As George Steiner has put it, "the events of 1789 to 1815 ... interpenetrate common, private existence with the perception of historical processes."[44] The voice came to matter a great deal in this interpenetration. Aesthetic nationalism wanted texts to "function as technically extended voice,"[45] as Marc Redfield has put it. In 1808, Johann Gottlieb Fichte gave the first of his *Reden an die Deutsche Nation* (*Addresses to the German Nation*) in Berlin, which framed German nationhood in terms of a receptivity to a particular kind of speech and a particular kind of voice. "I speak for Germans only,"[46] Fichte announced in opening his lectures—"for," in this instance, likely meaning both standing in for someone else and to the benefit of, or addressed to someone. Germans were the source of his speech, and they were the only legitimate recipients of it. Even if they were to encounter the live speech in dead letters, Fichte expressed the hope that "a part of the vital force with which these addresses perhaps seize you remains also in its mute transcript." Fichte generally privileged the "vital" force of the speaking voice—the eventual task of the printed addresses was to rouse Germans further afield, as though they were in the lecture hall with him. Against the atomism and "selfishness" of the Enlightenment Republic of Letters, Fichte invoked the centering, gathering

---

42 *Gesellschaftsblatt für gebildete* Stände, Vol. 3 (1813), 304.

43 Ibid.

44 George Steiner, *In Bluebeard's Castle: Some Notes towards the Redefinition of Culture* (New Haven, CT: Yale University Press, 1971), 12.

45 Marc Redfield, *The Politics of Aesthetics: Nationalism, Gender, Romanticism* (Stanford, CA: Stanford University Press, 2003), 71.

46 Johann Gottlieb Fichte, *Addresses to the German Nation* (Cambridge: Cambridge University Press, 2008), 10.

force of enunciated German.[47] The voice—coming from a German, addressing itself in German and addressing only those who understood German—would, Fichte hoped, call into existence a national community: "In the spirit whose emanations these addresses are, I behold the concrescent unity in which no member thinks the fate of another [member] foreign to his own."[48] After the Napoleonic Wars came to a close, the ability to speak freely and publicly—the raised voice unafraid of censorship—became an important aspect of liberal politics, influential in the art and literature of Restoration Era Vienna and elsewhere.[49] For nationalists, meanwhile, the ability speak with one voice was an inescapable part of national self-construction. Wherever they were raised, then, voices encountered, gathered, created groups, often large groups.[50] While the audiences at the *declamatoria* were generally small, and usually hailed from traditional theatergoing classes, the broader ability of the voice to speak to and for the mass, the people, the nation lurked as a horizon of possibility behind the performances.

In this context, hearing a voice was more important than hearing what it had to say. In his *Handbuch der Declamation* (*Handbook of Declamation*, 1813), Heinrich August Kerndörffer distinguished between the "relative beauty" of speech, which attaches to declamation "in relation to its content," and "absolute beauty" of speech that is independent of it.[51] Declamation for him centered the directness of this transmission of affect, almost independent of content. In his *Abhandlung über den Ursprung der Sprache* (*Treatise on the Origin of Language*, 1772) Herder had proposed that it is the role of "tone of a feeling to put the sympathetic being into the same tone."[52] By the time the various declamators took to their stages, spoken German was likewise understood as constructing and enabling sympathy, literally a feeling-along or feeling-together. But what is more, the kinds of togetherness that spoken German was taken to vouch for had become huge in scope, imagining ultimately an entire linguistic community as capable of responding to a performance in unison.

---

47 Alexander Aichele, "Ending Individuality: The Mission of a Nation in Fichte's *Addresses to the German Nation*," in *The Cambridge Companion to Fichte*, ed. David James and Günter Zöller (Cambridge: Cambridge University Press, 2016), 257.

48 Fichte, *Addresses to the German Nation*, 11.

49 Michael Kohlhäufl, *Poetisches Vaterland: Dichtung und politisches Denken im Freundeskreis Franz Schuberts* (Kassel: Bärenreiter, 1999), 42.

50 John Neubauer, *The Persistence of Voice: Instrumental Music and Romantic Orality* (Leiden: Brill, 2017).

51 Heinrich August Kerndörffer, *Handbuch der Deklamation* (Leipzig: Fleischer, 1813), 5.

52 Johann Gottfried Herder, *Abhandlung über den Ursprung der Sprache* (Leipzig; Brandstädter, 1901), 32.

Gustav Anton von Seckendorff (1775–1823) was both a sought-after reciter (under the stage name Patrik Peale) and a theorist of recitation.[53] In 1816, Seckendorff was appointed professor of aesthetics in Braunschweig, and his *Vorlesungen über Deklamation und Mimik* (*Lectures on Declamation and Expression*) appeared in the same year. Theorists like Seckendorff hitched their aesthetic wagon to musical theory, just as the practice of recitation yoked its fortunes to musical performance. Not only were recitation evenings usually reliant on musical interludes, accompaniment, or melodramatic structures. Theoretically, too, they borrowed their concepts, aesthetics, and, as we shall see, pedagogy from the field of music. Seckendorff's *Lectures* were first published with an accompanying volume of musical arrangements. Christian August Semler, in his essay "Über Deklamatoren und Deklamatoria" (1810), called for accompaniment by string instruments and wanted those instruments to intervene into the performance in a vocal mode: they were mean to ring out as a "humming" (*summen*) and "whispering" (*flüstern*) in the background.[54]

Apart from pragmatic considerations, there was an important methodological reason for this close link to music theory: music theory made giant strides during this era, and was understood as objective, scientific, and eminently translatable. While the sounded-out *Declamatorium* constituted a nationally bounded relationship between orator and audience, the rhetorical theory of the time sought to link speech to a broader, perhaps even universal public. For decades, the philosopher and translator Christian Gotthold Schocher teased his magnum opus, entitled *Uebersicht der declamatorischen Melodiezeichnung als das einzige Mittel, Grundsätze und Regel in der Declamation herzustellen* (*Overview of Declamatory Melodic Line as the only Means to Postulate Principles and Rules in Declamation*), but never actually published it. Nevertheless, his title is instructive: the point was to turn to music in order to universalize and systematize declamation—and indeed to systematize the communication of emotion (which was taken to be the point of tone). While this would seem to make declamatory theory an ill fit for the kind of instinctive linguistic community that reviewers and audiences sought in the *declamatoria*, it is likely it wasn't understood that way. From the Napoleonic Wars to the early Biedermeier period, different parts of Germany and different segments of German society varied widely in how much purchase feelings of patriotism had on the broader public. After and during the Wars of Liberation, for instance, patriotic fervor ran high in Prussia, whereas it was muted in some of the southwestern states. In German-speaking Austria and

---

53 Lodewijk Muns, "Gustav Anton Freiherr von Seckendorff, alias Patrik Peale: A Biographical Note" (2016): https://lodewijkmuns.nl/GAvS2016.pdf.

54 Christian August Semler, "Über Deklamatoren und Deklamatoria," *Zeitschrift für die elegante Welt* 136 (1810): 1098.

among German speakers in Bohemia, the question of which nation spoken language referred back to was an even more fraught one. At the same time the question of nationhood was insistently linked to feeling in common—it depended on other people speaking the same language feeling the same way one did about the nation. The question of how to universalize a particularized enthusiasm was thus front and center as a political-aesthetic problem—and music seemed to offer a solution.

This close connection between declamation and music was also reflected in practice and one evening of performances in particular highlights the tension this could entail between aesthetics and nationalism. On December 15, 1839, the writer and critic Moritz Gottlieb Saphir (1795–1858) put on an evening of declamation in the Theater in der Josephsstadt, Vienna. Saphir, a merciless critic and satirist with a strong local following, had branded the evening as "Saphir's Akademie und humoristische Vorlesung" ("Saphir's Academy and Humoristic Reading"), but the talent on display was serious. As the *Oesterreichischer Zuschauer* notes, previous editions had focused on declamators performing poetry, but the centerpiece this evening was a different kind of vocal performance: the host Saphir himself gave a prepared lecture entitled "Steam Power, Horse Power, Human Power, Money Power etc., or: How Many Powers Does Man Require in Order to be Right and Truly Stuck." The *Zuschauer* judged it "rich in pointed and diaphragm-splitting ideas," and compared the attunement between the master of ceremonies and his audience to an electrical charge: "like an electric spark" his wit "shot through the theater," and even during the "more weighty flashes of thought unveiling and illuminating the secrets of human nature and life," he provoked many a "yes, it's true" from the audience. Other performances of the evening included a traditional *Declamatorium* featuring ballads written by Saphir.

To conclude the evening, however, the singer and composer Benedict Randhartinger (1802–1893), once a good friend to Franz Schubert, sang his arrangement of a ballad by Johann Christian, Freiherr von Zedlitz, called "Die nächtliche Heerschau" ("Nocturnal Roll-Call," sometimes also translated as "Napoleon's Midnight Review"), accompanied on the piano by none other than Franz Liszt.[55] Zedlitz's poem makes a natural fit for the stage, but it makes a strange fit for an evening like Saphir's "humoristische Vorlesung." Like Goethe's "Danse Macabre," it is another gothic ballad about the dead not staying buried. But where Goethe's poem seems at most like an oblique commentary on the dead bodies stacking up across Europe during the Napoleonic Wars, "Die Nächtliche Heerschau" explicitly talks about the hecatomb. In the ballad a skeletal tambour, once a member of Napoleon's army, emerges from the ground to awaken his dead comrades across Europe

---

55 *Der Oesterreichische Zuschauer* 4, no. 154 (December 25, 1839): 1576.

and North Africa: those frozen in the Russian steppes, and those buried in the sands of Egypt. Eventually they are joined by Napoleon himself, "the dead Caesar," who reviews their spectral parade in an Alsatian field.

"Nächtliche Heerschau" first appeared in Zedlitz's 1828 collection *Todtenschauen*.[56] In the years that followed, the poem was made public in various ways. Even before Randhartinger premiered his version, Carl Loewe (1832/33, op. 23) and Robert Schumann (1840, WoO 11, no. 2) had set it for piano and voice. The poet also offered it to Franz Schubert, who however decided to use Wilhelm Müller's *Die schöne Müllerin* instead.[57] Martin Röder (1851–1895) (op. 4, no. 1) would later compose a piano part to accompany a recitation of the poem. Emil Titl (1809–1882) turned it into a cantata for male voices and large orchestra. Anton Hackel (1799–1846) set it for voice and piano, an arrangement that became popular in a transcription for voice and guitar by Anton Foreit. And in 1906, the composer Paul Ertel (1865–1933) turned it into a symphonic poem (op. 16), which was later transcribed for piano by Friedrich Hermann Schneider. It seems the musical side of this remediation was fully aware of the declamatory and theatrical side. The framing of Röder's piece makes clear just how much older forms of recitation survived through the more mediated institution of publishing: Hofmeister's *Verzeichnis*, which collected new musical publications on an annual basis, lists "Nächtliche Heerschau" as a piece "for declamation with pianoforte,"[58] while the catalogue of the publisher C. F. Kahnt lists it as a "melodrama with pianoforte accompaniment."[59]

The poem was quickly anthologized, and made its way into poetry collections for students of German as a foreign language.[60] The editor G. A. Hanisch included the poem in his anthology *Der Deklamator* (1858); a book intended, according to the subtitle, as a collection "of poems well-suited to public declamation" along with "instructions on how to present them." "Die nächtliche Heerschau" thus had a career in recitation beyond staged productions by professionals like Saphir's—it was supposed to initiate laypeople into the proper techniques of reciting poetry. Hanisch, who presents each of the poems in his collection with some specific purpose in mind, offers

---

56 Johann Christian, Freiherr von Zedlitz, *Todtenkränze: Canzonen* (Vienna: Wallishauser, 1831).

57 Susan Youens, *Schubert: Die schöne Müllerin* (Cambridge: Cambridge University Press, 1992), 2.

58 Friedrich Hofmeister, *Hofmeisters Handbuch der musikalischen Literatur* (Leipzig: Hofmeister, 1881) 8:92.

59 *Verzeichnis des Musikalien-Verlages von C. F. Kahnt Nachfolger* (Leipzig; C. F. Kahnt, 1890), 145/46.

60 See, e.g., Bernhard Roelker, ed., *A German Reader for Beginners* (Cambridge, MA: Bartlett, 1854), 63–65.

the following gloss on what exactly the hobby declamator is supposed to take away from "Nächtliche Heerschau": "This poem contains a brilliant declamatory music, which the poet brought about through the construction of his verse, and which we must strive to reproduce."[61] Hanisch suggests starting "in low tones" and keeping "speaking extremely slowly," and then charts in detail a gradual escalation both in terms of speed and emotional pitch. Where Randhartinger, Loewe, and the other composers seemed intent on imbuing the declamation with a dynamic plot, Hanisch guides his reader/student through one uninterrupted increase in emotional pitch. This difference may well be owed to a difference in their intended publics: Randhartinger and Loewe sought to make mourning appropriate for the larger (if not quite public) gathering, whereas Hanisch's instruction book intended to make public emotionality suitable for the domestic sphere.

One of the unspoken questions that seems to have occupied all of these different versions in one way or another is the one raised by Saphir's evening: just how serious is "Nächtliche Heerschau"? What kind of emotional presentation and response does it demand? From the beginning the poem had a strange tendency to attract unseriousness: the first parody, "Das tägliche Spektakel," was available in print by 1830; another, "Eugenien's Verzweiflung," appeared in 1870. The music that various composers wrote as accompaniment to Zedlitz's poem leaned heavily into an ostentatious militarism, shot through, depending on the version, with a pronounced sense of mourning, or instead an equally pronounced sense of irony.

Saphir programmed it as part of a largely humoristic evening, but Randhartinger's setting is actually one of the more serious versions of the poem: Randhartinger splits Zedlitz's long poem into separate sections (Schumann, by contrast, leaves off Napoleon altogether, while Loewe compressed internal stanzas). The song opens with a dramatic, even bombastic chorale, which the piano casts as a dark march, which suddenly turns to pathos-laden legato as the dead climb from their graves. Then the piano intones a literal reveille, which ushers in a calmer, ethereal, less declamatory middle section, in which the piano rather hesitantly reminds us of the military theme. As the "dead Caesar" arrives on the scene, the piano withdraws into a more restrained set of chords, while the voice (a soprano) intones a darkly jubilant and highly emotional version of the opening chorale. All militarism at this moment is banished into the piano accompaniment: what the piano seems to read as a march, the voice can register only as incalculable loss.[62]

---

61 G.A. Hanisch, Der Deklamator: Theoretisch-Praktische Anleitung der freien Vortragskunst und Mustersammlung (Munich: 1858), 26.

62 Michael Kohlhäufl, *Poetisches Vaterland: Dichtung und politisches Denken im Freundeskreis Franz Schuberts* (Kassel: Bärenreiter, 1999), 93–97.

Loewe's setting draws on a similar bifurcation, but tells a different story about the same tale. The vocal part (a tenor) is far jauntier than in Randhartinger's version—almost by necessity, as the driving piano arrangement pushes the voice along with a surprisingly uptempo march, given the story. Loewe's piano gives the proceedings a comical note, ornamenting a simple march beat with a surfeit of trills, triplets, sextolets, and little fanfares. The overall effect is of a piano accompaniment that in vital respects undercuts the vocal part—the piano drives the voice along, and forces it into a humorousness that feels at times inappropriate. One gets a sense that this voice would like to stop and recollect, but it receives no affordance to do so. There is an affective dimension to Zedlitz's poem, which the voice strains to unearth, but which the piano accompaniment stifles time and again. This seems to be a deliberate choice on Loewe's part. There are other songs of the era that manage to combine a military theme with a high emotional charge—Schumann's "Der Soldat" (one of the *Five Songs*, op. 40) is a striking example. Loewe stages the story of Napoleon's midnight parade as a site of always already frustrated emotional expression. If Hanisch turned to the poem to illustrate just how fully the human voice could capture a truly outlandish account of equally outlandish suffering, Loewe's song registers serious doubt to that score.

## The Printed *Declamatorium*

Balladry certainly had its role to play in public performances, but as Irmgard Weithase has made clear, the genre was not the best showcase for the affective focus of the era's declamatory style: the great reciters were supposed to mimic psychology, not the clatter of hooves.[63] Nevertheless, the ballad dominated in another aspect of public declamation: its teaching. While Seckendorff, Stein, and their peers were touring the German stage, a steady stream of handbooks offered to teach the layperson to recite poetry effectively, and provided a selection of texts putatively best suited to the project (*Mustersammlung*). Dozens of such collections appeared in the early part of the nineteenth century, and they survived the *Declamatorium* by decades. By mid-century the professional *Declamatorium* had lost what luster it once possessed. Reports of the form had never been without a hint of condescension, and as other forms of public performance professionalized the format was left behind. In Karl Immermann's 1836 novel *Die Epigonen* we meet an aging actor who, once he can no longer hold the stage, becomes a teacher and, once he begins losing his memory, "went through the lands and patched together the occasional *Declamatorium*

---

63 Weithase, *Geschichte der deutschen Vortragskunst*, 107.

in some corner or other of the world."[64] But beyond the ephemeral popularity of this format or that, the *Declamatorium* may well have fallen victim to a broader shift in the way media was disseminated and received. Indeed, the 1830s and 1840s saw a wholesale transformation of how music and the spoken word coexisted on the German stage.

Speech accompanied by music was in general in full retreat: the melodrama, still a mainstay in theaters during the age of Goethe, was close to extinct, and operas were abandoning recitativo structures in favor of through-composed ones.[65] But like many forms that were pushed off the professional stage, public recitation made itself even more keenly felt in semi-private settings. Impresarios and theater directors may no longer have programmed recitation evenings, but clubs, schools, workplaces, and families kept the practice alive. At the same time, as the ballad moved from the public stage into more private settings, it did so only through public mediation: after all, amateurs more so than professionals depended on what was published, and on what was recommended for recitation by the cognoscenti.

And yet, both the affects and their patriotic framing that had brought the public *Declamatorium* to such prominence during the first decades of the century persisted even as declamation became domesticated.[66] On July 26, 1829, Prof. Aloys Klar at the Karl Ferdinand University Prague organized his ninth annual "Celebratory Declamatorium" (*feierliches Declamatorium*) of students of philosophy. It can stand in for many such evenings of the era, even though, unlike musical evenings of the 1820s and 1830s, there is a pronounced localism to what the professor's students performed. Klar was a professor of classical philology, but the program was largely German-focused.[67] The program notes list the following pieces:

1. A prologue, spoken by Johann Hanner, a second-year student of philosophy
2. Libussa's Prophecy by Clemens Brentano, spoken by Jakob Jakowitz

---

64 Karl Immermann, *Werke*, herausgegeben von Benno von Wiese (Frankfurt a.M., Wiesbaden, 1971–1977), 2:58: "Nachdem er wegen schwindenden Gedächtnisses verabschiedet worden war, zog er durch das Land, und stoppelte noch hin und wieder ein Deklamatorium in irgendeinem Winkel zusammen."

65 Thomas Betwieser, *Sprechen und Singer: Ästhetik und Erscheinungsformen der Dialogoper* (Stuttgart: Metzler, 2002), 86f.

66 Günter Häntzschel, "Die häusliche Deklamationspraxis: Ein Beitrag zur Sozialgeschichte der Lyrik in der zweiten Hälfte des 19. Jahrhunderts," in *Zur Sozialgeschichte der deutschen Literatur von der Aufklärung bis zur Jahrhundertwende*, ed. Günter Häntzschel (Tübingen: M. Niemeyer, 1985), 203–33.

67 Aloys Klar, *Zum neunten feierlichen Deklamatorium der Hörer der Philosophie und der Prager Hochschule* (Prague: Pospissil, 1829), n.p.

3. "Sankt Johann von Nepomuk," spoken by Franz Schäffer
4. The ballad "Die Heilung und das Vögelein" by the Bohemian Romantic Karl Egon Ebert, spoken by Johann Kinzel
5. A Horatian Ode, recited by Oswald Leubner
6. "Der blinde König" by Ludwig Uhland, recited by Johan Matausch, a first-year student in philosophy
7. A Czech excerpt from Karl Egon Ebert's epic "Wlasta," recited by Wenzel Bechyne
8. "Albrecht Dürer," by J. G. Seidl, spoken by Franz Geyser
9. The ballad "Pippin der Kurze" by Friedrich Karl Streckfuß, recited by Joseph Ressel
10. A recitation from the *Iliad* by Wilhelm Dolezal, second-year in philosophy
11. A monologue from Schiller's *Wallensteins Tod*, spoken by Franz Bernert
12. "Labindo alla tomba di Belforte," spoken by Joseph Krzikawa
13. "Das Unglück der Weiber" by Johann Fürchtegott Gellert, spoken by Johann Hanner
14. "Der Kaiserhügel, a ballad from the age of the last French war," spoken by Menzel Klapper
15. An epilogue spoken Joseph Krzikawa

The majority of these texts were drawn from a *Auswahl von Gedichten zu deklamatorischen Übungen* (*Selection of Poems for Declamatory Practice*) published by Prof. Klar himself. Several things stand out about this collection: while there is a smattering of classical texts, most of the readings are drawn from fairly contemporary works in German and Czech. And while there is a clear nationalist tinge to the readings, the position of the Karl Ferdinand University was unusual enough to warrant including texts trafficking in, or even combining, nationalisms of different nations. Libussa (the German name for the Czech Libuše[68]) is the mythic founder of Prague—she appears here both in a German text by Clemens Brentano and in a Czech translation of Ebert's German-language poem.[69] While the concessions to the local culture and the multilingual Austro-Hungarian Empire are particular to Prague, similar evenings across the German-speaking world fused the kind of international canon characteristic of classicism with a specifically national set of texts.

Another respect in which Prof. Klar's evening is representative: the texts being recited are not exactly ones that have remained their authors' most enduring works. Nevertheless, his selections were mirrored in many other

---

68 John Pizer, "The Disintegration of Libussa," *Germanic Review* 73, no. 2 (1998): 145–60.
69 Karl Egon Ebert, *Wlasta: Böhmisch-nationales Heldengedicht* (Prague: Calve, 1829).

*Mustersammlungen* of the age—Streckfuß's ballad "Pippin der Kurze," for instance, seems to have been a favorite in German high school classrooms for much of the mid-nineteenth century. What we find in the *Mustersammlungen* and the amateur declamation evenings that drew on them is another canon of poems, one that persists perpendicular to the strictly literary canon. For while the selections were of course about voice, about cadence, about music, the editors compiling the *Mustersammlungen* did also make claims for literary quality. In his advertisement for his 1844 *Declamatorium für die Jugend (Declamatorium for the Youth)*, Johann Nepomuk Vogl made very clear that his poems were not merely chosen for what lessons in oratory they imparted, but for quality as well: "the ballad and the lyrical poem . . . should only bring us the accomplishments of dignified and recognized authors and composers."[70]

Four things stand out about this canon: (1) Unlike the repertoire of staged recitation, this canon disproportionately relied on balladic forms—they made up the vast majority of texts collected for learners. In fact, the more overtly didactic a collection was, the stronger it tended to rely on ballads. (2) The ballads these books collected were not the ones that ballad collections meant for readers tended to gather. Little overlap, for instance, exists between the ballads collected in Joseph Braun's collection *Deutsche Romanzen, Balladen und Erzählungen (German Romances, Ballads and Stories)* of 1840 and those collected by Vogl's *Declamatorium für die Jugend (Declamatorium for Young People)*, even though the two collections were published a mere four years apart. In terms of aims, Braun's was virtually indistinguishable from Vogl's: he targeted "the hearts of [Germany's] youth," wanting to provide them "a view into the intellectual richness of its people," weaving "a new, albeit weak, bond of love for this beautiful Fatherland."[71] But Braun's is probably the most bookish such collection of the 1840s—heavy in annotation and context, it clearly is a reader's object. After about 300 pages of mostly ballads, Braun's volume spends another 300 pages providing careful and engaging annotation. Its table of contents is encyclopedic and largely reflects what would be collected in a similar book today—lots of Bürger, Goethe, Schiller, Romantics, ending with Freiligrath and Platen. Vogl's *Declamatorium für die Jugend*, by contrast, for all its emphasis on "recognized authors and composers," gathers an entirely different set of classics and even a markedly different set of authors.

At the same time, (3) the ballads that Seckendorff and colleagues offered to the public for amateurs to hone their craft were not the ones they usually recited on stage. Nor were they the ones that entered the canon as *Lieder*. Generally, the printed *Declamatoria* contained a far higher number of humorous

---

70 Reprinted in Johann Nepomuk Vogl, *Declamatorium für die Jugend* (Vienna: Tendler, 1844), n.p.

71 Joseph Braun, *Deutsche Romanzen, Balladen und Erzählungen* (Frankfurt: Sauerländer, 1840), viii.

poems than their public cousins. They tended to draw from a narrower ambit of genres and ages (often privileging the recent past), and they tended to shirk the classicist trappings that had always been at least part of public performance. It is also worth noting that the poems collected in them were not ones that lent themselves to excessive emoting. Whenever the gentlemen compiling these anthologies took the stage, observers complained of their hamminess. When the reciter's role became more widely disseminated, the same theorists were at pains to rein in the histrionics. Some of this clearly has to do with a question of amateurism and professionalization. The diffusion of printed *Declamatoria* coincided with a period during which acting was further professionalized in the German-speaking world—new, more varied stages played to larger audiences in a broad range of settings.[72] And, much like musical pedagogy, declamation pedagogy depended on establishing and enforcing a divide between what was appropriate and permissible for professionals versus for enthusiast. The discourse at the time marshaled a broad phalanx of concepts around taste, propriety, and seriousness to enforce this divide in the case of music, seeking both to establish "commonalities among diverging types of musical performers" and to distinguish what they did from the broad mass.[73] Given the incredible size and influence of the burgeoning musical-pedagogical complex at the time, it seems that analogous version of these concepts operated in and around *Declamatoria* as well.

Finally, (4) the ballads in these books are not the ones that have remained canonic, nor do they coincide with those ballads that first established the form in Germany. For instance, in G. A. Hanisch's collection from 1858 we find not a single ballad by Goethe and only one by Schiller—Hanisch appends a note singling out the poem as difficult and "not recommended" for public performance by novices. The printed *Declamatoria* thus seemed to constitute an in-between canon: one that was somewhere between art object and use object, somewhere between the Olympian heights of the Weimar classicists and the poetry of the people. Genius aesthetic and declamation did not mix. Friedrich Kramer's *Athenäum für Freunde der Deklamation* (*Atheneum for Friends of Declamation*, 1817) does not even identify the authors of the texts in its main corpus—leaving it to the reader to consult an (incomplete) appendix to figure out authorship.[74]

One early influential collection of this type was Theodor Heinsius's *Bardenhain für Deutschlands edle Söhne und Töchter* (*Bardic Grove for Germany's Noble Sons and Daughters*, 1809), which was followed by three more volumes

---

72 Erika Fischer-Lichte, *Kurze Geschichte des deutschen Theaters* (Tübingen: Francke, 1999), 184.

73 Celia Applegate, *The Necessity of Music: Variations on a German Theme* (Toronto: University of Toronto Press, 2017), 32.

74 Friedrich Kramer, *Athenäum für Freunde der Deklamation* (Kempten: Dannheimer, 1817).

over the next twenty years. The word *Barde* points emphatically backwards in time, but the "edle Söhne und Töchter" points just as emphatically into the future. Heinsius's foreword makes it clear that he understood the pedagogic dimension of his collection very differently from that of his stage-focused peers. Where the declamatory performers seemed to rely on the formal project of Fichte's *Addresses*, the magic appeal of the spoken German word, Heinsius's project was closer to the cultural politics Fichte's lecture series actually proposed: instilling a sense of national identity and social cohesion through an educational program. As per the subtitle, Heinsius intended his books as a "Schul- und Familienbuch" ("School and Family Book"); the fourth volume (published in 1825) is meant, again as per the subtitle, for "more advanced school classes, friends of the arts and domestic circles." The first volumes were initially sold on a subscription model, so we have some notion as to who were the books' early adopters. Most of them are indeed individual households rather than institutions. The bards of the series title bridged the slowly emerging divide between education as undertaken by, for, and in the public, and the kind of education one receives in the home.

As would be true for *Mustersammlungen* going forward, Goethe and Schiller are relatively sparsely represented (Solbrig's *Vademecum* of 1823 does not include a single ballad by either author). This is all the more surprising since, as Mary-Helen Dupree has shown, the *Schiller-Feier* or memorial performances of the prematurely deceased poet's work were an important contributor to the declamation boom in the first years of the nineteenth century.[75] The reason is probably that by 1809, the project of declaiming German poetry was understood to be prospective rather than memorializing. Sean Franzel has pointed to the importance of vocal performance in turning *Bildung* from a personal pursuit into "a national-political event."[76] In Heinsius's first volume there is a great emphasis on patriotic texts. Heinsius even includes an essay by Johann Gottlieb Fichte on patriotism and dedicates the volume to the Prussian Queen Luise. Later volumes of Heinsius's *Bardenhein* would come to include pieces not primarily intended for declamation but representing important poets that would otherwise have to be omitted (they also included much more Goethe and Schiller). This first volume, however, was meant to be sounded out. In his annotations and introductions, Heinsius worried about who might hear these poems and how they would hear them. And while ballads made up only a portion of the texts he gathered, they were the only one meriting specific contextualization: before introducing his first ballad (Schiller's "Bürgschaft"), Heinsius even gave his readers a quick rundown of

---

[75] Mary Helen Dupree, "Early Schiller-Memorials (1805–1808) and the Performance of Literary Knowledge," in *Performing Knowledge, 1750–1850*, ed. Mary Helen Dupree and Sean B. Franzel (Berlin: De Gruyer, 2015).

[76] Franzel, *Connected by the Ear*, 5.

the ballad form. In the ballad, he explains to his budding declamators, "what rules is not, as in the epic, the force of the free will, but rather the power of feeling."[77] As a result, his advice to his reader consists of a catalogue of affects; Heinsius's explanations are largely a careful explication of the affects mobilized by the different characters in a ballad.

Going forward, these collections tended to interpret poetry by simply sounding it out. The typical *Mustersammlung* would introduce its texts with a short annotation, which rarely revealed anything hidden or difficult to notice. They made no mention of historical context or the author. Especially when it came to ballads, this deictic mode positioned itself implicitly against any philological impulse. In their editorial notes, collections like Heinsius's and Solbrig's emphasized the supposed immediacy, even obviousness, of balladic storytelling: when a character in a ballad exclaims, "Oh, nein!" then the annotation will instruct that the performer should "register surprise." In her narrativized *Studies of Oral Presentation* (*Studien über den mündlichen Vortrag*, 1861), Agnese Schebest has one of her characters suggest that understanding too much of a text is in fact inimical to its heartfelt reproduction: "you will find in reciting [*Hersagen*] of long rows of verses that you are far more easily distracted by their meaning, instead of arriving at that calm contemplation by which you can draw one tone after the other from your breast."[78]

This curtailment and concentration of broader meanings is particularly obvious in a short collection from 1847 edited by M. L. Schreiber, *Der Geschickte Deklamator* (*The Skillful Declamator*). Schreiber gathers a great number of poems, almost all ballads, concentrating on the "newer and newest poets." Indeed, Schiller and Goethe put in short appearances, but the vast majority date from 1815 and onward. The collection is emphatically apolitical in its framing and doesn't actually annotate any of its poems, but it gathers a large number of writers who were either explicitly political or in fact exiled or censored for their work: Georg Herwegh, Heinrich Heine, Hofmann von Fallersleben, Ferdinand Freilingrath, and Anastasius Grün. Another set were the poets associated largely with the Wars of Liberation—Ernst Moritz Arndt, Theodor Körner, etc. These were highly political poems presented without explicit political framing. Whether under French occupation or under the regimes of the Metternich era, the poems that constituted this particular canon connected the sounding-out of German balladry to the problematic of the German nation. They appeared to invoke the national project, but just as often the destruction wrought by the Napoleonic Wars. While collections like Schreiber's were anxious to control and gloss appropriate affects, they

---

77 Theodor Heinsius, *Der Bardenhain für Deutschlands edle Söhne und Töchter: Zweiter Theil* (Berlin: Dieterici, 1819), 20.

78 Agnese Schebest, *Rede und Geberde: Studien über mündlichen Vortrag und plastischen Ausdruck* (Leipzig: Abel, 1861), 11.

seemed content to leave the strange, tangled undertows of jingoism and mourning for their (often young) readers to figure out. What information the reader was to glean from these collections remained largely unstated; how they were to feel about it was obsessively policed.

While Schreiber, Hanisch, Heinsius, and Solbrig each use a different annotation system for their collections, their notes generally aim to explicate the ballad's affective dimensions. At the same time, they seem deeply suspicious of the free flow of emotion. They are insistent about what emotions are or are not to be mimicked at any point in time. They are obsessed with the correct sequencing of affects, with vocal effects that set apart the different personae. Especially older *Mustersammlungen* emphasize the importance of learning to articulate proper, effective, and affecting German through poetry, but insist that such learning must not be overly spontaneous. G. A. Hanisch's 1858 collection *Der Deklamator* (*The Declamator*) collected twenty-six serious and twenty-three comic poems, the vast majority of which were ballads. To each poem Hanisch appended a set of footnotes explaining how each poem would test the reciter's rhetorical skill. Maximilian Langenschwarz's "Das Buchstabierende Kind" is supposed to teach "major/minor modulation," Gerhardt's "Der Bettler und sein Kind" how to gracefully jump from key to key. Franz Carl Weidmann's "Der Alte Hanns" alternates between a frame narration and dramatic monologue. Brunow's "Der Lohn" is supposed to teach the reader how to maintain vocal control during high-speed, high-intensity passages, and Langenzweig's "Der Scharfrichter" is meant to familiarize the reader with the correct use of pauses.

In other words, *Der Deklamator* modeled itself on a *Musikschule*, one of the hundreds of textbooks that were supposed to help young people, with or without the help of a teacher, learn a musical instrument. Hanisch intended to present the poems he collected as neutral, objective, and stable object lessons, much as a simplified Bach minuet might aid a young piano pupil in learning about chords. And yet, with literature things never were that simple: Hanisch's instructions frequently do deliver interpretations either covertly or without meaning to. Take, for instance, his presentation of the ballad "An einen auf dem Schlachtfeld ausgeackerten Schädel" ("On a Skull Dug Up on the Battlefield") by Johann Friedrich Kind. Kind was a popular writer of ballads at the time (both Carl Maria von Weber and Conradin Kreutzer set many of his poems to music), but is today mostly remembered as the librettist of *Der Freischütz*. The poem was rarely anthologized in explicitly literary collections even at the time, but it does show up in no fewer than three *Mustersammlungen* for declamation.

At least part of the appeal must have had to do with extra-vocal considerations. The poem tells of the aftermath of violence, and while the speaker claims to be unsure whether the skull in question was cracked by a sword or by his plow, he does seem sure that this man died in a group: "The others rest in their dark bed so quiet / Sometimes under flowers, sometimes under snowy cover."[79] "An einen auf dem Schlachtfeld ausgeackerten Schädel" may well have entered circulation as a mourning poem for the many nameless dead of the then-recent recent war. But it is likely that it remained popular in the oratorical guides from Kramer's *Athenäum* (1817) to Hanisch's *Deklamator* (1858) for a different reason: almost the entire poem is addressed at the titular object, and the second half of the poem ramps up the tension gradually. It is, in other words, a perfect object lesson in escalation. "How much I'd like to sound a summons out to you,"[80] the poet says and launches into a litany of questions:

| | |
|---|---|
| Warst du mein Bruder einst?—sprich, gaben deine Blicke | Were you my brother once?—speak, did your look |
| Dem Freund einst Blick und Gegenred' zurücke?— | Once return your friend's gaze and reply?— |
| Hat wirklich denn ein Geist in dir gedacht? | Did an intellect think inside of you? |
| Hast du gehaßt, geliebt, geweint, gelacht? | Did you hate, love, cry, laugh? |
| Weißt du denn nichts?—so gar nichts mir zu sagen? | Do you not know anything?—have you nothing to say to me? |
| Schläft sich's dort unten wirklich still und kühl? | Does one really sleep down there so still and cool? |
| Kannst schmerzlos du das Sonnenlicht ertragen? | Can you stand the sunlight without pain? |
| Weicht mit dem Tode jegliches Gefühl?— | Does death free you from all feeling?— |

In the 1858 collection, Hanisch's notes break down the poem into an economy of tone. The poem has altogether too many questions, which creates tonal problems. He proposes that they sometimes need to be intoned "as statements of fact." Each question requires, Hanisch thinks, a slight raising of the voice, but he admits that most laypeople are unlikely to have the required vocal range. Hanisch's workaround, namely that speakers should lower their pitch slightly from time to time, is not as interesting as the problem he identifies. Where a reader would see only somewhat monotonous punctuation, and subvocalization would simply yield a somewhat repetitive melody,

---

[79] "Die andern ruh'n im dunckeln Bett so stille / Bald unter Blumen, bald in schee'ger Hülle."
[80] "Und rief so gern dir ein Beschwörungswort."

Hanisch's demand for tonal cadence turns the poem's litany of questions into a serious difficulty.

This constitutes in its own way an interpretation of Kind's poem: There is something insatiable about the many demands the speaker puts to the object that cannot, after all, reciprocate. And it is reciprocity the speaker is ultimate asking after, if not for: the poetic "I" does not want the skull to look him or her in the eye; rather, the speaker wants to know whether the skull's eyes were once capable of looking at another, at "the friend." By forcing his (imagined) students to emote toward an imaginary inanimate object, that is, by forcing them to place upon that object ever more intense demands, Hanisch sought to instill in his readers/students a relationship to what someone else sees. Hanisch understood Kind's poem, and its escalating questions, as a poetics of public emoting, emoting for an audience.

At the same time, any demands the speaker makes in the poem are made as subvocalizations. The speaker does not literally call out to the skull; he rather contemplates doing so and runs through the questions he would put forth. Indeed, the very phrase where the questions are identified as a form of conjuring is in the subjunctive: "und rief so gern dir ein Beschwörungswort." The entire poem is about the wish to vocalize, about the limitations of vocalization. Yet it made its career, such as it was, in nineteenth-century publishing largely as something to be sounded out loud. Just as the ballad was often an oral form contemplating the limits of oral transmission, so ballad declamation was often positioned and understood as a meditation on voicing the limits of the voice. The sheer number of mourning poems that washed through the public *declamatoria* and then seeped into individual households made sure of that.

At the same time, if the ballad possessed a strong undercurrent of German national melancholy, that melancholy circulated far beneath the surface. German music pedagogy had largely emerged from language pedagogy—it was influenced by Pestalozzi, Herder, and Rousseau.[81] Now it was retransferred: in the *declamatoria* the logic of music education found itself imposed on semantic sound material. Since the object of this pedagogy was the development and schooling of a public voice, *Mustersammlungen* tended to underplay the complexity of the texts they collected. They favored texts, above all ballads, that carried straightforward meanings that, at least to the editors' minds, needed to be inhabited rather than decoded. The populist mythology around the ballad, which regarded the ballad as a spontaneous expression of Germanic spirit, no doubt did its part to create a sense that what students were declaiming was in a sense already securely in their possession.

---

81 Wilfried Gruhn, *Geschichte der Musikerziehung* (Hofheim: Wolke, 2003), 53.

When it came to technique, however, their thrust was anti-populist. Since they modeled their aesthetic program on music pedagogy, the propagandists of the declamatory arts viewed any and all untrained eloquence with a certain degree of suspicion. To them, most people were not innately disposed toward great rhetorical gifts any more than they were able to play the piano without training. Gustav Anton Seckendorff, for instance, derided those who "knew that speaking was a kind of music," but who would "compare it, in distinction to music in the narrow sense, with the song of a bird, and thought their forest songs [*Waldgesang*] and speech flowed from no higher musical law."[82] There was of course something self-serving about this sort of insistence on the importance of vocal education. Nevertheless, boosters of public declamation generally seemed to posit naturalness not as automatic, but rather something that came at the end of a rather labor-intensive process. This became particularly important once the voice to be molded through public recitation became increasingly understood as the "voice of the people." It was certainly true of those thinkers who set their hopes for a national revival on public recitation that, when they said that ballads or their public recitation represented the voice of the German people, they thought of this voice as more than just a given reservoir that simply needed to be tapped. And indeed many of their contemporaries would have likely agreed that this voice was something yet to be established, the skill something to be taught.

The notion that naturalness is ultimately something that one can work toward is a defining, if paradoxical, feature of nineteenth-century music pedagogy and musical appreciation. The eighteenth century may have had an interest in anti-theatricality and a studied naturalness as well, but it had not usually tethered that naturalness to the question of the nation.[83] This new master category gave the demand for naturalness a renewed disciplinary force. We see such studied naturalness in musical practice, in art appreciation, and in many other fields; and it was usually tethered to an outside, public authority. How the individual played, spectated, consumed through this demand for working hard on naturalness became itself a spectacle. Public declamation shared with these practices a profound tendency toward norming.

One of the reasons public recitation became so central to nationalist discourses around 1800 is that it put the repression of regional dialects on the stage. To recite publicly was to recite in *Hochdeutsch*, and in their guidebooks the declamators never tired of pointing out that their pupils were to recite the words as they were written. Their pronunciation, in other words, was to model itself on printed German (*Schriftsprache*), and teach students to leave

---

[82] Gustav Anton Seckendorff, *Vorlesungen über die Deklamation und Mimik* (Braunschweig: Vieweg, 1816), I:16.

[83] See, e.g., Michael Fried, *Absorption and Theatricality: Painting and Beholder in the Age of Diderot* (Chicago: University of Chicago Press, 1988), 102.

behind the tinge of their particular home soil. When Goethe first set out his "Rules for Actors" ("Regeln für Schauspieler"[84]) in 1803, he declared that the "first and most necessary rule" was that the actor "free himself from all mistakes of dialects and strive to attain a completely pure pronunciation."[85] It is clear that the type of "dialect" Goethe has in mind here is regional, but he uses the word "provincialism."[86] If the stage was a place for high German, *Mustersammlungen* extended its reach into the home. Later in the nineteenth century, the ballad would make a point of incorporating regional *argot*. Nevertheless, we can get a sense for how firmly public recitation chained the ballad to high German from the early recordings of ballad parody: often enough, the joke is simply that the poem is being recited in a Cologne dialect (Robert Nonnenbruch) or in Franconian (Karl Valentin).

Generally, the *Mustersammlungen* represented a double address to the nation: on the one hand, they exhorted each individual to school and even drill their voice, language, and memory. But on the other, the voice, language, and memory it sought to establish were *collective* in nature. Don't speak how you speak naturally, but speak how you speak naturally "as a German." Don't remember what you have experienced but the memories of your *Volk*. And don't read as though you might subvocalize to yourself, but read as though someone is listening.

---

84 Goethe never published these rules himself, but seems to have encouraged Johann Peter Eckermann to pull them together from various sources.

85 "daß er sich von allen Fehlern des Dialekts befreie und eine vollständige reine Aussprache zu erlangen suche" (Johann Wolfgang von Goethe, "Regeln für Schauspieler," in *Goethes sämmtliche Werke* (Stuttgart: Cotta, 1840), 35:435.

86 See also Irmgard Weithase, *Goethe als Sprecher und Sprecherzieher* (Weimar: Böhlau, 1949), 77.

# 3 | Balladic Consciousness

## *The Ballad on the Opera Stage*

By the end of Napoleonic Wars, the term "ballad" was everywhere in German-speaking Europe, but what connected the different poetic, popular, musical, and dramatic phenomena subsumed under the moniker emerged as a problem during this period. At the same time, the fact that the ballad came to be deployed across various media also turned it into an arena in which the interactions of the various arts could be formalized. It could help articulate, in other words, what constituted a *Lied*, a melodrama, an opera. It could outline how the literary text, the dramatic presentation, the musical accompaniment could and should interact. The operatic ballad was perhaps the biggest outlier. "Ballad operas" had of course existed in the eighteenth century, and ballads or narrative poems circulated through many operas of the first half of the nineteenth century as self-contained musical numbers. But by the time the ballad attained cultural dominance in Germany, the ballad opera of the eighteenth century and the self-contained musical number were starting to be seen as problematic. Did they not pull opera away from the sphere of "high" art, of organic form and sustained audience attention, and toward the distracted audiences cheering an indifferent cavalcade of disconnected songs according to the public's whims and fashions? Popularity had become a double-edged sword: it vouched for the authenticity of a work, but it also threatened to exclude it from the more rarefied pastures of art. The sub-genres of operas in which ballads circulated, or in which balladic subject matters succeeded, were frequently aligned with expanded audiences: genres whose spectacular mode of presentation and outsized affects were implicitly or explicitly geared toward the rising bourgeoisie.

This problem was compounded once the ballad emerged as a German national genre. After all, the late eighteenth-century *Singspiel* had had a comparatively easy time with the format. In particular, the romance, whether in narrative form or as a plotless love-song, found its place as one number among many. The most famous today may be "Im M\*\*renland gefangen war," which the servant Pedrillo sings in Mozart's *Die Entführung aus dem Serail* (*The Abduction from the Seraglio*, 1781). A "Spanish romance" in siciliano rhythm (4/6), accompanied only by pizzicato strings, the piece, and others like it, were meant to stand out from the rest of the opera. And its provenance connects it to a pan-European network of influences rather than a German national spirit. The use of plucked string instruments to indicate a troubardouric provenance likely comes from Jean-Jacques Rousseau's *Le devin du village*.[1] Mozart's romance inspired a small list of narrative romances with pizzicato accompaniment—from Beethoven's fairly derivative opening to the romance in his "Musik zu einem Ritterballet" ("Music for a Knightly Ballet," WoO 1) to Louis Spohr's *Zemire und Azor* (1819), with a great number of imitators in between. But these romances were drenched in musical exoticism, and the troubadour-inspired romances in the *opéras comiques*, above all those by François-Adrien Boieldieu (1775–1834), were understood as specifically French.

Once ballad and opera both started being thought of as national projects rather than foreign imports, their interactions began to name a problem. On the one hand, in the age of Romanticism ballad and opera in Germany increasingly partook of the same aesthetic trends. The rise of the ballad was shadowed by the rise of the Romantic opera, which overlapped with balladry both in terms of its subject matter (focusing as it did on supernatural tales) and in terms of its affects (uncanny possessions and destructive passions). Romantic opera was prevalent on German stages from the late 1810s, when the operas of E. T. A. Hoffmann were written and Carl Maria von Weber's early works premiered, until well into the 1840s. But if it was situated close to balladry, the German Romantic opera was sparing in its use of actual ballads. Heinrich Marschner's Romantic opera *Der Vampyr* (1828) included a ballad that explored the backstory of the main character. Conradin Kreutzer (1780–1849) pursued a different strategy in integrating ballad and opera: he expanded a balladic *sujet* into a three-act grand Romantic opera. His *Der Gang zum Eisenhammer* ("The Walk to the Foundry"), with a libretto by Johann Anton Friedrich Reil, premiered in Vienna in December 1837. The other attempts to bring these forms into alignment were made by German composers working in France, and in particular in the genre of *grand opéra*.

---

1 Jacquelin Letzer and Robert Adelson, *Women Writing Opera* (Berkeley: University of California Press, 2001), 119.

Giacomo Meyerbeer's *Robert le Diable* (1831) included a well-known ballad, but there are other examples that are today mostly forgotten. Friedrich von Flotow (1812–1883), for instance, was German-born but French-trained, and wrote many of his operas in French. *L'Esclave de Camoëns*, which premiered in Paris in 1843, and only later came to Germany as *Indra, das Schlangenmädchen* (premiered in Vienna in 1852), contains a lengthy ballad in its second act. In the first act of Jacques Offenbach's *Les Fées du rhin* (1864), a woman farmer named Hedwig sings a ballad about women singing too much. Just how shaky the canon of operatic ballads was is indicated by Carl Maria von Weber's usage of the term just twenty years before Wagner: he referred to a song in *Oberon, or The Elf King's Oath* (1826) as "Fatima's ballad" in his letters and diary, but the designation does not appear in the score itself.[2] The song itself is more of a longing ode to a faraway homeland, closer to Mignon's song from *Wilhelm Meisters Lehrjahre* (1797) than to "Der Erlkönig": "O Araby! Dear Araby, / My own, my native land!"[3]

The most enduring example of an operatic ballad is the ballad of the Flying Dutchman that Richard Wagner has Senta sing in the second act of the opera of the same name. And while Wagner knew only some of the works listed above, he was in dialogue with the various attempts to combine the two genres, and the various difficulties his predecessors had encountered in these attempts. Where Wagner's contemporaries either adapted a ballad into a three-act dramatic structure, or integrated a ballad into its dramatic structure, Wagner's *The Flying Dutchman* in a way does both. In his writings about the opera, Wagner describes the whole work as a ballad, but simultaneously integrates a discrete ballad into his conception. None of the antecedents he could have drawn on in his conception of the *Dutchman* had this specific feature. Senta's ballad is a number that appears to colonize, maybe even cannibalize, the work that surrounds it, and it reflects on questions of literary form as much as it reflects on musical questions.

Wagner's work not only incorporates a frankly literary ballad, but it also provides a covert theory of the ballad. Wagner wrote *Der fliegende Holländer* at the dawn of opera's mass age. After the end of the Napoleonic Wars, opera orchestras had swelled, massive choruses had begun to occupy the stage, and bombastic sets and special effects, from steam to gaslight, played to larger and less socioeconomically segmented audiences. A burgeoning musical and cultural press, in which both Heine and Wagner participated, expanded the audience of operatic works well beyond those actually in attendance. Wagner's interest in the ballad was founded on a question of how, in such a dramatically changed environment, music could create community and

---

[2] Carl Maria von Weber, *Reise-Briefe von Carl Maria von Weber an seine Gattin Carolina* (Leipzig: Dürr, 1886), 156.

[3] J. R. Planché, *Oberon: An Opera in Four Acts* (London: Lacy, 1865), 27.

make shared meaning. Wagner had initially intended *Der fliegende Holländer* to be his great success in Paris. It ventured, alongside *Rienzi*, most decisively into the vicinity of the *grand opéra*. *Holländer* teems with crowd scenes, and evinces a profound ambivalence vis-à-vis the wisdom and morality of the people. The work is not so much addressed to a national community as it is interested in how to turn a mass audience into a community. As a consequence, his framing of Senta's ballad—his theory of balladry—is less about the performance, the sounding out that had framed interest in the public declamators of decades prior, and more about receptivity on the part of an audience. Balladry, to Wagner, depends on a certain attunement. It reaches into its listeners and activates something latent, preexisting. Wagner's staging of Senta's song brings to the fore questions of the unconscious in balladry, of pre-discursivity and how discourse can activate it. Wagner's theory of the ballad comes neither from the field of poetics, nor from the theory of music. Senta's ballad draws on a tradition of literary ballads more so than the aforementioned operatic ones and takes its cue from a literary work rather than any musical one. It speaks to the ballad from the space between arts. And it is in this space that Wagner assigned the ballad its home and location—as affection, as distraction, as media.

## Missing Daniel

While *Der fliegende Holländer* was unique in how it blended the ballad and the opera, the idea that the ballad told a story about media and an audience's historical receptiveness or unreceptiveness to them was one it shared with important literary forebears and contemporaries, above all Heinrich Heine. Heine was among the canniest exploiters of the strange mix of rigidity and flexibility that had come to govern the ballad form in Germany from Bürger onward. The ballad's topics, its meters, its themes, its rhymes were often so predictable that the slightest tweak of formula became noticeable even to casual readers (or, in the cases traced in the previous chapter, listeners). Heine's "Belsazar" (1827), for instance, draws on a biblical story tailor-made for ballad-treatment: a hubristic individual (named in the title), an affront against a higher power, and a supernatural event that punishes him for it. But Heine's ballad is unusual in that it is a ballad centered on someone who isn't there—who is never named, never mentioned, never even alluded to. The poem tells the story of Daniel, the *mene mene tekel*, and the Babylonian tyrant whom the *mene mene tekel* is addressing. But it is missing Daniel.

The story the ballad should by rights tell is the following: Belshazzar uses the loot from the temple in Jerusalem to celebrate a raucous feast, in the process mocking the God of the Israelites. A disembodied hand appears and writes in golden script upon a wall. Belshazzar's wise men are unable to decipher the message, so Daniel is brought before the king. "The wise men, the astrologers, have been brought in before me, that they should read this writing, and make known unto me the interpretation thereof: but they could not shew the interpretation of the thing" (Daniel 5:15). Daniel deciphers the message—that God has weighed Belshazzar, found him wanting, and will punish him forthwith. It seems that Belshazzar heeds Daniel's interpretation (or at least puts some stock in it), but it does him no good: "In that night was Belshazzar the king of the Chaldeans slain" by invading Medians.

Heine's ballad follows this story faithfully, except for its central detail: the prophet and the deciphering of the writing on the wall. In Heine's version the king seems to realize that he has gone too far, that his hubris will be punished, before the writing appears. The writing, not Belshazzar's death, appears to constitute the punishment. Something supernatural happens, of course, but that something is utterly undramatic—it confirms what the king has already intuited, it pronounces a judgment that will only later be fulfilled. Robert Schumann set Heine's poem in a beautiful arrangement as his op. 57, and the song is remarkable for the way all the life and energy seems to drain from it just about halfway in. Even those techniques that tend to speed up reading or recitation (the repetition of "Und sieh! Und sieh!," for instance) in Schumann's arrangement become moments of retardation. The song grinds to a halt as it watches the fiery script unspool on the palace wall.

| | |
|---|---|
| Und sich! und sieh! an weißer Wand | Behold! Behold! Upon the wall |
| Da kam's hervor wie Menschenhand; | A thing—a hand—came in the hall; |
| Und schrieb, und schrieb an weißer Wand | And wrote in fire upon the wall, |
| Buchstaben von Feuer, und schrieb und schwand. | And wrote, and vanished in the pall. |
| Der König stieren Blicks da saß, | The king just sat there, goggle-eyed, |
| Mit schlotternden Knien und totenblaß. | With knocking knees, pale, terrified. |
| Die Knechtenschar saß kalt durchgraut, | The lackey troop, by horror bound, |
| Und saß gar still, gab keinen Laut.[4] | Sat cold and still, without a sound.[5] |

---

[4] Heinrich Heine, "Belsazar," in *Werke und Briefe in zehn Bänden* (Berlin and Weimar: Aufbau, 1972), 1:52–53..

[5] Heinrich Heine, "Belshazzar," in *Poems*, trans. Ritchie Robertson (London: Bloomsbury, 1993).

What sort of understanding do these lackeys share with their master? What makes them all fall silent? In lieu of Daniel to translate God's judgment, Heine relies on a kind of *sensus communis*—a mounting sense of collective dread that receives, even if it does not understand, the writing on the wall. In Heine's version of the story, the divine writing sits uncomprehended and incomprehensible at the center of Belshazzar's feast, foretelling a doom no one is able to articulate. "Die Magier kamen, doch keiner verstand / Zu deuten die Flammenschrift an der Wand."[6] ("Magicians came, yet none at all / Could decipher the flame script on the wall.") Schumann adds to this a more emphatic juxtaposition of the *spoken* or *sung* word (which is at least ideally the province of the ballad) and the *written* word—and it is the written word that emerges victorious. Because there is no Daniel to voice what is written—to sound out the *mene tekel upharsin*—all vocal discourse can do is stand stupefied before the flaming letters and contemplate their incomprehensibility.

Many of Heine's nineteenth-century readers wondered whether the ballad's disappearing act was meant to make a point about Judaism. Imagine a world without Daniel, it seemed to be saying, you may not like it one bit. But that leaves aside that, with Daniel missing, the central act of reading and interpretation in the narrative disappears as well. "Belsazar" revolves around a sign no one can interpret but that everyone understands. The odd status of the sign in Heine's poem has been read in terms of a revolutionary temporality: the judgment on Belshazzar's reign has been pronounced, the execution of that judgment is almost beside the point—you do not need Daniel as a weatherman to know which way the wind is blowing.[7] At a more fundamental level, the poem is about media: it is about the danger of speaking (especially when drunk on power and wine), and the danger of not being able to read. It is, in other words, a ballad about the very nexus of orality and literacy at which the ballad traditionally persists. But at the same time, its media arsenal is more variegated than one that would simply oppose the written to the oral. "Belsazar" centers a script that no one can comprehend, but that everyone senses *must* be comprehended, and that everyone does grasp even if they can't decipher it. "Belsazar" is poetry that is far more interested in what it means to be in an audience than what it means to be a speaker or singer. And this audience both does and does not grasp what they are witnessing: they may not understand what exactly God's judgment of Belshazzar is, but they are nevertheless seized by an instinct that he has been judged.

Heine's poem forces its reader, singer, or listener to replicate this troubled nexus of speaking versus reading, of repetition versus interpretation, of surface and depth. Because it is missing Daniel, there isn't much to be

---

6 Heine, "Belsazar," 1:53.

7 Winifred Freund, "'Allnächtlich zur Zeit der Gespenster': Zur Rezeption der Gespensterballade bei Heinrich Heine," *Heine Jahrbuch* 2, no. 1 (1981): 58.

done about the poem itself interpretively—all we can do is (orally) repeat it. In his 1914 text "Remembering, Repeating and Working Through," Freud points out that repetition is in many ways opposed to remembering, so that "something is 'remembered' that could never be 'forgotten,' since it was at no time noticed, was at no time conscious."[8] Poems like "Belsazar" force their readers to carry forward an unremarked, unnoticed absence. The poem stages a surface that misses the main point of the Daniel-story, namely Daniel himself. We can stare at its writing all we want, but no amount of scrutiny will bring Daniel before our eyes. But at the same time, the poem is absolutely overt about the fact that its readers are necessarily missing its point: it is the story about the need to understand a deeper meaning, and about living with the failure of doing so. The poem flaunts its own shallowness, but it understands that shallowness as a problem. "Belsazar" is a poem about a surface that enables and facilitates circulation; but it is also a poem about depths lost in such circulation—namely Daniel, namely the divine locution that speaks through the poem's indecipherable script. We will see in the next chapter that Heine's great antagonist, August von Platen, relied on the same dialectic of interpretive depth on the one hand and a circulation that depends on the absence of interpretation on the other. The poem can be repeated, can circulate, be anthologized, be recited, be assigned in class, because there is some object in it that has never come to consciousness. It thus becomes important to ask what kind of consciousness (and what kind of unconscious) ballads were taken to require for their ceaseless circulation.

Wagner had met Heine in Paris in 1840, during a period when his understanding of media, audience, and attention began to take the shape that would define his "music dramatic" output from *Der fliegende Holländer* onward.[9] They were first introduced by the dramatist Heinrich Laube, but were brought together by a ballad—Wagner decided to set to music Heine's "Die Grenadiere" ("The Grenadiers," probably 1820) in an especially commissioned French translation as "Les deux grénadiers" (WWV 60). Wagner also later acknowledged the stylistic debt his reviews and reports of the Paris operatic scene owed to Heine. But most important, perhaps, Wagner drew from Heine the central inspiration for *Der fliegende Holländer*. In his *Autobiographische Skizze* (*Autobiographic Sketch*, 1842), Wagner provided two accounts of what had inspired him to tackle this tale—one of them clearly mystificatory in the way Wagner's later origin legends tended to be mystificatory, the other quite pedestrian. According to the first version, Wagner encountered the legend

---

8 Sigmund Freud, "Erinnern, Wiederholen, Durcharbeiten," in *Gesammelte Werke*, ed. Anna Freud (Frankfurt: S. Fischer, 1969), 10:128.

9 Jeremy Coleman, *Richard Wagner in Paris: Translation, Identity, Modernity* (Rochester, NY: Boydell, 2019).

during an ocean voyage, in a downright Ossianic encounter, among "the crags of Norway," in between "the most violent of storms," where Wagner heard the story "from the seamen's mouths."[10] But, unlike later accounts, Wagner's early *Sketch* gives a second, supposedly coequal inspiration: "I had also," Wagner writes, "made the acquaintance of H. Heine's remarkable version of this legend," namely in Heine's *Salon*, which "placed within my hands all the material for turning the legend into an opera-subject."[11] This doubleness in the genesis of *Der fliegende Holländer* Wagner later seemed at pains to repress. But it in fact asserts itself powerfully in the opera itself, and above all in Senta's ballad at the heart of Act II—not so much in what the ballad says, but rather in what it does, how it interacts with the work that surrounds it, with its world and with its audience.

## Balladic Consciousness

The second act of Wagner's *Flying Dutchman* centers on one of those exaggerated scenes of domestic life that abounded in German opera in the first half of the nineteenth century: While the men attend to manly business somewhere outside, the women are playing dress-up, stitching up garments and spinning yarns. This is how the women spend their time while the men are out hunting in *Der Freischütz*, it's how they spend the domestic scenes in Marschner's *Der Vampyr*, and it is how they pass their time in the middle act of *Der fliegende Holländer*. The voices are impossibly high, the songs are marked as insipid and repetitive, drawing their content mostly from domestic trappings—the girls are spinning yarn and singing songs about spinning:

> Summ und brumm, du gutes Rädchen,
> munter, munter dreh dich um!
> Spinne, spinne tausend Fädchen,
> gutes Rädchen, summ und brumm![12]

A nineteenth-century audience would have recognized in their spinning circle a very specific form of orality.[13] The sheer drudgery of spinning meant that it was usually done in groups, and usually groups of women.

---

10 Richard Wagner, "Autobiographic Sketch," trans. William Ashton Ellis, in *Richard Wagner's Prose Works*, 1:14.

11 Wagner, "Autobiographic Sketch," 1:17.

12 Richard Wagner, *Der fliegende Holländer*, in *Gesammelte Schriften und Dichtungen* (Leipzig: Siegel, 1907), 1:268.

13 Harry Rand, *Rumpelstinskin's Secret: What Women Didn't Tell the Grimms* (London: Routledge, 2020), Chapter 3.

Such spinning groups frequently happened in private spaces, but had a semi-public quality: the spinning circle was where information and opinion were circulated; and they circulated in a context of collective, almost proto-industrial labor.[14] It is worth noting, then, that the scene with which Wagner opens his second act ought to be a complex, heteroglossic discourse with many participants.[15] That is not how *Der fliegende Holländer* presents it: Wagner has high voices sing a formulaic ditty in unison. Perhaps the reason is sexism, but, more important, the domestic songs need to be flat, shrill, and repetitive to contrast with the ballad that comes after. The women's discourse, Wagner wants his listeners to infer, largely feeds on itself—it doesn't rise to the level of genuine knowledge, but rather moves in extremely restricted vocal ranges and through profoundly circumscribed topics. It has all the repetitiveness and self-containment of gossip.[16] The story that irrupts into this happy chatter—about a cursed sailor and his black-sailed boat—is of course just as much hearsay as whatever these women are exchanging. But the opera works hard to pretend that this story—especially in the way it relates to knowledge and circulation—is of a different kind altogether.

There is among the amiable throng one malcontent unhappy with their stereotypically "feminine" pursuits, unhappy with the scene's self-containment, its domesticated self-referentiality. While the women tend to their spinning and to their songs, Senta, daughter of Dahland, has her mind on other things and rebels against their tonal and their conversational arsenal. She wants to hear—in the middle of all this repetitive motion—the story of the world out there, a story about breaking a cycle of repetition. Compared with the curse of domesticity, it seems, Satanic damnation is the lesser of two evils. The tale that Senta wants to hear, the tale that the other women refuse to tell her, is that of the Flying Dutchman, the sailor condemned to traverse the oceans in search of a woman who would redeem him. By the end of the scene, all eyes and ears are tuned to Senta, all the back-and-forth has ceased. Senta has turned the women, who were initially busy both creating and consuming discourse, into a passive, receptive audience. The story by which Senta deputizes the domestic throng into rapt attention enters the domestic space as a ballad. And though the ballad was, in the nineteenth century, widely regarded as a domestic genre, in Wagner's opera it seizes the domestic space and renders it profoundly uncanny.

---

14 Melanie Tebbutt, *Women's Talk?: A Social History of "Gossip" in Working-Class Neighborhoods, 1880–1960* (Aldershot: Scolar Press, 2008), 22.

15 See, for example, Susan E. Philips, *Transforming Talk: The Problem of Gossip in Late Medieval England* (State College: Pennsylvania State University Press, 2010), 178.

16 On the intimacy and self-containment of gossip as world-making, see Patricia Meyer Spacks, *Gossip* (New York: Knopf, 2012).

The scene presents the ballad as relying on a double consciousness: something calls forth the ballad from Senta, and something allows her environment to respond with appropriate terror. What has come over her? And what does Wagner want to come over us in watching her? The answer to this question concerns not just Wagner's view of a particular poetic genre, but instead cuts to the very core of his emergent operatic aesthetics. For Senta's ballad is supposed to stand in for the opera with which it shares a name. In his *Mittheilung an meine Freunde* (1851), Wagner calls the *Holländer* "a mythic-poetic creation of the folk: a primeval trait of human nature."[17] Senta's ballad became his *pièce-de-résistance*: for the ballad was not a number in an Italianate opera, something an enterprising director looking to fit in a second performance on the same night might cut out of the work. The ballad contained the spirit of the opera, and it was a new spirit, a more unifying spirit. Of course, as Carolyn Abbaté points out, *Der fliegende Holländer* remains in most respects a number opera, but it wants to be something different: "The *Holländer* numbers are beads jostling each other on a string, not the net of interwoven threads Wagner would later place before us."[18] Nowhere is the jostling, the straining toward a kind of integration that would forgo individual numbers, arias, and duets, more evident than in the core set piece, the ballad.[19] Wagner recognized as much, even toying with the thought of calling the entire opera a "dramatic ballad":

> Unconsciously I put in this [ballad] the entire thematic core of the opera's music; it was a compressed image of the entire drama, as it stood before my soul; and when it came to providing a title for the completed work, I almost had a mind to call it a "dramatic ballad."[20]

In this short passage, Wagner identifies three axes along which the ballad comes from a place of depth and instinct compared to traditional opera: a formal axis, a dramaturgic axis, and a poetological one. The ballad does what the opera does, but it does it to another faculty. It works "unconsciously," through our "soul," immediate like an image, compressed by something like a collective dream-work. Yes, even the designation of "ballad" occurs to Wagner spontaneously, instinctually ("ich hatte nicht übel Lust . . .").

---

17 Richard Wagner, *Schriften und Dichtungen* (Leipzig: Breitkopf & Härtel, 1911), 4:323.
18 Carolyn Abbaté, "Erik's Dream and Tannhäuser's Journey," in *Reading Opera*, ed. Arthur Groos and Roger Parker (Princeton, NJ: Princeton University Press, 1988), 138.
19 Carl Dahlhaus and Norbert Miller, *Europäische Romantik in der Musik* (Stuttgart: Metzler, 2007), 293.
20 Wagner, *Schriften und Dichtungen*, 4:323: "In diesem Stücke legte ich unbewußt den thematischen Keim zu der ganzen Musik der Oper nieder; es war das verdichtete Bild des ganzen Dramas, wie es vor meiner Seele stand; und als ich die fertige Arbeit betiteln sollte, hatte ich nicht übel Lust, sie eine 'dramatische Ballade' zu nennen."

And Senta's ballad enters the opera with the same uncanny mix of caprice and inevitability. In his essay on "Remembering, Repeating and Working Through," Freud writes that "the analysand *recalls* nothing of what has been forgotten or repressed, he acts it out."[21] This is what Senta does: seized by something beyond her well-appointed bourgeois lifeworld, Senta acts out the demonic story more than she recalls it.

Sometime in early 1845, about two years after *Der fliegende Holländer* premiered, the composer Otto Carl Claudius (1793–1877) sent an opera *précis* to Wagner in Dresden: it was his adaptation of Schiller's ballad *Der Gang nach dem Eisenhammer* (*The Walk to the Foundry*).[22] Wagner, although clearly wanting to be helpful, doesn't seem to have liked the reading much. He offers general praise, but clearly sees a difference between what Claudius does with Schiller's ballad and "how I would have been compelled to form the subject into a concentrated Whole."[23] Wagner equates this instinctual drive toward compression with a respect for the concision already inherent in the ballad form. Claudius had drawn his libretto less from the ballad itself, and instead from a pair of melodramatic adaptations by Franz Ignaz von Holbein from 1808. Wagner admonishes Claudius that "to begin with, your libretto has too many people and too many scenes."[24] He adds: "I wish you had had nothing more before you . . . than Schiller's ballad; you would have gotten much closer to a real opera that way."[25] In other words: being truer to the economy of means and instinctual purchase of the ballad form meant that the opera that might emerge from the adaptation would be "closer to a real opera." The question was less how to accommodate the ballad in the opera form as it existed at the time, but what a "real opera" would have to look like in order to accommodate the ballad. Given Wagner's reflections on opera and drama in the second half of the 1840s, it seems likely that Wagner regarded the ballad as an antecedent to the *Gesamtkunstwerk*. Its fusion of poetic forms hearkened back to the Greek theater and augured its even more comprehensive cousin, the Wagnerian music drama. Nor was he alone in suggesting as much in the 1840s. Worlds removed from pageantry, number-opera, and

---

21 "der Analysierte erinnere überhaupt nichts von dem Vergessenen und Verdrängten, sondern er agiere es" (Freud, *Gesammelte Schriften*, 10:112).

22 Claudius published a libretto to this opera, probably in 1854: Otto Carl Claudius, *Der Gang nach dem Eisenhammer: Romantische Oper in 3 Aufzügen* (Naumburg: Sieling, n.d.). Given the time that elapsed between the letter and the publication, it is unclear whether the published libretto is what Wagner was sent.

23 To Otto Karl Claudius, in Richard Wagner, *Sämtliche Briefe*, 2:439: "wie ich den Stoff zu einem konzentrirten Ganzen zu formen mich gedrängt gefühlt haben würde."

24 Ibid.: "zunächst befinden sich in Ihrem Buche zu viel Personen und zu viel Szenen."

25 Ibid.: "Ich wünschte, Sie hätten . . . nichts vor sich gehabt, als Schiller's Ballade, so würden Sie der richtigen Oper bei weitem näher gekommen sein."

commercial song, the ballad seemed to Wagner's contemporaries to hail from an older place. Italians didn't have to invent it in imitation of little-understood Greek forebears, Germans didn't have to copy it from Italians and learn to stage it from the French. It wasn't kept away from the German language by political fiat until the days of Mozart. No, for them the ballad welled up from the soul of the people, the person singing it didn't speak for themselves. In his portrait of the composer Carl Loewe, the poet and theater-theorist Heinrich Bulthaupt suggested in almost proto-Heideggerian language that "the ballad sings through the singer."[26] Like young and naïve Senta, who with the first incantation of the storm-motif seems to transform before our eyes into something older, darker, the balladeer is possessed, overcome, inspired.

Wagner's writings about his Dutchman-opera look to the ballad as a legitimating *Urform* for the new kind of opera he is envisioning. But legitimation works the opposite way as well. One of the features Wagner lamented about the modern opera was the autonomy of stage and audience vis-à-vis one another. He was famously critical of Italian opera houses where, he thought, the stage provided nothing more than pleasant distraction over chatter. At the same time, Wagner worried about foreign-language texts or unintuitive plots that washed over their audience without caring whether they were being understood. The ballad became a useful vehicle for imagining an opera that would bridge such modern problems of spectatorship: for one, because it presupposed a more originary and organic scene of reception, and for another because it brought that scene of reception onto the stage. In *Der fliegende Holländer*, we witness Senta reciting and we see her audience be affected by her recitation in certain ways. Ballads frequently imagine the scene, or a possible scene of their reception. They have an idea of who they want to speak to, want to be spoken to. The poetic locution has a place in the poem's diegesis itself. There is a song being sung and it turns out to be the poem, there's a story being told and it is being told to us, specifically us—for safekeeping, as a warning, as important information. Although few are as explicit in their framing as Rudyard Kipling's early poems published as *Departmental Ditties and Ballads* and *Barrack-Room Ballads* (1892 and 1899 respectively), Kipling's poems make explicit what was in the nineteenth century widely understood: ballads have a social function that is inscribed into both their form and content, usually a function for a specific community.[27] Kipling's title signals that his poems emerge organically from an identifiable milieu. They tell the sort of stories soldiers relate to each other over a pint in an officer's club; and we, as their addressees, are not eavesdroppers on their

---

26 Heinrich Bulthaupt, *Carl Loewe: Deutschlands Balladenkomponist* (Berlin: Imberg & Lesson, 1898), 2.

27 Rudyard Kipling, *Ballads and Barrack-Room Ballads* (New York: Macmillan, 1899),

conversations, we become their barrack-room audience in reading the poem, an audience that may soon share the same tale at another mess hall. The poet casts him- or herself as a mere stenographer of a pre-existing discourse, even as the poetic form does its best to render this claim implausible.

In a strange way, then, even though he is attempting an unprecedented fusion of genres, Wagner has the two forms vouch for each other's authenticity. He positions the opera, or rather the kind of opera he is starting to want to compose, as organic and integrated precisely because it incorporates and combines its elements as instinctively and immediately as the ballad unites the dramatic, the lyric, and the epic. And he positions the ballad is authentic because the opera allows us to watch it being sung, gives us a peek into the *milieu* and the time period that supposedly gave rise to it—some Nordic folk huddling in trepidation while a possessed individual draws from ancient memory the dark tale of the flying Dutchman. In the German case, it is clear that much of it—the ballad as an effect of a *Volksgeist*, the ballad as a social pursuit, the imagined scene of reception—is purely fictional. Such fictions are what render the ballad what Susan Stewart has called a "distressed genre"[28]— just like a leather jacket distressed to simulate years of wear and tear when in fact it is only a few weeks old, the nineteenth-century ballad carries history (or historicity) inscribed in its form that it doesn't factually have. Wagner searched long and hard for an authentic German past to put on the stage, so long and so hard in fact he had to invent it. This put him in a uniquely fortuitous position in reflecting on the kind of double consciousness required by the ballad-form as it became popular in Germany in the quarter-century before his birth. It is easy, in other words, to see the moments where Wagner seems to fully commit to the idea that the ballad is a straightforward product of the soul of the people. But through them runs at all times a counter-current: an awareness that this aboriginality is a possibly a fictive conceit. That balladry is a modern practice of which modernity has forgotten that it is modern.

## Senta's Ballad

Reading Senta's ballad as more than an exemplar of the form, but rather on some however inchoate level a theory of it—a theory of its provenance, its hold on an audience, and its means of circulation—means looking both at the way the ballad unfolds in its operatic environment, and the way it works in itself. The word "ballad" had of course great ubiquity in 1840s Germany, but what exact aesthetic objects were to be subsumed under the

---

28 Susan Stewart, "Notes on Distressed Genres," in *Crimes of Writing: Problems in the Containment of Representation* (New York: Oxford University Press, 1991), 87.

name was not always clear. Rather than exploit this ambiguity, as Robert Schumann and Franz Liszt would do only shortly after *Der fliegende Holländer*, Wagner inserts himself into a very clear lineage with his libretto, and it is not a musical lineage. In composing Senta's ballad, Wagner draws on a discrete number of earlier operatic ballads, which flesh out the backstories for the frequently supernatural denizens of Romantic operas by Marschner and Meyerbeer. Specifically, Wagner followed them in structuring the ballad dramatically and situating it within the broader work. In Marschner's *Der Vampyr* (1828), young Emmy tells the story of the Vampire, and even though Wilhelm August Wohlbrück's libretto calls the song a "romance," it is clearly a gothic ballad. Thomas Grey suggests that Wagner's use of the operatic ballad owes the clearest debt to Meyerbeer's *Robert le Diable* (1831) and the ballad "Jadis regnait en Normandie."[29] Both "Jadis regnait" and Emmy's romance play off the single (female) voice relating the ballad against a broader chorus representing an audience reaction.[30] As Carolyn Abbaté and Roger Parker point out, "Jadis regnait" sets up not only the opera's anti-hero, it also showcases several important motifs of the opera in a way that anticipates Wagnerian leitmotif technique.[31] And, again like the romance of the Vampire, and unlike "Jadis regnait," the ballad occurs somewhat awkwardly as a retarding moment in the very center of the opera.

Like these earlier ballads, Senta's ends without the kind of traditional moral or narrative closure we would expect from a literary ballad. As Grey has pointed out, while the written/spoken ballad is by its very nature a closed form, operatic ballads were by nature of their integration into a larger whole often open-ended—they provided backstory and then deliberately failed to provide closure.[32] Both musically and dramatically, Senta's final outburst and imaginative rewriting of the text anticipates the main action of the opera, leaving the ballad interrupted: the ballad's coda (in B flat major) anticipates the opera's final bars. When Senta declares that she wants to be the woman who releases the Dutchman from his terrible fate, she seems to posit the entire opera as the final stanza of the ballad.

If the lineage of operatic ballads is a comparatively short one, another line of descent weighs far more heavily on the text Wagner has Senta sing. It is a literary line. There is in Wagner's oeuvre no other piece of text that so readily submits to the conventions of an extra-operatic genre. Given its variable line lengths, the way it organizes its strophes as a sequence of narrative functions, the

---

29 Thomas S. Grey, *Richard Wagner: Der fliegende Holländer* (Cambridge: Cambridge University Press, 2000), 73.

30 Hans Gaartz, *Die Opern Heinrich Marschners* (Leipzig: Breitkopf & Härtel, 1912), 33.

31 Carolyn Abbaté and Roger Parker, *A History of Opera* (New York: W. W. Norton, 2015).

32 Grey, *Richard Wagner*, 81.

text is fairly recognizably a literary *Kunstballade*. The alternation between narrative form and repetitive elements, as well as the disruptive moment of a possible release from fate, likewise would have been familiar to Wagner less from the work of other composers than simply from the poetry that he had grown up with and that had guided his first efforts in composing for voice. That is to say, it came from the poetry of Romanticism, from Goethe and Schiller. Wagner was working through his own Romanticism in positioning Senta's ballad within his "dramatic ballad," but it was largely Romantic literature rather than music.

The music takes care to emphasize the ballad as a linguistic creation—the descending fourth that opens each strophe has none of the dreaminess of, say, the inverted A flat major chord that opens Chopin's Ballade No. 1 in G minor (1831). Rather, it simulates on a musical level the searching gesture, the way rhyme and repetition seem to dig into an ancestral past, to claw things from it half-remembered. The idea of the ballad as a skaldic mission of recovery was an exclusively linguistic matter—it is a metafiction absent in the famous ballad settings by Loewe and Schubert—Wagner here tries to simulate it in music. At the same time, of course, the music can signal what material it seeks to retrieve: the interval simply reverses the first interval of the Dutchman-motif. What flares up spontaneously from the past in the Dutchman-motif, Senta has to dig down for.

Johohoe! Johohoe! Hojohe!
Traft ihr das Schiff im Meere an,
blutrot die Segel, schwarz der Mast?
Auf hohem Bord der bleiche Mann,
des Schiffes Herr wacht ohne Rast.
    Hui!—Wie saust der Wind!—Johohe! Hojohe!
    Hui!—Wie pfeift's im Tau!—Johohe! Hojohe!
    Hui!—Wie ein Pfeil fliegt er hin,
    ohne Ziel, ohne Rast, ohne Ruh!
Doch kann dem bleichen Manne Erlösung einstens noch werden,
fänd er ein Weib, das bis in den Tod getreu ihm auf Erden!—
Ach! wann wirst du, bleicher Seemann, sie finden?
Betet zum Himmel, daß bald ein Weib Treue ihm halt!

*Gegen das Ende der Strophe kehrt Senta sich gegen das Bild. Die Mädchen hören teilnahmvoll zu; die Amme hat aufgehört zu spinnen.*[33]

Heigho! ho! heigho! ho! heigho! ho!
Did you encounter the ship at sea
With blackened mast and crimson sail?

---

33 Wagner, *Der fliegende Holländer*, 1:271.

On deck you see a pale-faced man,
the ships mater who never sleeps.
>    Huzza! Hear the wind! Heigho! Heigho!
>    Huzza! Hear the whistling in the rigging! Heigho! heigho!
>    Huzza! Like an arrow she leaps,
Without port of call, without rest, without peace!
But one day this pale man might be saved,
If he found a woman that was true to him until death! --
But when will you find this woman, oh pale seaman?
Pray for the man at sea, That
woman true to him be!

*Towards the end of the stanza Senta turns towards the painting. The girls listen in rapt attention; the nursemade has ceased her spinning.*

Wagner was never short of exacting in his libretti (which he called "poems"), but Senta's ballad is unique in how closely it mimics a printed poem. Each strophe breaks down into three parts: the first four lines (starting with "traft ihr") are kept in a fairly traditional ballad meter, an iambic tetrameter, with perfect rhymes. The next four lines break with that rhyme scheme. In fact, it is hard to say what the rhyme scheme even is. Parts of the line retain the iambs, but overall the anapest rules: "ohne Ziel, ohne Rast, ohne Ruh." More likely, though, the lines simply have no unifying rhyme scheme. What regularity there is seems owed to the speed with which Senta bellows out the line onstage, as though the psychic pressure of the anxiety that grips her in recounting the story pressed the words into this form. In the next four lines, the poem's rhythm calms down, as Wagner turns to another technique recognizable from literary ballads: the manipulation of line length for dramatic effect. The two lines that start with "Doch kann," fifteen syllables each, almost read as an iambic hexameter, but by now the melody of Senta's song is dominated by pre-existing thematic material, and so "Mann" becomes "Manne" and "einst" becomes "einstens." The line is a hair's breadth away from being poetry, so to speak, but "Manne" and "einstens" are tokens of the reassertions of the operatic. Language doesn't reign supreme here, it shares space with its sister arts and has to pay homage to them. The final two lines of the refrain are simply operatic discourse: they signal out to Senta's onstage audience, and are picked up by them.

It is worth noting that the libretto gets most stridently literary at the moment one would expect a ballad to be most "popular." The refrain is, after all, an "orality effect" of the ballad: it is supposed to make it easier to remember and recite. Whether it constitutes a remainder of the ballad's oral transmission, or an effect intended to create the fiction of such transmission, it functions like the "hook" of a pop song, lodging its cadence and melodic particularity in our memory. Wagner recognized this, when in his *Zukunftsmusik*

(1860) he links the "Eindringlichkeit" of the ballad to "a folk-like refrain" ("ein volksthümlicher Refrain").[34] This Senta's lines most decidedly are not. There is nothing popular about these lines; we can almost hear the prompter in his wooden box guiding the singer through their tricky syntax. Wagner thus confronts his audience with two facts: that he relies on literary modes in Senta's ballad; and that those literary modes get overwhelmed or undercut not so much by the *musical* material, but by peculiarly *operatic* issues of performance. From the first the orality of Senta's poem stands in tension with the actual oral performance of the text on stage.

There are some significant deviations from the form, most centrally in strophic structure: Wagner follows the ballad form in dividing off separate sections. Most ballads alternate at most between stanza and chorus, or between two rhyme schemes or meters within each stanza, Wagner reproduces this effect through melody. There are three motifs that each demarcate clearly defined sections of Senta's ballad: there is a stanza with a churning, incantatory motif that we find only here in the opera—these are the text passages that emphasize fate, repetition, and punishment. They are in each case followed by a second stanza set to the famous storm-motif from the overture. This section is far more dynamic, far more impressionistic in its narration ("ohne Ziel, ohne Rast, ohne Ruh'"), only to then segue into the placid pastures of the redemption-motif, as the refrain rehearses each time the same text describing the Dutchman's possible redemption. Then, as the orchestra returns to the minor fourth that constitutes the opening bar to the opera, we return to the lilting drudgery of the stanza.

These segues in a sense give away the game. The transitions in Senta's ballad turn it into the shadow of the overture to *The Flying Dutchman*, and in a way they turn the ballad into an overture in itself. And this matters, given Wagner's own aesthetic predilections, and his stated ambitions for *The Flying Dutchman*: Wagner thought of the ballad as a "compressed image of the entire drama as it stood before my soul." And "compressed image of a drama" is probably not the worst description of the genre. But it is utterly inapt for the overture: the overture doesn't condense anything, it packs together an expository catalogue of themes just so the customer can browse the product before fully committing to buying it. It is not a seed for anything, isn't even a mise-en-abyme, but rather resembles the Dutch paintings by David Teniers and others showing off the art galleries of aristocratic collectors. The overture is, in other words, all the things that neither the ballad nor the total work of art was supposed to be: non-German, tinged with the values of eighteenth-century courtly society, and more about displaying goods than about the spontaneous upwelling of the spirit.

---

34 Wagner, *Gesammelte Schriften und Dichtungen*, 7, 121.

## Mary's Refusal

In theorizing the ballad through Senta, Wagner clearly conceives of the form as primarily concerned with transmission. Senta, as Wagner's early French prose draft has it, repeats "an ancient ballad which she had often heard sung by her maid, and which she herself repeats every day."[35] She brings it into the merry gaggle of girls not just to frighten her friends, but rather to contaminate them with the ballad's story. After her first strophe, Wagner's stage directions tell us that "the girls listen in rapt attention; the wet nurse stops spinning yarn" ("die Mädchen hören teilnahmvoll zu; die Amme hat aufgehört zu spinnen"). After the second run-through, we are told that "the girls are seized by the story and quietly sing along the final couplet" ("die Mädchen sind ergriffen und singen den Schlußreim leise mit"[36]). And by the end, the girls carry the tune for Senta who is overcome with the story she's been telling. As Wagner's friend and future father-in-law Franz Liszt put it in 1854, to her terrified audience "the fiction almost becomes reality."[37]

Senta seeks to transmit more than just information, the simple story of the cursed Dutchman. She wants to transform her listeners into future tellers of the tale. Once she is done with them, they're in a trance like hers, spinning yarn is far from their minds, and they've stopped serenading a spinning wheel and offer salvation to a diabolical captain instead. If Wagner posits the ballad as a state of consciousness more than a mere receptivity to information in this scene, that consciousness is not quite as straightforwardly engendered and transmitted as the stage directions would make it seem.

In this context, it is interesting how much time Wagner's characters spend bargaining over who has to tell the story, and bargaining over who even knows the story. Initially, Senta asks Mary, her nurse, to recite the ballad, something she has clearly done before (even though the final version of the libretto makes no mention about how often as the French prose sketch does). Mary demurs and refuses to blacken their idyll with the Dutchman's tale—it isn't clear why she's switched tunes. Then it turns out Senta knows the story and the song already. And she tells Mary not to chastise her for her fascination, for it is Mary who caused it in the first place:

| Was hast du Kunde mir gegeben,— | Why did you have to tell me the story |
| Was mir erzählet, wer er sei.—[38] | Why did you tell me who he was.— |

---

35 Cited in Grey, *Richard Wagner*, 172.

36 Wagner, *Der fliegende Holländer*, 1:272.

37 Franz Liszt, *Sämtliche Schriften: Dramaturgische Blätter* (Wiesbaden: Breitkopf & Härtel, 1989), 93.

38 Wagner, *Der fliegende Holländer*, 1:269.

Senta sings her song, sings of the cursed Dutchman and the woman who alone can set him free, and in the end cries out that she would like to be that woman. The audience knows that she will get her wish: Her father has bartered the girl off to the Dutchman. The salvation she would like to be, she already is when she sings about it. When the Dutchman walks into her parlor she recognizes him immediately—from the ballad, from her dreams, and from the portrait of his conveniently kept around. When he finally gets around to his big reveal in the third act, no one other than Dahland seems overly surprised.

Much has been made of the fact that the true source of uncanniness in this is not the cursed sailor, but young Senta. What on earth makes this happy girl want to insert herself into a horror story, what occasions her obsession with killing herself for a centuries-old captain with few prospects other than the ultimate release of death? More important, Senta's knowing complicity in her own undoing makes the story starkly unsuspenseful: the structure of the ballad is the structure of the opera—the three acts are simply a procrustean stretch of the tiny nugget of story contained in Senta's ballad. Here Wagner goes beyond well beyond the antecedents in Meyerbeer and Devrient—their ballads fill in important details of the story, Senta's turns the rest of the opera into tautology. Senta begs Mary for a ballad that it turns out she knows only too well. Senta blames Mary for implanting in her brain a story that only fleshes out what she's already dreamed. The girls find themselves transformed by hearing a story they already know. The Dutchman's big reveal tells Senta only what she's sensed all along.

Daniel Albright once referred to Senta's strange mode of asking about things she already knows, seeking answers she already possesses, as "diabolical,"[39] but that misses the fact that Senta's mode of knowing is replicated on a formal level by the opera itself: the ballad, which pretends to be part of the opera, actually *is* the opera, not *in nuce*, but *in toto*. The ballad form's promised integration of the lyric, dramatic, and epic modes, which moved Goethe to propose that it constituted the *Urei* of all three, presages the integration of media in the opera. That means that not only Senta becomes "diabolical" in Albright's sense by telling the ballad: we become diabolical alongside her. In *Der fliegende Holländer*, this seems to be the mode of consciousness presupposed by the ballad. It is a mode in which nothing that is known is news, in which all shock is supposed to be a shock of recognition, of realizing that one may not have previously known it like this, but one has known it all along. As Wagner puts it in his *Bemerkungen zur Aufführung der Oper*, Senta's dreamlike state is not to be understood "in the sense of a modern, pathological sentimentality" ("im Sinne einer modernen,

---

39 Daniel Albright, *Music Speaks: On the Language of Opera, Dance, and Song* (Rochester, NY: University of Rochester Press, 2009), 39.

krankhaften Sentimentalität"). "Much to the contrary," Wagner continues, "Senta is a hearty Nordic girl and even in her seeming sentimentality she is entirely naïve" ("Im Gegentheile ist Senta ein ganz kerniges nordisches Mädchen, und selbst in ihrer anscheinenden Sentimentalität ist sie durchaus naiv"[40]). The consciousness that Senta imparts on her listeners by the power of her voice and her performance thus functions as a kind of germinal form for the kind of attunement Wagner's opera requires from its audience. But Wagner is careful to complicate that consciousness—in a move that puts the lie to the common picture of Wagner as a supremely unironic depth-monger. I have already pointed to the troubling echoes of the overture in the ballad, which seem to place its origins in an eighteenth-century court-theater, not some half-timbered inn by a craggy coast. I have also pointed to the fact that although Wagner talks about the ballad as a "folk song" in his prose drafts, by the time he composes out the ballad it very clearly is a self-consciously literary construction.

But even within the stage action itself, there is an interesting disconnect between the claims to a lived-in orality on the one hand, and the far more mercenary travels of the printed word on the other. The first two lines of the ballad violate one of the characteristic parameters of a ballad. Senta's ballad is a poem for an audience. In singing it, she adopts a persona and through that persona tells a story to an implicit audience. The interesting twist Wagner puts on the ballad's implicit situational aspects is that the audience she *actually* addresses on stage is *not* the audience she seems to be addressing in the poem, and conversely, that the audience she interpellates in the poem is nowhere to be seen on stage:

Johohoe! Johohoe! Hojohe!
Traft Ihr das Schiff im Meere an.

The women are in their domestic situation precisely because they are not at sea. Their place is the home, and their men's place is the open ocean—their songs make reference to the sea only to point to a lack ("My love is out on the ocean," "Mein Schatz ist auf dem Meere draus"). This is part of why they are initially resistant to hearing the ballad, and why Mary decides to keep spinning rather than recite it. The question "Traft Ihr das Schiff im Meere an?" thus cannot possibly apply to these fishermen's and tradesmen's wives—they do not go anywhere where it would be possible to encounter the Dutchman. That is after all the logic of the Satanic curse under which the Dutchman labors: for seven years he encounters only men. Every seventh year he gets to go on land, and only there does he get his shot at women, and at redemption.

---

40 Wagner, *Schriften und Dichtungen*, 5:167

The first line, which could just as easily have appealed to our having *heard* about the ship, rather than interpellating us as potential first-person witnesses, thus on the one hand invokes the implicit scene of reception, and telegraphs that that scene of reception differs from the one we are witnessing on stage. Whether the point is that the song is not really Senta's to sing, whether Wagner seeks to imbue her rapture with a gendered dimension, turning the young girl into a sailor, or whether the point is that in the moment of hearing even the landlubber ladies can transform imaginatively into seafaring scallywags, the ballad opens on a moment where form becomes visible as form, formula as formula. We are led to think we are watching something like the *Urszene* of the ballad on stage, where a singer adapts and imparts to this specific audience this pre-existing story. But in the end Senta provides us with a pre-formed story, insensate to her audience, fixed and static as though reading from a book. She will *end* the poem by "improvising"[41] a line *in viva voce*, but she opens it by hewing to the dead letter.

## Means and Ends

Goethe's "Betrachtung und Auslegung" of his "Ballade vom vertriebenen und zurückkehrenden Grafen" (1821) opens with a general description of the ballad form. It is famous for the already cited formula that in the ballad the three elements of poetry lyric, dramatic, and epic are "not yet separated," but instead "still together as though in a single living original egg [*in einem lebendigen Urei*],"[42] an egg that the poet may only "incubate" ("bebrüten"), in order that its contents may soar into the heavens by their own strength. Less famous is the reason Goethe gives for this poetic egg—and most readers of the short piece will probably have forgotten that Goethe gives a reason for it at all. It does appear to be an explanation where none seems to be required—the years around 1800 thrilled to things that were originally and unconsciously unified, only to be pulled apart and separated into carefully circumscribed entities in secular modernity. Why would such originary unity require something as modern as a reason; how would it even allow for one?

But Goethe insists that the ballad is "mysterious," but not "mystical"— and that it is an *Urei* not simply because it is old. Rather, it combines the three forms of poetry to a purpose, even if that purpose is no longer truly ours in repeating the form. "For the singer has his object, his figures, their deeds and movements *so deep in his mind* that he does not know how to call them into the light of day" ("Der Sänger nämlich hat seinen prägnanten

---

41 Grey, *Richard Wagner*, 82.
42 Johann Wolfgang von Goethe, *Goethe's poetische und prosaische Werke in zwei Bänden*, ed. Friedrich Wilhelm Riemer and Johann Peter Eckermann (Stuttgart: Cotta, 1832), 1:432.

Gegenstand, seine Figuren, deren Thaten und Bewegung *so tief im Sinne*, daß er nicht weiss, wie er ihn ans Tageslicht fordern will"[43]). Rather than suppose that the unity of the three forms of poetry is an effect of the ballad's unconsciousness, its absolute character, to speak with Hegel, Goethe proposes that the unity is required precisely to make certain events conscious. Goethe's term *Urei* combines the *Ur* of the poet's morphological studies (*Urpflanze*) with a kind of organicist metaphor of supersession (think for instance of Hegel's description of the flower as the negation of the seed in the preface to the *Phenomenology*). This makes it tempting to think of the *Urei* as an immediate, undetermined origin point that then got alienated *into* its separate component arts, which only became what they became through the determination that is inherent in all negation. It is tempting, in other words, to think of Goethe as relying on a narrative akin to the one offered around the same time in Hegel's *Lectures on Aesthetics*.

But the fact that that unification served a purpose—it made things easier to remember, it made stories easier to follow for the audience—all of that smacks of the kind of means/ends-thinking and shallowness that nineteenth-century observers were otherwise loath to admit existed in the form. Precisely because they are too "so deep in his mind," the things the ballad wants to talk about need to be dug up using certain techniques. The ballad form is not the effect of depth, it is its negation: it is an attempt to bring things "into the light of day," to make them sparkle, to make them easy to picture, easy to share, easy to sing, easy to memorize. There is nothing instinctual about the ballad, its operations are a matter of expediency, technology before there was technology.

This is why Wagner's scenic framing of Senta's ballad recitation is so significant: in his prose drafts, Wagner has the story of the Dutchman burst forth from some deep place, some substrate of the *Volksgeist*. In the actual opera, the story bursts forth from the furniture, from interior decoration. It is after all the painting that first puts Senta under the Dutchman's spell. Nor is Senta really sharing a story in reciting the tale: perhaps it is too much to say everyone knows it—but it's been on everyone's lips, or everyone has heard it. For all its ubiquity, the poem doesn't prime them when a man steps into their world who seems to match its description, match its predicament, even match the portrait. The ballad has blended into the bourgeois *intérieur* to the point that it becomes pure circulating language without referent. Senta's ballad, inspired by a painting, memorized in childhood, and expressed in song, has run the typical *parcours* that takes the nineteenth-century *Kunstballade* through the bourgeois *interieur*—the only thing that's missing is for Senta to sit down at a piano to intone her dark tale.

---

43 Goethe, *Goethe's poetische und prosaische Werke*, 1:432.

But that does not serve to make it somehow less authentic a ballad. Much the contrary. For if the ballad in its composition includes a fantasia about composition and transmission, it also instantiates an actual line of transmission. By the time Wagner had Senta intone her ancestral song, as we have seen, ballads in the world outside of the opera house had become sources of collective consciousness, teachers of memory, popular as song, sources for shared jokes and parodies. There is something intrinsic to these poems that makes them so memorable, so adaptable. If every ballad set up two worlds, one within its fictive universe, and one in the social one, one did not therefore replace the other—rather the two existed always in a tension. The same Wagner that could laud the ballad as a "mytho-poetic creation of the folk" can also kibbitz that ballads "keep all the hurdy-gurdies in the land busy until every piano demands to have them at home as well."[44] Wagner wasn't necessarily distinguishing between two *types* of ballads, but rather working and feeling his way through two aspects of the same form. The ballad knows two kinds of circulation, two kinds of repetition—the demonic-folkish "Johohe" on the one hand and the hurdy-gurdy on the other.

Granted, Wagner's origin story for his opera seems to put him in the folkish camp—the ballad that turned out to be the unconscious seed for the entire work that emerged from that seed in one organic whole and was therefore better than those mechanical contraptions of Aubier, Meyerbeer, and even Weber. At the same time, Wagner's origin story is, as so often, at best a half-truth. And in this case—unlike the florid "self-fashionings" in which Wagner almost compulsively engaged, from his misdating his discovery of Schopenhauer all the way to the La Spezia event that postdated the melodies it supposedly gave rise to[45]—Wagner almost seems to want us to call him out on his obfuscation. For unlike his later operas, *The Flying Dutchman* has a rather clear source text, which could not be more different from the one Wagner seems to invoke through Senta.

Senta presents her ballad as something that is always known, something the invention of which always predates each invocation—before she knew it, Mary knew it; before Mary knew it, there was the painting, etc. But the ballad's story has a precisely datable origin, and it has nothing mystical about it. While it shares narrative features with Coleridge's *Rime of the Ancient Mariner*, Wagner's plot actually comes detail by detail from Heine's *Memoiren des Herrn von Schnabelewopski*, a satirical fragment from 1834. There, the narrative of the *Holländer* shows up as a stage show the titular gentleman witnesses, and part of the joke in the episode is that although Mr. von Schnabelewopski misses most of the play action due to an amorous adventure, the action is so schematic that he's not missing much. He reports the action, but seems to

---

44 Wagner, *Schriften und Dichtungen*, 10:140.
45 Katherine Rae Syer, *Wagner's Visions: Poetry, Politics, and the Psyche in the Operas through "Die Walküre"* (Rochester, NY: University of Rochester Press, 2014), 24.

find little meaning in it. At the end he reports: "The moral of the piece is that women have to look out, lest they accidentally marry a Flying Dutchman; and us men can see from the play that, in the best case, women will be our downfall."[46] As Grey has put it, Wagner adapted "Heine's ironic-humorous literary vignette," but "purged it of all modern irony."[47]

Whatever its merits as a life lesson, Heine's cheeky moral at the end of his "vignette" points to the fact that Wagner not only attempted to de-ironize Heine's story, but also sought to grapple with the ironies of spectatorship. Put simply, the type of spectatorship exemplified by Mr. von Schnabelewopski is miles apart from the one Wagner imagined for his operas. Why Wagner would draw on an outline for an almost comically untheatrical opera to structure his own libretto has been much debated in Wagner-scholarship.[48] Stranger yet: Heine presents "his" *Holländer* in bits and pieces, since Schnabelewopski is otherwise occupied, yet Wagner uses those bits and pieces as his whole plot.[49] Why does Mr. Schnabelewopski not pay more attention? Heine's narrator suggests two reasons: Because he is distracted by a love plot of his own, and because "the fable . . . is certainly known to all of you" ("Die Fabel . . . ist euch gewiß bekannt"). The very familiarity of a tale, it turns out, can breed distraction. In his music theoretical works, Wagner lauded the ballad for its reduction and containment. It is why he chose the form as his guide in plotting *Holländer* after all. But when we look at the origin of the *Holländer*-story, we find something quite apart from the reduction to the essential that comes from centuries of oral tradition, from stories shared in hushed voices over a campfire or declaimed on the market square, from Herder's "ewigen Erb- und Lustgesang eines Volkes"[50]— we find instead the reduction that comes from overhearing a story, but walking out halfway through. A compaction by distraction rather than concentration.

And, remarkably given the self-image Wagner cultivated throughout his career, Wagner makes no real effort to banish the spirit of distraction from his tale of Nordic authenticity. The Schnabelewopski-version of consuming a cultural object like a ballad remains in operation throughout *Der fliegende Holländer*. Wagner barely changes Heine's story, he maintains all the difficulties Heine's narrator identifies in the subject matter. Most centrally, he manipulates his story in a way that strikingly repeats the mistakes of which he accused Otto Carl Claudius's version of "Der Gang nach dem Eisenhammer"

---

46 Heinrich Heine, *Werke und Briefe* (Berlin: Aufbau, 1972), 4:79.

47 Grey, *The Flying Dutchman*, 86.

48 On the various possible paths of inspiration for Wagner's Dutchman, see: Dieter Borchmeyer, *Drama and the World of Richard Wagner* (Princeton: Princeton University Press, 2003), 80.

49 Carl Dahlhaus, *Richard Wagners Musikdramen* (Hildesheim: Friedrich, 1971), 15.

50 Herder, Von Deutscher Art und Kunst, in *Sturm und Drang: Dichtungen und theoretische Texte in zwei Bänden*, ed. Heinz Nicolai (Munich: Winkler, 1971), 1:262.

in 1845: Wagner takes the ballad's one-act structure and turns it into a three-act opera by a procrustean wizardry that seems threadbare and undynamic even at casual inspection. As Carl Dahlhaus pointed out, only by having characters discover and forgetting secrets, only by inventing characters solely for the purpose of slowing down the stage action, does Wagner manage to make his ballad stretch for three acts—it is never a good fit for them.[51]

And yet, given the degree to which Wagner's opera is not just interested in the "mytho-poetic creations of the *Volk*," but in the conditions of particularly modern spectatorship as well, the rickety construction seems to make a point about balladry and modernity in its own right. The story without origin is tacitly understood to be a fiction, a useful fiction that launches the ballad on its own path of circulation, of being heard, misheard, appropriated, misappropriated, drained of its meaning and given new meanings. Wagner hides the Schnabelewopski-origins of the Senta-ballad, but not so thoroughly that the ballad may whelm up, like the E flat major chord of the *Rheingold*-prelude, from some sort of primordial ooze. Instead those origins are erased to enable ceaseless circulation, from Dahland to Mary to Senta back to Mary and to Erik, in order to authorize such ubiquity that when the man the ballad is actually about appears on stage, he becomes an afterthought to the ceaseless circulation of his own legend. As Wagner presents it in *Der fliegende Holländer*, balladic consciousness is precisely unmindful. And he may well intend this as a portrait of modern media circulation: for whatever vaunted origins contemporaries were wont to suppose for the ballads they recited, there was little denying that those ballads often required little mind. They could enter one's milieu as the melodious unspooling of a memorized poem, as a misremembered nugget of wisdom, a forgotten quote, a parody with no particular point to it. The joy of repeating it was often a joy of parroting, of letting a text spool through you while bypassing any depths that the lyric would normally touch. Citing a ballad elicits a flash of recognition, not a communication in any real sense.

The ballad that Senta produces feels similarly citational. Although clearly a narrative poem, Senta's ballad is rather bad at narrative sequence: the three stanzas seem poised again and again to tell the story in sequential form, but they never actually manage to do so. The overall impression is that of a story overheard. Its reciter relates to the poem the way Mr. von Schnabelewopski relates to the performance of the fictional Flying Dutchman play: her attention dashes in and out. Wagner seems to have sensed that the ballad drew on both: intimations of depth (quaint and curious volumes of forgotten lore, the *Volksgeist*, etc.), and realities of publication, anthologization, memorization, and popular song. This doubleness is what made the ballad such a characteristic, and such a potent, form in the nineteenth century and particularly

---

51 Dahlhaus, *Richard Wagners Musikdramen*, 19.

in nineteenth-century Germany. As we have seen, the German ballad was uniquely able to mediate between its own fictive provenance (the fictiveness of which it wore on its sleeve more openly than its British cousin, for instance) and the fact that it was destined for circulation in emerging enterprises in publishing, pedagogy, and music. The ballad is inscribed with both the fictive depth, the fictive past circulation from which it supposedly springs, *and* with the new, and often distinctly modern, modes of circulation to which it would immediately submit as a written, fixed document. In addition to being "distressed" genre, then, we could say the ballad is a photographic one—it feigns an aura, which it laments as always already evaporated, but it feigns it as a means to authorize an entirely anti-auratic set of practices.

## 4 | Memorizing Ballads

*Pedagogy, Tradition, and the Open Secret*

*Fame is a form—perhaps the worst form—of incomprehension.*
J. L. Borges, "Pierre Minard, Author of the Quixote"

Why do we recite a poem? Why do we commit it to memory? Most poems are agnostic on the matter, but ballads are an exception. Many, though not all, have an answer for such questions; they tell us why someone cared, and why we should too. If we recall them, if we repeat them, we participate in their drama in some way. Consider, for instance, those ballads which present themselves as the fulfillment of a promise or an obligation on the poet's part. We might call this moment the "balladic charge": someone who cannot speak for him or herself charges the poet with carrying forward a story that would otherwise disappear from the annals of history. When in Henry Wadsworth Longfellow's "The Skeleton in Armor" (1841) the titular creature appears to the poet, he has just such a reason for his visit:

> I was a Viking old!
> My deeds, though manifold,
> No Skald in song has told,
> No Saga taught thee!
> Take heed, that in thy verse
> Thou dost the tale rehearse,
> Else dread a dead man's curse;
> For this I sought thee.[1]

[1] Henry Wadsworth Longfellow, *The Poetical Works* (London: Routledge, 1891), 15.

The skeleton in armor seems to think that Longfellow's own time, Longfellow's nation, and perhaps the ballad form itself make a better fit for the Viking's tale. Skalds and epic sagas may not sing of the simple, everyday heroism of the immigrant, of the lowly heroism of the non-aristocrat, of less-than-glorious deeds—but a ballad, conveyed to a nation of immigrants whose heroism remains resolutely quotidian and non-aristocratic, just might provide a better vessel. And just for insurance, the skeleton in armor threatens the poet with a dread curse—surely not a bad motivation for putting a pen to paper.

But a balladic charge is deeply ambiguous, a letter entrusted to us sealed and with unclear intent. We agree to carry forward the poem, perhaps knowing what it signifies, perhaps ignoring entire dimensions of it. The very ease of its passage—its limpid cadence, its speaking roles, its lulling rhymes—makes it dangerous cargo. After all, carrying it and understanding it are very different things. What, then, are we to make of a poem that drafts us not only into carrying forth its tale, but that even drafts us into the poem's cadence itself? A poem that sings of a wave, that purports to *be* that wave, and in its final couplet suggests that to repeat its cadence is to become part of that wave? Repeating it, we become elemental:

| | |
|---|---|
| Sangen's, und die Lobgesänge<br>    tönten fort im Gothenheere;<br>Wälze sie, Busentowelle, wälze sie<br>    von Meer zu Meere![2] | Far and wide the songs of praise<br>    resounded in the Gothic host;<br>Bear them on, Busento's billow, bear<br>    them on from coast to coast![3] |

The imperative in the second line addresses itself to a river, but it isn't hard—in the final line of a poem—to feel oneself interpellated as a reader. We, too, are to "bear on" what we have witnessed. In a poem that begs to be memorized, to be repeated, the balladic charge (to recall the dead king of whose burial it tells) turns the listener into part of a wave—we are the medium by which the "songs of praise" move, by which they redound through the ages. Get swept up in me, the poem says, and you will be carrying me forward in turn.

Frances Yates once argued that Dante's *Divine Comedy* could be understood as "a kind of memory system for memorizing hell,"[4] and indeed memory and the duty to memorize has frequently had a moral, even religious dimension. It is noticeable that this dimension is largely missing in the ballad: these

---

2 August Graf von Platen, *Werke in zwei Bänden*, ed. Kurt Wölfel and Jürgen Link (Munich: Winkler, 1982), 1:9.

3 August von Platen, "The Grave in the Busento," in *The Poetry of Germany*, ed. and trans. Alfred Baskerville (Philadelphia: Schaefer & Conradi, 1873), 235–36.

4 Frances A. Yates, *The Art of Memory* (London: Bodley Head, 2014), 104.

poems may at times impart easy morals, but more frequently they tell deeply ambiguous stories, stories in which guilt, transgression, and punishment are misaligned or confused. They refuse easy identification, and frequently side with antiheroes, outsiders, and transgressors. Often, especially in murder ballads and gothic ballads, they treat outrageous cruelty with less outrage than would be seemly. This renders the connection between memory system and morality a deeply strange one: we feel compelled to memorize these poems, but we do not fully know why. Friedrich Nietzsche in *The Gay Science* proposed that "rhythm is compulsion; it creates an insuperable desire to give in, to join in, not only one's feet, but one's soul follows the beat."[5] The rhapsode of the Dionysian detected in the ravishments of rhythm an amoral, inescapable force. No assignment in a moral system guides our retention, in many cases not even the simple guidance provided by utility. When Wagner's Nordic village in *The Flying Dutchman* circulates the dark tale of the titular specter, and then fails to recognize that specter when he walks in the door, the opera seems to raise a similar question: what is the point in remembering? What's the use of all the beautiful memorability?

## Properly Swept Up

Likening the flow of poetic language to that of water seems to be as old as thought about poetry itself. The ancients variously understood the flow of the voice, poetic prosody, and the flow of poetic inspiration to be like the course of a river. Virgil's third *Eclogue* ends with an exhortation to "claudite iam rivos, pueri; sat prata biberunt" ("close the floodgates, boys; the meadows have drunk enough"[6])—the canal locks must be closed lest poetry's endless stream inundate already sated fields. Dante in turn greets his Virgil at the outset of the *Inferno* as "quel Virgilio e quella fonte che spandi di parlar si largo fiume" ("that Virgil, that fountain which spreads forth so broad a river of speech"[7]).

The Cyrenean poet Callimachus (second century BC) extended the likeness even further than Virgil had: he compared baggy epics to huge rivers heavy with sediments, while good poetry was a short clear stream still close to its spring.[8] In Roman thought what Cicero termed the *flumen orationis* ("river

---

5 Friedrich Nietzsche, *Werke in drei Bänden* (Munich: Hanser, 1954), 2:92.

6 Virgil, P. *Vergili Maronis Opera: The Eclogues and the Georgics*, ed. John Conington (London: Whittaker, 1881), 50. All translations from the German, French, and Latin, unless otherwise indicated, are my own.

7 Dante Alighieri, *Inferno*, trans. and ed. Robert M. Durling (New York: Oxford University Press, 1996), 30–31.

8 Prudence J. Jones, *Reading Rivers in Roman Literature and Culture* (Lanham, MD: Lexington Books, 2005), 55.

of speech") or *flumen verborum* ("river of words"[9]) was becoming so commonplace that it barely functioned as a metaphor anymore—it simply became another word for oration.[10] In the eighteenth century, Batteux's *Principes de la littérature* similarly opined that "tout discours est un ruisseau qui coule" ("all discourse is a flowing stream"[11]). The hermeneut's job consisted to some extent in arresting that implacable flow, ushering it into new channels, straightening out its meanders, and plumbing the depths "beneath" the undulations. Quintilian, in his *Institutio Oratoria* (ca. AD 95), suggested that "channeling" the imposing flow of rhetorical discourse *in rivos* facilitates "crossing" that flow ("qualibet transitum praebent"), that is, comprehending the text.[12]

From the moment the *Kunstballade* rose to prominence in Germany at the end of the eighteenth century it placed great emphasis on the "river that flows." The implacable flow of poetry, and what it meant to get to its bottom, played no small part in the genre's wide circulation across media. August von Platen (1796–1835), one of the masters of the genre, not only seized the metaphor of the river-like flow of poetry, but understood the poetic effects of this metaphor as an important benchmark for the fate of poetry in the modern age. For Platen the ballad's emphasis on flow in the wake of Bürger's *Lenore* proved "the possibility of a melodic effect of the German language."[13] The fact that the ballad managed to recreate the melodious effects of classical form in a modern vernacular vouched for the very possibility of harmonizing classical and autochthonous forms of poetry. Platen himself turned to the semantic field of water whenever he outlined his requirements for poetic language. In a note in his diary recording the composition of a poem, Platen expresses the hope "that the hexameters, and in particular the pentameters, should flow well and without fault."[14] In a short epigram entitled "Gerechte Rache," ("Justified Revenge") he describes how "his hexameters undulate [*wogen*]," and how his "masculine spirit," in an allusion to the primordial waters of Genesis, "hovers over the pentameters!"[15]

---

9 Marcus Tullius Cicero, *M. Tulli Ciceronis Academia* (London: Macmillan, 1885), 316.

10 Larue Van Hook, *The Metaphorical Terminology of Greek Rhetoric and Literary Criticism* (Chicago: University of Chicago Press, 1905), 12.

11 Charles Batteux, *Principes de la littérature*, 5 vols. (Paris: Saillant & Nyon, 1774), 5:102.

12 Quintilian, *Institutio Oratoria* (Cambridge, MA: Harvard University Press, 1980), 5.13.13.

13 August von Platen, *August Graf von Platens sämtliche Werke*, ed. Max Koch, 12 vols. (Leipzig: Max Hesse, 1909), 10:123.

14 August von Platen, *Die Tagebücher des Grafen August von Platen*, ed. Georg Laubmann and Ludwig von Scheffler, 2 vols. (Stuttgart: Cotta, 1900), 2:53.

15 Platen, *Platens sämtliche Werke*, 4:203.

Even in the context of a genre whose meter strove for a "melodic effect," however, Platen's "Das Grab im Busento," written in 1820, stands out, since it deals so explicitly with a flowing river and its poetic powers. The poem imitates the flow of the river Busento, utilizes the river metaphor to describe its own sonorities, and makes the river its real protagonist. What is more, its imitative flow gave the poem a peculiar afterlife: "Das Grab im Busento" quickly became one of the most frequently memorized poems of the nineteenth and early twentieth centuries, drilled into the heads of *Gymnasiasten* throughout the *Kaiserreich* and beyond. It is a poem about the transmission of historical memory intended to be itself readily memorized, that is to say, to participate in this process of transmission. But the historical memory contained in the poem turns out to be more complicated than those imperial pedagogues who made their students memorize it might have thought—and so is what the poem thinks we transmit through its memorization. Nineteenth-century pedagogy often opposed memorizing a poem's flow and analyzing it. Platen's "Grab im Busento" draws on this opposition, but plays off those "melodious effects" that invite us to tarry with the poem's surface against those other effects that draw us into its depths.

Platen's ballad both describes and performs a poetic burial, in which the poem's one solid object, the king's dead body, is dissolved into the literal *flumen* and the metaphoric *flumen cantionis*:

| | |
|---|---|
| Nächtlich am Busento lispeln, bey Cosenza, dumpfe Lieder, | By Cosenza, songs of wail at midnight wake Busento's shore, |
| Aus den Wassern schallt es Antwort, und in Wirbeln klingt es wieder! | O' er the wave resounds the answer, and amid the vortex' roar! |
| Und den Fluß hinauf, hinunter, zieh'n die Schatten tapfrer Gothen, | Valiant Goths, like spectres, steal along the banks with burned pace, |
| Die den Alarich beweinen, ihres Volkes besten Todten. | Weeping over Alaric dead, the best, the bravest of his race. |
| Allzufrüh und fern der Heimath mußten hier sie ihn begraben, | Ah! too soon, from home so far, was it their lot to dig his grave, |
| Während noch die Jugendlocken seine Schulter blond umgaben. | While still o' er his shoulders flowed his youthful ringlets' flaxen wave. |
| Und am Ufer des Busento reihten sie sich um die Wette, | On the shore of the Busento ranged, they with each other vied, |
| Um die Strömung abzuleiten, gruben sie ein frisches Bette. | As they dug another bed to turn the torrent's course aside. |
| In der wogenleeren Höhlung wühlten sie empor die Erde, | In the waveless hollow turning o' er and o' er the sod, the corse |

| | |
|---|---|
| Senkten tief hinein den Leichnam,<br>   mit der Rüstung, auf dem Pferde. | Deep into the earth they sank, in<br>   armor clad, upon his horse. |
| Deckten dann mit Erde wieder ihn<br>   und seine stolze Habe, | Covered then with earth again the<br>   horse and rider in the grave, |
| Daß die hohen Stromgewächse<br>   wüchsen aus dem Heldengrabe. | That above the hero's tomb the tor-<br>   rent's lofty plants might wave. |
| Abgelenkt zum zweyten Male,<br>   ward der Fluß herbeygezogen: | And, a second time diverted, was<br>   the flood conducted back, |
| Mächtig in ihr altes Bette<br>   schäumten die Busentowogen. | Foaming rushed Busento's billows<br>   onwards in their wonted track. |
| Und es sang ein Chor von Männern:<br>   Schlaf' in deinen Heldenehren! | And a warrior chorus sang, "Sleep<br>   with thy honors, hero brave! |
| Keines Römers schnöde Habsucht<br>   soll dir je dein Grab versehren! | Ne'er shall foot of lucre-lusting<br>   Roman desecrate thy grave!" |
| Sangen's, und die Lobgesänge<br>   tönten fort im Gothenheere; | Far and wide the songs of praise<br>   resounded in the Gothic host; |
| Wälze sie, Busentowelle, wälze<br>   sie von Meer zu Meere![16] | Bear them on, Busento's billow, bear<br>   them on from coast to coast![17] |

Platen's poem closes by linking two kinds of flow: that of the river and that of the Gothic song, which corresponds to that of the poem itself. It is the story of a watery burial told in a limpid cadence clearly evocative of the river Busento itself. Nary a nineteenth-century discussion of the poem fails to dwell on the poem's "almost Lied-like" cadences, which "come so close to being music, that they appear to be composed [rather than written]."[18] But, when it comes to the poem as well as to the song it depicts, melodic flow is a means to an end: the nineteenth century understood the rhythm of the ballad form as a way of orally transmitting cultural and historical memory. For the writer Willibald Alexis (1798–1871), the ballad preserved a function that had attached to poetic rhythm at the very dawn of human culture: "rhythmic sentences and verses meant to preserve the memories of prehistory or a truth discovered in prehistory."[19] This is

---

16 Platen, *Platens sämtliche Werke*, 1:28.

17 August von Platen, "The Grave in the Busento," in *The Poetry of Germany*, ed. and trans. Alfred Baskerville (Philadelphia: Schaefer & Conradi, 1873), 235–36.

18 Karl Barthel, *Vorlesungen über die deutsche Nationalliteratur der Neuzeit* (Gütersloh: Bertelsmann, 1879), 434.

19 Willibald Alexis, "Ueber Balladenpoesie," *Hermes oder kritisches Jahrbuch der Literatur* 21, no. 1 (1824): 1–113, here: 11.

a function that "Das Grab im Busento" invokes explicitly by making the "Busento's billow" an extension of the Goths' "songs of praise." The poem both relies on a propulsive cadence and reflects what the flow of "Busento's billow" and "song of praise" might accomplish—namely, to carry forth memory, but also to hide from memory.

"Das Grab im Busento" deals with two moments of remembrance, which are diametrically opposed in their particular parameters. There are, for one, the songs of the Gothic host, to some extent identical with the ballad itself and explicitly likened to the Busento's waters. The "Busentowelle" is to carry the song from ocean to ocean; the melodious flow of water and song ensures the transmission of the memory of King Alarich and his early end. If the first moment of memorization comments on the poem's form, the second moment of memorization is central to the poem's plot: the burial of Alarich itself. Here the Goths make their king deliberately unavailable to memory, remove him from the world of memorialization, and do so yet again by the flow of the river.

The Busento's waves (and the poem that mimics their flow) are both a means of spreading memory, and of making a thing unavailable for recovery, for memory. The poem tells the story of this unavailability, and thus stages the concealment of the beloved body, as an object of both poetic reflection and desire. This it does almost by necessity, since the boy king, young and beautiful, is the only concrete person the poem ever presents us with—otherwise, the poem's cast of characters consists of whispering waves, shadowy Goths, and their echoing song. Among these impersonal, disembodied, and diffuse folk, the king's dead body is starkly concrete, the most "real" character the reader encounters in the poem. Add to this the fact that Platen makes his Alarich much younger than his historical counterpart and gives us intimations of his physical beauty, and the dead boy king casts a disturbing allure over the poem's otherwise shadowy proceedings. We are to understand the song as but an ersatz for a now-invisible body, a body we are asked to understand as a potential object of our desire.

The strange double position occupied by the poem's flow, the way it makes visible and conceals, removes from language and brings into language, speaks to the contradictions of the ballad form itself. It is likely that Platen burdens his poem in this way to test and interrogate a form that was, at the time he wrote "Das Grab im Busento," increasingly becoming the primary way in which Germans experienced and received poetry. "Das Grab im Busento" plays with the opposition of transmission and concealment, passive reception and critical dissection when it comes to both the king buried underneath the river Busento and the ballad that tells his story. Passive surrender to cadence and flow, and its opposite, hermeneutic intervention, were central terms in the ballad's meteoric career in the nineteenth century more generally, and

Platen's poem is in dialogue with the ideology that would crucially inform that career.

## Memory and the Ballad Form

When Goethe posited the ballad form as the "living original egg" ("lebendiges Urei") of all the elements of poetics, he also suggested that this kind of poem "may only be incubated" ("nur bebrütet werden darf"), rather than, say, cracked open.[20] If the ballad was a more fully integrated poetic form, an archaic throwback to a time before poesy split into "three basic types," its unity rendered it at once more robust and more fragile than those "types" that descended from it. Its unity testified to its secure anchorage in the everyday life of the *Volk*, but at the same time rendered it highly vulnerable to dissection—it is poetry that tolerates only gentle "bebrüten." Nineteenth-century nationalism's preference for instinctual and unspoken community over *Gesellschaft*, which required mediation or interpretation in order to communicate, quickly claimed the ballad form for itself. One was not supposed to bring too much critical force to bear on these poems (to channel their waters, to speak with Quintilian), and there wasn't much to be gained by it if one did. There is something in the sonic and narrative organization of ballads that ensures that these poems don't require interpretation, and, indeed, they are not conducive to interpretation.

The immediacy that supposedly characterized the transmission of balladry was seen to derive in no small part from the form's tendency toward straightforward rhythm, cadence, and rhyme. When Platen insisted on the "melodische Wirkung" of the ballad, the historical dimensions of melody extended beyond the possibility of recuperating (antique) totality under modern circumstances, and to the preservation of oral forms in literary culture. Samuel Taylor Coleridge encapsulated the Romantics' sense of the ballad's relationship to orality when he wrote that "before the introduction of writing, metre . . . possessed an independent value as assisting the recollection, and consequently the preservation, of *any* series of truths or incidents."[21]

But it was not meter alone that imbued the ballad with its "value as assisting the recollection." When the first German ballads arrived on the British Isles, audiences were "electrified," according to Walter Scott, because the translations "boldly copied the imitative harmony of the German,"[22]

---

20 Johann Wolfgang von Goethe, *Goethe's poetische und prosaische Werke in zwei Bänden*, ed. Friedrich Wilhelm Riemer and Johann Peter Eckermann (Stuttgart: Cotta, 1832), 1:432.
21 Samuel Taylor Coleridge, *Biographie Literaria* (London: Rest Fenner, 1817), 69–70.
22 Walter Scott, "Essay on Imitations of the Ancient Ballad," in *Walter Scott's Poetical Works* (Edinburgh: Cadell, 1847), 554–68, here: 564.

which they similarly understood as markers of the form's origin in oral traditions. The German ballad of that era trafficked almost obsessively in "imitative harmony": galloping horses, whispering brooks, howling winds—they all were lovingly encoded into the rhyme scheme, the rhythm, and the cadence of the individual stanzas.

As Coleridge's and Scott's remarks make clear, the ballad's imitative cadence was informed not just by a particular poetics, but also by a theory of cultural memory and its transmission. Unlike meter, which in modern vernacular languages often required going against both the grain of everyday language and its onomatopoetic power, "melody" or "imitative harmony" was immediately accessible. *Pace* Quintilian no one had to reroute their flow into canals in order to understand these poems—anyone could hear Wilhelm's horse galloping through "Lenore," or the slinking of the bucket-wielding broomsticks in "Der Zauberlehrling," the click-clack of the bones in "Der Totentanz," or the whispering flow of the Busento in Platen's poem. Like the fairy tale, the *Lied*, and Wagnerian *Stabreim*, the ballad was supposed to have risen from a deep wellspring of Germanic authenticity rather than the persnickety rulebooks of classicist aesthetics. For Coleridge, Alexis, and Platen, the highly memorable flow of the ballad constituted a relic of a time when ballads were passed along orally, or were in turn used to pass along news, folklore, and history—as Alexis puts it, "history and poetry were originally one and the same; only with the growth of writing the two came apart."[23] The speaker's memorization of the poetic flow was identical with the "recollection, and consequently the preservation," of the events recounted in it. The fact that its "imitative harmonies" allowed the ballad to be easily memorized and transmitted thus amounted to an "orality effect" that convinced readers that the form had once been an organic part of everyday life, of the history of the *Volk* and of popular culture.[24]

But even as its authenticity was fetishized, the ballad's link with the *Volk* was always ambivalent. After all, the *Kunstballade* was meant to at least partially divest itself from the mnemonic aspects of the *Volksballade* (its ease on ear and mouth); it was meant, to some extent, to resist easy memorization. It is rather ironic that it was mostly *Kunstballaden* that wound up furnishing the objects of memorization for generations of nineteenth- and twentieth-century Germans. This irony finds its expression in a telling anecdote Freud relates at the outset of his *Psychopathologie des Alltagslebens* (1907). After debating with "a younger colleague" about the forgetting of poems, the colleague volunteers to have himself tested. The colleague chooses "Die Braut von Korinth" ("The Bride of Corinth"), "a poem of which was very fond,

---

23 Alexis, "Ueber Balladenpoesie," 11.
24 See Maureen McLane, "Ballads and Bards: British Romantic Orality," *Modern Philology* 98, no. 3 (2001): 423–43.

and that he thought he knew it by heart, or at least several verses of it"[25] ("welches Gedicht er sehr liebe und wenigstens strophenweise auswendig zu können glaube"[26]). The first stanza goes off without a hitch, Freud reports. But by the beginning of the second stanza the young colleague gets into trouble. Freud compares the text his friend recites with the actual text of Goethe's poem and the two differ as follows. The young colleague recites the following stanza:

> Aber wird er auch willkommen scheinen,
> Jetzt, wo jeder Tag was Neues bringt?
> Denn er ist noch Heide mit den Seinen
> Und sie sind Christen und—getauft.

The actual stanza reads:

> Aber wird er auch willkommen scheinen,
> Wenn er teuer nicht die Gunst erkauft?
> Er ist noch ein Heide mit den Seinen,
> Und sie sind schon Christen und getauft.

The trouble Freud's "young colleague" runs into while trying to recall the stanza's second line ought to be familiar to anyone who has struggled to recite a poem memorized years ago. It is clear that the colleague still remembers the original line's cadence, namely that it was a question; he also gets the overall rhythm and line length right (for instance, substituting the stress-unstress sequence of "jeder" for "teuer"), though he disrupts the poem's actual (and rather complicated) meter. Most centrally, however, although he has already successfully recited the poem's first stanza, he supplies a line that does not follow the original's rhyme scheme, one of the few uncomplicated aspects of Goethe's "Braut von Korinth." The two psychoanalysts decide that the interpolated rhyme pertains to the young colleague's preoccupation with professional rejection, which led him to repress the line in which the *Jüngling* is forced to "teuer" "die Gunst erkauf[en]." Freud's reading suggests, then, that the poem we recall always provides a double record; that it is shadowed by language that has circulated through us, but has not been retained or absorbed, that we have not wished to absorb or refused to absorb.

The most interesting meta-theoretical aspect of Freud's investigation of memorization in this passage is that he and his young colleague treat

---

25 Sigmund Freud, *The Psychopathology of Everyday Life*, trans. Anthea Bell (New York: Penguin, 2002), 19.
26 Sigmund Freud, *Zur Psychopathologie des Alltagslebens* (Berlin: Karger, 1907), 15.

Goethe's rather idiosyncratic poem as a constant rather than a variable. They are interested in the external material the young colleague supplied, rather than in the way that that supplied material ran afoul of Goethe's text, where it was inserted, and how it fits with the larger poem. In pursuing a "psychopathology" of our mental operations, Freud and his colleague are concerned with how the human unconscious can influence recall; that such recall will also depend on its object is naturally of lesser interest to them. But the object of recall is particularly remarkable in this case—the young colleague picks not just any arbitrary object for his recitation test, but a highly peculiar one: "Die Braut von Korinth" is a uniquely hard poem to memorize. Goethe's ballad is set in classical Greece, even though it utilizes its classical setting to tell a profoundly gothic tale.[27] This generic doubleness renders the poem's form similarly complex: the meter is highly varied, mixing pentameter, tetrameter, and adding lines in trochaic trimeter, giving the poem a vaguely classical cadence, and one exceedingly rare for a ballad. The rhyme scheme follows up the traditional ABAB stanza with an uncanny appendage in the shape of three more lines (ABABCCB). Goethe also tends to maintain each line as a semantic unit, such that each line introduces new information at least semi-independent of the information of the previous one.

The result is a poem starkly removed from the sing-songy catchiness of most (if by no means all) ballads of the era. More to the point: far from a parapraxis, the young colleague's misremembering is actually an entirely appropriate way of engaging with Goethe's poem. We are not meant to memorize "Die Braut von Korinth"—doing so does not bring out something intrinsic in the ballad, but rather ignores resistances that are very much the poem's own. Memorizing ballads was a prime form of interacting with this part of the canon (to the point that Freud's colleague naturally turns to a ballad to test his memory rather than, say, to a soliloquy), but the canon was not always or not entirely amenable to this kind of appropriation. The possibility of memorization was both anchored deep in the ideology of the ballad form, but insofar as the *Kunstballade* sought to divest itself from popular sources it also had to take a more nuanced position vis-à-vis the possibility of memorization.

As a poet anxious to mediate classical meter and a Romantic emphasis on the nation, Platen was uniquely aware of this tension at the heart of the *Kunstballade*. In an early text he heaped scorn on the "coiffed singers of the Fatherland" ("frisierte Vaterlandssänger") for their pretensions to a new orality. "Those ancient bards of Teutonia, whom you seek to emulate, sang about the battles and victories of their heroes,"[28] but uncritically resurrecting

---

27 John R. Williams, *The Life of Goethe* (London: Blackwell, 1998), 107

28 Platen, *Platens sämtliche Werke*, 11:118: "Jene alten Barden Teutonias, denen ihr nachstreben wollt, besangen die Schlachten und Siege ihrer Helden."

their craft resulted only in ridiculousness—the moderns may still produce ballads, "but none of them are 'Die Braut von Korinth'."[29] "Das Grab im Busento," by contrast, seeks to synthesize the metric sophistication of "Braut von Korinth" with the mnemonic ease of the "old bards" that others attempted to emulate so poorly. The poem employs a highly regular trochaic tetrameter, a classical meter that Platen imported into German with a skill unmatched by others. At the same time, the poem relies heavily on Scott's "imitative harmony," and it is, unlike "Die Braut von Korinth," an exceedingly easy poem to memorize. It thus seeks to harmonize those elements in the ballad form that solicit memorization and those that frustrate it. And the poem's ending at once celebrates the memorializing function of the ballad and its potential for stymieing such memorialization.

Platen was well versed in the subject: that the "wogen" of his meters made his poems easy fodder for memorization was something that Platen fully realized, but he was also himself passionately devoted to appropriating the poetry of others in this way. He resolves in his diaries in 1818 to "learn by heart a few poetic pieces in each language that I understand, and to repeat them frequently"—starting with Hamlet's famous soliloquy.[30] Indeed, this is how he seems to have internalized Hafis's poetry, especially the Ghazals.[31] If "Das Grab im Busento" is extremely solicitous of the powers of human memory, that solicitousness was something the poet very much intended. Indeed, it appears that he was acutely aware of memorization's ideological charge. Platen's poem invites its reader to let the waves carry him, and insists that letting oneself be carried means abnegating a certain kind of understanding.

Memorization became if anything a more dominant a way of appropriating the canon in the decades after Platen's death. The memorization of poetry attained particular importance in the pedagogy of the German Empire, and when it came to poetry the stock repertoire was actually quite limited.[32] The Domgymnasium in Naumburg (Saale), for instance, whose headmaster Prof. Dr. Albracht provided parents with an exhaustive *Übersicht über die absolvierten Pensen* for Easter 1893, gives us a glimpse of the poems the *Gymnasiasten* of the *fin-de-siècle* were expected to have under their belt. "The following pieces were learned by heart" ("Auswendig gelernt sind"[33]), Albracht begins, and

---

29 Ibid.: "aber es ist keine Braut von Korinth."

30 August von Platen, *Die Tagebücher des Grafen August von Platen*, ed. Georg Laubmann and Ludwig von Scheffler, 2 vols. (Stuttgart: Cotta, 1900), 2:130: "in jeder Sprache, die ich verstehe, zwei poetische Stücke auswendig zu lernen und sie stets zu repetieren."

31 Platen, *Die Tagebücher des Grafen August von Platen*, 2:461.

32 Martina Lüke, *Zwischen Tradition und Aufbruch: Deutschunterricht und Lesebuch im Deutschen Kaiserreich* (Frankfurt: Peter Lang, 2007), 364.

33 Heinrich Sieling, ed., *Jahresbericht Domgymnasium zu Naumburg a. S.* (Naumburg: Heinrich Sieling, 1893).

lists about twenty poems—only one of them, Friedrich Schiller's *Siegesfest*, is not a ballad (*Jahresbericht*).

If teachers, headmasters, and imperial functionaries had a clear preference for ballads, they further favored either ballads that unfolded in a classical setting (Schiller's "Kraniche des Ibykus" and "Die Bürgschaft") or those that retold historical events. Psychological ballads (like those of Annette von Droste-Hülshoff), ballads in fairy tale settings, or gothic ballads were entirely missing—and while Freud's young colleague dutifully turns to Goethe when he decides to test his memorizing mettle, the German Empire's charges were primarily treated to Schiller ballads, while those of his famous friend were almost entirely absent.

What did Albracht and his teachers hope to gain through this memorization? The terms in which nineteenth-century pedagogy tended to understand memorization mirror those that "Das Grab im Busento" deploys with respect to its "main character" Alarich and his memory. Prime among these is a supposition that informs childhood education to this very day: memory was passive, while understanding was active, and rote memorization did nothing to aid understanding, as children were drilled to repeat sequences of German, Latin, Greek, and chemical or binomial formulae with little or no insight as to what they signified. The defenders of memorization seem to have reasoned similarly, but insisted that in some cases understanding a poem was simply not as important as knowing it by heart. They attributed value to the mere *Überlieferung* of information, absent any serious hermeneutic intent. Truly grasping *Überlieferungen* did not require trying to understand them, but rather surrendering to the meanings they supposedly carried independent of critical intervention.

This exact case was made by the conservative pedagogue Karl Georg von Raumer (1783–1865) in the 1840s; the way he made it also points to the provenance of this manner of legitimating memorization, namely the liturgical role of memorization and knowing by heart. If we shouldn't make children memorize something that they hadn't fully grasped before, Raumer argued:

> In that case [we] should neither make them learn the small Lutheran catechism nor Bible verses and religious songs by heart. After all they deal with secrets of the faith, which the intellect of even the longest human life will not plumb to their full depths. . . . It is after all a gracious and wise institution of our dear Lord, that He endowed us with a mental storeroom, in which we may stow away seeds for the future.[34]

---

34 Karl Georg von Raumer, *Geschichte der Pädagogik* (Stuttgart: Liesching, 1847), 34.

Understanding might one day follow from memorization, but it did not have to precede memorization. Memorization was in fact an act of humility, of safe-keeping things that one was not as of yet ready to fully submit to the intellect.

Other conservative education scholars even suggested that understanding was actually detrimental to memorization, and that what we would today call a "close reading" of a poem should be avoided, if students were to successfully commit a poem to memory. In his book on the craft of teaching, Albrecht Goerth, headmaster of the higher and middle girls' school in Insterburg, East Prussia, recommends having children memorize poems "in a goodly selection, and fairly large number," but suggests "not discussing the content at all."[35]

To some extent this came with the territory: often enough young people were simply given the assignment to memorize "a poem" from a particular selection and many such poems likely went undiscussed in the classroom. Insofar as discussing the poetry before recitation was necessary at all, it should be limited only to "explications of words and facts, including metaphors," and leave aside "all unnecessary pondering [*Klügeln*], namely any kind of moral application."[36] The fact that the headmaster would consign the "moral application" to "unnecessary pondering" speaks to the single-mindedness with which memorization was pursued in pedagogy during the turn of the century—but also to the related fact that ballads were supposed to be immediately comprehensible, thereby accommodating themselves to this sort of use. This sort of rationale, as much as a young nation's obsession with imagining its own history, seems to have stood behind the preference given to historical ballads often dealing with heroic individuals—they were widely regarded as unambiguous, straightforward narratives and clear moral lessons, thus requiring no *Klügeln* before thirty-five tenth-graders were set loose on them.

While this manner of proceeding would likely provoke apoplexy in American readers reared on generations of close reading in its various historic guises, Goerth's understanding of these poems to some extent followed their self-understanding as outlined above. In the specific case of "Das Grab im Busento," Karl Storck's late nineteenth-century *Deutsche Literaturgeschichte* described the poem's formal construction as "simpler and therefore also more folk-like."[37] It was a ballad's proximity to oral *Volkstum* (the heredity of the people) that made it intuitively comprehensible and easy to remember. After

---

35 Albrecht Goerth, *Die Lehrkunst: Ein Führer für Lehrer und Lehrerinnen, welche sich in ihrem Beruf zur Meisterschaft ausbilden wollen* (Leipzig: Klinkhardt, 1886), 78.

36 Goerth, *Die Lehrkunst*, 78.

37 Karl Storck, *Deutsche Literaturgeschichte* (Stuttgart: Muth, 1903), 358.

all, as we have seen, the popular songs and poems from which most nineteenth century critics thought the ballad descended, were seen as less aesthetic products in their own right than vehicles of transmission for news, history, and moral lessons. Just as a listener on a medieval marketplace, or around a highland hearth, was supposed to glean the popular ballad's meaning without intervention on the bard's part, so teacher Goerth provided his charges with a treasure trove of oral history, which they could commit to memory and meditate on at their own leisure. Platen similarly linked memorization and authentic German culture: "Come, boys, shake the dust of the classroom, and instead of your Roman vocabulary learn by heart the poem of your forefathers!" Repeating the "Gedicht eurer Väter" inside (Platen was referring specifically to the *Nibelungenlied*) meant rehearing what the ancient Germans had heard around the campfire, it meant returning Germanic orality to the modern age: "We want to listen to those noble deeds to which the ears of our forefathers thrilled!"[38]

The ease with which the ballad could circulate and be memorized constituted, for Platen as for Goerth, a return to oral tradition. Children didn't need to know much about the time in which the ballad was set, or about the form's historic or generic antecedents—all they needed to do was follow the ballad's mellifluous cadences, which would lead them to the origins of their nation and *Volk*. Ballads were a form that had sprung spontaneously from the *Volk*, and could be just as spontaneously grasped. Because its undulating cadence made for easy memorization on a practical level, and suggested that it spoke of and from the very origins of German nationhood and literature on an ideological level, "Das Grab im Busento" became a veritable mainstay in the era's classrooms. When Goerth singles out Platen's poem as particularly well suited for memorization, he picks up both on its poetic simplicity and on the fact that it functions well without previous introduction: "It is necessary only to explain, or maybe to repeat, who Alarich was, how he came with his army of Goths to Cosenza in southern Italy."[39] Goerth's opinion that Platen's ballad required little explanation seems to rest on more than just the poem's straightforward construction and plot, and ultimately on its ease on voice and memory.

While Goerth's pedagogical assessment postdates Platen's poem by nearly a century, Platen was aware of the fact that the ideology of memorization distinguished between repetition and understanding, and that it tended to favor simple revocalization over the attempt to approach national poetry through *Klügeln*. This was a fact the poet seems to have confronted with some ambivalence: again and again, he noted in his diaries when he met someone who

38 Platen, *Platens sämtliche Werke*, 11:155.
39 Goerth, *Die Lehrkunst*, 78

had memorized several or even many of his poems, sometimes as a sign that that someone appreciated his genius, sometimes with a tinge of annoyance. In 1834 his friend Fugger introduced the poet to a general's wife in Munich, "a woman, who seems to know all my poems by heart and who spends all her time with them. Of my other works she seemed to take no notice."[40] Here, then, the poet treats memorization as a replacement for "real" engagement with the poet's work—in German he characterizes the time she spends with his works a mode "occupying" herself ("Beschäftigung"), rote and devoid of comprehension. There are clear gendered valences to Platen's dismissal—the general's wife memorizes his poems because she has nothing better to do. There is another mode of comprehension he would have preferred—less repetitive, more incisive, more penetrative, more masculine. Of course, he would have been aware that that with which she "occupied" herself, he had offered for exactly this sort of treatment. And yet it was somehow not right, not authentic. "Das Grab im Busento" turns the ballad's attempt at a restitution of oral tradition into its central plot point. But that plot suggests something else as well: the river carries the song of Alarich, but it also hides the physical Alarich beneath its waves.

## Memory and Concealment

For the nineteenth-century readers of "Das Grab im Busento" there seems to have been nothing hidden underneath the poem's implacable phonetic stream, but when Friedrich Gundolf in 1920 lauded Platen's "euphony and choice of words" ("Wohllaut und Wortwahl"),[41] he was likely aware that the very placidity of the waters masked hidden compartments in the depths. Gundolf was a member of the quasi-religious group gathered around the poet Stefan George (1868–1933). The members of George's "Circle" put great stock in the idea that poetry had an esoteric and an exoteric side, that great poetry, in other words, had secrets to keep. In the case of von Platen, this was almost certainly right: The story of "Das Grab im Busento" tells us as much, staging a scene of disappearance, erasing even the traces of that scene, and then working to get the reader to doubt whether there ever really was such a scene: the Goths bury their leader and reroute the river over his grave to preserve his memory and his legend from the meddlesome "Romans" who might exhume and desecrate him. The "Busento's billow" invoked at the poem's close is thus as much about the passing-on of memory as it is about its dispersal. What is more, the ballad's plot undercuts the idea that one could

---

40 Platen, *Die Tagebücher des Grafen August von Platen*, 2:955.
41 Friedrich Gundolf, *George* (Darmstadt: Wissenschaftliche Buchgesellschaft, 1968), 78.

fully entrust oneself to the ballad's flow in a way that would bypass the need for interpretation. The poem's final line may exhort its reader to tarry with the flow of the waves, to follow them out to sea, but the ballad's plot tells us that this is to some extent a piece of misdirection from the beautiful king in shining armor buried beneath its flow.

Platen's prosodic choice, a trochaic tetrameter, is both essential to that misdirection, and represents a tipping of the poet's hand. As indicated above, a trochaic tetrameter is a rather counterintuitive meter for a ballad, precisely because its regularity can be inanimate and unsettling. Classical trochaic tetrameter, unlike its German form, which since Gottsched had been a heroic meter, was a comedic one instead. The Greeks had turned to this meter for humor, because they regarded its uniform flow as slightly ridiculous. It was also usually a choral meter, and not surprisingly did not seem to lend itself to one central fantasy subtending much balladry, that of a lone skaldic bard singing to a rapt audience. While most of the great ballads of the nineteenth century provided the basis for any number of musical settings for one singer, most of the song settings of Platen's poem were not for single voice, but choral arrangements, most prominent among them two settings for men's chorus by Friedrich von Gernsheim (1839–1916) and Johann Baptist Zerlett (1859–1935).

For Platen, the trochaic tetrameter's extreme evenness seems to ally the implacable churning of the poetic rhythm with the flow of the water itself. This equation is both a matter of Scott's "imitative harmony" and something more metaphysical. The poem's final image, of the river's waves carrying the sound of the Gothic song, suggests that the king's memory survives not in the shape of a statue, a marked grave, or a body, but rather in rippling and dissipating waves. The poem is just as depersonalized and disembodied as the young king's memory. Similarly, the traditionally choral implications of trochaic tetrameter serve to disperse and render less concrete the vocality of the poem. The "song" the poem allies itself with is thus explicitly placed on the side of the concealing flow; the poem's single concrete "object," the king's dead body, is successfully hidden by the end. The ballad's meter is both distractingly perfect and emphatically inanimate; it, too, tells the story of a concealment and dispersal—there once was a singular subjectivity, an individual body here, but it has been hidden and dissolved.

Why would Platen's poem both perform and tell the story of this misdirection? Platen wrote "Das Grab im Busento" in Erlangen, "une petite ville assez pitoyable" ("a small, rather pitiful town") where he had moved from Würzburg in October 1819 and where he found himself "sans amis, sans aucune connaissance, tout-à-fait abandonné" ("without friends, without any acquaintances, totally abandoned"[42]). The reason for his relocation was a compromising love letter he had sent to a fellow student at Würzburg, Eduard

---

42 Platen, *Die Tagebücher des Grafen August von Platen*, 2:329.

Schmidtlein. The object of his affections had recoiled from Platen's "detestable missive" ("schimpfliche Schreiben"), and had added "that all would have to react this way, who read this overflow of disgusting depravity."[43] This phrase seems to have made Platen fear that Schmidtlein might make the letter public. His "exile" in Erlangen was thus a move to conceal his homosexuality, to cover, protect, and keep private his personal life. Not long after Platen's arrival in Erlangen another budding relationship (with Hermann Freiherr von Rotenhan) foundered on similar shoals, an experience that led to Platen's writing of "Das Grab im Busento." The "overflow" ("Ausfluß") of his forbidden longing for Schmidtlein, which he had unwisely let slip from his control, had brought him to this place; the famous poem he would write here was all about the poet controlling the flow of prosody, of information.

Platen's first journal entry from Ansbach on March 28, 1819, recounts the following episode: the moment he arrived in Ansbach, Platen sent a letter to Schmidtlein (whom he calls "Adrast" in his diaries[44]), justifying himself and bitterly protesting Schmidtlein's treatment of him. Rather certain that the other man would refuse to accept the letter, or read it if he did, Platen memorized the content of his letter and reproduced it in full in his diary. Even if Schmidtlein were to read it, Platen requested that he make the missive disappear: "I have a right to request that you burn the letter, which you may not even deign to answer, upon reading it."[45] Memorization thus becomes the only trace of a text that has to disappear; only the passivity of memory can safeguard the scandal that, were it to remain a physical letter, might yet be exposed to the cruel light of analysis. Schmidtlein seems to have obliged, and until Platen's diaries were published in the early twentieth century, the words of the letter were lost to history. Safekeeping and memory, intrusion and interpretive disturbance—these were the overriding themes of "Das Grab im Busento"; and for the Platen of early 1820, they seem to have had to do with matters of privacy and sexuality.

Few recent analyses of the poem have proceeded without remarking on the irony that its reception diverged so thoroughly from the situation that gave rise to it. As Germany's national and imperial project consolidated in the course of the nineteenth century, Platen's cry of lament was increasingly understood as a historical ballad extolling Germanic *Kameradschaft* and self-sacrifice against the pettiness of the "Romans" of the world. In this transformed understanding the poem became one among many novels, poems, and quasi-scholarly treatises that sought to understand Germany's

---

43 Cited in Heinrich Detering, *Das offene Geheimnis: Zur literarischen Produktivität eines Tabus von Winckelmann bis zu Thomas Mann* (Göttingen: Wallstein, 1994), 101.

44 see Christian Mücke, *"Bleibe ich doch wunderbar unglücklich": Platens Aufenthalt in Würzburg 1818–1819 und seine Liebe zu "Adrast"* (Würzburg: Osthoff, 1993).

45 Platen, *Die Tagebücher des Grafen August von Platen*, 2:238.

new national role and mission by telling stories of noble Germanic tribesmen and the decadent Romans they overran.

If the stock repertoire of ballads usually memorized consisted of long history-poems describing historical, preferably medieval scenes, heavy on pomp and action and light on psychology, it is perhaps not surprising that the origin of "Das Grab im Busento" as a poem of love and loss came to slide out of view in such company. Often the *Lehrpläne* of the Second Empire place the poem not in the German classroom, but rather in history lessons, almost as a primary document of ancient Germanic tribal customs and burial practices. While the poem's martial reinterpretation became canonic, Platen's homosexuality, spelled out for all to read in Heinrich Heine's infamous attacks on the poet, was universally ignored in the *Kaiserreich* and after. Even after Platen's diaries and letters were published in the early 1900s and 1910s, at which point the biographical basis for many of the famous historical poems should have been evident, Platen scholarship danced around the issue for another half-century. (One exception may have been the aforementioned George-circle, which proved unusually attuned to homoerotic subtexts, being centered around barely concealed homosexuality as a constituting secret itself.)

By that point, however, there emerged the opposite tendency: to understand Platen almost entirely in light of the highly revealing letters and diaries, and the poems as almost direct abreactions of the poet's inner torment as evidenced in those letters and diaries. They saw Platen as essentially at the mercy of homoerotic impulses, which he sought to (unsuccessfully) repress or sublimate in his poetry. Hubert Fichte, in a seminal essay on Platen, wrote that the poet "not only had to struggle with the transfiguration of nature into art, but with the transfiguration of disdained nature."[46] But at least in the case of "Das Grab im Busento," Platen disturbs not with involuntary insights into the failed sublimation of "disdained" desire, but rather with an almost teasing alteration between disclosure and concealment that Heinrich Detering characterized as "the open secret."[47] In Platen's case this "open secret" is perhaps more open than in others: the poem's historic garb is both chosen carefully enough to license the decades of misreading the poem received, and pulled away sufficiently to give the reader (or memorizing student) a glimpse into an elusive and fragile nugget buried under the poem's sparkling, efficient flow.

Paradigmatically, Peter Bumm, Platen's most recent biographer, calls the reception of "Das Grab im Busento" a "Mißverständnis": "a lover's complaint

---

46 Hubert Fichte, *"Deiner Umarmungen süße Sehnsucht": Die Geschichte der Empfindungen am Beispiel der französischen Schriften des Grafen August von Platen-Hallermünde* (Tübingen: Rive Gauche, 1985), 36.

47 See Detering, *Das offene Geheimnis*, 79.

in historic disguise appeared to the reading public a poetic contribution to German nationalism."[48] While Bumm is certainly right that the nationalistic reading that made "Das Grab im Busento" a perennial favorite of the *Lesebücher* of the German Empire requires exquisite critical blinders, turning "Grab" into a historical ballad is not exactly a misunderstanding. This is not just a poem that is "in historic disguise," as Bumm would have it, it is also a poem about history, about the transmission of knowledge and remembrance—hardly something that is true for most love poems. And yet "Das Grab im Busento" is precisely that, a history poem about desire and a love poem about historical memory. Given this unusual mixture, cast in a form as explicitly popular as the ballad, it is little wonder that "Das Grab im Busento" was easily and frequently misinterpreted. By embedding and encoding the personal within the historical, and then turning encoding and embedding into historical indices, Platen both seduces the reader into misinterpretation and then reminds him of the fact that he is missing something.

What Bumm and others discount is that the poem's strange double career has its origin in the text itself and is in many ways solicited by it: the way in which "Das Grab im Busento" dissolves its one recognizable object into an ever more ethereal ensemble can be read (à la Bumm) as a chillingly lonely and lifeless lament for that lost body, or one can read it as the joyous sacrifice of the individual body to the greater group, as the dead Alarich is dispersed into the "Gothenheer" and its patriotic songs. At the heart of the poem's disappearing act lies a reversible figure, and those who drafted "Das Grab im Busento" into a project of German chauvinism emphasized (by and large correctly) the same aspects of the poem that most forcefully raise the issue of homoeroticism.

Conversely, the dominant nineteenth-century reading, in which the king's body is simply dispersed into the community of mourners, could not readily account for the mournful specificity with which the poem endows Alarich. The insistence that Alarich died "allzufrüh" ("Ah! too soon"), that he was "fern der Heimat" ("from home so far"), and that he still had his "Jugendlocken" ("youthful ringlets' flaxen wave"), makes it clear that Alarich matters as more than just a token of a community. There is an individual story, and a profoundly alienated one at that, being buried here by a faceless mob, and the "Heldenehren" of which that mob sings give no account of this part of the individual.

Indeed, while the poem traffics in such seemingly universal Romantic shibboleths as yearning, youth, and exile, Platen's use of these tropes is comparatively specific—this dead boy's youth, his exile, and his yearning for

---

[48] Peter Bumm, *August Graf von Platen: Eine Biographie* (Paderborn: Schöningh, 1990), 232.

Rome do not represent features of human existence as such, but they are unique to this individual. In particular, Platen's poem deploys homelessness differently than many Romantics who tended to "transcendentalize" such homelessness. Gundolf claimed that Platen was incapable of "true homesickness"[49] for the world of antiquity (as opposed to Goethe and Hölderlin), but Platen's yearning and exile are not signs of generalized nostalgia for an antique plenitude; they instead feed on a quite actual threat of exile and of public scandal. Platen felt "homesick" because of the episodes with Schmidtlein and Rotenhan, not on account of metaphysics. From the very beginning, Platen connected his "homelessness" to his homosexuality, well before he was effectively exiled on account of it.

In a sonnet entitled "Es sehnt sich ewig dieser Geist ins Weite" (1826), the poet writes: "Doch wer aus voller Seele haßt das Schlechte, / Auch aus der Heimat wird es ihn verjagen, / Wenn dort verehrt es wird vom Volk der Knechte" ("Whosoever from the depth of his soul hates the mean / From his homeland it will drive him far / If there the mean is venerated by a tribe of servants").[50] In Platen's work, homelessness is almost invariably connected to *Vertreibung*, to being chased out by a "Volk der Knechte" or the "schnöde" Romans of "Das Grab im Busento." Of course, the historic Alarich was chased nowhere, he died in the pursuit of conquest, but Platen's insistence that he died "allzufrüh und fern der Heimat" (though the historic Visigoth king was well near forty by the time he died in Cosenza) seems to integrate him into this narrative of expulsion from the *Heimat* by the "tribe [*Volk*] of servants." It is the Romans with their "schnöde Habsucht" ("lucre-lusting") who drive the Visigoths to bury their leader under the river.

The infamous outing by Heinrich Heine, the so-called Platen-Affäre that precipitated the poet's semi-voluntary exile from Germany and ultimately delivered him to the same fate that befell Alarich, was still a few years in the future at the time Platen wrote "Das Grab am Busento." Nevertheless, fear of this kind of publicity clearly subtends the poem and its desire to protect a beautiful tragic corpse from the viciousness of a nattering populace. If the poem does bear the traces of such fear, however, they are owed to a very canny game on his part with insight and concealment. By insisting on questions of *Heimat* and by making Alarich into a boy king of sorts, Platen actively invites the reader to make the connection both to homoeroticism and to the fate its revelation might (and ultimately would) force upon the poet himself.

But while male beauty and its tragic fate are very much on the surface of the poem, it actually tells the story of their submersion. The beautiful boy and his exile are, by the poem's end, at the bottom of the Busento, as the

---

49 Gundolf, *George*, 39.
50 Platen, *Werke in Zwei Bänden*, 1:399.

king's loyal servants express their hope that the grave may be "unversehrt." As noted before, the poem mixes its preoccupation with remembrance with terror about the possible violation of the deceased's memory. The story told in "Das Grab im Busento" is primarily one of concealment—not of remembrance but of the disabling of remembrance. Alarich's men honor his memory not by erecting a memorial, but rather seek to ensure that no reminder exists, safe the one they know to be hidden beneath the waves. Not only do they seek to make Alarich unavailable to memorialization, they seek to prevent his unavailability from being noticed. Alarich is not only handed over to forgetting, his forgetting is in turn forgotten. Not for nothing does their burial method (placing the dead king on his horse and setting both into a hole in the ground) resemble nothing so much as an equestrian statue. Indeed, it seems surprising that the German *Kaiserreich*, with its well-documented and enduring predilection for equestrian statues, did not notice the telling strangeness of building someone a statue underwater.

Another one of Platen's poems, written in February 1820, and thus immediately after "Das Grab im Busento," plays the same game of concealment in plain sight.[51] Platen begins it by insisting that the poem's addressee (i.e., Rotenhan) "never seek to know my secret," while drawing all the more attention to the existence of such a secret:

| | |
|---|---|
| Erforsche mein Geheimnis nie, | Never seek to know my secret, |
| Du darfst es nicht ergründen, | You must not get to its bottom, |
| Es sagte dir's die Sympathie, | This much sympathy would tell you, |
| Wenn wir uns ganz verstünden.[52] | If we fully understood each other. |

In fact, Platen bases this poem around a very similar dynamic as "Das Grab im Busento": true understanding (of a person, in this case) requires a lack of knowledge. Digging for the "secret" is a sign not just of a lack of sympathy, but a lack of understanding. Sympathy and understanding are matters of concealment, of letting sleeping dogs lie; it is clearly the same desire for sympathetic opacity that lies behind the Visigoths' burial of their beloved leader. But where "Erforsche mein Geheimnis nie" does not specify the medium of this sympathy-inspired opacity, "Das Grab im Busento" makes that medium its main topic—the mellifluous whisper of the river itself.

If the Goths' diversion of the flow is something of a poetic act, it is one performed to prevent what Quintilian characterized as the basic hermeneutic

---

51 Platen, *Die Tagebücher des Grafen August von Platen*, 2:366.
52 Platen, *Platens sämtliche Werke*, 2:74.

act: channeling and digging. After all, the Goths pursue this forgetting of forgetting in order to ward off diggers: "Keines Römers schnöde Habsucht soll dir je das Grab versehren" ("Ne'er shall foot of lucre-lusting Roman desecrate thy grave"). The Romans threaten to violate Albarich's grave trying to lay hold of that body and his "stolze Habe"; their "Habsucht" is hermeneutic insofar as it seeks to concretize (into a particular body and its physical accoutrements) a king the poem is seeking to render ethereal. The legend cancels out the physical body and its physical location. Alarich needs to be forgotten lest diggers know where to start shoveling. That the *Römer* would do what the Goths did—dig another riverbed, reroute the flow, dig down in the "the waveless hollow" ("wogenleeren Höhlung")—means that the Goths fear not some unprecedented act on the part of the Romans, but rather the repetition of their own actions. The poem tells us of an act of diverting and channeling language but tells us that that act must not be repeated.

"Das Grab im Busento" thus suggests that this flow, which conceals the beloved body and which is so central to the poem's ethics, is simply the flow of the lyric itself; the poem's way of making opaque is precisely the beautiful *flumen orationis* itself. "Erforsche mein Geheimnis nie" hints at something similar at its resolution:

| | |
|---|---|
| Was um mich ist, errät mich nicht, | What is around me does not guess me, |
| Und drängt und drückt mich nieder; | And presses and pushes me down; |
| Doch, such ich Trost mir im Gedicht, | But I in the poem my solace seek, |
| Dann find ich ganz mich wieder![53] | Where I can find myself whole again! |

Here, then, the poem simply offers surcease from the coldness and the lack of understanding of the outside world (the "Volk der Knechte"); it is neither a way of communicating the self, nor is it a way of concealing it. "Das Grab im Busento," on the other hand, makes the latter link rather clearly: the flow of poetry, like the flow of water, is a means of enforcing an ethical engagement with a lost object, that is to say one based not on probing or digging, but on a sympathy built on not fully penetrating it.

The effort of channeling and directing the flow of poetic language is thus not a matter of expressing biography, personality, subjectivity, or even just voice, but rather of concealing all of them as much as possible. The "avarice" ("Habsucht") to be thwarted is nothing other than the attempt to exhume biographical or embodied concreteness from its grave beneath the melodic flow of balladic form. "Sympathie," on the terms of the contemporaneous "Erforsche mein Geheimnis nie," means to submit to, or to remain in the

---

[53] Ibid., 2:74.

thrall of, the pellucid poetic *flumen*, and not to channel or reroute its waters. If "Das Grab im Busento" stages the dissolution of the solid object of mourning into a potentially infinite poetic flow of mourning song, then the reader is exhorted to forget understanding and to stop probing "underneath" the concreteness of the sonic flow—to memorize in Goerth's sense. We are exhorted, on ethical rather than pragmatic grounds, to read the poem without probing, to memorize its surface flow rather than diverting the flow for purposes of digging. In opposition to Virgil's image of the poem's floodgates having to be closed, lest it pour endlessly, Platen's poem ends with a call for precisely such endless proliferation.

Here, then, the mnemonics of the ballad form are seemingly turned on their head: rather than aiding memorization and *thus* memory (as in the idea of a *Moritat* or *Volksballade* passed from fairground to marketplace and from town to town), "Das Grab im Busento" seduces its reader into memorization in order to preserve its watery grave *from*, rather than *for* memory. This may well be what Freud's discussion of Goethe's "Braut von Korinth" points toward: in the *Kunstballade*, memorization stands in an almost antagonistic relationship to the poem, it goes against the grain of the poem. Only the failure of memorization reveals the poetic flow's unconscious. That flow, in Platen's case, is alluring and seductive, but it also manages to be unsettling. Platen, like Goethe, chooses a meter that does not exhaust itself in onomatopoeia, but rather draws attention to its artifice—what Gundolf called Platen's false "Heimweh."

Gundolf of course assumes that Platen imitates antique form because he seeks to get back in touch with a kind of plenitude associated with antiquity. But as we have seen, Platen's poem actually relies on a disconnect between modernity and antiquity: it resurrects the antique *flumen orationis* without regard for the fact that its preconditions are lacking in modernity. This disconnect registers in the rhythm of the poem, which manages to at once be comfortingly flawless and to arouse suspicion by dint of its flawlessness. According to the ideology of the German ballad in the early nineteenth century, the ballad reunited the different lyric arts into the *Urei* of poetry. "Das Grab im Busento" by contrast showcases the fact that it is partial, that the very perfection of its trochaic flow hides a lack, another dimension that the poem itself has removed beyond recovery, and that nevertheless beckons from beneath the waves of discourse. In this way the generations of memorizing *Gymnasiasten* did not "misunderstand" the poem, they followed its dynamics and respected the fact that, with Alarich lost, all we have are the waves of the Busento.

5 | The Ballad and the Family

A child being put to bed is a defining fantasy of the nineteenth century. Granted, parents put their children to bed before it, sang them songs, or told them stories. But it was the nineteenth century that obsessively analyzed and sought to structure that quotidian transaction, that both provided it material aplenty and sought to give it a form—from the Brothers Grimm's *Hausmärchen* to Marcel Proust's bedtime vigils, from the dreams Novalis gives to his Heinrich von Ofterdingen to the ones Sigmund Freud analyzes for the Wolf-Man. And, as Maria Tatar has argued, the question of what exactly is transacted and transmitted in this scene—whether, for instance, a child is meant to be put to sleep or kept awake by the physical object of the book or the story it contained—was itself deeply ambiguous, which pointed to the unsettled questions of whether what was transmitted in this manner was conscious or unconscious.[1] Some of the fascination stemmed from a renewed interest in the etiology of the individual psyche, and from the realization of how much of it could be located in early childhood. It was also bound up with a renewed emphasis on affection in childrearing. As M. O. Grenby has noted, after the "business of the day" "the childhood's bedtime was the ideal moment for the performance of parental duty."[2] But on another level, it reflected the fact that intergenerational transmission had lost some of the imperturbable self-evidence it may have once possessed. In the oedipal age, in an age that understood itself as making a "modern" break with the past, the question of how lessons, stories, and spirit moved from generation to

---

1 See Maria Tatar, *Enchanted Hunters: The Power of Stories in Childhood* (New York: W. W. Norton, 2009).

2 M. O. Grenby, *The Child Reader, 1700–1840* (Cambridge: Cambridge University Press, 2011), 207.

generation felicitously, and what might disrupt their movement, became the source of immense anxiety.[3] By the mid-nineteenth century, the ballad became wrapped up in this anxiety.

The ballad form was, in some ways, a technology of transmission. Herder had called it "the eternal song of inheritance"[4] of the common folk: it was eternal, but driven by passions that could be reactivated anew again and again with each generation, in each family unit. Yes, you transmitted it as a people, but not necessarily in public; around a fire in a faraway farmhouse, just you and your children might do the bidding of this "eternal song" of the "spirit" of the people. As Lutz Röhrich has pointed out, many classic folk ballads deal with irruptions of incomprehensible, cosmic forces (evil spirits, divine retribution, the vagaries of fate and fortune), but dramatize these conflicts by staging them as intrafamilial disagreements, conflicts, or dramas.[5] The art ballad frequently follows this convention: Goethe's "Der Erlkönig" manages to telescope questions of natural and supernatural world, of free will and fate, into an intergenerational epistemic disagreement between father and son, which takes up the bulk of the poem's drama. A poem like "Der Erlkönig" operates, both on a plot level and as form, by placing the ineffable into an emphatically domesticated context. Ballads frequently concretized the obscure, mystic atmosphere of the supernatural occurrence into a more recognizably human, and frequently familial, squabble—and thereby made it portable, tellable, and relevant to people among whom it was repeated. This was probably why Herder also thought it was an "ancestral" or "hereditary" song: something that is with a people, though not as a cold tradition growing more distant with each generation but rather something that belongs to each generation anew.

And it was something that was sounded out by each generation anew, that was vocalized by one generation for the next. In the nineteenth century, the matrix of intergenerationality always jostled against another one, that of gender. There were no "parents" who could or would recite poems or nursery rhymes to their "children," there were mothers and fathers reciting for their daughters and sons. Nursing and caring were how gender roles were instantiated for the parental generation and were inscribed in the filial generation.[6] Stories like Heinrich Hoffmann's immensely influential

---

3 Adrian Daub, *The Dynastic Imagination: Family and Modernity in Nineteenth Century Germany* (Chicago: University of Chicago Press, 2021).

4 Herder, *Von deutscher Art und Kunst*, 258: "der ewige Erb- und Lustgesang des Volks."

5 Lutz Röhrich, *Gesammelte Schriften zur Volkslied- und Volksballadenforschung* (Münster: Waxmann, 2002), 85.

6 See, for instance, Tamara S. Wagner's brilliant analysis of Anne Brontë's description (and critique) of how child-rearing served to gender (in this case single) parents and children in *The Tenant of Wildfell Hall*: Tamara S. Wagner, *Infancy, Infant Care, and Nineteenth-Century Popular Culture* (Oxford: Oxford University Press, 2020), 172.

*Struwwelpeter* (first published in 1844, but made iconic via the illustrated edition of 1845) introduced the reader to a group of children typifying the excesses of childhood. Individual poems are about "bad Friederich" who tortures small animals, little Konrad who sucks his thumb, "Suppen-Kaspar" who refuses food. "Zappel-Philipp" won't sit still. The one girl among them is Pauline, who plays with matches when she has been told by her father not to, and burns to a crisp. But the children are almost all boys and the excesses are all emphatically masculinized. Hoffmann's attempt to teach young people was really an attempt to think through the education of young boys—in fact, he explicitly wrote the book as a father for his son.[7]

When poetry drew on the familial scene, it sometimes reconfirmed this kind of gender construction. But just as frequently it problematized it. Peter Cornelius (1824–1874) considered himself a "poet-composer" and composed almost exclusively for voice.[8] In his setting of Annette von Droste-Hülshoff's "Das Kind" from 1862, he registers and amplifies an ambivalence vis-à-vis gendered intergenerational transmission. Droste-Hülshoff's poem may speak of a generic "child" in its title, but in the text itself, the poem makes explicit that it is about a boy:

| | |
|---|---|
| Wär' ich ein Kind, ein Knäblein klein, | Were I a child, a tender boy, |
| Ein armes, schwaches, geliebtes, | Poor, weak, and doted on, |
| Daß die Mutter mich wiegte ein | So mother would rock me to sleep |
| Und süße Lieder mir sänge! | And sing sweet lullabies to me! |
| Blumen brächten die Sklavinnen auch, | Slaves would bring flowers, |
| Mit dem Wedel wehrten die Fliegen; | Would shoo flies with a swatter; |
| Aber Zillah, mich küssend, spräch: | But Zillah, kissing me, would speak |
| "Gesegnet, mein süßes Knäbchen!"[9] | "Be blessed, my sweet little boy!" |

The gender dynamics of Droste-Hülshoff's text are vertiginous. By the time Cornelius is done with the short poem, they are doubly disorienting. The poem is in the subjunctive throughout—it is a poem that imagines emotional closeness and physical intimacy, but that in its grammar acknowledges distance and mediation. On a first level, a female

---

7 David Blamires, *Telling Tales: The Impact of Germany on English Children's Books, 1780–1918* (Cambridge: Open Book, 2009), 337.

8 Hellmuth Federhofer and Kurt Oehl, *Peter Cornelius als Komponist, Dichter, Kritiker und Essayist* (Regensburg: Bosse, 1977).

9 Annette von Droste-Hülshoff, "Das Kind," in *Gesammelte Schriften*, ed. Levin Schücking (Stuttgart: Cotta, 1879), 1:425.

poet imagines herself a young child, but specifically a boy, and conjures into being an increasingly elaborate (female) support staff of mother, slaves, and a nanny to help care for herself. There is a second level, however, which Cornelius emphasizes by giving the song to a tenor voice to sing: the poetic "I," implicitly masculinized in Droste-Hülshoff's text, but rendered as a heroic tenor by Cornelius, imagines itself in a stereotypically "feminine" position: "poor, weak, loved," an object of song, of fanning, of kisses. But what is more, the tenor ends the song impersonating the nanny "Zillah," blessing the child in a high vocal register. The tenor voice puts on a vocal drag to reaffirm its own masculinity by addressing itself from a feminized perspective.

Another aspect of Droste-Hülshoff's poem that Cornelius's short arrangement cannily amplifies concerns the sheer excessiveness of the infantile demand. A mother gently rocking him is perhaps not too much for an infant to ask—but certainly by the moment the imagined child begins asking for slaves to shower him with petals, the infantile demand attains a degree of measurelessness that begins to seem monstrous. The young boy (who, recall, is really the projection of an adult man) lets his demands run wild, until it emerges as a demand for total submission and subservience—one marked as profoundly masculine in the nineteenth century. Cornelius amplifies this by playing up the sweetness of the pretend-boy's melodies, as his tenor, and his masculinized subjectivity, get lost in the sheer jouissance of the imagined situation, knowing full well that Droste-Hülshoff's words will fatally reframe that sweetness. The moment at which an adult imagines intergenerational transmission, the moment at which an adult man seeks to give voice to the intergenerational scene, that scene becomes inevitably, inescapably uncanny. Both Droste-Hülshoff and Cornelius in their ballads and ballad settings respectively seem intent on amplifying rather than negotiating that sense of uncanniness.

Insofar as it participated in intergenerational transmission, the ballad intervened into childhood development later than nursery rhyme, picture book, or fairy tale. In Germany, ballads were a thing of elementary school *Lesebücher*, of poetry anthologies given as communion gifts, of learning to read and recite and memorize.[10] They were not nursery rhymes, even if their joyful wordplay could sometimes make them sound that way. They were adventure fictions and scary stories, and they presupposed a basic understanding of story to work on their young audiences. There were schoolyard games based on (sometimes half-remembered) old ballads—at the end of the nineteenth century, Franz Magnus Böhme collected dozens of them, many combining an

---

10 See Emily C. Bruce, *Revolutions at Home: The Origins of Childhood and the German Middle Class* (Boston: University of Massachusetts Press, 2021).

old text with strange and intricate bodily rituals.[11] The ballad was recognizably part of the project of guiding the young in some fashion—the implicit morals of its storylines about hubris and punishment, its historicist appeal to the wisdom of bygone ages and generations could feel pedagogical.[12] Many an art ballad, maybe most famously "Das Riesenspielzeug" by Adelbert von Chamisso, has at its core a moment of paternal admonishment.

The many seductions of the ballad—the fact that it often had exciting plots, a memorable meter, and an intuitive cadence—also made it a useful pedagogic vehicle. Ballads often told tales of reward and punishment, but they were themselves reward: the sugar that could make the bitter medicine of morals and history go down more easily. Nevertheless, by mid-century a number of writers used the family scene as a way of disrupting the logic of transmission that made the ballad such a standby in schoolhouses and music recitals. They sought to unsettle the way so many ballads pretended to stage an intergenerational dialogue, only to eventually retreat into a discourse of fate, resignation, and hubris punished. Even though they did not explicitly theorize the form, it appears that for them, the formal and thematic self-control of the ballad reiterated the inertia, solidity, and force of the family line. And for them challenges to that inertia, disruptions of that force could be lodged in the ballad. A balladic poetics of sisterhood functioned as precisely this sort of challenge.

Sisterhood in these poems disrupts descent as a mode of ascertaining transmission. These ballads describe a sisterhood that seems to exist at the exclusion of intergenerational family structures: sisters are ballad subjects because they have no mother. As has long been noted by scholars of fairy tales, this is a deeply telling omission. As Friedrich Kittler has argued, "the construct of the originary text, which has no basis in the real, can be possible only through a parasitic relation to the Mother's Mouth."[13] By absenting the mother, these ballads create deeply questionable narratives unwilling either to construct an "originary text" of the kind Kittler describes, or to construct such a text in a threadbare, unconvincing way. Perhaps the clearest reflection of this dynamic comes in a poem outside the German tradition, and a poem that is not immediately recognizable as a ballad, even by the relaxed standards established in the English-speaking world by Wordsworth's and Coleridge's 1801 *Lyrical Ballads*. Christina Rossetti wrote "Goblin Market"

---

11 Franz Magnus Böhme, *Deutsches Kinderlied und Kinderspiel* (Leipzig: Breitkopf & Härtel, 1897), 550.

12 For the implicit "pedagogy of fear" in fairy tales, see Maria Tatar, *Off with Their Heads: Fairy Tales and the Culture of Childhood* (Princeton, NJ: Princeton University Press, 2020), 22f.

13 Friedrich Kittler, *Discourse Networks 1800/1900* (Stanford, CA: Stanford University Press, 1990), 86.

in 1859 and published it in 1862. Its story certainly qualifies as balladic: two sisters, Lizzie and Laura, live by themselves in the woods; Laura is tempted by the Goblins who each evening proffer their wares across the glen. Quickly she becomes addicted to their fruit, and returns to the glen each night. After she can no longer afford her addiction, and slowly begins to age and wither away, Lizzie tries to buy the fruit for her. When the Goblins realize she is buying for her sister, they set upon her and try to force-feed her their fruit. Lizzie escapes, and tells her sister to drink the fruit juice off her body. Repulsed by the fruit, Laura falls into a deep sleep, but wakes up cured.

"Goblin Market" is a story of redemption that would not be out of place in a German ballad of the same era—but Rossetti's telling of it doesn't quite fit the mold. The meter is irregular, and varies between three and four stresses; the rhymes vary between simple ABAB couplets and far more complicated schemes, while the internal rhymes and assonance give the poem the structure of a nursery rhyme. At 567 lines, it goes on far too long to tell a properly balladic story, indulges in exhaustive lists and fanciful digressions, and foregoes any metafictional markers that would give it an air of minstrelsy. None of these generic markers need to be determinative, of course, for "Goblin Market" is balladic enough, a just-so ballad. As a consequence, its nineteenth-century readers oscillated on what genre to ascribe to the poem and, by extension, whom they believed the poem was for.

In a 1863 article on the poem in *Macmillan's Magazine*, "The Hon. Mrs. Norton"[14] (the social reformer Caroline Norton, who was in fact a friend of Rossetti's[15] ), suggested that readers "not too rigorously inquire," and describes "Goblin Market" as "a ballad which children will con with delight, and which riper minds may ponder over, as we do with poems written in a foreign language which we only half understand."[16] Norton did not explicitly say what made the baggy, epic "Goblin Market" a ballad to her mind—but, given that she was friendly with Fanny Mendelssohn-Hensel and conversant with the German tradition, there is a good chance the answer depends on German and musical reasons.[17] More directly, though, it appears to be the "delight" of children that marks "Goblin Market" as a ballad for her—a departure from her contemporaries, who, as Dieter Petzold has shown, tended

---

14 Caroline Norton, "'An Angel in the House' and 'The Goblin Market'," *Macmillan's Magazine* 8 (May–October 1863) (London: Macmillan, 1863), 398.

15 Rosemary T. Vanarsdel, "Macmillan's Magazine and the Fair Sex: 1859–1874 (Part One)," *Victorian Periodicals Review* 33, no. 4 (2000): 375.

16 Norton, "'An Angel in the House' and 'The Goblin Market'," 402.

17 See Fanny Mendelssohn-Hensel, *Tagebücher* (Leipzig: Breitkopf & Härtel, 2002); Marie Mulvey-Roberts and Ross Nelson, eds., *The Selected Letters of Caroline Norton* (London: Taylor & Francis, 2021), 154.

to think of ballads precisely as naïve without being targeted explicitly at children.[18]

Today scholars seem much less ready to credit the first part of Norton's description ("a ballad which children will con with delight")—we have gotten lost in the easily guessed-at depths, have lingered on fruit-juice-stained lips and heaved sighs, have offered queer readings and deconstructions, and have perhaps neglected that the poem, for all its alluring depths, has an equally seductive innocent surface. "Goblin Market" is intended to be two things to two audiences, and Norton imagines that the poem accomplishes its mission only by being both. The poem's dual address is as a moment of intergenerational transmission: parents and their children read or hear the same verses, but each party hears or reads quite different things. This may well be why Norton identifies "Goblin Market" as a ballad: ballads frequently function as intergenerational communications. An older speaker tells a younger listener about the past and initiates the younger listener into certain wisdoms and moral precepts. Ballads are lessons for a time before there are lessons; like fairy tales they may teach something without the pupil noticing it.

Norton does not say who the "riper minds" are who may "ponder" the hidden depths beneath the childish delight. There is no indication that just because a poem has a didactic angle, it was therefore read by parents or caregivers to the children under their tutelage. "Goblin Market" is at any rate too long for use as a bedtime story. But the poem's assonance and sound-painting, its seductive lilt and cheeky internal echoes, nevertheless speak of the maternal body, speak of it moreover at the moment at which it begins to recede into the distance. The poem offers its own viscous, "sugar-sweet" sap in the shape of its gorgeous sonorities that can almost be better enjoyed without fully understanding the words.

> And whisper'd like the restless brook:
> "Look, Lizzie, look, Lizzie,
> Down the glen tramp little men.

At the same time, the poem's villainous, seductive Goblins are masters of signing: where the sisters Laura and Lizzie lie self-sufficiently in each other's arms, the Goblins we meet are "Signalling each other, / Brother with sly brother." Their seduction is to some extent the seduction of signification, the pull of the Symbolic. The somatic pull of the poem's sonority, by contrast, which draws the sisters back toward each other with dreamlike ease, emerges from what Julia Kristeva has called the "semiotic." As Judith Butler has put it, for Kristeva "in its semiotic mode, language is engaged in a poetic

---

18 Dieter Petzold, *Das englische Kunstmärchen im neunzehnten Jahrhundert* (Berlin: De Gruyter, 2015), 61.

recovery of the maternal body, that diffuse materiality that resists all discrete and univocal signification."[19] Kristeva's "revolution" in poetic language attaches to the rhythm, rhyme, and homophony—all the sense that we can make without attending to the meanings of the words themselves.[20] It is clear that some of the crucial "semiotic" dimensions of poetic language Kristeva identifies are curtailed somewhat in balladry: ballads are narrative poems and tend not to thrive on the kind of Mallarmean polysemy that Kristeva clearly has in mind. The ballad's plurivocality is, as Goethe already observed, closer to the orderly dialogue of the drama than to the sudden upwelling of new voices in lyric discourse. And yet: few poems can speak as eloquently to the seductiveness of rhythm and cadence, of play and onomatopoeia, as the ballad—and can speak about them to a younger audience. And of course, as Walter Ong would point out, a parent encountered "Goblin Market" as a printed, fixed object, a reified thing in a visual realm, whereas the child listening encountered it as a sonic event, with all the instabilities, mishearings, and ambiguities that entailed.[21]

If Kristeva had turned her attention to the ballad, she might have envisioned it as an index of the maternal body under encroachment from the Symbolic. In other words: if the gorgeous chaos of lyric poetry speaks to us of the limitless communication between infant and mother, the ballad is about the narrowing of that communication, where the mother's heartbeat, the tone of her voice, and the smell of her skin are still an intrinsic part of the communication, but so are the words she is speaking, and the lesson she is consciously seeking to impart. Perhaps this is the existential note behind Caroline Norton's puzzlement as to where the meaning of "Goblin Market" is to be located: we can imagine a childlike hearing of the poem, and a highly suspicious hearing (or more likely reading) of it, but neither mother nor child can clearly locate themselves along the spectrum between the extremes. How much does the child understand? Which fruits will the child feast on: the sonic extravagance of lines like "She suck'd and suck'd and suck'd the more," or the measured life-lessons like "Twilight is not good for maidens"? And which of these lines prompted the mother to reach for the book in the first place?

By both relishing the pleasures of the semiotic *and* rhapsodizing their symbolic overcoming, "Goblin Market" makes the reader choose, or perhaps rather locate him- or herself in a process of maturation: are we still infantile enough to thrill to the sound of sucking, or are we adult enough to listen to the serious morals imparted in the poem? I am avoiding the more inclusive "themselves" advisedly in this context, because when "Goblin Market" asks

19 Judith Butler, *Gender Trouble* (London: Routledge, 1990), 112.
20 Julia Kristeva, *The Revolution in Poetic Language* (New York: Columbia University Press, 1984), 179.
21 Walter Ong, *Orality and Literacy* (London: Routledge, 2003), 119.

us to locate ourselves, it is asking us to locate ourselves in a gendered matrix as well. Rossetti's most famous collection of nursery rhymes puts the sheer love of sound in its title: the volume is called *Sing Song*. Here the mother's body is an explicit subject, in the dual sense that a lot of the rhymes talk of parents and that many of them are meant to be enunciated by parents. But the words enunciated are about loss. Often enough the rhymes and rhythms that assure the child of the present parents articulate the possible absence:

> My baby has a father and a mother,
> Rich little baby!
> Fatherless, motherless, I know another
> Forlorn as may be:
> Poor little baby![22]

The retreat and the persistence of the maternal body together structure the prosody of "Goblin Market." Its disappearance triggers the events told in the poem, and its return vouches for the safe deliverance from those events. Laura and Lizzie appear close to the point of incest, and their world seems almost perfectly self-enclosed; we never hear of parents, an extended family, and until the very end nothing of children.[23] The only men we meet are the "queer brothers" peddling their Goblin wares in the forest. Unperturbed by reproductive sexuality, the two sisters live "Cheek to cheek and breast to breast / Lock'd together in one nest." And we get a sense that they might well remain forever unperturbed until Laura's curiosity, and her expeditions into the forest, bring change into their idyll:

> Evening by evening
> Among the brookside rushes,
> Laura bow'd her head to hear,
> Lizzie veil'd her blushes:
> Crouching close together
> In the cooling weather,
> With clasping arms and cautioning lips,
> With tingling cheeks and finger tips.

Lizzie and Laura are quite enough world, maybe even quite enough thrill, for one another—and yet the forest disrupts their self-sufficiency. Jill Rappoport has pointed out that sisterhood seems rather utopian in "Goblin Market," but it is noticeable that this utopia isn't exactly stable. For Rappoport, "Goblin

---

22 Christina Rossetti, *Sing Song: A Nursery Rhyme Book* (London: Routledge, 1872), 3.

23 Nancy Welter, "Women Alone: Le Fanu's 'Carmilla' and Rossetti's 'Goblin Market'," in *Victorian Sensations: Essays on a Scandalous Genre*, ed. Kimberly Harrison and Richard Fantina (Columbus: Ohio State University Press, 2006), 138.

FIG. 5.1 Frontispiece to *Goblin Market and Other Poems* (1862).

Market" tells the story of domestic femininity disrupted by the lure of consumerism (the open market), which Lizzie then in turn challenges in order to save her sister.[24] The sisters' domestic arrangement is always already under threat, and Lizzie's rescue mission cannot really remove that threat. Only leaving the idyll in a different direction, namely the transition from sisterhood to motherhood, brings the narrative to a definitive close.

The famous frontispiece by Dante Gabriel Rossetti in fact suggests that the sisterly self-enclosure somehow produces the temptations offered by the Goblins—temptations only voided by the intergenerational family line. Dante Gabriel depicts the sisters in close embrace, almost like twin fetuses in the womb (Fig. 5.1). The Goblins parade through a sort of iris in the background. The two worlds of the poem, the enclosed domestic sphere and the seductive world outside, are each reduced to a bubble. The sisters' bubble gets its shape from the heads and arms of the girls, which naturally describe a circle. The Goblin-bubble seems to derive its shape from some contrivance: we are seeing a fragment of a larger scene, there are Goblins outside of

---

24 Jill Rappoport, *Giving Women: Alliance and Exchange in Victorian Culture* (New York: Oxford University Press, 2012), 92.

the frame or window or lunette—whatever allows us to see the Goblins also imbues them with a shape that the sisters arrive at spontaneously, as a tangle of limbs and faces. Whether the new invention of the photographic lens stands behind it, or some older visual trick[25]: the Goblins beckon through an optic of the sisters' making, produced through their self-generated occupation of visual space.

Of course, if Caroline Norton is right, it is probably through this generation of a moral out of a story that Goblin Market enters the realm of balladry. While the poem lingers with the fruits and forests, remains occupied with its lilting, dreamy lists, it is far closer to a nursery rhyme. Once it reveals itself, or reinvents itself as a didactic poem, it is much more clearly a ballad: the point of the story is no longer the pleasure of the telling, but rather something to be refined from it, like sugar from its fruits.

In more than one way through balladry speaks tradition: mother had an ulterior motive for telling you this story. She coated it in just enough rhythmic sugar, but by the end you can taste the medicine. Often in the nineteenth century, balladry was understood as the act of passing something on, its voice was that of the forebears, and the young listener had absorbed their wisdom, their falsehoods, their prejudices long before they could say to themselves, like little Marcel, "I am falling asleep." And yet balladry also resisted this patrilineal, or matrilineal, or really any lineal thrust—it has picked up the slack where, as in the case of Rossetti's "poor little baby," there is no father or no mother to give voice to the past and to impose it on the future.

> Days, weeks, months, years
> Afterwards, when both were wives
> With children of their own;
> Their mother-hearts beset with fears,
> Their lives bound up in tender lives;
> Laura would call the little ones
> And tell them of her early prime,
> Those pleasant days long gone
> Of not-returning time:
> Would talk about the haunted glen,
> The wicked, quaint fruit-merchant men,
> Their fruits like honey to the throat
> But poison in the blood;
> (Men sell not such in any town):
> Would tell them how her sister stood
> In deadly peril to do her good,

---

25 Allen Staley, Christopher Newall, Tim Batchelor, Alison Smith, and Ian Warrell, eds., *Pre-Raphaelite Vision: Truth to Nature* (London: Tate Books, 2004).

> And win the fiery antidote:
> Then joining hands to little hands
> Would bid them cling together,
> "For there is no friend like a sister
> In calm or stormy weather;
> To cheer one on the tedious way,
> To fetch one if one goes astray,
> To lift one if one totters down,
> To strengthen whilst one stands."

In these final stanzas, the self-containment of Dante Gabriel Rossetti's frontispiece gives way to an extension in time, and sisterhood, with all its mysterious glories, becomes a teaching of motherhood.[26] These final lines also turn the story into a message: we get a reassuring sense of why it is being told and what moral it is meant to impart. Readers have puzzled ever since *Goblin Market* was published whether the moral imparted in this final turn is really borne out in the poem that precedes it—but it is clear that, even if it were, there is a pronounced break in these final lines, one that concerns the poetics of the poem and the familial status of its characters. Story turns into teaching; and the sisters turn into mothers.

It is hard not to think of these twin transformations as parallel processes. Sisterhood becomes a story to be told to one's children, a steadying moral to be imparted, when before it behaved more like a destabilizing, disquieting force. Siblinghood becomes, in other words, a mere buttress in intergenerational transmission. The verticality that was missing from the sisters' mysterious dyad (where are the parents?) now drafts this very mystery into its service (the sisters are now parents). At the same time, the pleasure of communication from body to body becomes mediated through discourse—maternal presence is transformed into maternal teachings. Communication loses its beautiful, luxuriating pointlessness, leaves behind the nursery, and enters the stultifying atmosphere of the classroom.

Preoccupations with what is passed on in poetic genres generally understood to be child-friendly were not unique to Great Britain. In fact, given the centrality often accorded to balladry in the idea of a "national" education project in Germany, it cannot surprise that they surfaced there with much greater starkness and virulence. But these preoccupations also first emerged among poets who were forerunners of German realism, and rather than the luxuriant symbolism of *Goblin Market*, the ballads of Friedrich Hebbel (1813–1863) and Annette von Droste-Hülshoff (1797–1848) tended to address questions of family by playing with perspective, with temporality, with omniscience.

---

26 Janet Galligani Casey, "The Potential of Sisterhood: Christina Rossetti's Goblin Market," *Victorian Poetry* 29, no. 1 (1991): 70.

Hebbel appears to have completed his family ballad "Vater und Sohn" the same year Christina Rossetti published "Goblin Market." And in writing it, he responded to similar pressures as the "balladic" ending Rossetti gave "Goblin Market." In a diary entry from October 1862, Hebbel notes that he removed a stanza from "the ballad," which most scholars believe must have referred to "Vater und Sohn."[27] If that's true, Hebbel's lapidary note hides a rather revolutionary intervention into his poem: for the lines Hebbel removed (and which he notates in his diary) belong to a narrator, who comments on and explains the characters' psychology. The poem we have today has some rudimentary descriptive narration, but is largely made up of dialogue—and much of the poem's capacity to disturb comes from this willingness to let the characters discourse dominate the story.

What is lost when one narrates family? What does that Archimedean focalization outside the family unit obscure? "Goblin Market" provides a suggestion: it risks turning the vagaries of emotional life into a lesson to be imparted; it risks turning family into a standing reserve for melodramatic convention; it risks turning the nursery rhyme into a ballad. Where "Goblin Market" wound up capitulating to this balladic demand, Hebbel and Droste-Hülshoff both experimented with ballads that problematized the narrative, the melodramatic, the dynastic dimensions of family. In doing so, they problematized the notion of tradition itself, for which and of which the ballad cannot help speaking.

## Balladic Inheritance

If the ballad was, as we have seen in Chapter 1, widely regarded as a more compressed form of the epic, this compression had to do with its function—namely the fact that the ballad was occupied with a process of transmission. The ballad was supposed to pass down orally, impress itself on listeners rather than readers, and eventually be impressive enough to inspire those listeners to pass it on in turn. Writing after the Ossian controversy, in which Dr. Johnson had challenged the idea that a poem of the length of, say, *Fingal* or *Temora* could be passed down effectively in an exclusively oral culture, the thematic compression and formal precision of the ballad came to vouch for its connection to the *Volk* and pre-literary traditions.

Throughout the nineteenth century, this compression was often understood in terms of tidiness. Unlike the lumbering epic, the jagged novel, the ballad condensed and domesticated the great wide world. It was an efficient housekeeper, requiring little foreknowledge and little afterthought.

---

27 Friedrich Hebbel, *Tagebücher* (Berlin: Behr, 1904), 4:343.

Frequently, most clearly in Franz Lucas's 1906 dissertation on the topic, Droste-Hülshoff's *Kleinepik* is understood in terms of its "art-economic purposes [*kunstökonomischen Zwecken*]"[28]—linking the form to the *oikos*. Such a view understands Droste-Hülshoff's perspectival compression and unclear focalization as a form of good housekeeping: the poet reaches for epic effects in a folk-song-inspired genre, and the only way to make them fit is to work with quasi-novelistic techniques.

But in fact Droste-Hülshoff's domestic scenes used the ballad form's inherent compression to play off the epic, dramatic, and poetic against each other in ingenious ways. And they seem to have done so to complicate the popular perception of ballads—not so much with regard to its roots in domesticity, but rather with regard to the valorization of oral transmission that lies implicit in the form. While the dominant ideology celebrated the family as a locus of direct, uncorrupted, and instinctual transmission of value, the family became for her a place where orality revealed itself to be profoundly uncanny and deeply compromised. Others proceeded the same way: telling stories about the family to talk about the nature of orality, of tradition, of *Geist*. Droste-Hülshoff and Hebbel formulated implicit critiques of a genealogical theory of balladic transmission, that is to say a theory that understood the process by which *Volksballaden* survived in a population in essentially familial terms. Their critique proceeds by turning the family into a subject of the ballad. Both poets frequently treated family relationships as primarily concerned with transmission (of affect, of knowledge, of identity), and understood this transmission as somehow interrelated with the transmission effected in and through the ballad. They reflected on the bonding and restrictive force of family and analogized it with the bonding and restrictive force of poetic form. In terms of its form, the ballad pretends not to have been invented. Like an heirloom of which no one can say exactly when it came into the family, it is handed down and passed on, and if its origins are supposed to be murky, the line and lineage it traces in the process of its transmission are supposed to be deeply meaningful. Ballads belong to national families, and what speaks through them was understood to matter differently to the individual depending on whether they belonged to that national family or did not.

In this, it strikingly resembled other kinds of inheritance the nineteenth century worried about: what, in a society increasingly dominated by bourgeois values, was the role of hereditary and traditional roles, fiefdoms, privileges? How much freedom did the individual organism have before the will of the species, the drift of its genetic material, its familial or

---

28 Franz Lucas, *Zur Balladentechnik der Annette von Droste-Hülshoff* (Münster: Regensberg, 1906), 32.

national unconscious? Legal theorists debated the question of whether transmitting one's individual will to future generations through testaments was a practice to be encouraged at all. Broadly speaking, proponents of positive law (for instance, Savigny) emphasized the importance of inheritance and inherited will, while natural law theorists tended to regard it as problematic and hubristic to want to project one's own will past one's own death—among the latter camp numbered Annette von Droste-Hülshoff's favorite cousin, Clemens August. In his *Lehrbuch des Naturrechts oder der Rechtsphilosophie* (*Textbook of Natural Law or the Philosophy of Right*, 1823), he writes that "the will of a deceased is a ground that does not demand respect from anyone."[29]

Droste-Hülshoff understood herself as someone who would live on through future legacy rather than contemporary presence. In fact, she famously insisted that she did not care to have a contemporary reception: "however, I'd like to be read in a hundred years."[30] Inheritance, legacy, and transmission mattered to her quite intensely, and yet she was all too aware of the risks and strictures of such acts of bequeathing.[31] The ballad "Vorgeschichte (second sight)" from 1840/41 picks up on this problematic of transmission: how does one impose one's will into the distant future? And how does one deal with the past's will reaching out into one's own present? A *Freiherr* finds himself awake at night, worrying about his son, a sickly child who is the last scion of an illustrious family line. Each night he puts the boy to sleep before an immense, looming family tree "in nigh endless row."

| | |
|---|---|
| Hat er des Kleinen Stammbaum doch | He's had the small one's family tree |
| Gestellt an des Lagers Ende, | Placed at the foot of his bed, |
| Nach dem Abendkusse und Segen noch | So that after the goodnight kiss and evening prayer |
| Drüber brünstig zu falten die Hände; | He can lovingly fold his hand over it. |
| Im Monde flimmernd das Pergament | The parchment flicker in moon's glow |
| Zeigt Schild an Schilder, schier ohne End'.[32] | Showing crest upon crest in nigh endless row. |

29 Clemens August von Droste-Hülshoff, *Lehrbuch des Naturrechtes oder der Rechtsphilosophie* (Bonn: Marcus, 1831), 105 (§55).

30 Droste-Hülshoff to Elise Rüdiger, July 24, 1843; cited in Gustav Sichelschmidt, *Allein mit meinem Zauberwort: Annette von Droste-Hülshoff* (Düsseldorf: Droste, 1990), 256.

31 Adrian Daub, *The Dynastic Imagination: Family and Modernity in Nineteenth-Century Germany* (Chicago: University of Chicago Press, 2021), 44.

32 Droste-Hülshoff, *Gesammelte Schriften*, 1:284.

Eventually the *Freiherr* has a vision of a funeral, only to realize he is witnessing his own. But the mystical vision of how powerless he is before his family's ultimate demise leads to a moment of empowerment, an empowerment (not insignificantly for a supposedly originally oral form) through writing:

| | |
|---|---|
| Dann hat er die Lampe still entfacht, | The baron sets his lamp alight, |
| Und schreibt sein Testament in der Nacht.[33] | and writes his testament that very night. |

As Ulrike Vedder writes, the poem strongly links "having visions and genealogy"[34]—in "Vorgeschichte" it is a matter of a particular kind of sight, but more generally in Droste-Hülshoff we could speak of a connection between genealogy and visibility. What stories are recorded, passed on, or even tellable in the first place has to do with genealogical and familial structures. But what Vedder does not specifically thematize is the poem's form itself: the ballad, which manages to combine the family tree (with "crest upon crest in nigh endless row") with the premonition that inspires the writing of a will. The poem is about an ambient, haunting vision of past and future (the old baron finds himself beset by things barely seen and barely heard, which he decides he "must see" and "must hear") that inspires a very precise genre of written transmission. Not only does Droste-Hülshoff's ballad seem to contain a theory of family inheritance, but it allegorizes the origin myth of the form of the *Kunstballade* itself: it transforms an uncertain, instinctive, sensuous form of transmission into a carefully regulated (and written) form. It is, however, to put it mildly, an ambivalent allegory. In many ballads, balladic knowledge presents a kind of heterodox history-writing, compensating for the defects of the "official" version. In "Vorgeschichte" the ballad records something not being recorded, transmits something that cannot and will not be transmitted. The *Freiherr*'s ghostly vision of his own death will pass down to no one; his last will and testament can.

This was more than a shift in content, involving instead a reconceptualization of how the ballad form preserved and transmitted its content. While they still were not "social ballads" in the mode of the later nineteenth century, Droste-Hülshoff's works in the genre poems no longer accept the ballad's modes

---

33 Ibid., 1:286.
34 Ulrike Vedder, "Erbe und Literatur," in *Erbe: Übertragungskonzepte zwischen Natur und Kultur*, ed. Sigrid Weigel, Stefan Willer, and Bernhard Jussen (Frankfurt: Suhrkamp, 2013), 128.

of transmission as an unproblematic given (aping oral modes of tradition). What families transmit from generation to generation emerges as a problem analogous to what the ballad transmits and how. Droste-Hülshoff's "Die Schwestern" deals with a single generation: the poem constructs a story of sisterhood, but it foregrounds the question of *who* exactly is constructing it. In other words, it takes the father's visionary double perspective in "Vorgeschichte" and problematizes it; in the process, it problematizes and reconceptualizes the very origin myth of the ballad. Droste-Hülshoff was keenly aware of sisterhood as a category that subtended both unusual autonomy for a woman, and indentured her to her relatives ("the helpful fifth wheel," or "das hilfsbereite fünfte Rad," as she puts it in the poem "Auch ein Beruf"[35]). "Die Schwestern" is unusual in that it offers not so much a philosophy as a poetics of sisterhood, one that raises questions of who gets to narrate in poetry, and who gets to constitute a poetic tradition.

"Die Schwestern" is another exceedingly long poem. In its four parts it tells the story of Gertrude and Helene. In the first part, Helene has not returned from an errand in town and a Gertrude rushes half-mad through the forest searching for her. The second part tells of what may have been a missed encounter between the two women in town years later. In the third part, Gertrude finally finds her sister's corpse washed up at the shore—Helene, apparently now a well-known prostitute, has drowned. In the fourth part we learn that Helene's death drove Gertrude into madness and eventual suicide—she is said to haunt the grove where the narrator, an aristocratic hunter traveling with his servant (*Bursche*), comes to stalk his prey.

Or at least, that is the story the reader is eventually led toward. While the mode of narration is realist throughout, Droste-Hülshoff's poem mimics Gertrude's cognitive processes—her desperate, confused attempts to bring into some sort of order a mad, incomprehensible rush of events is mimicked in the poem's episodic narration. But this desire for order is double-edged: like Gertrude, the reader is invited to construct meaning and coherence, and seduced into forgetting that these are constructions. Especially when the poem's narrator enters the scene at the very end of the poem, the question of what, if any, legitimacy these shopworn narrative constructions possess is thrust to the forefront of the poem. "Die Schwestern" is rife with melodramatic plot points, but again and again the reader is made to doubt that those plots accurately describe what is going on. The poem is rife, even overripe, with gothic and melodramatic trappings, from rocky outcroppings to dark forests. In the first section of the poem a group of workers at the local mill listen to the "mad ghost among the firs" ("irre Gespenst im Tanne"), a ghost that turns out to be Gertrude—very much alive, very much sane, and

---

35 Droste-Hülshoff, "Auch ein Beruf," in *Gesammelte Schriften*, 1:372.

very much in need of their aid. She will end up mad and a ghost, of course, but at this moment Gertrude is simply a desperate woman in a desperate situation. It is a male gaze, as secure as it is blinkered, that turns her into a gothic trope, and ultimately into a self-fulfilling prophecy. Again and again, Droste-Hülshoff's poem trots out hoary tropes only to reveal that they are tropes—and usually a sign that men are telling stories rather than accurately describing the world around them.

The poem's lingering questions about its central (and titular) relationship ultimately become questions about knowing as such. Throughout "Die Schwestern" the narrator seems afflicted by a curious set of tropic confusions, for instance, an inability to distinguish between the act of gazing and the human eye. The third section begins with an extended metaphor about gazes, although in most cases it seems the poem wants us to imagine it said "eyes" when it said "glances":

| | |
|---|---|
| Zehn Jahre!—und mancher der keck umher | Ten years—and many who once alert |
| Die funkelnden Blicke geschossen, | Sent radiant gazes around them, |
| Der schlägt sie heute zu Boden schwer, | Now cast them aground with heavy heart, |
| Und mancher hat sie geschlossen.[36] | Or have closed them altogether. |

This is likely not an accidental slippage. The inability to distinguish between visual organ and the specifically subjective act of looking marks a central lacuna that comes to structure the poem as a whole: gradually "Die Schwestern" becomes less about looking at a story, and more about who is looking and what it means that they are looking. And even when it comes to the central scene of the long poem's plot—Gertrude leaning over the dead Helene—the narrator constructs a drama of glances and eyes that works hard to suggest a moment of recognition, but one that seems mostly owed to the narrator's poetic handiwork.

In "Die Schwestern" little can be assumed to be straightforwardly factual. We first meet Gertrude as a "ghost in the firs" as imagined by a group of handymen, and by the end of the poem she indeed conforms to their melodramatic projection. Accepting this ending means to credit a series of male gazes with an objectivity that elsewhere in the poem (including in the very first scene) they manifestly do not possess. We are led to assume that the drowned woman is Helene and has worked as a prostitute. But it is a gaggle of male sailors who identify dead Helene (bulging with lake water) as a local prostitute; it is our male narrator who claims that Gertrude went

---

36 Droste-Hülshoff, *Gesammelte Schriften*, 1:311.

mad, and who claims that she haunts these woods. Why would we believe them? If we do believe them, "Die Schwestern" functions as the story of a family undone by the disappearance of parental authority. Helene has been entrusted to Gertrude by her dying mother, and while there is no father in the picture, Gertrude early in the poem invokes a substitute father figure— "Our Father, Who art in Heaven." Neither real nor spiritual parent provide succor to the sisters and so their bond cannot survive their tribulations. But crediting this reading indeed requires that we believe every conjecture made by a male figure in the course of the poem. The reading of "Die Schwestern" as carrying a profoundly paternalistic message constitutes an itself paternalistic imposition of meaning on facts that may well not support it.

The most important projection, however, has long slipped past us by the time we become suspicious. It is almost at the end of this lengthy poem that the narrator makes the somewhat startling admission that the sisters of the title may be anything but. Why did one break down at the sight of the other's corpse? The reader has been led to assume that their connection is somehow established or explained, but it turns out their relationship lingers only as a suspicion:

| Ob ihres Blutes? man wußte es nicht! | On account of their blood? it's hard to know! |
| Kein Fragen löste das Schweigen[37] | No question resolves the silence |

At this moment, Droste-Hülshoff's ballad stakes a claim for the powers of poetry. The ballad can do what all other questioning is unable to accomplish: it fills the silence that surrounds, that in some sense constitutes the sisters' sisterhood. That would put "Die Schwestern" in a whole class of nineteenth-century poems that celebrate poetry's ability to speak for things that the prose of the world has no access to (the nocturnal vision behind the prosaic writing of the will in "Vorgeschichte," for instance). But that would require that the narrator knows more than the mere observer, who, we are told, doesn't know whether Gertrude and Helene are sisters.

As Susanne Kord has pointed out, the tropes of sentimental discourse were, from the eighteenth century onward, one mechanism by which women whose relationship seemed to be more-than-friendly were rendered safe.[38] Lauren Shizuko Stone has likewise pointed to the narrative tropes

[37] Ibid., 1:314.
[38] Susanne T. Kord, "Eternal Love or Sentimental Discourse?," in *Outing Goethe and His Age*, ed. Alice A. Kuzniar (Palo Alto, CA: Stanford University Press, 1996), 231.

of omniscient narration in German realism as a "straightening" of potential queerness.[39] The omniscience by which the poem knows that Gertrude and Helene are sisters is just threadbare enough to watch the process of straightening happen. And this omniscience is to some extent identified with the ballad form itself, its promises, its capabilities, and its ability to tell and transmit clear and reproducible stories. The poem foregrounds this problem by actually staging a scene of balladic performance: the second part begins with a market day in town, with town criers, a hurdy-gurdy man, and even the harlequin-like buffoon-figure *Hanswurst*. This is the world into which the ballad imaginatively inserts itself, of which it pretends to be a surviving sediment. It is the world to which its stories once sought to appeal. The melodramatic contrivances on which Droste-Hülshoff has "Die Schwestern" depend are those of the broadsheets: murder, sex, depredation, long-delayed reunions, madness, hauntings.

In many a ballad, the reader is supposed to be able to imagine a lone bard, ancient minstrel, or else a carnival barker telling the story, which means it has to be focalized through a single, personalized voice. But that personalization only goes so far; the speaker remains to some extent identifiable yet anonymous. "Die Schwestern" begins with what appears to be a narrator who stands outside the action, but who toward the end appears on the scene. Even before this the narrator of "Die Schwestern" is fairly idiosyncratic. The long poem opens and closes on an identical couplet, a reverie about nature that frames the story and its mood, or perhaps suggests the story to the narrator in its entirety. Throughout the poem, pronouns like "I" and "we," and asides about what "we" know and agree on, foreground the fact that here *one* person is speaking to another person, or more likely persons. When the narrator does appear in the poem, he does so with far more dramatic specificity than the usual ballad speaker: he is probably a he, for one, since we meet him hunting with a rifle; he is wealthy, wealthy enough to have a manservant, and he is from the same area as the sisters. The unspecific scene at the beginning of the poem's second section—the carnival with its stories offered as popular entertainment—is but a feint. The scene of narration is far closer to the one characteristic of the German novella in the mid-nineteenth century: its unreliable narrator communicates across identifiable, real-world class, regional, and gender divisions.

These fairly explicit class and gender markers lend an entirely new valence to the question of why he tells this story of sisterhood. On a sentimental reading, "Die Schwestern" testifies to the fact that the ballad form can salvage

---

39 Lauren Shizuko Stone, "'Is that your sister or your husband?' Literary Realism, Ahmed's Queer Phenomenology, and Döblin's *Two Girlfriends Commit Murder by Poison*." Lecture, Stanford Department of German Studies, 06/01/21.

and preserve what the world of men doesn't and cannot know—namely that Gertrude and Helene are long-separated sisters. But the emphasis on gendered gazing and disciplining knowledge makes it clear that sisterhood may well be a male projection. Two women come to die in horrible but—in their society and social station—predictable ways, and a male gaze constructs the melodramatic structure around their deaths. But why is this projection necessary? Is it to account for Gertrude's intense affective outpouring at the sight of dead Helene—to suggest that the only reason one woman might mourn for another might be that she is a long-lost sister? Or is it simply that such melodrama makes for good, morbid entertainment for a wealthy hunter like our narrator and others like him? The poem doesn't say, but its paratextual arrangements (title, section breaks, etc.) suggest that constructing the sisterhood narrative matters immensely to the poem. It needs this to be true, even if perhaps it isn't.

It's easy to say that the ballad form speaks for the dispossessed, for those who don't usually get to narrate their own stories (the apprentice rather than the sorcerer)—but "Die Schwestern" submits the ballad's pretense at democratization to rather strenuous scrutiny. Just as plausible as the reading that the poem renders safe a heterodox counter-history is the reading that the poem imposes a masculinist fantasy cobbled together from conventional tropes on a relationship between two women that is in its own way heterodox and, in its intransparency and impenetrability, queer. This ambiguity in how we are to interpret the poem's very telling of its story places particular emphasis the repeated line that opens and closes the poem. It is a bit of nature lyric and first describes the scene of Helene's disappearance and concludes the poem by depicting the desolate landscape that inspires the male narrator to comprehend (or invent) the earlier scene:

| Sacht pochet der Käfer im morschen Schrein, | Gently clicks the bugs in rotting lumber, |
| Der Mond steht über den Fichten.[40] | The moon stands above the spruce trees. |

The poem ends with its own inspiration. And the nature of this inspiration is precisely the question: is nature suggesting something to our narrator, something that society has perhaps repressed? Or does nature simply function here as the instigator for a melodramatic flight of fancy? We cannot know, of course. But it is worth noting that in closing with its opening, the poem actually resolves nothing. Rather, the poem once again problematizes

---

40 Droste-Hülshoff, *Gesammelte Schriften*, 1:314.

its balladic character, this time not in terms of tropes or narration, but in terms of repetition. The question of what it means that the line is repeated in each of the poem's two worlds (the hunter-narrator's and the possible sisters') leads to another, much broader one: what does it mean that ballads are repeated?

Friedrich Hebbel raises just this question in the ballad "Vater und Sohn." For decades the ballad form had contained the dream of a story handed down from generation to generation, passed along orally without ever requiring the brittle supplement of the printed page. Hebbel's ballad presents that fantasy as a nightmare: he presents a shadow of violence, guilt, and madness being handed from generation to generation. The ballad form recapitulates (and in a climactic moment of possible salvation comes to disrupt) a familial form of inheritance.

## The Weight of History

On October 8, 1862, Hebbel jots down a quick anecdote in his diary. It concerns an ekphrastic rather than narrative poem, but a poem that likewise deals with family. His daughter (Christine or "Titi," then fifteen years old) recites his poem "Drei Schwestern" ("Three Sisters"), a poem, Hebbel notes, "of which I had no idea that she knew it by heart." According to Hebbel, "Titi" ends up profoundly amused by her father's poem—though the question is why.

> When she gets to the passage "She barely knows that she is a girl," she hides behind her mother and begins to laugh heartily. I thought she might be making the connection with herself and betray as much with her laughter. But it was actually the result of an even greater naïveté. She thought the verse too stupid, since "even the youngest would know that she is a girl."[41]

The poem in question is a description of Palma Vecchio's painting of three sisters. It, like Droste-Hülshoff's "Die Schwestern," is a poem about the mysteries of sisterhood. But unlike Droste-Hülshoff, and perhaps not unlike her narrator, Hebbel in his poem fills in the mysteries by overinterpreting. Palma Vecchio's painting is subtle, and while it is strange to treat a poem like a piece of art criticism, the poem almost asks its readers to: how much of the poem's psychological detail, how much of its life philosophy, how much of its moralizing, can we really make out in Palma Vecchio's painting?

---

41 Hebbel, *Tagebücher*, 223.

| | |
|---|---|
| Der einen zuckt es schmerzlich um den Mund, | One has a painful pinch around her lips, |
| Sie trug den Kranz der Schönheit, voll und rund, | She carried the wreath of beauty full and round, |
| Doch glitt er schneller, als sie's je geglaubt, | But swifter than she supposed it slipped from her, |
| Hinüber auf der Nächsten schlichtes Haupt, | Onto the simple head of the next sister, |
| Und still empfindet sie die Macht der Zeit | And quietly she feels the power of time |
| Im ersten Schauer der Vergänglichkeit.[42] | Shuddering at the first hint of transience. |

Hebbel opens them poem by acknowledging that every emotion ascribed to the three young women is in fact a male projection, and a projection borne out of a kind of paternalistic impulse. For the story the painting tells the poetic I, that the three girls are starting to cope with adulthood, with the inevitable fading of youth, is an emphatically sentimental one, whereas the three girls are being described in all the physical expressions of naïveté popular at mid-century:

| | |
|---|---|
| Drei Schwestern sind's, von sanftem Reiz umstrahlt, | Three sisters, enveloped by a gentle charm, |
| Ihr eigner Vater hat sie uns gemalt, | Their own father painted them for us, |
| Sich ähnlich an Gestalt und an Gesicht, | They look alike in body and in face, |
| Sogar an Augen, nur an Mienen nicht, | Even in their eyes, but not their expressions, |
| Und lieblicher hab' ich den Horentanz | Never have I seen in lovelier shapes |
| Noch nie erblickt in seinem Zauberglanz. | The magic glow of the dance of time. |

Note that Hebbel ascribes to his own daughter a similar naïveté: He is surprised she knows the poem, misunderstands her amusement. He initially believes she is thinking of herself, but comes to realize that she simply doesn't understand what womanhood signifies within her father's poem.

---

42 Hebbel, "Drei Schwestern," in *Sämtliche Werke in zwölf Bänden*, ed. Adolf Stern (Berlin: Knaur, 1908), 6:219.

Like the huntsman's reading of sisterhood in Droste-Hülshoff's ballad, his sentimental pleasure at her naïve acceptance of her father's description of a young girl's fate is deeply paternalistic. And yet, there is more going on in Hebbel's little note: for ironically, young Christine actually rewrites her father's poem. At least the published version renders the line in question as: "Die dritte hat noch eine lange Frist, / Sie weiß noch kaum, daß sie kein Kind mehr ist." Young Christine turns that into "Sie weiß noch kaum, daß sie ein Mädchen ist."[43] The third sister is on the cusp of adulthood without realizing it; Christine's version doesn't realize she is a girl.

Given the age of the three women Palma Vecchio depicts, Christine's amusement at the line would—at least given the prejudices of the time period—make sense. But perhaps that isn't the motivation of Christine's, conscious or unconscious, reworking of her father's line. She ascribes to the youngest of the three women a degree of naïve grace that, at least for the mid-nineteenth century, transcends the bounds of common sense: and she turns a story of aging and maturation, seemingly accidentally focused on three women, into a story about gender. She intensifies and thereby makes visible that these women mean only insofar as men force them to mean, by either pictorial or poetic means. And given that Palma Vecchio imposes meaning on his daughters, and "Titi" recites a poem by her father, the little episode seems to speak to the role of paternalistic inheritance in art: how fathers force their offspring to realize meaning they have imposed on them.

This is an abiding fascination of Hebbel's balladry as well, to the point where ballads may be seen as inheritances of just the kind that Hebbel's fathers force upon their reluctant offspring. The unusually long ballad "Vater und Sohn" ("Father and Son") is perhaps most blunt in making this link, but many of the poems collected in Hebbel's *Ausgabe letzter Hand* under the rubric "Balladen und Verwandtes" ("Ballads and Related Matters") treat the passing-on that happens in ballads and the passing-on of (often undesirable) familial traits as analogous. In the poem "Aus der Kindheit,"[44] for instance, another largely dialogue-based ballad, a mother (at the behest of an absent father) forces her son to drown the family cat, and almost ends up killing the boy in the bargain. In "Der Haideknabe,"[45] the conflict is between a master and his apprentice. In "Das Kind am Brunnen,"[46] a young child almost falls into a well while their wet nurse sleeps. It is especially sleep and dreams that seem to lend sharp contours to familial relationships, relationships that are frequently characterized by violence, deprivation, and suffering.

---

43 Hebbel, *Tagebücher*, 223.
44 Hebbel, "Aus der Kindheit," in *Sämtliche Werke in zwölf Bänden*, 6:57.
45 Hebbel, "Der Haideknabe," in *Sämtliche Werke in zwölf Bänden*, 6:33.
46 Hebbel, "Das Kind am Brunnen," in *Sämtliche Werke in zwölf Bänden*, 6:46.

In the poem "Auf eine Unbekannte,"[47] which was set by Peter Cornelius (op. 5, no. 3), Hebbel makes clear that relations like these are about more than mere blood kinship. There the poet speaks of "mysterious hours" where "nature" grants human beings the gift of fellow-feeling: "Perhaps then these most transient association / familiars are made more familiar" ("Vielleicht wird dann zu flüchtigstem Vereine / Verwandtes dem Verwandten nah gerückt"). What is at stake in these moments of relatedness throughout Hebbel's poetry is the ability to empathize, to genuinely interact in the first place. The question that preoccupies these poems does not so much concern whether family can transmit. Instead, family becomes a bellwether for whether transmission is possible at all, whether it is worth it—and what, if anything, human beings can share with one another. Imagining this moment of sympathy, Cornelius's song setting decides on escalating agitation, the tenor rising both in pitch and in emotional register (marked *bewegter* and *noch bewegter* in the score)—before it abruptly calms down at the final line that imagines that "it is your feeling, which courses through me" ("Ist's dein Empfinden, welches mich durchzückt"[48]). It is another person's feeling that finally brings the singer a certain measure of calm, that gradually slows down the vocal line, that moves it from a mezzoforte to a piano and eventually a reflective, inward pianissimo. Significantly, it is not the feeling of "familiarity" (*Verwandtschaft*) that the music seems to find relaxing, not the feeling in parallel with another. It is rather the other person's feeling by itself. Projecting feelings onto another, soliciting feelings from another, imposing feelings on another, in these songs is exhausting and ultimately violent business. The hoped-for redemption is to feel kinship with the other by not having feelings of one's own at all.

Behind such impositions and projection lurks again and again the question of gender. It is noticeable that these poems were rather unpopular when it came to song settings—"Der Haideknabe"[49] exists in a setting for recitation with piano accompaniment by Robert Schumann, but many of these social ballads seemed to repel composers when it came to the traditional *Lied*-form. Schumann focused on scenes of childhood with particular interest—the *Kinderszenen*, op. 15, remain mainstays in the repertoire—and therefore also seems to have found Hebbel's family-related texts most interesting. However, he consistently de-balladized the poems in the process: he largely avoided poems with too much action, he complicated the often starkly dichotomized dialogues. By the same token he removed their specific genderings. In "Wiegenlied am Lager eines kranken Kindes"[50] (op. 78, no. 4), he relies

---

47 Hebbel, "Auf eine Unkekannte," in *Sämtliche Werke in zwölf Bänden*, 6:66.
48 Hebbel, "Auf eine Unkekannte," in *Sämtliche Werke in zwölf Bänden*, 6:66.
49 Hebbel, "Der Haideknabe," in *Sämtliche Werke in zwölf Bänden*, 6:35.
50 Friedrich Hebbel, "Wiegenlied am Lager eines Kranken Kindes," in *Sämtliche Werke: Historisch kritische Ausgabe*, ed. Richard Maria Werner (Berlin: Behr, 1904), 7:166.

on two voices, tenor and soprano, to address the child together. He further removes a stanza of Hebbel's that identifies the speaker as the mother, giving the text to a parental couple to sing instead. Rather than a balladic drama of different voices, then, the song creates a united, and fairly static parental function, and likewise makes Hebbel's "mein Knäblein" ("my boy") into a gender-neutral "Kindlein."

Schumann's choices in adapting Hebbel's poetry were likely primarily owed to aesthetic considerations and preferences. Nevertheless, in their totality they probably do constitute something of a reading of Hebbel's family poetry. Schumann sensed that there was something that required stabilization in Hebbel's scenes of intergenerational transmission. Just like Droste-Hülshoff, Hebbel seemed to worry about what tradition leaves out—unlike her, it was not with the intention of transmitting new stories from new speakers, but instead with a view to escaping from the suffocating strictures of having to transmit. "Vater und Sohn" pushes this sense of suffocation to a breaking point—and perhaps as a result, it seems to have never been set to music. "Vater und Sohn" tells a straightforward story, a gothic whodunit of sorts, but in so doing manages to reflect on, and trouble, the very lucidity of the story and its telling. Whatever it makes clear it indicts; and whatever it manages to make murky it tends to regard as a source of hope. A grandfather has made his grandson set fire to their house, and his son decides to put an end to the old man ("So steck ich dir heut das Ziel") and thereby to his deviltry. This is presumably to protect the boy from following in the grandfather's footsteps, although it turns out the father himself is following in his father's footsteps: repeating his father's patricide with his own father.

The poem outlines a lineage consisting not just of the three generations that interact in the poem proper, but also of past and future generations. But the poem's central gesture, that of inheritance from father to son, confuses its meaning more than it clarifies it. The poem is called "Vater und Sohn," but the poem is really talking about *three* different relationships that can be characterized in that way: the grandfather and his father he slew, the grandfather and the father who wants to kill him, and lastly the father and the son who may be next in the parricidal line, but who is, as of the time of narration, simply a mute onlooker.

"Wer hat die Kerze ins Dach gesteckt?"
Mein Sohn, dein Knabe tat's!
"Sein Arm ist zu kurz, wie hoch
   er ihn reckt!"
Ich hob ihn empor, er erbat's.

"Who has put the candle to the roof?"
My son, your boy did it!
"His arm is too short, no matter
   how much he stretches!"
I raised him, he asked me to.

The father drags his own father out of the house toward "the black gulch," the young boy mutely following along. The grandfather who has cacklingly goaded his son into further violence up to now, suddenly shows fear—fear of his own father.

| | |
|---|---|
| Wer fault denn dort? "Mein Vater, Sohn, | Who rots down there? "My father, son, |
| Schau, eben zeigt er sich!" | See, now he shows himself!" |
| Wem droht der Schatten? | Who does the shadow threaten? |
| "Wem sollt er drohn?" | "Who do you think? |
| Dem Mörder, und das bin ich! | His killer, and that killer is I! |

Just as the father seems about to add another patricide to a long line of them, he realizes that his young son has followed them. Seeing his boy's face finally stills his anger and interrupts the hereditary violence.

| | |
|---|---|
| Ihn graust, er zieht mit der Rechten schnell | He shivers in dread, and draws with his right hand |
| Sein Kind zu sich heran, | His boy toward him. |
| Und reicht die Linke auf der Stell | And extends his left hand then |
| Dem bösen Vater dann. | To the evil father. |
| "Steh auf, und steckst du auch morgen mir | "Get up, and even if tomorrow |
| Die Hütte ganz in Brand, | You set the whole house ablaze, |
| Ich setze den Stuhl in der neuen dir, | I'll put down in the new house your chair |
| Der in der alten stand."[51] | Which was in the old one." |

The ballad's story is concerned with the transmission of knowledge from one generation to the next, but it is the grimmest knowledge imaginable. The father has witnessed his grandfather's murder, and the realization that his son might do the same eventually stays his hand. The poem's first stanza is all about the fire, which the little boy has set, but which his father correctly surmises was set at the grandfather's instructions. Knowledge moves through the patriarchal line; it, like murderous madness, is an acquired trait that is passed down the family tree, as though on the Y-chromosome. But the same relationship that vouches for knowledge in the poem's story comes to undercut it in its form.

[51] Hebbel, "Vater und Sohn," in *Sämtliche Werke in zwölf Bänden*, 6:230.

That's because the poem deliberately compounds generations upon each other, and insists on narrative repetition so obsessively that it is often hard to parse *which* father does what to *which* son at any one point. The poem delights in maneuvering different relations next to each other, usually through apostrophe and repetition: "Mein Sohn, dein Knabe tat's," "Mein Vater, Sohn," "Mein Sohn, mein Sohn, nicht dorthinein." What moves the strange carousel of appellations in Hebbel's ballad is the linguistic fact that "father" and "son" are sliding signifiers, that, in other words, everyone has a father, but that the locution "my father" only rarely means the same person in two instances. Hebbel uses a similar effect to confuse killer and victim in the similarly bleak ballad "'s ist Mitternacht." But in "Vater und Sohn," this slide works only because of the poem's determinism: we cannot distinguish the various fathers and sons by their actions, because they all behave (at least initially) in the same murderous way.

What complicates matters further is the use of quotation marks throughout. These aren't strictly necessary in ballads, many were printed entirely without them in the nineteenth century. Hebbel includes them to offset the different dialogue partners (one person speaking in quotation marks, the other speaking in the same *Schriftbild* as the poem's narrator)—but in a way that again confuses rather than clarifies who is speaking. Sometimes the father's discourse is marked by quotes and the son's is presented as just plain poem-text, at others the reverse is true. And again, it is very difficult to determine who is screaming bloody murder, since both candidates are interchangeable in their murderousness.

Just as in Droste-Hülshoff's "Vorgeschichte," the poem plays with a juxtaposition between oral tradition and written transmission. And, as in Droste-Hülshoff's "Vorgeschichte," the intergenerational trauma that constitutes the family can really only be dispelled by written transmission—the quotation marks that promise to bring order into the balladic rendition of that trauma. "Vater und Sohn" performs a failure of orality: The poem's penchant for apostrophizing and repetition makes it a very tough poem to read or hear. Although "Vater und Sohn" is entirely about acts of oral transmission of knowledge, it crucially depends on the written form, above all the magic of the comma, which helps us make at least some sense of who is talking to whom at different moments. Writing down the events gives rise to a kind of civilizing process: fathers and sons no longer wantonly collapse into one another, we are able to prize apart one generation from the next. The comma creates a caesura in the heedless repetition of the previous generations' crimes and defects—a tradition of murder and mayhem that writing does all too well to disrupt.

As different as Hebbel's and Droste-Hülshoff's poems are, they coincide in this distrust of the patriarchal power of orality. If the ballads collected in Schiller's 1797 *Almanach* tended to celebrate (with some reservation) the wayward, heterodox, and anarchic power of oral literature against the stern "Wort und Werke" and "Brauch" of the sorcerers of this world, Hebbel, Droste-Hülshoff, and many others in their generation (Heinrich Heine and August von Platen, for instance, both born the same year as Droste-Hülshoff) tended to be far more suspicious of the oral. *Volkes Stimme* to them spoke not truth to power, but spoke rather power, the power of tradition, the force of habit, the inertia of patriarchy.

# 6 | The Ballad and Its Narratives

Since 1852, Friedrich Hofmeister's annual *Verzeichniss sämmtlicher in Deutschland und den angrenzenden Ländern gedruckten Musikalien* endeavored to collect all the sheet music published in the German-speaking world that year. In its 150 pages, Hofmeister's *Verzeichniss* for the year 1857 lists a little more than fifty musical pieces that their publishers designated as "ballads." Some are reissues or transcriptions, though the great majority reflect works first published in 1857. The number of pieces advertised as ballads is not huge, but what is striking is their broad range: Hofmeister's guide carefully distinguishes between different instrumentations and ensembles, and ballads are dotted throughout the categories. There are song settings and pieces without words. There are pieces that refer to a specific poem, there are others that do not. Some pieces, both instrumental and for voice, have titles that hint at a narrative, while others are just called *Ballade*. In some, a second instrument (the cello or the flute, for instance) doubles for the human voice, but many are simply for a single pianist.

The publishing house Kistner in Leipzig had put out a piano ballade by Ignaz Moscheles (op. 128), Luckhardt in Kassel sold a piano ballade (op. 60) by Friedrich Wilhelm Markull, and Spina publishers in Vienna published a piano ballade by Franz Jüllig (op. 15). Theodor Oesten's "Chromatopen, 12 brilliant *Tonstücke*" contain a ballade as part of a cycle, as do Ferdinand Hiller's *Vermischte Klavierstücke* (op. 66) and K. Merz's *Morceaux mignons*. And of course, several publishers pushed new and reissued piano transcriptions of operatic ballads, including one of Senta's ballad from *Der fliegende Holländer*. Carl Schuberth's *Morceaux characteristiques* for piano and cello contain a "ballade élégiaque," and Friedrich August Kummer's *Pièces de salon* for the same instruments include another setting of Senta's ballad. Hofmeister's compendium contains plenty of traditional ballad settings—for solo voice (Loewe's setting of Luise von Plönnies's "Der kleine Schiffer," op. 127), for chorus and soloists (H. Stiehl's "Der kühne Schiffer," op. 33), and dramatic scenes (the posthumous publication of Schumann's "Des Sängers Fluch," op. 139) either with piano or with full orchestra (Richard Würst's "Der Wasserneck," op. 30, which Hofmeister's *Verzeichniss* calls a "lyrical ballad" even though the publisher calls it a "lyrical cantata"). The *Verzeichniss* even lists one song setting in Swabian dialect ("Der Hans und 's Bäsle," by a certain C. Binder).

Given the massive growth of musical publishing in the German-speaking world by the mid-nineteenth century, the fact that ballads would appear at different segments of that market, targeted at professional singers and amateurs, at individual musicians, single households, and choral societies, is not altogether surprising. But it is nevertheless worth reflecting on the fact that by 1857 a musically inclined reader was as likely to encounter the word "ballad" on their piano, in their choir, or at their local orchestra as on their bookshelf. Sheet music at this point had a reading public and it seems that consumers largely accepted that the term "ballad" had such a broad range of applications. In previous chapters we have seen that the literary ballad had always had an unusually clear imagination of its own scene of reception, which meant that this newly expanded range of what a ballad *could* be and how it *could* be received stood in some tension with an equally developed sense of what a ballad was and what it wasn't.

This tension allowed composers to think through the relationship between music and literature, and between the popular and the elite. Just as audiences accepted written ballads as part of what they encountered in their everyday lives as literature, so did the musical public that constituted itself in Germany in the first part of the nineteenth century use balladry to habituate itself to certain concepts of what music was and how it could be shared. So, rather than a nostalgic fallback to older modes, the ballad was a way in which a musical modernity could enter the concert hall and the private home, even if the *sujets* of the pieces themselves were about thundering steeds and valiant knights.

Individual ballads tell stories, but the genre itself tells stories as well. Just-so stories about information passed along, lost or rediscovered, about collective memory and the spirit of the people. Even though this metanarrative of balladry was usually an artifice, the demand it placed on its audience was perfectly real. The very process of grasping what a ballad was trying to say told you where you landed in that metanarrative. Were you one of the moderns who had fallen away from the authentic oral culture from which the ballad hailed? Or were you resurrecting that earlier, more authentic culture? The fact that simply hearing the ballad meant telling oneself a story made the ballad a convenient object lesson for a musical public still coming to understand itself as such. In *Opera and Drama*, Richard Wagner had criticized contemporary music as "resembling the clavichord": "in it, each unit does the work of a community, but alas! In bare abstracto."[1] As they melded the supposedly collective genre of the ballad with more individualistic forms, composers specifically engaged with the question of how interpretation could become "the work of a community."[2] And in this context, interpretation meant largely the interpretation of narrative—not so much to fully understand it, but to ask after it in the right way. As John Daverio suggests in discussing Schumann's "Ossianic" compositions, supposedly Nordic forms (such as the ballad) became one way in which the programmatic was imported into and anchored in music.[3] To understand the narrative of a ballad meant to understand a narrative about the ballad—about art's position, and yes about the individual's position, in society.

All the newly invented forms that in the 1830s, 1840s, and 1850s went by the old name of "ballad" had to them a pedagogic element, constituted an attempt to form and mold interpretive communities, to mediate between elite and popular culture. As Jonathan Bellman has pointed out, "the ways in which music might recount a narrative were evolving in the first half of the nineteenth century."[4] What was also evolving was the sense of an audience for which these narratives ought to be made intelligible and meaningful. The ballad, a poetic genre that was supposed to come from and speak to the common *Volk*, seemed to raise this exact question of what it meant for a story to be meaningful for a particular community. The ballad and its many intermedial transfers were thus caught up in this evolution, but more important, they furnished a convenient arena for it. If composers wanted to figure out how music told stories, and wanted to impress their sense of musical narrative on an expanding audience for instrumental music, the ballad was a perfect vehicle through which to do that. Ideological questions of the imagined community of the German nation interacted with ideological questions of a far less imaginary crowd—the concert-going public.[5]

The orbit and immediate forerunners of the so-called New German School (*Neudeutsche Schule*) played a particularly significant role in this development. If the ballad was well-positioned across the different categories of Hofmeister's *Verzeichniss*, the "New Germans" and their great inspirations

---

1 Richard Wagner, *Opera and Drama* (Lincoln: University of Nebraska Press, 1995), 123.

2 See Mark Berry, *Treacherous Bonds and Laughing Fire: Politics and Religion in Wagner's "Ring"* (London: Routledge, 2016), 20.

3 John Daverio, "Schumann's Ossianic Manner," *19th Century Music* 21, no. 3 (1998): 247–73.

4 Jonathan Bellman, *Chopin's Polish Ballade: Op. 38 as Narrative of National Martyrdom* (New York: Oxford University Press, 2010), 35.

5 James Garratt, *Music Culture and Social Reform in the Age of Wagner* (Cambridge: Cambridge University Press, 2011).

Liszt, Wagner, and Schumann were responsible for a lot of it. And composers like Felix Draeseke, Joachim Raff, and Wendelin Weißheimer pushed the borders of balladry even further. Their efforts did not win widespread recognition even at the time; most of the works were only moderately successful and are largely forgotten today. But they speak to a historic moment in which the supposedly ancient genre of the ballad helped articulate something like a modern sense of musical audience and reception. As the case of Weißheimer makes clear, why they would turn to the ballad was not always clear. The young Weißheimer wrote a version of "Das Grab im Busento" for male chorus (premiered 1857), before he ever encountered Liszt's music, which made the most explicit case for the use of poetry in music.[6] It seems that for those composers seeking to experiment with form at mid-century, balladry simply was in the air.

When Weißheimer first came to work with Liszt in Weimar in 1860, the older composer decided to program a symphony based on Schiller's "Ritter Toggenburg" written by Weißheimer for a concert at court. It was a great honor, of course, but there was a problem: Weißheimer would not be able to see his own work performed, since "a concert at the grand ducal palace was restricted to the court and to nobility, and bourgeois subjects were excluded." But Liszt had a suggestion: "Simply put on a topcoat and a white cravat, take a violin, walk in with the violinists and act as though you were playing along." Weißheimer thus mimed his way through the premiere of his own symphony. After the performance, Liszt revealed the ruse to the Grand Duke and his wife. "Her Royal Highness," Weißheimer wrote in his memoirs, "asked after my sequence of thoughts [*Ideengang*] in the piece, since the program, with its note [that the symphony was an] 'Instrumental Introduction to Schiller's Ritter Toggenburg' had given her too few indications."[7]

The scene suggests how balladry connected diverse audiences and modern performers, how it provided a meeting ground both universally acknowledged as necessary and understood as somewhat fraught. At the same time, the meeting of aristocrat and burgher, of audience and composer, of enthusiast and professional takes place by way of the question of how to bring a literary program to bear on a piece of instrumental music. What unites the Grand Duchess of Saxe-Weimar-Eisenach and the young composer is the question, not his answer; the matter of his *Ideengang*, not some precise argument about compositional logic. The Grand Duchess desires "Deutung," which in context probably doesn't mean so much interpretation as an index,

---

6 Wendelin Weißheimer, *Erlebnisse mit Richard Wagner, Franz Liszt und vielen anderen Zeitgenossen nebst deren Briefen* (Munich: Deutsche Verlags-Anstalt, 1898), 60.

7 Weißheimer, *Erlebnisse mit Richard Wagner, Franz Liszt und vielen anderen Zeitgenossen nebst deren Briefen*, 57.

a hint. She asks about how she can connect a text she knows well to a piece of music she is encountering for the first time, not for him to do it for her.

## "Finding Words Again": The Instrumental Ballad Comes to Germany

It is tempting to read the move toward aesthetic politics among the New German composers as a displacement of energies left homeless after the unsuccessful revolutions of 1848.[8] But at least when it came to the ballad, the aesthetic politics in question had predated 1848 by some time. When the ballad began to establish itself as something other than a sub-form of the *Lied*, it did so with an implicit politics. And it maintained that politics after expanding into an even greater range of musical fields after 1848. Robert Schumann, in his function as critic rather than in his role as composer, would shape this initial broadening in the German-speaking world, without actually contributing to it. His wife-to-be Clara Schumann wrote a piano ballad in 1836 (op. 6, no. 4). And when Frederic Chopin published his Ballade No. 1 in G minor (op. 23) in 1835, Schumann decisively shaped its German reception (and indeed its reception until today). Chopin would dedicate the second ballade (in F Major, op. 38) to Schumann in 1839.

Schumann's most significant intervention into the reception of Chopin's ballades was likely the attribution of a literary basis to the pieces. It is disputed why exactly Chopin designated his four piano pieces as ballads: Günther Wagner and James Parakilas both suggest that Chopin meant to draw on the literary theories of the Romantic age.[9] Wiesław Lisecki instead proposed that Chopin intended to draw on the root meaning of the ballad—the ballad a *ballata*, a piece for dancing, rather than on poems for the piano.[10] The lineage Chopin was aiming for, he suggests, was a strictly musical rather than literary one. Karol Berger, by contrast, has suggested that especially the G minor ballade seems designed to bring to mind a literary rather than strictly musical rhetoric: the famous opening largo sounding "as if the speaker were short of breath or, better, still turning in his mind the subject of the about-to-be-opened story."[11]

---

[8] James Garratt, *Music, Culture and Social Reform after Wagner* (Cambridge: Cambridge University Press, 2010), 156.

[9] Günther Wagner, *Die Klavierballade um die Mitte des 19. Jahrhunderts* (Munich: Katzbichler, 1976), 113.

[10] Wiesław Lisecki, "Die Ballade von Frederic Chopin: Literarische oder musikalische Inspirationen," *Chopin Studies* 3 (1990): 305–18.

[11] Karol Berger, "The Form of Chopin's Ballade, Op. 23," *19th Century Music* 20, no. 1 (1996): 48.

Whatever Chopin's initial motivation, it is clear that Schumann seems to have been determined to understand the pieces in terms of an emphatically literary poetics. And it is equally clear that he was determined to link the new genre to a poetics with overt political investments. In an 1836 letter, Schumann told the conductor and theory teacher Heinrich Dorn (1804–1892) that Chopin had played the ballade in G minor for him, calling it Chopin's "most inspired work."[12] But his most significant framing came in one of the earliest reviews of the Ballade No. 2: there he called the first ballade "one of [Chopin's] wildest, most peculiar compositions," and lauded the second as "no less fantastical and inspired"—a vocabulary frequently employed for pieces in what John Daverio called the "Ossianic manner" in German Romantic instrumental music. But most significant, he hinted at how these works might be interpreted: Chopin had told him, Schumann reported, "that he had been inspired to write his ballads by a few poems of Mickiewicz," and adds that "in reverse a poet would have an easy time finding words again for this music."[13]

This brief remark seems to have launched more than a century of attempted pairings, and seems to have reinterpreted the generic contract implicit in the term "ballad." Unlike in the English-speaking world where Chopin's op. 23 was known as a "ballade," but "Sven Vondvedt" was a "ballad," German had to reconcile the same term with very different applications. But what is remarkable is probably less that they did so, but how easily they did. The way Chopin and Schumann together brought the piano ballad to Germany asked audiences to locate the ballad in two narratives: an internal one (what might be said to happen in a piece), and a second external one (what might be said to happen through the playing of a piece). And here the reception of Schumann's interpretation became just as important as the reception of the pieces themselves. Schumann only reports that Chopin was "inspired" by "a few poems." The possibility that these poems may have globally inspired this set of piano pieces was very quickly discarded in favor of the idea that an individual poem of Mickiewicz must have inspired each of the four ballades. Rather than derive something more general from a collectivity of poems—a mood, say, or an atmosphere—the conventional wisdom crystallized around the idea that Chopin had removed words from Mickiewicz's poems just as Schumann claims another poet could "find words again" (*wieder finden*) for the instrumental music. It treated the piano ballad as a Song without Words.

There is, as Bellman notes, something very strange about this: none of the poems usually adduced as inspirations for Chopin's ballades were designated as a ballad by its author.[14] Likewise, the mechanism Schumann's interpretation

---

12 Sept 14, 1836, cited in Judith Chernaik, *Schumann: The Faces and the Masks* (New York: Borzoi, 2018).

13 Robert Schumann, *Gesammelte Schriften über Musik und Musiker* (Leipzig: Breitkopf & Härtel, 1914), 32.

14 Bellman, *Chopin's Polish Ballade*, 20.

imputes to Chopin's writing process makes no mention of a direct transference of a specific poem's words or narrative into an instrumental piece. Schumann simply writes that "a poet would have an easy time finding words again for this music: it stirs the innermost." What makes for the translatability of poem to music and potentially back to words is the intensity of feeling transported, not a kind of narrative clarity.

This was, as Carl Dahlhaus pointed out, the sense of poetic meaning-making that guided Liszt's invention of the genre of *Symphonische Dichtung* in the 1840s—one that is diametrically opposed to the modernist understanding of that term: rather than *Dichtung* operating with words, poetry became the carrier of transcendent ideas.[15] In his landmark study of the instrumental ballad, James Parakilas suggests that Chopin basically performed the musical equivalent of what the twentieth century would call a structural analysis—rather than a specific tale, the piano ballade brought together narrative elements in a sequence that resembled the narrative elements of a ballad. It was, as Parakilas writes, a schema that depended on a prestabilized legibility of a certain set of formal or generic features to a certain kind of audience.[16] But of course the certain audience is key: unlike the immediate intelligibility of a narrative, the idea of generic features depends on a community that can properly respond to, or be taught to respond to, those features. To be an instrumental balladeer was to rise to some extent out of the mere narrative or musical towards a theory of communication. It was a way to be part of a phenomenon, and to be above it at the same time.

The ballad, by dint of its reliance on tropes, its familiar story beats, makes amateur structuralists of all of us. It seems Schumann understood the generic contract involved in Chopin calling his op. 23 a *Ballade* as follows: it commits the listener to bringing certain modes of literary reception to bear on the piece, without suggesting that those modes of reception necessarily map one-to-one onto music. As Bellman points out, "by virtue of its title, the ballad genre, even at this nascent point, implied a kind of narrative coherence and cohesion"[17]—in the ballad, fantasy, improvisation, feeling were somehow structured and guided. While Schumann does not make this explicit, it is not hard to guess why he and others thought reception of the ballads required structure and guidance. In the piano ballade, the bard figure has become the virtuoso: the tricky A flat major chord that opens the Ballade No. 1 bears little resemblance to the kinds of pseudo-harp arpeggios that

---

15 Carl Dahlhaus, "Dichtung und Symphonische Dichtung," *Archiv für Musikwissenschaft*, No. 39 (1982), 237–244.

16 James Parakilas, *Ballads without Words: Chopin and the Tradition of the Instrumental Ballade* (Portland, OR: Amadeus Press, 1992), 32/40.

17 Bellman, *Chopin's Polish Ballade*, 17.

had traditionally signaled balladic narration, for instance in opera. The story may be the same, but the scene of production and reception has altogether transformed. This is folk-likeness (*Volkstümlichkeit*) for the age of the mass audience. As balladry migrated from one medium to the other, Schumann's interpretation of the new genre insisted that there was some stable balladic core to be carried over from voice to piano. But it is important to note that his interpretation also involved the assumption of a decisive reconfiguration of its constituent units.

Jim Samson proposes several reasons for Chopin's balladic turn, and they may well hold true beyond the individual biography. He points out that the ballade (along with the first scherzos Chopin wrote sometime around his arrival in Paris) signaled a move away from the concert forms characteristic of Vienna classicism. Indeed, in this context the ballad, as an emphatically or even anti-classical literary form, was rhetorically powerful in asserting a caesura vis-à-vis what had come before. Samson also points to the fact that the ballad arrived at a moment when the piano had attained its dominance in nineteenth-century musical life, specifically its public dimensions, a "flamboyant, cosmopolitan and above all commercial concert life of a newly influential middle class."[18] Of course, much of this public performance was centered on the kinds of works one would have encountered in Hofmeister's 1857 *Verzeichniss*: potpourris, rondos, fantasias usually arranging or extemporizing on the work of others. Samson points out that works of this type were characteristic of Chopin's early output during his Warsaw years. The ballad was the moment he broke from it.

While Loewe's ballad settings were both performed in concert and sold to individual consumers for home use, Chopin's piano ballads depended on the increasingly public function of virtuosity: while they could be produced by a talented amateur in their own parlor, in other words, the piano ballades seemed to call out for a public. The ballades were not intended as the kind of showy compositions with which one could dazzle a well-heeled gaggle of burghers at a musical soirée. But their very designation as ballads carried a reminder of a kind of organic musical life that the figure of the bard-as-virtuoso seemed to fatally undercut: they relied on a profound asymmetry of performer and audience, of spectacle and consumption. It was almost as though interpreters like Schumann sought to hold at bay the scandal of a ballad circulation that could somehow do entirely without words. Not a ballad without narrative necessarily, but a ballad without a recognizable, easily retold narrative. After all, retelling was what ballads were all about. Insofar as they are ballads, Chopin's pieces are distinctly modern in that they presume

---

18 Jim Samson, *Chopin: The Four Ballades* (Cambridge: Cambridge University Press, 1991), 2.

FIG. 6.1 Johannes Brahms, 4 Ballades, op. 10, no. 1 (1854) with Brahms's designation "After the Scottish Ballad 'Edward' from Herder's *Stimmen der Völker.*"

that their performance arrests rather than extends circulation: What "plot" there is, what "dialogue" exists in the music, can no longer be paid forward. There is no re-creating it somewhere else, no holding it safe in one's mind to pass along at a later time—this parlor, this concert hall, this recording, is the end of the line. Its audience is not an audience of plausible repeaters, but an audience of mere listeners. Piano balladry is not storytelling, but it seeks to strongly resemble it.[19]

In the decades that followed, German composers tended to solidify the literary associations Schumann had first stoked.[20] Even as the piano ballade established itself as a musical genre of its own, composers were insistent to anchor it in the literary ballad tradition. When Johannes Brahms's Four Ballades op. 10 appeared with Breitkopf & Härtel in 1856 (Fig. 6.1), the composer made sure to place the note "Nach der schottischen Ballade: 'Edward' (in Herder's 'Stimmen der Völker')" before the first of the four pieces.[21] Even if he didn't provide a direct literary antecedent, Brahms's ballads seemed to gesture toward literary form.[22] Carl Tausig's op. 1c (1860), although an arrangement of a now-lost orchestral version, became well-known largely as a brilliant piano concert piece. Tausig (1841–1871) included the subtitle "Das Geisterschiff" on the cover, but interestingly didn't include the author of the text (Moritz von Strachwitz). Rather than attempt to resolve the

---

19 Charise Y. Hastings, *The Performer's Role: Storytelling in Ballades of Chopin and Brahms* (PhD diss., University of Michigan, 2006).

20 Wagner, *Die Klavierballade um die Mitte des 19. Jahrhunderts*, 71f.

21 William Horne, "Brahms's op. 10 Ballades and His *Blätter aus dem Tagebuch eines Musikers*," *Journal of Musicology* 15, no. 1 (1997), 98–115.

22 Ting-Chu Heather Shih, *"The" Four Ballades, Op. 10 of Johannes Brahms: A Song Cycle without Words* (DMA diss., Boston University, 2005).

ambiguous residue of literary balladry that Schumann had identified in, or possibly projected, onto Chopin's creations, the New German school seemed to want to maintain it.

## "Once Again a Ballad": The Origins of the Choral Ballad

After years of writing almost exclusively for solo piano, Robert Schumann's output in the 1840s veered decisively toward the voice, mostly in the shape of non-narrative songs. Among Schumann's extensive corpus of *Lieder* for voice and piano of the 1840s, there are some ballads, but most of his output consisted of non-narrative songs. Cycles such as *Liederkreis*, *Frauenliebe*, *Dichterliebe*, and *Myrthen* drew on the poetry of Heine, Rückert, Eichendorff, and Chamisso; were generally highly lyrical; and eschewed the dramatic trappings characteristic of, say, Loewe's ballad compositions. While impressive, the ballads—for instance, *Belsatzar* and *Die beiden Grenadiere* (both based on ballads by Heine)—were decidedly secondary.[23]

By 1850, when Schumann took over as chief conductor in Düsseldorf, both Schumann's attitude toward the voice and his attitude toward the ballad seem to have undergone another shift.[24] "The range of Schumann's Düsseldorf works," writes Martin Geck, "is vast: at one end of the scale are the intentionally popular choral ballads . . . , at the other the hermetic violin sonatas and the *Songs of Dawn*."[25] Schumann's only (and rather unsuccessful) opera *Genoveva* had its premiere in 1848, and the *Requiem for Mignon*, the 1852 Requiem, several oratorios, and a motet were written during this period.[26] But during the last years of his creative life, Schumann drew on the ballad-canon for an unusual form, namely large-scale choral works: alongside Uhland's "Des Sängers Fluch" (op. 139, 1852), the same poet's "Der Königssohn" (op. 116, 1851), and the works "Vom Pagen und der Königstochter" (op. 140, 1852) and "Das Glück von Edenhall" (op. 143, 1853) each draw either their subjects or their very words from that trove of ballads assembled in the first decades of the nineteenth century.

---

23 Susan Youens, *Heinrich Heine and the Lied* (Cambridge: Cambridge University Press, 2007), 194.

24 Lawrence Kramer, "A New Self: Schumann at 40," *Musical Times* 148, no. 1898 (2007): 3–17.

25 Martin Geck, *Robert Schumann: The Life and Work of a Romantic Composer* (Chicago: University of Chicago Press, 2013), 230.

26 Jürgen Schaarwächter, "Sublimierte Dramatik oder Klassizismus: Zu Schumanns Vokalkompositionen mit Orchester ab 1846," *Archiv für Musikwissenschaft* 54, no. 2 (1997): 152.

While Schumann had previously written more traditional ballad-settings for piano and voice, these new pieces were somewhere between the *Lied*, the cantata, opera, and oratorio.[27] They seemed to definitively exceed what ballad settings had been capable of since Zumsteeg's and Zelter's first settings; at the same time they didn't follow the logic of subsumption and expansion that Wagner had tested out in *Der fliegende Holländer*. Schumann's newfound devotion to the ballad form does not seem to have impressed his contemporaries very much, nor have his concert ballads endured in the canon the way his song cycles of the same era have. When in the spring of 1853, Schumann got in touch with the music critic Richard Pohl, who had adapted "Der Königssohn" and "Vom Pagen und der Königstochter," with plans for a new collaboration, the younger man reacted with dismay—"Once again a concert ballad,"[28] Pohl complained. Pohl's worries about the genre stemmed from a sense that it was borrowing from literature while riding roughshod over a certain literary logic. "It's easy to say to say we should adjust the manner of speaking to Uhland's," Pohl wrote to Schumann, "but how could we be completely successful in that? Or at least be seen to be successful by the demands of the [music] critics?"[29] Those critics, as well as audiences since, have largely agreed with him: as Geck notes, the trio of concert ballads is "rarely performed today."[30]

Where Loewe's and Schubert's ballads accommodated themselves to a newly emergent culture of domesticity, Schumann's grand choral ballads were written with another emergent cultural institution in mind: the lay chorus. As we will see in more detail in Chapter 7, the nonprofessional male choir was largely understood as a new phenomenon in the nineteenth century, and, especially for more nationalist observers, it resounded with the echoes of the popular uprising against the French in the 1810s. Decades later, the nationalist historian Heinrich von Treitschke noted Zelter's foundation of Berlin's *Singverein* in 1808 as an early stirring of German national spirit, and claimed (incorrectly) that the many similar *Vereine* and *Liedertafeln* were a largely North German (and thus ultimately Prussian) invention. "In the Prussian national army," he adds, "there was no end to cheerful singing during the war; Lützow's volunteers had a trained choir, and their example was, after the peace, imitated by many of the Prussian regiments."[31]

---

27 Michael Jarczyk, *Die Chorballade im 19. Jahrhundert* (Munich: Katzbichler, 1978), 13.
28 R. Larry Todd, *Schumann and His World*, 256.
29 Letter Pohl to Schumann, July 8, 1851 (cited in Sauerwald, 438).
30 Geck, *Robert Schumann*, 231.
31 Heinrich von Treitschke, *Treitschke's History of Germany* (New York: McBride Nast, 1916), 2:294.

For democrats and reformers the chorus was likewise an object of intense political preoccupation. It democratized the production and the reception of music, it mediated between high art and popular culture. When the composer, music teacher, and revolutionary writer Johanna Kinkel died in 1858, she left behind the novel *Hans Ibeles* (published in 1860), in which the main character expresses his dismay at the notion that the people are disconnected from true art: "With how much joy does the poor artisan take a much-needed hour from his breadwinning in order to sing in the chorus of a *Musikverein*? Don't hundreds stand still silently and intently listening, when a truly great, elevating composition is played outdoors?"[32] The very ubiquity of choral singing vouched for an organic integration not just of musical life, but of the people. Schumann's choral works of the 1850s, written like *Hans Ibeles* after the catastrophe of 1848, partook of the same musical politics.

In truth, Zelter's *Liedertafel* was a far more professional affair than later choral societies—its members were largely trained singers and musicians rather than amateurs. The impulse toward a democratization of voices came from Hans Georg Nägeli's *Gesangsbildungslehre für Männerchor* (1817), and thus from Switzerland rather than Prussia. But whatever the historical sequence, the idea that the spontaneous raising of a group of (usually male) voices had immediate political significance was widespread in the early to mid-nineteenth century. In that context, as Burkhardt Sauerwald has pointed out, it cannot count as accidental that Schumann discovered the nonprofessional chorus after the failed revolution of 1848.[33] It also surely isn't an accident that he turned to a crop of uniquely politicized authors, including Ludwig Uhland (1787–1862), to furnish his subjects, and that he brought that nonprofessional chorus onto the stage to sing ballads.

Schumann was not alone in bringing together an expansion of the musical means of production with poets associated with the struggle for democratization. In his study of the Uhland-adaptations of Schumann, Kreuzer, and Silcher, Sauerwald has shown that their choral versions of Uhland's ballad were all pitched at a particular kind of chorus. For while Schumann's orchestral parts and solo voices are somewhat demanding, the choral part seems targeted at amateur voices.[34] Silcher and Kreuzer went even further in this regard, seemingly keen to keep their versions of *Des Sängers Fluch* accessible to nonprofessional vocalists and instrumentalists alike. But in some way, Schumann presents the more interesting solution: his cantata mediates

---

32 Johanna Kinkel, *Hans Ibeles in London: Ein Familienbild aus dem Flüchtlingsleben* (Stuttgart: Cotta, 1860), 55.

33 Burkhardt Sauerwald, *Ludwig Uhland und seine Komponisten: zum Verhältnis von Musik und Politik in Werken von Conradin Kreutzer, Friedrich Silcher, Carl Loewe und Robert Schumann* (Berlin: lit Verlag, 2015).

34 Ibid.

between the inclusiveness of amateur performance and the exclusivity of virtuosic performance. It is neither fully geared toward lay musicians, nor public in a professionalized, commercialized sense. As Celia Applegate has pointed out, for Schumann and many liberals of his generation, "the all-important aspect of their work was its publicness, not its politics." Moreover, "the publicness that concerned them was emphatically not that defined either by commerce or by state authority."[35] Insofar as the various players in Schumann's monumental ballads were gathered as an audience around the singing of ballads, they could stand in for a public that was neither about commerce nor about the state.

But of course they were not just singing ballads: what ballads the professional soloists and the amateur chorus rehearsed were embedded in a full concert piece that runs about forty minutes. In *Des Sängers Fluch*, the large scale, the collective nature of these compositions ran up against the admittedly contained scope of the German art ballad. In purely formal terms, the main reason Schumann got interested in them seems to have been the same that made Wagner center *Der fliegende Holländer* on a ballad ten years prior: a concern with a cohesive whole. The choral ballad was intended to take the place of non-staged excerpts of select snippets from popular operas.[36] Of course, it was still created by either distending an existing short text, or (more frequently) by grafting several literary texts together and hoping for some congruency—but at least their connection was motivated by considerations of drama rather than simply of popularity.

Portions of Schumann's music clearly hew to what John Daverio called Schumann's Ossianic mode, characterized by "a pervasive melancholy tone" and "invocations of the harp."[37] At the same time, its fanfares, the simple triadic harmonies, and the many fifths and octaves draw from Schumann's "chivalric" song cycles, such as *Dichterliebe*.[38] But unlike, say, the composer's *Romanzen und Balladen* (op. 67), *Des Sängers Fluch* doesn't sustain either tone throughout. The question of balladry is here referred to a larger whole: the Ossianic mode has a function to fulfill within a totality. The source for Schumann's efforts may well have been Nils Gade's 1846 cantata *Comala: A Dramatic Poem*, which drew on Macpherson's Ossian for its text, but on several of Gade's ballad settings in its musical arrangements.[39] So from the first,

---

35 Celia Applegate, "Robert Schumann and the Culture of German Nationhood," in *Rethinking Schumann*, ed. Roe-Min Kok and Laura Tunbridge (Oxford: Oxford University Press, 2011), 7.

36 Sauerwald, *Ludwig Uhland und seine Komponisten*, 340–42.

37 John Daverio, "Schumann's Ossianic Manner," 247.

38 Jonathan Bellman, "Aus alten Märchen: The Chivalric Style of Schumann and Brahms," *Journal of Musicology* 13 (1995): 117–35.

39 R. Larry Todd, *Mendelssohn-Essays* (New York: Routledge, 2008), 62.

the choral ballad brought together two things: a broad collective, a large audience, for a sung ballad, and a not-so-covert pedagogic impetus, a desire to get the collective to listen to ballads in the right way, yes, to listen to art music in the right way.

Uhland's poem "Des Sängers Fluch" ("The Minstrel's Curse") is well chosen for exploring these and related questions: the poem celebrates the spontaneous power music can have even over untrained audiences, but it just as severely cautions against bad listening practices. As so often in balladry (think of Heine's "Belsazar," explored in Chapter 3), the right way to listen or to read is fairly obvious and democratically available, but that does not mean that no wrong way to listen or to read exists. And precisely because listening or reading incorrectly makes you immediately a minority among the rapt host, it is coupled with denunciation—almost everyone gets it, and if you don't there is something deeply wrong with you. In the poem, as in Schumann's oratorio, two bards arrive at a royal court. Their song melts everyone's heart: courtly irony collapses as genuine feeling envelops all. It is precisely this genuine aesthetic response on the part of his courtiers that outrages the king. Even though their song is not political, he understands the bards' purchase on their audience as competition, as a form of political seduction. Their voices are doing something that only his voice should by rights be allowed to do. "You have beguiled my people, beguile you now my queen?"[40] ("Ihr habt mein Volk verführet, verlockt ihr nun mein Weib?"), he screams as he thrusts his sword into the younger bard. But as the title intimates, the singer's voice wins out. Leaving the blood-stained hall, the older bard curses the palace and the king: may the king's name ring out voiceless into thin air.

| "Dein Name sei vergessen, in ew'ge Nacht getaucht, | "Thy name shall be forgotten, steeped in eternal night, |
| Sei, wie ein letztes Röcheln, in leere Luft verhaucht!"[41] | And, like a dying rattle, in empty air take flight!"[42] |

King and bard both seem to understand their friction as one between competing voices. The king recognizes in bardic singing a kind of usurpation of his power. And the bard uses his curse to limit the king's power to the present, to withhold it from posterity. He can do this because letting kings' names ringing out after their deaths is a bard's stock-in-trade. "Des Königs

---

40 Ludwig Uhland, "The Minstrel's Curse," trans. Margarete Münsterberg, in *A Harvest of German Verse* (London and New York: Appleton, 1916), 99.

41 Ludwig Uhland, "Der Sängers Fluch," in *Gedichte (Ausgabe Letzter Hand)*, ed. Hartmut Fröschle and Walter Scheffler (Munich: Winkler, 1980), 252.

42 Uhland, "The Minstrel's Curse," 99.

Namen meldet kein Lied, kein Heldenbuch; / Versunken und vergessen! das ist des Sängers Fluch" ("No songs, no book of heroes the monarch's name rehearse; / Dissolved in night, forgotten! That is the minstrel's curse.") Uhland's poem closes. And indeed Uhland's ballad remains faithful to the terms of the bard's curse, doesn't utter the king's name or describe his kingdom. Indeed, it's worth reflecting that the ballad, with its love of generics ("the singer," "the king"), is uniquely suited to carrying out such erasure. For Uhland a ballad is ultimately the best revenge. While Schumann shared Uhland's politics, his version of the story has an altogether different political economy of posterity altogether—if for no other reason than that it cannot consign the king to silence the way Uhland does.

On June 25, 1851, Schumann wrote to Pohl that "it occurred to me that many a ballad with little effort and good effect could be treated as a concert-musical piece for solo voices, chorus and orchestra."[43] It is a strange, almost cavalier outline of the task—"little effort" (*leichte Mühe*) seems strangely mercantile framing for such an undertaking—but both the composer and his increasingly frustrated librettist seemed to agree that directness and naturalness were of paramount importance. The balladic material needed to be translated without being distorted—the very directness of its appeal (its "good effect") depended on it. This makes *Des Sängers Fluch* an excellent test case for what counted as directness: what in the ballad needed to be preserved? What did Schumann want to ensure the audience got out of it? And how did one go about preserving it? The answers to all these questions are deeply revealing.

The cover of the posthumous edition refers to the piece simply as "a ballad," but if that is what it is, it is a ballad of ballads. Pohl's libretto brings together the narration from Uhland's ballad, a few recitatives and duets with text by Pohl, and snippets from various songs by Uhland. What results from this montage can at times resemble an oratorio in the vein of Schumann's earlier *Das Paradies und die Peri* (op. 50, 1843), but in scale and length calls to mind Felix Mendelssohn-Bartholdy's cantata *Die erste Walpurgisnacht* based on poetry by Goethe (op. 60, 1830/1843). Unlike Goethe's *Die erste Walpurgisnacht*, which was written for music (though the intended arrangement by Carl Friedrich Zelter never materialized), Uhland's compact poem made an awkward fit for the cantata form, something Schumann, all his talk of "little effort" notwithstanding, seems to have recognized.

*Des Sängers Fluch* combines several texts in a way that seems, as in Wagner's *The Flying Dutchman*, to propose something akin to a theory of the ballad. For rather than expand the ballad, filling it with incident and additional characters, Schumann largely chooses to refract the plot of Uhland's ballad

---

43 Quoted in Martin Demmler, *Robert Schumann: "Ich hab im Traum geweinet": Eine Biographie* (Stuttgart: Reclam, 2006), 227.

internally through a mise-en-abyme. The work opens with a short orchestral prelude and a narrative introduction by an alto solo voice, declaiming the first three stanzas of Uhland's poem. The narration begins as a *Lied*, but increasingly turns into a recitativo. Then the first character in the story speaks: one of the two singers, here called a "Harfner," sings the text Uhland gives him to say in the ballad. A fairly straightforward operatic duet follows with a text by Pohl.

After an orchestral fanfare, the narrator returns and picks up Uhland's ballad text. The king, the young singer, and the queen each has a brief aria (the text of each by Pohl), and then the bards launch into their first of three songs. This one ("In dem Thale der Provence") thematizes the origins of Minnesang and is partly based on the poem that opens Uhland's cycle *Sängerliebe*. The chorus of courtiers chimes in to express its admiration for the song, and the king demands a second song, "a legend [*Sage*] of olden days, when only the sword decided and blood paid for blood." That second song turns out to be another ballad by Uhland, "Die drei Lieder," the story of a king demanding three songs from a wandering bard—a choice the king, not entirely shockingly, takes to be a reference to himself. Specifically, he seems to think the ballad refers to him killing his brother and claiming the throne. At this point, it is the queen's and the courtiers' turn to demand a song "the German hymn, a song of freedom of a beautiful age," and the two bards comply—the lyrics to their final song are a rearrangement of the closing stanzas of Uhland's "Gesang und Krieg."

Each balladic performance within the ballad, then, is performed for an audience that has specifically requested it. Where Wagner's *Flying Dutchman* positions the balladic audience as a predominantly receptive one, largely at the mercy of the music and the ancient tale that seizes them, Schumann and Pohl present a democratized and dynamic relationship between singer and audience. The king, the queen, and the courtiers may have little choice but to be affected by the singers' ballads, but they have a choice in what type of ballad they would like to hear. They make specific requests for how they would like to be seized by ancient tales. While Uhland's ballad leaves out the song that sets the catastrophe in motion, Schumann and Pohl give the audience three separate songs that bring about the murder—they want the audience to recognize what in Uhland was ineffable as profoundly discursive and political. Aesthetic response and aesthetic choice are forms of political positioning. For all its ancient garb and chivalric fanfares, then, Schumann and Pohl want to politicize aesthetic recuperation: choose your nostalgia wisely, they seem to say, for it may determine your politics.

At the same time, the persistent internal mirroring in Pohl's organizational scheme also pushes the relationship of part and whole to the forefront. Pohl's solution to the problem of how to turn a short poem into a large-scale musical piece was to extend the original ballad by adding different songs and ballads by Uhland—by his own count about fifteen of them. This was not Schumann's initial solution to the same problem: he had asked his librettist to simply fill in the ballad, keeping the same meter and cadence as the original poem, something Pohl thought simply couldn't be done. In trying to avoid simply "watering down" the original ballad, as he put it, Pohl turned to the author Uhland as the unifying authority. His aim: "Let Uhland speak for himself."[44] The poet even makes a tongue-in-cheek appearance in the libretto. The two bards claim to have learned the second song they sing for the king "from Master Ludwig's mouth, when we came this way through Swabia"—a clear reference to Ludwig Uhland, who was born in Tübingen.

In expanding Uhland's ballad, then, and expanding it in a way that retained a certain coherence and formal rigor, Pohl and Schumann seem to have made the same assumption about what their audience needed to get from the choral ballad—in a word: coherence—but very different assumptions of what their audience would bring to the ballad. Both Pohl's and Schumann's solutions assumed a certain foreknowledge on the part of the audience and sought to leverage that foreknowledge in specific directions. Where Pohl assumed that an audience would either know or somehow sense that the different numbers used to stretch out the original balladic story came from the same author, namely Uhland, Schumann seems to have thought that the audience might notice inconsistencies in the language or meter of the libretto. As in Schumann's imbrication of instrumental ballade and literary genre, the composer intended to instill a hermeneutic process in his audience, one that made certain assumptions of what that audience brought to bear "naturally," and certain assumptions about what aesthetic categories they needed to develop.

## "Lenore" at 100: The Symphonic Ballad

Ten years after Schumann had sought to fit Uhland's ballad *Des Sängers Fluch* for a choral garb, the ballad's migrations brought it into the sphere of the symphonic poem. In 1860, as we saw, Wendelin Weißheimer premiered his "Toggenburg" in Weimar. In 1863, Hans von Bülow premiered an orchestral ballade based on "Des Sängers Fluch" in Berlin (op. 16). It was recognizably a symphonic poem that hewed closely to Uhland's plot. But more than plot, Bülow's orchestral ballad seemed intent on mimicking certain balladic effects: what Schumann had achieved by multiple voices, von Bülow recreated through leitmotif technique. The specifically balladic attunement between singer and audience that Wagner's *Flying Dutchman* had put on stage, Bülow brought out through sly motivic resonances. Like Schumann, Bülow not only

---

44 Letter Pohl to Schumann, July 8, 1851 (cited in Sauerwald, 438).

filled in the song that is missing in Uhland's poem, but in fact made it the center of the piece—a plaintive melody that begins with an arpeggio for solo cello, but is later taken up by the orchestral collective.

Although well-received at the time, none of these orchestral ballads was exactly influential—in fact, the most lasting legacy of Bülow's work may have been that while he was busy rehearsing the piece, his friend Richard Wagner and his wife Cosima struck up their fateful friendship.[45] The symphonic ballad did not occupy pride of place within the broader field of the symphonic poem—as James Parakilas has written: "orchestral *ballades* are simply those symphonic poems that happen to have ballads for their poems."[46] And while in Germany a number of composers from the New German orbit contributed to the genre in the 1860s and 1870s, the form would become influential only much later and outside of Germany: the genre's true heyday were the 1890s, and it proved most influential in France (where Paul Dukas wrote perhaps the most famous orchestral ballad of all, *L'apprenti sorcier* [1897]), in Scandinavia (where a young Jean Sibelius wrote the symphonic ballad *Skogsrået* in 1894[47]), and in Eastern Europe (where Bedřich Smetana, Antonín Dvořák, Peter Ilyich Tchaikovsky, and many others composed in the form).

And yet, the very fact that the orchestral ballad depends for its definition on its literary origin puts it at an interesting nexus in the development of the theory of program music and its relationship to the theory of literature. While symphonic poems generally were concerned with tone painting, the symphonic ballad in particular sought to emulate highly specific plots. The German ballad was regarded as being about compression, and that meant about moments of intensity, rather than about the kinds of episodic or picaresque narratives that, say, Strauss could rely on for his *Till Eulenspiegel*, Emil Niklaus von Reznicek for his *Schlemihl*, or Ernst Boehe for his *Odysseus*. As a result, as Parakilas notes, "while narrative action might be barely suggested in other symphonic poems, it is the shaping force in most orchestral *ballades*."[48] This is particularly true for Gottfried August Bürger's ballad "Lenore," which is mostly concerned with a single action—a wild ride. Bürger's poem tells the story of a woman left behind when her beloved Wilhelm goes off to war. When Wilhelm returns one night to invite her on a ride, Lenore, blinded by love or no longer caring to read

---

45 Oliver Hilmes, *Cosimas Kinder: Triumph und Tragödie der Wagner-Dynastie* (Munich: Siedler, 2010).

46 Parakilas, *Ballads without Words*, 204.

47 Veijo Murtomäki, "Sibelius's Symphonic Ballad *Skogsrået*: Biographical and Programmatic Aspects of His Early Orchestral Music," in *Sibelius Studies*, ed. Timothy Jackson and Veijo Murtomäki (Cambridge: Cambridge University Press, 2001), 107.

48 Parakilas, *Ballads without Words*, 204.

the warning signs, climbs onto his ghostly steed. In a wild hunt, spectral Wilhelm and Lenore rush toward what turns out to be his grave, and disappear together to hell.

The poem was widely renowned for its use of rhythm and assonance. An exponent of storm-and-stress aesthetic, Bürger wanted the form of "Lenore" to arise fairly directly from the content narrated, rather than being imposed on it from the outside. This organicism didn't prevent it from circulating widely and in a dizzying range of media: It found admission into rarefied collections of poetry, while also circulating widely in so-called *Liedflugschriften*, broadsheets that were often colorfully illustrated in the manner of traditional murder ballads. It was also an early and highly successful export item. As we have seen, in his "Essay on the Imitation of the Ancient Ballad," Sir Walter Scott had singled out "Lenore" for its "imitative harmony,"[49] specifically the way the thunder of hooves seemed to echo through the poem's breathless meter. Visual representations of Lenore's wild ride proliferated in print, in etchings, in paintings—with the most famous ones by Louis Boulanger, Lady Diana Beauclerk, and William Blake. "Lenore" quickly inspired song settings, by Josef Javůrek, Johann Friedrich Reichardt, and Johann Zumsteeg,[50] a melodrama by Antonín Reicha, as well as an *opera semi-seria* by the Italian composer Saverio Mercadante. Precisely because the meter seemed to give the ballad its own native music, several composers decided not to give the text to any voice to sing. Richard Kügele (op. 8) and Franz Liszt (S 346) both composed melodramatic accompaniments for declamation (see Chapter 2).

Finally, the year Bürger's poem turned a hundred years old, it inspired both a symphonic poem and a symphony, the former by August Klughardt, the latter by Liszt's erstwhile assistant Joachim Raff. Raff published his work as a symphony, even though part of it is quite obviously a symphonic poem; the younger Klughardt, wishing to cede him pride of place, published what is recognizably a four-movement symphony as a "symphonic poem in four parts."[51] Raff's Symphony No. 5 (op. 177) had its premiere in 1870 and went on to immediate success, even if it, like its composer, is little remembered today. The story of "Lenore"'s peregrination across media is also a story about form, form un-imposed and re-imposed. "Lenore" began its life as a poem the form of which was supposed to flow organically from its content. The meter of "Lenore" was the beat of hooves, not the dictate

---

49 Sir Walter Scott, "Essay on the Imitation of the Ancient Ballads," in *The Poetical Works* (Edinburgh: Black, 1875), 1:269.

50 Lorraine Gorrell, *The Nineteenth Century German Lied* (Pompton Plains, NJ: Amadeus, 1993), 18.

51 Alan H. Krueck, "A Tale of Two *Lenores*—or Is It Three?," http://www.raff.org/support/download/krueck/krueck_theree_lenores%20.pdf.

of the Alexandrine; its assonances and rhymes the whispers of nocturnal nature, not of poetic contrivance; its repetitions and onomatopoeias were supposed to be the rumblings of the unconscious mind, not the waxings of a clever wordsmith.

This emphatic balladic spontaneity clearly informs its resurrection a hundred years later as a symphonic poem, a genre for which very similar claims were extended. And yet, when Raff deals with the subject matter, he integrates the symphonic ballad into a traditional sonata-form symphony. Raff was deeply attuned to Liszt's reasons for championing programs, yet he varied his approach to programs throughout his career. For one, he never used the new hybrid genre of "symphonic poem" championed by his mentor, preferring to work in the forms that constituted the symphonic poem's ancestry—the symphony (of which Raff wrote eleven) and the overture (of which he wrote at least ten, one of which is today lost). His symphonies integrated their programs with the sonata form. Moreover, the kinds of programs Raff relied on could range widely: his tetralogy of seasonal symphonies, as his Alpine Symphony and his Forest Symphony, are really more characteristic and ekphrastic pieces; then there is Symphony No. 6 (op. 189, 1873), known today mostly by its program: "Gelebt: Gestrebt, Gelitten, Gestritten, Gestorben, Umworben" ("Lived: Striven, Suffered, Fought, Died, Sought After"). But in a work like the Symphony No. 6, the unifying program Raff provides really serves to animate a fairly traditional sequence of movements, true to what William Newman has called program music's "double-function form"[52]: living and struggling happen in an expository Allegro non troppo, suffering and fighting happen in a Vivace, the third movement signifies death with a Funeral March, and the remembrance part closes out the affair in a chorale in Allegro.

The "Lenore" symphony is different. Rather than double-function form, Raff relies on a gradual change of form into function. The first two movements—an Allegro and an Andante quasi larghetto subtitled collectively "The Happiness of Love"—hew to the kind of generalized programmatic writing that characterized most of Raff's symphonies. The third and fourth movements play by different rules, although those rules are not immediately made clear. At some point the four-movement symphony transforms into a symphonic poem, which shadows the narrative of the ballad quite scrupulously—although interestingly the point at which it begins to do so is difficult to pinpoint. It certainly isn't at the beginning of the third movement, or at the beginning of the final movement, which is actually subtitled

---

52 William Newman, *The Sonata since Beethoven* (Chapel Hill: University of North Carolina Press, 2018), 134.

"ballade." There is thus one form, the symphonic poem, nesting inside the sonata form, but it nests uncomfortably and messily.

Unlike a musical *ekphrasis* (say, Rachmaninoff's "Isle of the Dead"), turning a ballad into a symphony involves the interpretation of one temporal medium by means of another. And here it mattered that in the case of "Lenore" the temporality of the poem's cadences would have been immediately present for much of the symphony's audience. The listener of Raff's symphony who had never read or heard Bürger's poem simply did not exist. Many listeners in 1870 likely could have recited it from memory. That makes it significant that little of the ballad's "native" rhythm or narrative cadence survives in Raff's symphonic treatment in the first three movements. There is no sense of the high drama in which ballads traditionally traffic, and which was so highly prized in the antiquarian revival around the turn of the nineteenth century. Only the fourth movement ("Reunited in death, Introduction and ballad") actually follows the sequence of events presented in Bürger's poem. It abandons the ABA-structures that persist in movements I through III, and relies on reprises of thematic material from all previous movements. The rhythmic structure suddenly takes on a recognizable "balladic" form, as Raff emulates Bürger's celebrated metric re-creation of spectral Wilhelm's wild ride in musical form, and the unremitting meter of its balladic narration becomes a breathless perpetual motion in the low strings, as the woodwinds and later the trombone raise the tension, accelerating throughout the movement until Wilhelm and Lenore reach the gravesite.

It's tempting to surmise that Raff presents only this fourth movement as a symphonic poem "in all but name,"[53] as Jonathan Kregor has done, and to treat only this movement as a one-to-one transposition of Bürger's ballad (it is only here, 150 pages into the score, that "nach Bürgers Lenore" is added). But that neglects the fact that the first three movements *do* recapitulate events related in the ballad; they simply don't present them in the sequence they are related there. Narratologically speaking, the four movements lay out a program that follows the *récit*, but not the *narration* of the ballad: the events of the first three movements are present in Bürger's poem only in analeptic insertions, whereas only the fourth goes through the gesture of narrating. The symphony thus acknowledges its own structure as a kind of epic storytelling, whereas the ballad presents the story of a compressed episode. In the course of Raff's Symphony No. 5, we witness one kind of storytelling, and then follow its compression into another, a balladic, mode of storytelling. This compression allies symphonic poem and balladic storytelling, symphony and epic storytelling.

---

53 Jonathan Kregor, *Program Music* (Cambridge: Cambridge University Press, 2015).

## "The Secure Bed of a Unitary Thought": The Symphonic Poem and the Ballad Form

If the invention of the genre of *Symphonische Dichtung* took recourse to a specific understanding of *Dichtung* as the carrier of transcendent ideas, it sought to thereby – by a sort of generic fiat – also guard against a charge of arbitrariness when it came to the relationship between language and music.[54] The ballad emerged from the same ideology of the poetic: rather than a specific reconstruction of popular poetry, it drew on a supposed core essence of a particular folksong and simply gave it a new outward poetic shape. This was how Johann Gottfried Herder had presented his folksong collection *Stimmen der Völker in Liedern*. When Johannes Brahms turned the ballad "Edward" from this collection into the basis of his piano ballad op. 10, no. 1, he simply extended the idea of poetic translatability that had guided Herder in compiling the *Stimmen* in the first place. The reason neither Herder nor Brahms took himself to be unduly manipulating their sources by re-writing and remediating them was that both adaptations to them presented the idea "behind" the folk song. Poet-compiler, as well as composer, could make dramatic changes, or bring a tale into an altogether new medium, and the poem remained essentially the same thing. The tone poem was able to draw on this understanding of poetry, to derive aesthetic plausibility and intelligibility from it. Liszt's tone poems were neither translations nor adaptations of literary language into new language—they took an idea or mythic kernel that preexisted its own literary assertion and gave it musical shape. This was why most "symphonic poems" did not take their names from novels, plays, or stories that existed in only one version—they drew on the mythic building blocks "behind" canonic texts. And however infrequently ballads were the quarry from which symphonic poems were drawn, it would have been deeply plausible to most Germans of the 1850s that balladry did something rather similar.

At the same time, the symphonic ballad came with one peculiarity, at least in the German context: while the stories behind the ballad were (usually falsely) assumed to be ancient myths, they were famous in one specific linguistic guise, famous moreover to the extent that people could recite them by heart, or sing them in their musical song settings. And as the debate over Schubert's and Loewe's variant interpretations of Goethe's *Erlkönig* made clear, listeners and musicians alike were loath to surrender their hermeneutic ownership of specific interpretations of the ballads.[55] The composer was, in

---

54 Hans Heinrich Eggebrecht, *Musik im Abendland* (Munich: Piper, 1991), 671.

55 Christopher H. Gibbs, "'Komm geh' mit mir': Schubert's Uncanny *Erlkönig*," *Nineteenth Century Music* 19, no. 2 (1995): 115–35.

the final analysis, also a first reader, with all the potential for reinterpretation and misinterpretation that entailed. The very currency of the ballad thus challenged its assimilability into the new form of the symphonic poem. The musical ballad had great currency among Liszt's students, but in two distinct, almost contradictory modes that drew on two distinct understandings of the ballad. Hans von Bülow, for instance, wrote a well-known "Ballade" for piano op. 11 in the Lisztian mode, but also wrote the aforementioned "orchestral ballade" (op. 16) based on Uhland's "Des Sängers Fluch." Whereas op. 11 is a dreamy piece, narrative and clearly dialogical, the "orchestral ballade" is essentially divided into three narrative tableaux (the court, the song, the curse), the middle of which—the bard's song—takes up the vast majority of the piece. These two pieces envision an altogether different of audience for themselves: in op. 11 the listeners *are* the ones hearing the ballade, in op. 16 we hear an orchestra stage for us the telling of a ballad and its effect on *its* listeners.

In the case of Raff's "Lenore," this understanding is reflected above all in the strange ways in which the symphonic poem stands throughout in dialogue with the more expansive, more conventional form of the symphony. The symphonic poem is supposed to dissolve the four-movement structure of the symphony, while somehow preserving its elements; embedding this embryonic symphony within an actual sonata form creates an informative tension. Since the motivic material for the symphonic poem comes entirely from the first three movements, the symphony seems to make Liszt's argument that the symphonic poem constitutes a sort of sublation of symphonic form—but why would Raff choose to undercut that argument by preserving the forms supposedly made irrelevant by his final movement?

The answer likely lies in how Raff wanted his listeners, familiar with Bürger's text and familiar with a canon of ballads that asked them to imagine themselves as a particular kind of audience, to make sense of the developmental schema of his piece. Just like Liszt, Raff drew on the literary hermeneutics that developed in Germany out of the critical philosophy of Kant, as well as Romantic responses to that philosophy. After all, both ballad and symphonic poem were models for the kind of understanding that did not proceed from pre-existing form, but rather established parameters for understanding dynamically. And it was this *dynamism* that was the form's real point. Both genres were supposed to organically create their own form. This was possible because the understanding of program common in the New German School took the program to establish the autonomy of musical form. The ballad sprang up as a reaction to the rule-aesthetics of the eighteenth century, the symphonic poem was an initial reaction against the sonata-form. While program-music's detractors tended to see the narrative dimension of the program an addition, a crutch, a guardrail through the roiling cauldron of the music of the will, its advocates, as Richard Strauss insisted, saw the "poetical program" as a step in "the creation of new form," that is to say the form-giving impulse *of* the will freed from the constraints of traditioned musical form.

Liszt's essay "Berlioz und seine Harold Symphonie" of 1855 charged that proponents of "absolute music" proceed from the assumption that music, through a process of historical trial and error, had worked to an incontrovertible set of forms that were inviolable.[56] While a mischaracterization, it points to the fact that Liszt thought of compositions adhering to a program, borrowing a pre-existing schema from a literary text, an historic event, or a preformulated sequence, as freeing themselves from old schemata. This seems counterintuitive: program music inserts a musical text into a literary tradition, and yokes, for better or for worse, its own prerogative for formal invention to centuries-old dictates. And yet, Liszt thought of this act as liberating. Liszt defined a program as

> Some sort of preface added to the pure instrumental music in comprehensible language, with which the composer undertakes to protect the listener of the arbitrariness of poetical exegesis vis-à-vis his work, and to direct their attention in advance to the poetical idea of the Whole.[57]

On the face of it, this characterization seems to confirm the worst stereotypes about program music. At the same time, it's hard to fathom just why this sort of description would have appealed to someone like Wagner: the insistence on "verständliche Sprache" as opposed to the churning incomprehensibility of musical syntax, seems to turn Schopenhauer on his head. Schopenhauer had understood music as the language of the Will, the other arts (above all the language-based ones) as expression of the Will's self-alienation into discrete individual objects—the world of "representations" (*Vorstellungen*) beholden to the *principium individuationis*. Language, in Liszt's description, seems designed to safely return music from the limitless world of the Will to such specific *Vorstellungen*—a horror for any Schopenhauerian.

Dahlhaus made the case for the debate over program music as a deeply conflicted response to Schopenhauerian aesthetics of music. With regard to the passage from Liszt just cited, it is worth pointing out what Liszt is not saying: the "verständliche Sprache" of the preface is not required to aid the listener hopelessly at sea in the limitless ocean of musical material. It is rather required in order to curb our associations in order to free them—to rein in a *Willkür* without limit, logic, or purchase. In surrendering to language, Liszt seems to think, neither composer nor listener surrenders interpretive

---

56 Franz Liszt, "Berlioz und seine Harold-Symphonie," in *Gesammelte Schriften* (Leipzig: Breitkopf & Härtel 1882), IV:92.

57 Ibid., IV:101.

freedom, but rather actualizes it. Hegel's *Philosophy of Right* provides a classic explanation of why *Willkür* is not freedom. In arbitrariness, our freedom is purely formal, that is, it has no content and no reasons to guide—and it therefore is no freedom at all, because a form that does not generate its content out of itself is not truly autonomous. Liszt had read Hegel, but he would have encountered this theory of freedom largely as a social philosophy, and largely through the *Aesthetics*.[58] His concern was with what an arbitrary interpretation said about an individual's position in the broader polity. To be seized by a work of art was meaningful only when others were seized similarly for similar reasons. And the categories by which one understood one's experience both needed to emerge spontaneously and needed to be broadly shared. After all, as Hegel had argued, the mere ability to pick from whatever options occur to us is not freedom, because it makes us dependent on whatever options occur to us. It is a purely appetitive kind of freedom, and makes us dependent on our impulse and circumstances—and these are contingent. "It is inherent in arbitrariness that the content is not determined as mine by the nature of my will, but by contingency; thus I am also dependent on this content, and this is the contradiction which underlies arbitrariness."[59]

This is the discourse upon which Liszt's characterization of interpretive freedom relies. The "arbitrariness of poetical exegesis" is not in fact true autonomy. Autonomy proceeds not by the connections of subjective wish and arbitrary object, but is rather governed by *rules* (*nomoi*), which rules are however self-legislated. Liszt's essay on Berlioz suggests that program music alone can be autonomous, because a program allows music to generate formal laws out of itself. It is, Liszt says in the Berlioz essay, a matter of "schematisieren" rather than "fixieren" musical meaning—"channeling the all-powerful waves of eddying tones into the secure bed of a single unitary [*eines einheitlichen*] thought that determines them."[60] The key word here is not the *eines*, it is *einheitlich*. Liszt's point is not that the thought needs to be the same in the composer's brain as in the listener's: what matters is that it is sustained, rather than being buffeted by sensory inputs this way and that.

Raff's "Lenore" responds to two challenges of aesthetic politics that Liszt's conception of program music was intended to address. The first concerns a kind of democratization of aesthetic response: how does one ensure that an audience comes to its understanding (and indeed the very categories of its understanding) of a piece of art independently while at the same time ensuring that its experience and response are collective and shared? The second one

---

58 Franz Liszt, *Die Zigeuner und ihre Musik in Ungarn*, in *Gesammelte Schriften* (Leipzig: Breitkopf & Härtel, 1883), 6:15.
59 G. W. F. Hegel, *Elements of the Philosophy of Right* (Cambridge: Cambridge University Press, 1992), §15; 49.
60 Liszt, "Berlioz und seine Harold-Symphonie," IV, 103.

concerns contextualization: in order to expand from the particularized aesthetic experience toward a political horizon, the audience must be guided on how to relate part to whole. This had been implicit in Schumann's framing of Chopin's ballades already: these were not interesting little concert pieces; to listen to them meant to listen for an entire cosmos that lay behind them. It has also been implicit in Schumann's choral ballads: to enter into a ballad recitation by a chorus meant to enter into a balladic world, to construct a specific mode of receptivity. In both respects, program music seemed to respond to challenges that bourgeois realism sought to address in literature: how to create collectivities of taste and reception out of an expanding readership, how to educate receptivity, but without imposing modes of receptivity from the outside.[61]

The problem of the whole and how it might be perceived asserts itself in Raff's symphony even on a notational level. Raff's careful metronomic markings in the score reveal something that a listener does not perceive: all four movements are actually the same tempo, even though we experience them as shifting. It's a trick Raff was generally fond of, but he uses it almost obsessively here. These regularities in the score that the listener does not perceive, but that nevertheless inform our hearing of it, clearly owe something to the ballad aesthetics of the time, which likewise posited a form that *appeared* simple, varied, and incidental, but which actually contained a certain unified *Weltanschauung*. The metronomic markings implicitly posit the four movements of the sonata form as alienations of certain determinate aspects of the one, indivisible *Urei* of the ballad, as Goethe put it. Under the objective optic of the measure the wild ride has already started with the first bar, but it remains latent and implicit until it culminates in the compressed, climactic moment of the fourth-movement ballad. Likewise, it is not so much that the ballad only grinds through pre-existing thematic material furnished by the first three movements; instead, the first three movements isolate and hypostatize what exists in an inseparable unity in the ballad movement.

The importance placed on an understanding of the *totality* in Raff's symphony, and its close link to *genre*, is instructive beyond the relationship to balladry. It also points to the way in which experience and subjectivity are present in program music—namely, *not* as psychological content, but rather as a hermeneutic horizon. As Jaroslav Volek has pointed out, one can understand a program in the Lisztian mode as a "meta-sign"[62]: It expresses an idea about the expressibility of ideas in music. In his 1906 book *Das Erlebnis und die Dichtung*, Wilhelm Dilthey called this *Erlebnis*. Dilthey's concept has

---

61 Fritz Martini, *Deutsche Literatur im bürgerlichen Realismus, 1848–1898* (Stuttgart: Metzler, 1981), 370.

62 Jaroslav Volek, "Programmusik aus semiotischer Sicht," *Archiv für Musikwissenschaft* 39, no. 4 (1982): 234–23.

frequently been charged with psychologism, but at least his concept of "experience" is, if anything, proto-existentialist: in his preface he calls it "connection [*Zusammenhang*] of action, suffering, dying with the final grounds of our *Dasein*"[63]—a sense, in other words, for the what it is to be a human possessing a perspective and particular mode of being-in-the-world. Program does not mean a simple, tautological re-narration of some text, nor does it mean a specific set of associations that we are forced to follow like viewers of a film[64]; it is rather the sense that the concatenation of musical ideas corresponds to some sort of subjectivity that alone, rather than tradition or genre, accounts for its form. Whether we can follow every element in that chain does not matter; whether we get every element right matters even less; the supposition of a chain and the acceptance of that chain as formal principle is what is central. "We mean the program in prose or verse attached to purely instrumental music," Liszt writes, "which . . . points the listener towards determinate thoughts and images, which the composer seeks to unroll before him."[65] Rather than a set of empirical states rendered in tones, programs concern the very communicability of empirical observation rendered in tones. The *Zuhörer* in this passage is not spoon-fed specific *Gedanken*; it is not browbeaten into a unified response with all other listeners to a piece. Rather, Liszt thinks the composer provides the listener with hints, not so much hints at the "specific thoughts and images" that he is seeking to unroll, than hints at the *fact* that he is trying to unroll them. The program communicates primarily the fact that it is seeking to communicate.

This is why a Schopenhauer disciple like Wagner still could take a positive view of a music that appeared at first blush to subjugate itself to the dictates of language, and thus to representation. The sequence of events that constitutes the program, the reality effects that appear in the score, belonged to the thing in itself, not to the phenomenon, to the world of the will, not to the world of representation. The sequence of events was not an outside addition to the roiling of musical matter; it mapped that roiling itself. To its proponents, program music was more absolute than absolute music. And it was receptive to traditional stories not so much because they were traditional stories, but because they modeled what spontaneous receptivity could look like in an age of mass audiences and mass communications.

Raff's symphony works toward moments when form no longer suffices to guide our understanding of the symphony, and toward other moments where program does not suffice. The transition into the program is highly

---

63 Wilhelm Dilthey, *Das Erlebnis und die Dichtung* (Göttingen: Vandenhoek & Ruprecht, 2005), 10.

64 Theodor Reik, *The Haunting Melody: Psychoanalytic Experiences in Life and Music* (New York: Farrar, Straus & Young, 1953).

65 Liszt, "Berlioz und seine Harold-Symphonie," IV, 100.

ambiguous, and neither is our stay in the world of Bürger's ballad ever entirely comfortable: the third movement ("Zweite Abtheilung: Trennung, Marsch") is a fairly traditionally structured ABA-movement. The movement opens and closes with a march, which builds in a constant crescendo, followed by a simple trio, then the march sets in again and slowly fades away. Raff's own statements suggest that this movement depicts an army coming to town, Wilhelm bidding his love farewell, and then marching off with the soldiers. This would mean that this movement still forms part of the backstory, rather than the poem's plot. At the same time, Bürger's ballad *does* open on an arriving army, but it is the army returning from Bohemia sans Wilhelm. A listener primed to recognize the elements of Bürger's ballad in Raff's program might thus be forgiven for assuming the truly programmatic section of the symphony commences halfway into the third movement (with the reprise of the march)—Raff's own daughter in her biography of her father seems to do so.

While Raff is in fact quite careful in following Bürger's poem in the fourth movement of the symphony, he appears equally at pains throughout to omit easily identifiable turning points. Three of the poem's most iconic moments—Lenore not seeing Wilhelm return from the war, Lenore blaspheming against the divine order, and Lenore and Wilhelm's disappearance into his grave—are pointedly omitted. The point seems to be that the third movement becomes something of a pivot: we cannot exactly say *when* the program becomes balladic (when, in other words, prehistory becomes story), and the better we know the source text the harder it gets. And indeed the symphony concludes with a rewriting of the story. Bürger's tale ends with Lenore in Wilhelm's grave and dancing spirits intoning the moral of the story: that it's wrong to vituperate against God in the interest of love. As Raff signals with his title for the final movement ("Reunited in Death"), he reads the ballad entirely differently—and he closes with a moment of apotheosis, a gorgeous closing choral in E major (unlike Henri Duparc's symphonic poem of the same year, which closes on a decidedly downbeat note). Whatever it is meant to depict, it's clear that it's not a young woman's entombment in her fiancé's coffin. Whether Raff borrows the transfiguration-ending from Karl von Holtey's "patriotic play with song" based on Bürger's poem (1829), which includes a more hopeful coda after the final verses, or whether it comes from the most famous instance of redemption snatched from the jaws of damnation, the conclusion of Goethe's *Faust*—the effect is the same: the more well-versed the listener is in the ballad, the more they will be surprised by where the music takes them.

# 7 | The Ballad, the Public, and Gendered Community

For his thirty-third birthday in 1843, Clara Schumann gave her husband the gift of several songs. One of them is a highly dramatic setting of Heinrich Heine's "Lore-Ley." Heine's poem was even then most famous in a folk-song setting by Friedrich Silcher from 1837. In 1841, Franz Liszt had set the poem as a languid, through-composed *Lied*. Clara Schumann's version steered clear of both extremes, producing a coherent, atmospherically rich ballad that feels deliberately anachronistic in parts. As Caitlin Miller has pointed out, Clara and Robert tended to record their mutual musical gifts to one another in their marital journal, and although "their reactions are generally quite positive and encouraging,"[1] this particular one elicited a rather terse note from her husband: "Clara as always gave me presents."[2]

Heine's "Die Lore-Ley" (1824) is a strange text: it starts with a famous, ambiguous lyrical incantation ("Ich weiß nicht, was soll das bedeuten," "I know not what causes my sadness"), and it concludes with a fisherman drowning in the Rhine. In other words, the poem begins as something else, but approaches being a narrative poem by the end of its six short stanzas. With its hammering piano triplets, its constant sforzandos, and a tempo designation of "Schnell" (Silcher's dreamy, even-keeled setting of the same text

---

[1] Caitlin Miller, "'Und das hat mir ihrem Singen, Die Lore-Ley gethan': Subjectivity and Objectification in Two Heine Settings," in *Women and the Nineteenth-Century Lied*, ed. Aisling Kenny and Susan Wollenberg (London: Routledge, 2016), 243.

[2] Gerd Nauhaus, *The Marriage Diaries of Robert & Clara Schumann: From Their Wedding Day through the Russia Trip* (Boston: Northeastern, 1993), 197–98 (op. cit. Miller in Kenny and Wollenberg, 243).

is a rather unhurried Andante), Clara Schumann's "Lore-Ley" rather clearly reads Heine's text as a ballad, where Silcher presents a *Lied*. In fact, the song clearly echoes Schubert's setting of "Der Erlkönig" (op. 1), of which she owned an autograph, a gift from one of Schubert's friends during her extremely successful concert tour in Vienna in 1837/38.[3]

This is all the more noticeable as Heine's "Die Lore-Ley" is not a straightforward example of any of these things: the poem deliberately confuses its timeline, as well as the relationship between the fairy tale of the Lorelei the narrator recollects and the drowning she brings about (possibly in the narrative present). While it is clear that the poem features a narrator and a fisherman, it is unclear who is speaking at which point: does the first stanza represent the fisherman's thoughts before the events described in the third stanza, or are the two spectator and object? Heine's poem can be read as a meditation on the destructive magic of nature, or as a commentary about the lure of poetry about the destructive magic of nature. Clara Schumann, who was an exacting reader and deeply annoyed with song settings that ran roughshod over the authorial intent of a poem, must have been aware of this ambiguity—yet it is striking how far she goes in banishing it.

Schumann chose to read "Lore-Ley" as a *Schauerballade*: a ballad of psychological horror à la Johann Rudolf Zumsteeg.[4] As a musical choice, this isn't altogether surprising—the form was quite popular and it allowed for some truly evocative voice writing. But especially when it came to questions of gender, Schumann's choices had deeper ramifications. In Heine's poem, we find a clearly male narrator at a safe remove from the dangerous feminine lure of the Lore-Ley. As the poem goes on, that remove is gradually eroded, and by the end the narrator either drowns (if he indeed is identical with "the mariner" [*der Schiffer*] identified in the third person in the song's third stanza), or he at least imagines himself in the position of a sailor being lured to his death along the Rhine.

Like Schubert's "Der Erlkönig," Clara Schumann's "Die Lore-Ley" takes what, in Liszt's hands, for instance, is a gradual intensification of dread and suffuses it evenly throughout the piece. Both singer and piano accompaniment start the song distressed—even though Heine's opening lines speak of "sadness" rather than any agitation. This has the strange effect of making the song both more and less dramatic than it could be—the emotional pitch is high, but it does not intensify as the dreamy reverie gives way to a lethal threat. It also makes it impossible to separate cleanly between the tale and its telling: the very mode of access that gives rise to the story, the

---

3 Nancy B. Reich, *Clara Schumann: The Artist and the Woman* (Ithaca, NY: Cornell University Press, 2013), 57.

4 Ibid., 237.

"tale of old times" that is stuck in the narrator's mind, appears to be part of the problem.

Heine's poem stages a gradual transition from melancholic detachment to a sense of existential threat—Clara Schumann, by positioning the whole poem as a horror ballad, suggests that even the initial apparent detachment lives in terror of the Lorelei. The opening line (literally: "I don't know what can be the meaning") in her hands is not some wistful balladic engagement with a distant myth; it is the terrified explanation of a skipper already worried about the supernatural siren. That is to say, Schumann implicitly positions balladic recall as always already overly involved, as always already terrified, as ultimately a bit hysterical.

At the same time, the song gives the male-focalized narration to a female voice to sing. The vocal part goes as high as an F5, calling for a virtuosic and rather straightforwardly gendered performance. A poem that concludes with a rather pointed warning about the destructive effects of the female voice becomes, in Clara Schumann's hands, a celebration of the same. The song undercuts the narrator's presumptive masculinity (the kind of person who goes around collecting legends in nineteenth century German literature is almost always male, and the kind of person who hikes to, and contemplates, haunted natural sights is likewise) by having the song sung by a woman. And it goes further by attaching the nimbus of anxiety, even hysteria, that envelops the arrangement with its pulse-quickening triplets and sudden jumps from low to high pitches to (a) a male narrator and (b) to the ballad form itself.

Whether in the privacy of the home or in public, it did not take much for the ballad to become ensnared in questions of gender. It fit snugly into both, but, as Schumann's setting makes clear, its ready participation in various spheres and settings could easily turn into a problem. To be sure, the topics and stories ballads transported often tended toward the conventional, especially when it came to attitudes around gender—chaste maidens, faithful knights, humane queens, and children in terror abounded. But the sheer diversity of forms through which the ballad insinuated itself into everyday life created a mismatch between the conventional stories being told and the modes of their telling. Clara Schumann had a broad set of models in different media to draw on when she sat down to compose "Die Lore-Ley," and her choices were able to position balladic narration as a form of male hysteria.

Questions of gender in balladry were always also to some extent political: they concerned the organization of gendered bodies in space, and they concerned how their organization related to the nation. At the same time, the reverse was also true: the organizations that singing gave rise to were taken to communicate not just essential facts about gender, but also about the political history of gender more broadly. This is true even of a piece like Clara Schumann's "Loreley"—for the very simple reason that it remained an, apparently rather unloved, spousal gift. The song was not published during

Clara's lifetime—it never quite escaped the Schumanns' domestic, private lives.[5]

The idea that ballads spoke to forms of togetherness, often forms lost to time, was common in nineteenth-century Germany. And the look back in time often linked performing specifically to gendered groups, the further back, the more starkly gendered. When in 1861 the Swiss classicist Johann Jacob Bachofen first presented his theory of the ancestral "mother right" (*Mutterrecht*), he proposed that in ancient Greek "music, tone, rhythm" without sung text one could detect remnants of a "material-feminine" aesthetic, vestiges of an archaic "gynocracy" that had otherwise been erased from history[6] And when, almost forty years, later the young ethnologist Heinrich Schurtz proposed that rather than the matriarchate the original form of human sociability was the "confederation of men" (*Männerbund*), he likewise imagined that song had a role to play in its formation: some tribes on the northeastern coast of German-colonized Papua New Guinea, he reported, constituted separate same-sex houses for men. They did so by scaring off the women with their flute playing and their singing.[7] To nineteenth century Germans single-gender spaces thus told profoundly political stories about the very roots of human communal life. And they may well have projected them into the distant past, because such questions dominated their own world. There were questions around which emotions singing could and should project, and how they shaped social space by being projected in this way. There were questions around instrumentation, about how voice and instrument represented individuality or larger collectives. There were questions around professionalism and dilettantism. And there were questions about privacy and publicity: what it meant to raise one's voice alone or in groups, in the salon at home, at church or on the concert stage.

## The Ballad in All-Male Environs: A *Sängerkrieg* in Berlin

Of course, all-female communities were considered more remarkable. Somewhat harder to spot are spaces and practices that, in nineteenth-century Germany, entwined the ballad with male homosociality—partly because male homosociality was so thoroughly normalized that it barely registered

---

5 Susan Youens, *Heinrich Heine and the Lied* (Cambridge: Cambridge University Press, 2007), 241.

6 Johann Jakob Bachofen, *Das Mutterrecht* (Stuttgart: Krais & Hoffmann, 1861), 371.

7 Heinrich Schurtz, *Altersklassen und Männerbünde: Eine Darstellung der Grundformen der Gesellschaft* (Berlin: De Gruyer, 1902), 222.

and was rarely reflected upon. One place where it was, were the literary societies that renewed the German literary ballad around the middle of the nineteenth century. Closed literary societies sprang up across Germany in the early nineteenth century, part of a veritable boom in private clubs. Philosophical societies, music societies, societies for the fine arts, and literary societies proliferated, and almost all of them were more or less exclusive. They benefited from an upwelling of patriotic feeling just as much as from the fact that their patriotism was not particularly politically focused. At the same time, they were concerned with the constitution of certain markets: the proliferation of choral societies tended to change the calculus on publishing certain works of classical music; *Kunstvereine* like the ones in Karlsruhe (founded in 1818), Munich (1823), and Düsseldorf (1829) shaped the art market and promoted certain artists and works.[8]

On the whole, as we will see, choral and musical societies were less inclined toward what Heinrich Schurtz, Herbert Schmalenbach, and Max Weber would later identify as the *Männerbund*. Nor do they seem to have been as selective when it came to social class. In literature, though, the ingroup/outgroup dynamic seems to have been rather pronounced: literary associations behaved in ways reminiscent of the *Burschenschaften* (university fraternities) of their day—rituals, code names, hazing, and bizarre traditions included. Even before he relocated to Berlin in 1845, Theodor Fontane began attending the meetings of one such literary *Verein* called *Der Tunnel über der Spree* (Tunnel above the Spree). Fontane was introduced to the *Tunnel* by Bernhard von Lepel in 1843, was admitted into the society in 1844, and remained a member until 1865, serving intermittently as its secretary and leaving ample testimony as to the activities and organization of the group.[9]

The *Tunnel* was founded in 1827 and met weekly on Sundays at a few locations around Berlin. In his autobiography, Fontane mentions a mural that immortalized the group at the Café Belvedere, which then sat between the St. Hedwig's Cathedral and the Opera Unter den Linden. It exemplified, Fontane notes, "a nice piece of Old Berlin," probably because its tone seems to have been jocular: Hugo von Blomberg (1820–1871) was depicted "in a jersey with a sash, as a juggler on two horses, likely to signify that he worked as painter and poet. To his right sat I, in the costume of a Douglas or Percy on a rocking horse tilting my lance against another knight, most likely a competing balladeer."[10]

---

[8] Helmut Blazek, *Männerbünde: Eine Geschichte von Faszination und Macht* (Berlin: Links, 1999), 79.

[9] Joachim Krueger, "Der Tunnel über Spree und sein Einfluß auf Theodor Fontane," *Fontane-Blätter* 4, no. 3 (1978), 201–25.

[10] Theodor Fontane, *Von zwanzig bis dreißig* (Berlin: Fontane, 1898), 271.

As the (now long-lost) mural makes clear, a sense of male-on-male competition suffused the proceedings of the *Tunnel*, and both in terms of form and content that competition drew on the ballad form. The spirit of competition was, as the mural also makes clear, fairly tongue-in-cheek. However diverse was the *Tunnel*'s membership, in terms of age, profession, and social station, the ballad was central to its core rituals. The *Tunnel*'s membership included the ballad composer Carl Loewe, the painter Adolph Menzel, the opera singer Franz Betz, high-ranking administrators such as the Prussian minister of culture Heinrich von Mühler, many Prussian officers, but above all literary authors and translators. Some, like Emmanuel Geibel and Christian Friedrich Scherenberg, were relatively well known in their day, but are largely forgotten today (ironically, it was Geibel who mocked the *Tunnel* as an *Kleindichterbewahranstalt*, an "Asylum for Minor Poets"[11]). Others, above all Fontane and Theodor Storm, remain household names.

At the group's Sunday meetings, members presented previously unpublished works, referred to in the *Tunnel*'s jargon as "Späne" ("woodchips"). In 1853, the minutes of the *Tunnel* (likely written by Fontane) noted for the year the following distribution of "Späne": 90 works were presented ("bringing the number of *Späne* since the foundation of the society to 5082"), consisting of "42 songs, 30 ballads, six essays, three each of speeches and dramatic works, and a monodrama with choirs, a diploma and a statue."[12] The literary was thus the central, but not exclusive focus of the society. Nevertheless, the group's occasional prizes were awarded entirely to literary works. Works of music and the visual arts were welcome, but screened, as it were, outside of competition.

The privacy of a club is generally of a specific kind. Unlike that of the family, it cannot pretend to naturalness. Its codes and nicknames have something fanciful, its idioms a forced chumminess. The same was true for the *Tunnel*: every "rune" who was admitted into the circle had to choose a code name, which, in the tradition of masonic lodges, seems to have been intended to erase class differences. The group had its lingo, its traditions and rituals, all of which, judging from the protocols, created distinction for distinction's sake, for sharply demarcating an inside from an outside. There were, in other words, no mysterious inner workings to the club, just mysterious nomenclature for decidedly mundane goings-on. The intergenerational element by which older members supported and guided the work of younger members gave the group something familial. At the same time, the *Tunnel* was also about networking, and members were not squeamish about helping their fellows.

11 Paul Heyse, *Jugenderinnerungen und Bekenntnisse* (Berlin: Hertz, 1900), 87.
12 "Geschichte des 26. Tunneljahres (1852/53)," 3.12.1853. In Theodor Fontane, *Fontane, Autobiographische Schriften* (Berlin: Aufbau, 1982), 3/1:335–340.

This makes the importance of balladry within the *Tunnel über der Spree* an interesting object for study. We have encountered the ballad as a public-facing object, meant to activate patriotic fervor or preserve unofficial history. We have encountered the ballad as a familial object, giving shape to the practices of the private sphere. But the *Tunnel* exemplifies something different: its emphasis on balladry had definite political dimensions—the club's poet members stressed the patriotic, the collective in balladry. But at the same time, the club was deliberately insular, keeping its inner workings obscure and secret. While the *Tunnel*'s members discussed taking a public position during the revolutionary year of 1848, they ultimately decided against it. It seems to have been the only time this question raised itself for them in the nearly seventy years of the club's existence.

So what kind of politics is embodied in an organization like the *Tunnel über der Spree*? As Gudrun Loster-Schneider has argued, the *Tunnel*'s very heterogeneity represented a strange (but far from atypical) entwinement of the political and the apolitical.[13] The *Tunnel* brought together representatives of the Prussian state and vociferous critics of that state; in order to allow them to inhabit the same space, the *Tunnel* insisted on leaving politics at the door. "How else," Fontane remarks in his memoirs, "would 'Minister von Mühler' have been able to coexist with Löwenstein of the [satirical magazine] Kladderadatsch."[14] Of course, as Loster-Schneider points out, this was necessary only because the club's members had fairly opposed political convictions to leave at the door. As Ernst Kohler observed in a 1940 study of the "Tunnel," the group "did not have a great deal of philosophical interests, and politics were excluded by statute."[15] Nevertheless, this emphatically apolitical frame was itself political and bespoke a tacit sense of the baseline legitimacy of the status quo. Members who wished to mock and change the Prussian state were welcome; members who wanted to topple it were certainly not. The group's poetry was largely centered on patriotic themes, but its patriotism was closer in spirit to nascent Realism—characterized by an abiding respect for the life rhythms of the local populace—than the openly revolutionary literature of the Romantic and *Vormärz* periods.

Among the group, Fontane was most exacting in seeking out the origins of the ballad. Fontane would do much to modernize the genre in Germany. But for him any ballad was nevertheless also a look back—back to the Middle Ages, back to the eighteenth century, back to the origins of the German art ballad tradition. In the autumn of 1848, Fontane read Percy's *Reliques of ancient*

---

13 Gudrun Loster-Schneider, *Der Erzähler Fontane: Seine politischen Positionen in den Jahren 1864–1898 und ihre ästhetische Vermittlung* (Tübingen: Narr, 1986), 39.

14 Fontane, *Von zwanzig bis dreißig*, 267.

15 Ernst Kohler, *Die Balladendichtung im Berliner "Tunnel über der Spree"* (Liechtenstein: Kraus Reprint, 1969), 28.

*English Poetry* and Sir Walter Scott's *Minstrelsy of the Scottish Border*—the encounter with the English ballad was central to his output within the *Tunnel*, much of which consisted of adaptation and translation of Percy and Scott.[16] At the same time, as Michael White has pointed out, Fontane's translations were adaptive and forward-looking—he saw his versions of these texts "as part of an ongoing process of writing within a specifically German tradition," bringing "his text further from, not closer to, its apparent source."[17]

His discovery of Percy spurred him to great creativity: twenty-five of Fontane's just over 100 ballads are directly based on ancient English ones, with another twenty-five or so choosing the sort of topics an anglophone ballad might have plausibly taken on as its subject. This was at least in part due to the immediate audience for these poems, namely his fellow members in the *Tunnel*. In the *Tunnel*, Fontane wrote, "we had our own areas of specialization and lavished the most attention on them: for me all things Scottish, especially Mary Stuart, and all things Frederick the Great and Prussian."[18] In 1858, Fontane, by now extremely well established, returned to the *Tunnel* to read a few pieces. Among them was another one based on recent events.[19] "The Tragedy of Afghanistan" ("Das Trauerspiel von Afghanistan") tells the largely true story of assistant surgeon William Brydon's arrival in Jalalabad in the winter of 1842, the only survivor of an army of 16,000 that had set out from Kabul. Fontane's ballad imagines that, after taking in Bryden from the darkness and the snow storm, the British commander bade his garrison sing English tunes into the storm as a signal to any other survivors.

| | |
|---|---|
| Sie irren wie Blinde und sind uns so nah, | They walk like blind men, are nonetheless near, |
| So laßt sie's *hören*, daß wir da, | So let them hear that were are here, |
| Stimmt an ein Lied von Heimat und Haus.[20] | Start singing a song of home and house. |

The army sings for two nights straight, one popular song after the other. But of course "those meant to hear can hear no more" ("Die hören sollen, sie

---

16 Hans Rhyn, *Die Balladendichtung Theodor Fontanes* (Berne: Francke, 1914).

17 Michael White, "Herder and Fontane as Translators of Percy," in *Fontane and Cultural Mediation*, ed. Ritchie Robertson and Michael White (Cambridge: Modern Humanities Research Association, 2015), 115.

18 Fontane, *Von zwanzig bis dreißig*, 394.

19 Christian Grawe and Helmuth Nürnberger, eds., *Fontane-Handbuch* (Stuttgart: Kröner, 2000), 55.

20 Theodor Fontane, *Sämtliche Werke* (Munich: Nymphenburger, 1975), 20:160.

hören nicht mehr"[21]). The garrison's song turns, inevitably but imperceptibly, from a living signal, a sonic beacon by which other Englishmen might be guided, into a dirge for those who could have been guided by it. The songs don't change, but their audience, and thus their purpose does. Living exchange becomes inert, ritualized mourning. Fontane used the destruction of Elphinstone's army outside of Kabul as an opportunity to reflect nostalgically on a changing world—and to use public song as a way to trace that change. As in "The Tragedy of Afghanistan," Fontane frequently portrayed the constancy and immutability imputed to public song as a fiction, but one that alone made change traceable and measurable.

Fontane's works of the period oscillated between affirmation and problematization. As in later works, they frequently take recourse to an ironized nostalgia, or a sympathetic irony that leaves entirely open whether something that is in the process of disappearing deserves to disappear or not. Whether one wants to cast Fontane as a resigned conservative or a progressive with certain sympathies for the outmoded, there is ample evidence for both in his works and letters. The ballad form in particular lends itself to this suspension between a genuine longing for the past and a wallowing in its violence and danger: the ballad laments things only once they are safely gone, and it traffics in a kind of generalized nostalgia that does not have to come from a place of affirmation. In an environment like the *Tunnel*, this constitutive indecision was an asset.

If the *Tunnel* was not overtly concerned with day-to-day politics, it was very much concerned with gender politics, above all shifting codes of masculinity—codes that, especially during the era in question, were themselves implicitly political. Many of the practices around the circle's balladry were collaborative—Fontane presented his ballad "Der Verbannte" before the *Tunnel* in 1854, and a year later Carl Loewe published the work as his *Lied*-setting "Archibald Douglas" (op. 128).[22] But largely the *Tunnel*'s mode of balladry was characterized by playful competition. While there were several concurrent competitions (and constant grading of one another's literary work), the *Tunnel*'s ballad contest seems to have been the group's longest-running. The group's members explicitly compared their ballad contests to medieval rituals of masculinity, such as the Provençal art of a "gay science," but they did so in tones that suggested the outmodedness of such rituals.

All *Späne* submitted for consideration by the group were graded. The grading system (*sehr gut, gut, ziemlich, schlecht*, and *verfehlt*) smacked of the

---

21 Theodor Fontane, "Das Trauerspiel von Afghanistan," in *Sämtliche Werke* (Munich: Nymphenburger, 1975), 20:159.

22 Lorrain Gorrell, *The Nineteenth-Century Lied* (Pompton Plains, NJ: Amadeus Press, 2005), 229; Roger Fiske, *Scotland in Music: A European Enthusiasm* (Cambridge: Cambridge University Press, 1983), 96.

schoolhouse, and verdicts were frequently harsh. In other aspects, however, the format drew on far older models. In his recollections, Fontane cast it as "a kind of *Sängerkrieg*"[23]—the bardic competition that had long furnished the subject of ballads as well as their metafiction. Meaning: not only were there many ballads that dealt with the competitive composing and reciting of balladry, the ballad form itself frequently included a pretense that the poem emerged from precisely such a context. In the letters exchanged between Fontane, Geibel, and Heyse, for instance, the *Tunnel*'s balladeers cast themselves as late descendants of the troubadours and their "gay science."[24] It would still take another thirty years before Nietzsche made the phrase the title of one of his books, but what drew him to the term seems to have animated the balladeers of the *Tunnel* as well—the phrase was a memory of the onetime "unity of singer, knight and free spirit"[25] in early medieval Provence. There was a kind of organicist longing for unalienated, non-professionalized artmaking to these competitions.

Significantly, given that Fontane during those years seemed to strive for the establishment of a realist ballad, the *Sängerkrieg*-motif was profoundly associated with Romanticism. The medieval texts that are usually grouped as the *Sängerkrieg* were reintroduced by the Swiss philologist Johann Jakob Bodmer, Johann Christoph Gottsched's great antagonist and a champion of medieval literature. Bodmer had also been among the earliest ballad collectors in Germany, presenting several volumes of *Altenglische und altschwäbische Balladen* in the 1770s and 1780s. The poets of the *Tunnel* would follow the link he and Herder made between Anglo-Saxon subjects and ancient German ones.

Like the view of the ballad championed by Bodmer, the texts Bodmer collected of the *Sängerkrieg* likewise proved central to German Romanticism. The first sustained literary engagement had been Novalis's *Heinrich von Ofterdingen* (published posthumously in 1802), followed much later by E. T. A Hoffmann's novella *Der Kampf der Sänger* (1818) and Friedrich de la Motte Fouqué's play *Der Sängerkrieg auf der Wartburg* (1828). It was likely the anti-classicism that had long shaped the reception of these texts that made them a model for the members of the *Tunnel*. But even the medieval *Sängerkrieg* as a poetological model pointed both forward and backward. Admittedly, the members of the *Tunnel* practiced their singing competition in the spirit both of cheerful anachronism and nostalgia. When compared, for instance, to Richard Wagner's treatment of the same theme in *Tannhäuser und der Sängerkrieg auf der Wartburg* (1845), the members of the tunnel were

---

23 Theodor Fontane, *Sämtliche Werke* (München: Nymphenburger Verlagshandlung, 1959), 15:157.

24 Emmanuel Geibel and Paul Heyse, *Der Briefwechsel von Emmanuel Geibel und Paul Heyse* (Munich: Lehmann, 1922), 303n.

25 Friedrich Nietzsche, *Werke in drei Bänden*, ed. Karl Schlechta (Munich: Hanser, 1954), 2:1127.

not all too serious in their comparisons between their practices and the love lyric of the medieval poets. But it is worth noting the fact that these modern troubadours competed largely via the ballad, not via love poetry.

This was most likely owed to the prevailing winds in realist poetics at the time. In 1858, the literary critic and professor for literary studies Robert Eduard Prutz published *Die deutsche Literatur der Gegenwart, 1848–1858*, which took to task much of the post-revolutionary literary output in Germany and advocated for a realist poetics. That meant either texts about the everyday life of the *Volk*, or at least stories about its history. The enemy was in either case an overly subjective lyric poetry, and Prutz regarded the ballad as a possible corrective. At least, he thought, insofar as his contemporaries managed to keep their subjective associations and enthusiasms in check. For him, in the German poetry of his day the historical fact, centerpiece of an objective poetics, was all too often overpowered by the accidents of subject feeling (*Empfindung*). He complained how "the individual historic moments almost disappear under the breadth of the lyrical effusions [*Ergüsse*] or philosophical reflections; even the authentic ballad or romance is a rare thing, as the poet doesn't care much for the actual subject matter, but rather seems to serve as a starting point [*Anhaltspunkt*] for his subjective feelings and reflections."[26] It is clear that the way subjects and forms were distributed in the *Tunnel* aimed at something similar: the balladry practiced there was intended to center "the actual subject matter."

Beyond its implicit nationalism, privatizing the courtly models of the medieval period into an intramural club activity had a not-so-hidden political dimension. Louise Otto-Peters may have made the case more bluntly than most, but there was, in particular in comparison to the politicized poetry of the *Vormärz*-period and in the aftermath of the 1848 revolution, a widespread suspicion that a *Sängerkrieg* was really a mere matter of art for art's sake. As Peters wrote in that revolutionary year:

| | |
|---|---|
| Wohl giebt's noch Sängerkriege, | Of course there are still singers' battles |
| Aber in anderem Sinne | But they are fought |
| Als einstens der Sängerkrieg ward gefochten | In different sense from long ago |
| In deinen Hallen, uralte Wartburg. | In your halls, ancient *Wartburg*. |
| Krieger sind jetzt die Sänger | The singer now is a warrior |
| Gottentflammte begeisterte Volkstribunen.[27] | A divinely inflamed tribune of the people. |

---

26 Robert Prutz, *Die deutsche Literatur der Gegenwart, 1848–1858* (Leipzig: Voigt & Günther, 1859), 203.

27 Louise Otto, *Mein Lebensgesang* (Leipzig: Schäfer, 1893), 83–85.

The singer's war had changed. The modern troubadour no longer sparred with other singers, but rather tested his art against the forces of repression and reaction. Rather than entertaining the powerful he discomfits them. In this context, the *Tunnel*'s insistence on modeling ballad competitions on the *Sängerkrieg* (and calling them such) while mostly shutting out the outside world and its historic developments signaled a deliberate adherence to an older notion of the singer's power when more modern ones were available.

In his memoirs, Fontane remarks that, because "the ballad was both his domain and mine,"[28] Hugo von Blomberg emerged as his "allerspeziellste[r] Nebenbuhler," a word denoting a competitor for a lady's affection. But it is important to point out that the lady in question was, in this case, the approbation of other men. The ideology of masculinity that animated the *Tunnel über der Spree* combined the *ars amatoria* of the medieval *Minnesänger* with the single-sex environment of the *Männerbund*. For where the medieval balladeer (at least as imagined in modern ballads) performed for a mixed audience, wanting to make the men jealous and the women want him, the members of the *Tunnel* performed for, or at least sought to win over, an all-male audience. There may have been the occasional female performer in attendance, and perhaps some female "runes" (although none are noted in the protocols). But those members voting on the "Späne" were an all-male cohort. As Fontane would note later, the ballad competitions were like "Wartburg song festivals [*Sängerfeste*]," except "they lacked the ladies and the wreaths."[29]

Gender relations were a frequent topic in the poetry written by the *Tunnel*'s members. Moritz von Strachwitz's 1848 "Neue Gedichte" in fact open with a lengthy cycle of poems "Den Männern" and "Den Frauen"—there, again and again, he casts the poetic I as a beleaguered singer:

| | |
|---|---|
| Dir, edle Herrin, will ich bringen | To you, noble mistress, I'll bring |
| Des treuen Dichters Scheidegruß, | The faithful poet's parting words, |
| Ich weiß nicht, was ich werde singen, | I know not what I'll sing, |
| Wohl aber, daß ich singen *muß*. | What I know is that sing I *must*. |

Singing in these poems constitutes the spontaneous overflow of a masculinity under pressure. In general, many of the works of the poets from the *Tunnel*'s orbit present a portrait of masculinity under twin pressures from the

---

28 Fontane, *Von zwanzig bis dreißig*, 394.
29 Fontane, *Sämtliche Werke*, 15:158.

decline of chivalry and the fungibility of capitalism. As a poem by Strachwitz from the cycle "Den Männern" puts it:

| Kein Ritterschlag ist zu verdienen, | No knighthood can be earned |
| Da wo zum Ritter schlägt das Geld.[30] | Where money alone knighthood confers. |

In certain ways, the anti-commercial, anti-professional thrust of the *Tunnel* was in keeping with this critique of capitalist modernity. But in others, the group's poetry tended to mark as foolhardy and anachronistic precisely those practices and values that came to structure its own operations.

Paul Heyse, born in 1830, was introduced into the *Tunnel* in 1848 by his longtime mentor Emmanuel Geibel and joined the group in 1849. Heyse was at the time writing his dissertation on rhyme schemes in troubadour poetry, and immediately began participating in the club's competitions. He won the 1851 competition with the ballad "Das Thal des Espingo." The ballad provides a window into the process by which the "Späne"—unpublished, performed, and graded in private—found their eventual public. And it demonstrates how the members of the *Tunnel* in their balladic practice seemed to reflect on the strange genesis of their poetry—what it means for a poem formally committed to a heterogeneous public, and mixed-gender groups, to find its audience first in a private, single-sex environment.

In the case of "Das Thal des Espingo," the poem was published by Otto Friedrich Gruppe, a Hegel-student and philologist in Berlin as well as the editor of the *Deutscher Musenalmanach* founded by Adelbert von Chamisso and Gustav Schwab in 1830.[31] Gruppe approached the *Tunnel* in May 1851, asking for "patriotic contributions" to the 1852 edition.[32] The members of the *Tunnel* invited him to their meeting that August, and Gruppe was, as Fontane explained in a letter to Bernhard Lepel, "not particularly overjoyed by our prize-ballads."[33] Gruppe's objections seem to have concerned a certain lack of straightforwardness of the group's poetic output—Fontane confided to Lepel that he was sure Gruppe had not in fact understood most of the ballads. Nevertheless, in the end Gruppe's *Deutscher Musen-Almanach für das Jahr 1852* appeared with contributions from *Tunnel*-members such as Franz Kugler, Merckel, Lepel, Fontane, and Heyse—along with sixty others. Just a year later, Fontane wrote an anonymous review

---

30 Moritz von Strachwitz, *Sämtliche Lieder und Balladen* (Berlin: Grote, 1912), 122.

31 Otto Friedrich Gruppe, *Deutscher Musen-Almanach für das Jahr 1852* (Berlin: Reimer, 1852), 294.

32 Roland Berbig and Bettina Hartz, *Theodor Fontane im literarischen Leben* (Berlin: De Gruyer, 2000), 120.

33 Fontane to Lepel, August 21, 1851, in Theodor Fontane and Bernhard von Lepel, *Der Briefwechsel: Kritische Ausgabe* (Berlin: De Gruyter, 2006), I:274.

of the *Musenalmanach*, in which he singled out his *Tunnel*-friends for praise and otherwise ripped the publication apart.[34]

Heyse's "Das Thal des Espingo" puts the formulaic nature of the balladry practiced among the members of the *Tunnel* to good use: it is the sort of poem that leverages our familiarity, even overfamiliarity, with certain balladic tropes in order to make variations more noticeable.[35] For "Das Thal des Espingo" is essentially a ballad of supernatural seduction: an army of Moorish invaders crosses the Pyrenees, watchful of Basque fighters and bent on conquest. But when they reach the titular valley (in what is today Southern France), the sheer beauty of the setting recalls for the invaders their long-abandoned homeland. Throwing caution to the wind, they frolic in the pastures and the roses, go swimming in the Lac d'Espingo—and fall victim to their Basque enemies.[36]

In terms of its narrative structure, "Das Thal des Espingo" resembles the many ballads of the turn of the nineteenth century, in which men are led astray by natural forces (which often have a hint of the supernatural) and perish. But of course the titular valley and its fatal allure and the murderous Basques are not particularly supernatural. And whatever magic inheres in the titular valley's suggestion of *Heimat*, the Basque fighters (whose *Heimat* the valley is) seem immune to it. While Heyse casts the seduction of the *Heimat* in largely feminine tropes, the siren song of butterflies, jasmine, and narcissus only highlights the fact that there are no actual sirens in this song. Destruction is entirely a matter of (male) longing. In fact, even the opposing Basque forces never actually appear directly: they announce themselves as a threat early in the poem, and are implied as the Moorish army lets down its guard at the end of the poem. The community depicted in "Das Thal des Espingo" never meets an outside, an other—it yearns for its origins, and dissolves once it has found the simulacrum of that origin.

The poem thus deals with the gendered undoing of a single-sex group. The outside forces bringing about the army's destruction are only present by implication, and the explicit reason for the Moors' undoing offered in the poem is something generated by the all-male community itself—a homesickness and a desire for belonging that seems to equate its objects in each case with femininity. The poem's central problematic is masculinity: an all-encompassing, ultimately empty self-sameness subtended by a self-destructive nostalgia. It would go too far to suggest that Heyse won the *Tunnel* ballad-prize through a deeply unflattering portrait of the *Tunnel*

---

[34] Berbig, Hartz, *Theodor Fontane im literarischen Leben*, 122.

[35] Theodor Fontane and Paul Heyse, *Der Briefwechsel zwischen Theodor Fontane und Paul Heyse* (Berlin: Aufbau, 1972), 259.

[36] Theodor Storm and Paul Heyse, *Theodor Storm–Paul Heyse: Briefwechsel* (Schmidt, 1969), I:32.

itself—but it is nevertheless striking that both in terms of gender and in terms of privacy, "Das Thal des Espingo" represents a nightmare version of what an association like the *Tunnel* could be.

While no detailed protocol survives of Heyse's reading of the poem, it's clear from discussions of his other works from among the members of the *Tunnel* that they understood that his relationship to their form of sociability was shot through with a certain irony and separatism.[37] When Heyse presented his ballad "Wanda," members criticized the coldness of the poem and its heroine. With regard to a reading from "Francesca von Rimini," Fontane later wrote that the tragedy "lacked a necessary connection between the poet and his work," and was instead "more of a product of a *Bildung* and of a choice."[38] In other words, young Heyse seems to have refused the simulacrum of a collective poetics on which the *Tunnel* thrived: a close connection between a community, its practices, and aesthetic form.

At the same time, Heyse seems to have repeatedly made the lack of women among the group an implicit topic. In February 1849, Heyse presented a novella in verse ("Margherita Spoletina"), a work full of such frank eroticism that, as Wilhelm von Merckel's protocol notes, "the 'Tunnel' had to gather all its stoicism" and simply "express a smirking 'c'est bon'."[39] The homoeroticism of shared, if somewhat bashful, communal arousal is perhaps unremarkable for a group of ostensibly straight men—but it is worth reflecting on why von Merckel remarked on it explicitly in his notes. He sounds neither scandalized, nor simply amused by the moment. It seems to distill something of the sociability practiced in the *Tunnel* for him.

But, almost perforce for a successful ballad, these private reflections before a closed group did not remain long within the *Tunnel*'s confines. Josef Gabriel Rheinberger set "Das Thal des Espingo" as a ballad for an all-male chorus in 1865 (op. 51, published in 1869). Rheinberger retains the claustrophobic containment of Heyse's ballad and musically heightens it. The text of "Das Thal des Espingo" contains some gorgeous descriptions of the landscape, but instead of an idyllic interlude Rheinberger renders them in tones of immense foreboding. The entire eight-minute piece is rendered as one long *marche funèbre*—the rout of the Moorish forces, which occupies a single elusive stanza in Heyse's text, suffuses every measure of the choral ballad, even the more lyrical passages that depict their fatal yearning for their homeland. Part of this lugubrious effect stems from Rheinberger's instrumentation: rather than compensate for the uniformly lower vocal registers with a full palette of orchestral color, he skews his orchestra in the same direction. Bass, cello, and bassoon dominate, the clarinets remain in their lower range,

---

37 Kohler, *Die Balladendichtung im Berliner "Tunnel über der Spree,"* 360.
38 Fontane, *Von zwanzig bis dreißig*, 337.
39 Cited in Kohler, *Die Balladendichtung im Berliner "Tunnel über der Spree,"* 360.

and through it all the steady beat of a tympanum speeds the invaders to their deaths.

As such, Rheinberger's ballad traffics in a kind of deliberate redundancy: the chorus sings largely *unisono*, while the instrumental parts seem to have little autonomy vis-à-vis the singers. An early reviewer for the *Musikalisches Wochenblatt* called the work's atmosphere "oppressive," and he meant this as a compliment: an "oppressive mugginess of an incipient thunderstorm" ("drückende Gewitterschwüle") lingered over the piece, he claimed. By way of this oppressiveness Rheinberger imposes unity on Heyse's ballad—the choral ballad reveals itself as a dirge for an army of lost men well before the reader of the poem would know this, and certainly long before the soldiers themselves know.[40] Of course, this overall effect again seems to read the ballad in terms of gender: Rheinberger's instrumentation deliberately refuses to provide a counterweight to the hypertrophy of lower registers that comes with any composition for *Männerchor*, especially one for non-professional male voices (the reviewer recommended the work specifically for directors of choral societies, "since the technical demands never exceed what is right and proper"). The "oppressiveness" that the *Wochenblatt*'s reviewer noted is thus of a piece with the gendering of the piece's consumers—it is a work about male homosociality, written for a single-sex literary society, composed with a view to initial consumers who were likewise all men.

## "Hail, I Am Worthy!": Joining the All-Male Choir

As Rheinberger's setting of "Das Thal des Espingo" makes clear, when the musical ballad dealt with questions of gender in the mid-to-late nineteenth century, it was frequently by way of the gendered collective, especially the chorus. There existed an entire subgenre of ballads set for all-male choirs, and composers frequently drew for them on ballads that dealt with all-male environments: armies in the field, sailors on their ships, monks in their monasteries, knights on a quest for faraway women. As in the case of the *Tunnel über der Spree*, balladry was a way to articulate contemporary spaces and collectivities in terms of older ones, and emerging forms of masculinity in terms of traditional ones. The composer Rudolf Wagner alone wrote a choral "Ritterständchen" called "From the Days of the Minstrels" ("Aus der Zeit der Minnesänger," op. 127), "Donna Clara sits in Spain," a "Spanish ballad for male chorus" (op. 128), and "The Murderous Proprietor" ("Der Mordwirt"), an "uncanny ballad for male chorus" ("schauerliche Ballade für Männerchor,"

---

40 *Musikalisches Wochenblatt* 2, no. 44 (1871): 691.

op. 113). Friedrich Gernsheim rendered the all-male company of Goths in "Das Grab im Busento" in a ballad setting for male chorus (op. 52).

As noted in Chapter 6, this proliferation of all-male song settings was at least partially motivated by the boom in choral societies. These societies, which had sprung up across the German-speaking world, later to spread well beyond it, were even in the nineteenth century understood to be a new invention—the custom was, as *Meyers Großes Konversationslexikon* put it in 1908, "a child of the nineteenth century."[41] The phenomenon was generally agreed to have begun with Zelter's *Liedertafel* in Berlin in 1809. Like Zelter's club, the early choral societies were composed of professionals—librettists, singers, and composers—and they understood themselves as advocates for the form, seeking to stimulate the creation of a larger repertoire for male choir. But as the phenomenon spread, it tended to open itself to talented dilettantes, and to become less professionalized in two ways: *Verein* membership no longer consisted of professionals, and member activities were concerned with more than just putting on choral concerts.

Women occupied an ambivalent position vis-à-vis the choral movement. The boom largely involved men's choirs, even though there were also many women's choral societies. Ever since the Swiss music critic and pedagogue Hans Georg Nägeli, founder of the *Männerchor* in Zurich in 1810, had agitated for public singing as an aspect of public education, the spread of choral societies had had a whiff of the pedagogical. Being a choral director meant, after all, being half-artist and half-schoolmarm—which likely made it a more acceptable occupation for women than, say, orchestra conductor. And insofar as the chorus was meant to model a kind of unity of "the people," an aesthetic communication across all barriers, including women's voices in choruses was ideologically essential.[42] At the same time, women composers writing for the chorus often found receptive singers, but were prevented by the cultural mores of the time from actually presenting their work in public.

This was because organizing public singing by women was of course a form of organizing women. Besides *Lieder*, choral pieces were among the main fields in which German women composers found success in the nineteenth century. Many of Fanny Hensel's compositions for larger ensembles are cantatas (*Lobgesang*, *Hiob*, etc.) and dramatic scenes (*Hero und Leander*, *Szene aus Faust II*) for women's chorus, soloists, and piano or orchestra. Composing for women's voices in the plural went along with gathering

---

41 *Meyers Grosses Konversationslexikon* (Leipzig and Vienna: Bibliographisches Institut, 1908), 13:231.

42 Ryan Minor, *Choral Fantasies* (Cambridge: Cambridge University Press, 2012), 20–21.

women in public, or at least semi-public spaces—and it almost always meant taking them outside of the home. Louise Reichardt (1779–1826) founded a music school for women, as well as the first women's chorus in Hamburg (the *Gesangsverein*, founded in 1816).[43] Emilie Zumsteeg (1796–1857) founded the first *Frauenliederkranz* in the Kingdom of Württemberg.

As a result, many of the German women composers of the nineteenth century wrote particularly for vocal forms—Louise Reichardt wrote almost exclusively for solo voice or choir. Josephine Caroline Lang (1815–1880) was particularly noted for her *Lieder*, some of which were set for male choir by Felix Mendelssohn and Friedrich Silcher for the *Liedertafel* in Tübingen. Johanna Kinkel (1810–1858), a noted voice and piano teacher, likewise wrote mostly songs and cantatas. However important vocal music was to these composers, it is notable that ballads seem to have played a less than prominent role for most of them. Hensel wrote a large number of songs, but hardly any of the poems they are based on have narratives. The cultural bias that women were more "naturally" drawn to scenes of contemplation and passivity may have been one reason for this aspect of her selections. The widespread sense that fealty to the words of great (usually male) writers required a specifically feminine deference may have been another.[44] Lang is mostly known for her vocal compositions; her catalogue contains more than 125 *Lieder*, but only two of them are based on texts that resemble a ballad, and not one draws on the then-consolidating ballad canon as explored by Loewe, Schubert, and Schumann.

Some of this had to do with aesthetic partisanship—Lang was friendly with Felix Mendelssohn, Fanny Hensel, Ferdinand Hiller, and Clara Schumann, none of them particularly close to the New German champions of the ballad. But the main reason seems to have been that her art was indebted to a different understanding of Romanticism: Lang chose the poetic texts for her *Lieder* as a kind of artistic diary, and extensively annotated her songs to link them to her own autobiography.[45] This was to some extent a cover—these songs often made explicit points about history and politics—but they did so retaining a veneer of private communication.[46] And privacy in this case meant specifically a withdrawal from history, a rhetorical self-dehistoricization: Lang did compose battle songs, especially around the 1848

---

43 Iris Boffo-Stetter, *Luise Reichardt als Musikpädagogin und Komponistin: Untersuchungen zu den Bedingungen beruflicher Musikausübung durch Frauen im frühen 19. Jahrhundert* (Frankfurt: Lang, 1996)

44 Stephen Rodgers, *The Songs of Fanny Hensel* (Oxford: Oxford University Press, 2020), 82.

45 Harald Krebs, "Meine Lieder sind mein Tagebuch," *Musik in Baden-Württemberg Jahrbuch 2002* (Stuttgart: Metzler, 2002): 126.

46 Harald Krebs and Sharon Krebs, *Josephine Lang: Her Life and Songs* (New York: Oxford University Press, 2007), 229.

revolution, but unlike her other oeuvre these were never published during her lifetime. Her political songs, as her biographers note, were a local affair, "noticed only in Tübingen."[47]

This decision, however much gendered musical practice was at the heart of it, decisively shaped women composers' presence in emerging national repertoires, especially when those repertoires were more broadly suffused outside elite circles.[48] The large-scale choral performance, as Fiona Palmer has pointed out, functioned as a powerful figure for cross-class community, for commonality across differences, and for historicity as such. There was a memorability to choral events: they made as well as ordered history (for instance, in the frequently spectacular Bach revivals in Germany, or Handel revivals in England).[49] Women's singing, by contrast, was often tethered back to the home and understood as an extension of domestic social singing.[50] This tended to dehistoricize it.

Luise Adolpha Le Beau (1850–1927) was of a somewhat later generation than Zumsteeg and Lang, and her relationship to both history and the ballad was noticeably different. In fact, she used balladry to reflect on historical relationships having, however implicitly, to do with the gendering of history. Like many girls of the bourgeoisie (her father was a high-ranking officer in the army of the Grand Duchy of Baden), she was home-schooled—including in music, for which both her parents had pronounced enthusiasm. She later trained as a pianist with Wilhelm Kalliwoda and Clara Schumann, as well as composition with Josef Gabriel Rheinberger and his pupil Melchior Ernst Sachs.[51] Both of these latter men wrote ballads, and more specifically choral ballads (Rheinberger's op. 97 is *Clärchen auf Eberstein*, based on a ballad by his wife Franziska von Hoffnaaß, and Sachs composed his own choral version of the aforementioned "Thal von Espingo").

Her compositions found her working across the broad palette of pieces that composers could plausibly position as "ballads" in the second half of the nineteenth century. We have two ballads (op. 16, published in 1880) for

---

47 Ibid., 136.

48 Joep Leersen, "German Influences: Choirs, Repertoires, Nationalities," in *Choral Societies and Nationalism in Europe*, ed. Krisztina Lajosi and Andreas Stynen (Leiden: Brill, 2015), 14.

49 Fiona Palmer, "The Large-Scale Oratorio Chorus in Nineteenth Century England," in *Choral Societies and Nationalism in Europe*, ed. Krisztina Lajosi and Andreas Stynen (Leiden: Brill, 2015), 99.

50 Celia Applegate, "Building Community through Choral Singing," in *Nineteenth-Century Choral Music*, ed. Donna Di Grazia (New York: Routledge, 2013), 12.

51 Ulrike Brigitte Keil, *Luise Adolpha Le Beau und ihre Zeit: Untersuchungen zu ihrem Kammermusikstil zwischen Traditionalismus und "Neudeutscher Schule"* (Frankfurt am Main: Lang, 1996).

mixed choir and piano, one of them being that perennial evergreen, Ludwig Uhland's *Die Vätergruft*. Also in 1880 she wrote a ballad for baritone and orchestra based on the poem "Im Sängersaal" by Oscar von Redwitz (op. 22). In 1896 she published two ballads for piano and solo voice (op. 42). A few years later, she published a piano ballad in D-major (op. 47). These appear to have been some of the composer's more frequently performed and successful works—Le Beau's public presence as a composer rested at least in part on balladry.

In her memoirs *Lebenserinnerungen einer Komponistin* (1910), however, this range of works received a strange treatment. Le Beau explains that op. 22, and the two ballads in op. 42, were in fact revisions of works written by her father during his youth. "It always pained me," she wrote, "that I was not allowed to name my father as the author; but alas he did not want me to. But now the time has come for me to confess that the works are his and he is due all the recognition for them."[52] But Le Beau muddies the record throughout her memoirs, leaving open how significantly she revised her father's works (which would have been decades old by the time she published them). In the case of op. 22, for instance, she claims to have orchestrated as well as "revised" (*umgearbeitet*) her father's work, in order to perform it for the composer Franz Lachner.[53] And in the case of op. 16, she seeks to position another father figure in proximity to the ballad: she dedicated it to Sachs, "my friend and first teacher."[54]

Le Beau seems intent to present her balladic efforts as closely linked to various male figures. Few other compositions of hers come in for this kind of obsessive appeal to authority—but almost all her ballads do. And one of them may also explain why: the aforementioned op. 16 contains a setting of Ludwig Uhland's ballad "Die Vätergruft," the tale of a man joining a chorus of dead men. In the ballad, an old knight joins his ancestors in death, a story the ballad tells as a drama of voices: the old knight enters "den Chor" of his family chapel, which in German can refer to a chancel as well as a group of singers. His ancestors become present to him as a "wondrous song," and he raises his voice to join them. By the time he has finished speaking, the "ghostly sounds" have disappeared and he is joined with them in death's stillness.

Unsurprisingly, this drama of voices was frequently adapted for voice in the nineteenth century: Perhaps the only setting of the song that has endured in the repertoire is one composed by Franz Liszt (S. 281, 1844). Heinrich Esser (1818–1872) published a version for voice and piano in 1845. The

---

52 Luise Adolphe Le Beau, *Lebenserinnerungen einer Komponistin* (Baden-Baden: Sommermeyer, 1910), 9/10.
53 Ibid., 70.
54 Ibid., 72.

"Dichterkomponist" Peter Cornelius (1824–1874) wrote an a cappella version for solo bass and chorus, and Emil Naumann (1827–1888) set it as a *Lied* for piano and mezzo-soprano (1856). By their very arrangement, each of these decides to give voice to one party or the other in the vocal drama of Uhland's poem: is this the story of the knight, the story told by the knight, or the story of the "chorus" of ancestors?

Liszt too wrestled with the issue of which among the different parties to the ballad's story gets to actually frame the story. Rather than reflecting the poem's polyvocality by literally giving it to multiple human voices, Liszt sought for its reflection in the textures of the non-vocal accompaniment. It was an inclination that he never seems to have reconsidered: in his dying days Liszt returned to the song, but instead of amplifying the vocal part, he set the accompaniment for orchestra. Liszt's *Lied*-compositions tended to draw on other genres for dramatic effects, and this is particularly true for his ballads.[55] In "Die Vätergruft" it is a chorale-form that enters with the third stanza—around the time the text invokes the "miraculous singing" of the knight's ancestors, and we hear from the aged knight himself. Where other composers had sought to reflect perspectival shifts in the vocal parts, Liszt switches genre to replicate the shift in focalization in the ballad, combining church music and sonata form.

Le Beau, by contrast, resolves the drama of voices by handing the arrangement to four singers throughout—even before the dying knight joins the "chorus" of his ancestors, he is a part of a broader collective. Le Beau presents the ballad as a chorale in A minor from the first bar, and even introduces a kind of echo effect (accomplished by a slight delay in the tenor part) well before the old knight speaks diegetically, or even enters a tomb that could echo his speech. The effect is more than just an acoustic one, more than just an echo: Uhland's poem tells of a voice joining other voices, and Le Beau gets great mileage out of having the voices perform and re-perform that gesture of joining a chorus again and again. Given the ballad's drama of voices, however, it seems to matter which of the four singers speaks for whom. When the old knight addresses his ancestors collectively, for instance, the bass enters a quarter note before the other three voices (Fig. 7.1), which, given the tempo ("ziemlich langsam") almost inevitably gives his declamation of "Eure" something operatic, whereas the eighth notes sung by the remaining voices give their rendition the quality of a *parlando*. In this moment, in other words, it is clear who is speaking, who is addressing and who is being addressed by "Eure." Three bars later, that difference has evaporated (Fig. 7.2) and perhaps the most decisive declarative statement the old knight makes is intoned by

---

55 Jürgen Thym, "Crosscurrents in Song: Six Distinctive Voices," in *German Lieder in the Nineteenth Century*, ed. Rufus Hallmark (London: Taylor & Francis, 2009), 200.

FIG. 7.1 & 7.2 "Die Vätergruft," ballad by Louise Adolpha Le Beau, based on the poem by Ludwig Uhland.

all four voices in unison: "Heil mir," they sing speaking as one individual, "ich bin es werth"—"Hail me, I am worthy."

These kinds of gestures of asynchronicity and synchronicity are dotted throughout the piece—most frequently the tenor enters early, at other times the bass, at times soprano and tenor together. But neither soprano nor alto ever charges ahead by herself. This has the effect of marking out the stereotypically female voice as a late joiner. And perhaps this is by design: after all, it is not surprising that a female composer like Le Beau would have settled on the story of a late descendant's bid to join an all-male chorus, to mingle his voice with that of a set of (male) forebears. It is, after all, exactly what her song is doing. At the same time, the drama of accession into a broader collective, into a community across time, frames the soprano not as a supplicant. Its bid, like the old knight's, is premised on facing those forerunners on equal terms. "Hail, I am worthy," the old knight exclaims in joining his ancestral choir, and Le Beau renders the moment as one in which the piece's echo effects cease, where past and present fall into one. In the way Le Beau adapts this line, one can practically hear the composer carving out a space for herself in an ancestral line of classical composers.

The scene of narration imagined by balladry frequently juxtaposed an individual singer and his or her rapt audience. But as the case of Luise Adolpha Le Beau shows as much as that of Paul Heyse, in the nineteenth century balladry did not simply interpellate a crowd; frequently enough, it was understood to be produced by one as well. As a result, the concept of the ballad as a spontaneous production from the "spirit" of a *Volk* became identified, at least to some minds, with the very specific national community. Or at least it was used to attempt to conjure such a community into existence. This attempt will occupy us in the next chapter.

# 8 | The Ballad and the Sea

*Regionalism, Mourning, and the Modern National Imaginary*

*There is a narrowness in such a notion,*
*Which makes me wish you'd change your lakes for ocean.*

—Lord Byron, Don Juan

For George Borrow the ballad had come from across the sea. Borrow (1803–1881), a novelist and travel writer, largely made his name in English letters by translating, editing, and popularizing Danish, Norwegian and Icelandic, ballads, and part of his branding effort was to insist that these were more originary than their English or Celtic cousins. They were, according to Borrow, closer to the source, perhaps even themselves the source; the songs of the English minstrels were mere emanations of Scandinavian balladry. In his fictionalized autobiography *Lavengro*, Borrow's stand-in tells the following story of how he came into the possession of this Nordic treasure trove:

"A book," said I, "how did you come by it?"

"We live near the sea," said the old man; "so near that sometimes our hut is wet with the spray; and it may now be a year ago that there was a fearful storm and a ship was driven ashore during the night, and ere the morn was a complete wreck. When we got up at daylight, there were the poor shivering crew at our door; they were foreigners, red-haired men, whose speech we did not understand; but we took them in and warmed them, and they remained with us three days; and when they went away they left behind this thing, here it is, part of the contents of a box which was washed ashore."

"And did you learn who they were?"

"Why, yes; they made us understand that they were Danes."[1]

It doesn't seem as though we are supposed to take this story—itself balladic in its sensibility—as a window into its author's life. Even though Borrow's description here gives his rediscovery of the ancient Norse ballads a mystical hue, at other moments he is quite forthright that the ballad is above all a mercantile object.

In his essay on "Danish Poetry and Ballad Writing"[2] he proposes a comparatively unromantic origin story for it: the ancient Nordic bards were court-propagandists for their Viking lieges, and thus in a mutually beneficial business relationship with the Norse kings and chieftains; they would sing the king's praises, extol his success in war "so that he might requite them by transmitting their names to posterity." Throughout his essay Borrow is fairly cynical about this arrangement: in his telling, "the north soon became overstocked with poets" and the ballad became an export article, mirroring, but not quite coinciding with, the Norman conquests. So the Nordic skalds came across the sea to the areas raided by the very chieftains whose praise they now carried to the conquered courts.

Whether as a mystical object of epiphany or as a rather more pedestrian object of barter, the ballad comes from the sea. Or, perhaps better, it comes to us, its modern audience, from the sea. When Henry Wadsworth Longfellow in one of his ballads sought to construct a lineage for American balladry, he likewise sought to imbue it with a maritime ancestry. Much mystery surrounded a skeleton in armor discovered in 1832 near Fall River, Massachusetts, and in Longfellow's 1843 ballad, his poetic alter ego encounters the skeletal Viking who charges him with recalling the tale through a ballad: "My deeds, though manifold, / No Skald in song has told, / No Saga taught thee!" His "balladic charge" is twofold: tell my story, and Americanize my story. When the Viking (in pre-skeletal form) wants to sing his own story at a royal court in Norway, he cannot do so: "Mute did the minstrels stand / to hear my story."[3] What ties his tongue is that he doesn't have a story to tell that deserves epic treatment. By the time he visits Longfellow's narrator he has one that deserves something a little different—a ballad. His story is not heroic, or if it is heroic, it is so in a decidedly quotidian, anti-epic way: it is the non-aristocratic, stolid, protestant everyday heroism of the immigrant.

---

1 George Borrow, *The Works of George Borrow: Lavengro* (London: Constable & Co., 1923), 235.

2 George Borrow, *The Works of George Borrow: Miscellanies* (London: Constable & Co., 1923), 16:504.

3 Henry Wadsworth Longfellow, *The Poetical Works* (Boston: Houghton Mifflin, 1896), 55.

Longfellow's poem allies this more modest heroism with the ballad form itself—ballads are, or can be, properly American, precisely because they are not the outsized epics of the medieval sagas, of Homer or of Virgil. They are themselves modest, self-limiting, perhaps even a bit self-effacing, with all the fleetness, adaptability, and flexibility of an immigrant to the American continent.[4] It is a Viking, an arrival from across the Atlantic, who charges Longfellow's poetic I with bringing the ballad to America. The tradition Longfellow's ballad appeals to is one of discontinuity, of displacement. "Of course, I make the tradition myself,"[5] Longfellow wrote in a letter to his father. As he noted elsewhere, "the national ballad is a virgin soil here in New England, and there are great materials."[6] The charge, the first spark, the form to harness the virgin territory and to fertilize American storytelling into balladry comes from a Viking and across the ocean.

Borrow insisted that the ballad was a "compressed" epic. This is a juxtaposition we have encountered before: Dr. Johnson had dismissed Ossian's epic poems, claiming that at best their supposed editor James Macpherson had stitched together "wandering ballads." The cheerleaders of the ballad form had long insisted that ballads, albeit shorter, were themselves epic. And yet this put their efforts at collection and anthologization, which after all endeavored to put these wandering ballads back into some sort of totality, in a contradictory position: if these ballads were sufficiently epic in themselves, why did they need all the other ballads around them? If these ballads were only defective epics, diminutive epics, were not dismissals in the vein of Dr. Johnson's vituperations against Ossian altogether justified?

Perhaps, however, that was not the opposition the ballad's boosters had in mind. Dr. Johnson had dismissed Macpherson's bid to have Ossian's poems accepted as a national epic of the kind as were being discovered, or, in the absence of actual epics, invented throughout Europe—the *Nibelungenlied* in Germany, the *Kalevala* in Finland, the *Mabinogion* in Wales. Ballads were epic, but they were not national epics—the distinction that Borrow, who was harsh in singling out Macpherson for criticism, suggested was one between the all-encompassing national epic on the one hand and the partial epic of the ballad on the other. What those ships brought to England were fragments of a cosmos, not the full expanse of it. Ballads were regional rather than national.

---

4 This link is made more explicit in another Longfellow ballad, "The Village Blacksmith," which likewise refuses to center on any kind of exceptional heroism, instead singing a paean to the humble, quotidian heroism of doing your job: "Each morning sees some task begin, / Each evening sees it close; / Something attempted, something done, / Has earned a night's repose."

5 Cited in Longfellow, *The Poetical Works*, 52.

6 Cited in Claudia Stokes, *Old Style: Unoriginality and Its Uses in Nineteenth-Century US Literature* (Philadelphia: University of Pennsylvania Press, 2021), 160.

## "Doktor, sind Sie des Teufels?"—The North Sea

Compared to British traditions, German literature came late to the sea. In a country largely organized around extensive river systems, the sea was long a regional concern, and a whiff of provincialism attached to it always. If a poet wanted to reflect on the human condition or the nature of memory and consciousness, he or she talked about rivers and lakes. To speak of the sea was to speak of the specific regions abutting the sea. But before the mid-nineteenth century, few ballads made the sea their explicit topic. To be sure, there were several ballads about the sea as a metaphysical space, whether they dealt with enchanted islands (August Kopisch's "Die Wettersäule"), with the world under the sea (Schiller's "Der Taucher"), with the existential solitude of the sailor (a marooned seaman who perishes on the titular island in Adalbert von Chamisso's "Salas y Gómez"), or a drowned king kept alive by water spirits having to overhear songs about him from the surface in Heinrich Heine's "König Harald Harfagar." Joseph von Eichendorff's "Der Götter Irrfahrt" opens with a world-enveloping ocean—but the romance tells the story of how the gods accidentally raise land from the depths.[7]

There were several canonic ballads describing old or ruined castles by the sea—Goethe's "Der König in Thule," for instance, or Ludwig Uhland's "Das Schloss am Meere" (1815)—which used the sea as a metaphor for the transience of all things. Theodor Fontane's maritime balladry tells stories of nature punishing human hubris—albeit usually as part of Fontane's Anglo-Saxon fascination. "Goodwin-Sand" tells the story of the infamous sand banks in the Straits of Dover, while "Die Brück' am Tay" is about the collapse of the Tay Bridge in Scotland in 1879, "John Maynard" about a disaster on Lake Erie 1841. Ballads on Nordic themes frequently involved the sea: in Wilhelm A. Schreiber's "Der Schmied auf Helgoland" ("The Smithy on Helgoland," set to music as "Odin's Ocean Ride" by Carl Loewe) a harried rider appears before a smith on the isolated island of Helgoland, demanding new horseshoes for his steed—the god Odin, riding for battle. Karl Gottfried von Leitner's "König Hakons letzte Meerfahrt" ("King Hakon's Last Sea Voyage") describes a Viking fire burial. But even when a maritime theme almost forced itself upon the poet, German balladry remained curiously landlocked. While several of Fontane's Nordic ballads deal with sea voyages, just as many deal with nymphs, valleys, and cliffs around various lakes.

This changed by mid-century, largely because literature's focus shifted. Whenever literature refused any calling as exalted as talking about the human condition or the nature of *Bildung* and consciousness *tout court*, the sea and its surrounding regions became a powerful means of rebuttal. The

---

7 Joseph von Eichendorff, *Werke* (Munich: Hanser, 1970), 1:299.

sea made a materialist of the poet. If a literary text wanted to address such unclassical topics as modern technology, the nature of work, or "just" how people actually lived their lives, then sailors, traders, fishermen, and Wardens of the Levees were attractive subjects. If the sea connected the English ballad to its ancestry within world literature, it provincialized the German ballad.

By the late eighteenth century, Germans had begun to discover the coastline for themselves, and for the first time that meant all Germans. In what John Gillis has called "the second discovery of the sea,"[8] landlocked populations flocked to the shore not in order to cross the sea, but for the sea's own sake. They came for the wild landscape, for the healthy air, for the baths, and for the fauna. The institution of the sea bath was an import from England, but German luminaries like Georg Christoph Lichtenberg and Christoph Wilhelm Hufeland quickly popularized the salubrious effects of sea air and seawater among the largely landlocked population. In 1793, the first sea bath on the Baltic Sea opened at Heiligendamm, and in 1797 the first one on the Frisian shore of the North Sea opened in Norderney.

In 1825, Heinrich Heine came to Norderney to celebrate the successful defense of his dissertation. He would return in 1826. Norderney, a small speck of sand in the inhospitable sea, was at this point starting to attract wider crowds. Although the first efforts at opening a bath here had been undertaken by the East Frisian authorities, by the mid-1820s the island was a place "von Welt." The sea baths had been opened by the Prussian king. Since the Congress of Vienna, Norderney was part of the Kingdom of Hannover, and thus in some nominal way of the English Empire. The tiny island had suddenly become a part of a much larger cosmos. Not surprisingly, Norderney largely attracted the erstwhile combatants of the Napoleonic Wars. To entertain them, the island soon opened a thermal bath and a casino. The first *Kurpark* opened shortly after the Napoleonic Wars.

Most visitors do not seem to have come to Norderney as Germans exploring their own *Heimat*, but rather as visitors to an exotic land.[9] Heine wrote about the "Insulaner" as though he were a world traveler speaking about the denizens of Tahiti, and he semi-seriously describes them as childlike savages. In characteristically cheeky prose, Heine claims that the "Insulanerinnen" ("the women islanders") "in the end bear children who resemble the bathing guests."[10] He is immediately intent to dispel any suggestion that this is due to actual sexual contact between the women of

---

8 John R. Gillis, *The Human Shore: Sea Coasts in History* (Chicago: University of Chicago Press, 2012), 129–30.

9 On the ambiguities in the application of the term *Heimat* in nineteenth-century Germany, see: David Blackbourn and James Retallack, *Localism, Landscape, and the Ambiguities of Place* (Toronto: University of Toronto Press, 2007).

10 Heinrich Heine, *Reisebilder, Zweiter Teil*, 3:92.

Norderney and the bathers. Rather, he suggests, these children come about like young Otto in Goethe's *Wahlverwandschaften*, who looks nothing like his father, but instead resembles the man his mother was picturing while he was sired. Which means: the virtue of the island maidens is intact, thanks to "their ugliness and especially their smelling of fish," but they are objects of mainland desire, and the mainland visitors are objects of theirs. The bathing guests, too, separated by gender, but "not too separated," seem to ogle more than they fornicate.

For Heine, then, this happy isle and its sights, whether they be ugly native women or pretty bathers, are primarily touristic: one gawks at them, fantasizes about them, lets one's ego be stroked by the attentions of older aristocratic guests of the sea baths. As Lukas Bauer has argued, Heine's travel writing generally speaks to a tourist gaze and the concomitant commodification of experience, which together outline "for Heine a break in cultural cohesiveness." The tourist's gaze and that which attracted said gaze emerged for Heine as a coefficients of modernization processes.[11] Heine is aware throughout that this gaze, and his encounter with the sea shore more generally, is shaped by a historically specific mode of experience, namely tourism, rather than by some universal human need. Or rather, he conceives of it as a universal human need shaped by a historically specific mode of tourism.

This applies above all to the local folklore: Heine, a careful collector of local stories, equally at home in Christian lore, Judaic tradition, and Germanic myth, seems to make few efforts to track down local stories. Instead of the ethnological gaze of the Grimm Brothers, he trains upon these islanders that of the tourist—happy to project, unwilling to dig. "What must have happened on the soil, on which I now tread?" he wonders and never bothers to find out. At the same time, Heine seems to suspect that there never was some original Norderney before the swarms of tourists encroached upon it, and which the right questions might yet unearth. Perhaps what we take for old customs and folklore seem profound and meaningful only through the tourist's eyes, when in fact they are perfectly banal.

> An assistant principal who bathed here wanted to claim that once upon a time services were here conducted for Hertha, or better Forsete, of which Tacitus speaks with such mystery. If only those whose reports Tacitus relied on didn't err and mistook the bathing cart for the goddess's holy chariot![12]

---

11 Lukas Bauer, "'Sie durchziehen dieses Land in ganzen Schwärmen': Tourism as a Marker of Modernity in Heine's Reisebilder," *Monatshefte* 110, no. 4 (2018): 488.

12 Heinrich Heine, *Werke und Briefe* (Berlin: Aufbau, 1972), 3:104.

Tacitus, Heine suggests here, mistook for a religious rite what was simply commerce and exercise. Perhaps no more meaning attached to it than that people do not enjoy getting their feet sandy while wearing shoes. But he does nothing more than suggest this possibility, and in characteristic irony he leaves his suspicion suspended in midair, so that it almost boomerangs on him. After all, Heine's suspicion may be well founded, and the supposed wagon of Hertha nothing more than a primordial bathing cart. Or alternatively perhaps, Heine may simply be incapable of seeing in an ancient, ur-Germanic, deeply religious ritual anything more than his own bathing practice reflected back at him. Is Heine falling victim to typically touristic solipsism, or is he instead in danger of the tourist's equally characteristic exoticism?

In the poem "Seegespenst," of the first cycle of poems in *Die Nordsee*, Heine, perched on the side of a ship, contemplates the endless depths of the sea below ("Unendliches Sehnen, tiefe Wehmut / Beschleicht mein Herz"; "An infinite yearning and deep sadness / Steal into my Heart."[13]), only to get in his own way time and again. He opens with the line "But I leaned over the rail of the vessel," and throughout the poem the I is an "aber"—the thing that sticks out, the exception, the concession. The self, and more to the point Heine's self, is what gets between the oneness with the world that the sea suggests but cannot deliver. Repeatedly, the loss of self he seems to yearn for is made unattainable by his own overactive mind, his own projections, his own reminiscences. He gazes into the depths only to populate it with the legendary long-submerged city of Vineta, with a marketplace and cityfolk ("sedate-mannered men, dressed in black mantles"), he looks for a mermaid only to find an old flame, and when he is finally ready to make the balladic move and throw himself over the railing, the fisherman holds back the newly minted PhD with another biographical reminder:

| | |
|---|---|
| Aber zur rechten Zeit noch | But just in the nick of time |
| Ergriff mich beim Fuß der Kapitän, | The captain grabbed me by the foot |
| Und zog mich vom Schiffsrand, | And pulled me from the rail, |
| Und rief, ärgerlich lachend: | And cried with an angry laugh, |
| Doktor, sind Sie des Teufels? | "Doctor, what the devil's got in you?"[14] |

---

13 Heinrich Heine, "Sea Apparition," in Heinrich Heine, *The Complete Poems of Heinrich Heine*, trans. Hal Draper (Frankfurt: Suhrkamp/Insel, 1982), 142.

14 Heinrich Heine, "Sea Apparition," in Heinrich Heine, *The Complete Poems of Heinrich Heine*, trans. Hal Draper (Frankfurt: Suhrkamp/Insel, 1982), 143.

For better or for worse, Heinrich Heine recognizes in Norderney, in its religious lore and its legends, none other than Heinrich Heine. There are moments, of course, where he has what we might term universal experiences around the sea, but he pulls himself back time and again. In "Nächtliche Fahrt," one of the ballads collected in the *Romanzero*, he tells of a sea voyage that turns dangerous. Rather than universalizing the poetic I, the experience of peril at sea particularizes Heine. For in his moment of desperation, the poet calls out to the God of Israel in a particular Hebrew name, that of lord almighty (*shaddai adonai*).

| | |
|---|---|
| O steh mir bei, barmherziger Gott! | Oh be with me now, merciful god! |
| Barmherziger Gott Schaddey! | Merciful God shaddai! |
| Da schollert's hinab ins Meer— | It slips down into the sea— |
|   O Weh— |   oh woe— |
| Schaddey! Schaddey! Adonay!—[15] | Shaddai, Shaddai, Adonai. |

Is it Heine on that boat? It certainly isn't someone whom nineteenth century German readers would have understood as an everyman—the sort of everyman who could narrate, under cloak of anonymity, a traditional ballad. The moment the Hebrew prayer crosses his lips, the narrator is particular and particularized—and possibly particularized down to one possible identity, namely that of Heinrich Heine. Tacitus, the *Konrektor*, the bathers, the reader, and even Heine himself keep wanting to recognize in the characters, the landscapes, and stories of Norderney some sort of universality: humanity as such, Germany as a country, the ancient Germans as a race, maybe even (as in the poem "Im Hafen") the world spirit itself. But Heine suggests time and again that what we find in this search is ultimately ourselves—petty, individual, modern tourists afraid to get our feet sandy. At the shore, as Todd Pressner has put it, Heine encounters the particular that will not be sublated in Hegelian fashion into the universal.[16]

There are, to be sure, other moments in Heine's treatment of the North Sea, moments where it is man versus the elements, and the particular traveler is nowhere to be found. But even those poems tend to take one look at the sea and recoil into one individual's biography. One such poem finds the poet standing by the seaside, but as the waves push in they seem to propel him from the generality, the universality of the scene toward ever-greater biographical precision. In other poems in the cycle, looking out over the sea

---

15 Heinrich Heine, "Nächtliche Fahrt," in *Romanzero, Werke und Briefe in zehn Bänden* (Berlin: Aufbau, 1972), 2:56.

16 Todd Pressner, *Mobile Modernity* (New York: Columbia University Press, 2007), 134.

triggers visions of the Edda, of Viking warriors, of the Scottish Highlands—
here it returns the speaker to his cradle.

| | |
|---|---|
| Und die weißen, weiten Wellen, | And the broad-breaking billows, |
| Von der Flut gedrängt, | Impelled by the tide, |
| Schäumten und rauschten näher und näher— | Foamed up and roared in nearer and nearer— |
| Ein seltsam Geräusch, ein Flüstern und Pfeifen, | A strange sort of noise, a whispering and whistling, |
| Ein Lachen und Murmeln, Seufzen und Sausen, | A laughing and murmuring, sighing and soughing, |
| Dazwischen ein wiegendliedheimliches Singen— | Immingled with lullaby-like singing—[17] |

And just like that, on a single, admittedly long, word, "wiegenliedheimlich," the poem turns: the hesitant stabs at anthropomorphism become utterly dominant, the possibly metaphoric "sighing" becomes an utterly humanized "singing," and the uncanny sea becomes as *heimlich* as a mother's cradle song. We have moved from the most inhuman, impersonal, inhospitable, to its opposite—the childhood home. And the conduit by which this sudden transfer, or frustrating relapse, occurs is song, is story:

| | |
|---|---|
| Mir war als hört' ich verschollne Sagen, | I seemed to hear forgotten sayings |
| Uralte, liebliche Märchen, | And ancient beautiful legends |
| Die ich einst, als Knabe, | That once I heard as a boy |
| Von Nachbarskindern vernahm, | From the neighborhood children, |
| Wenn wir am Sommerabend, | When on a summer evening |
| Auf den Treppensteinen der Haustür, | We'd squat on the stone doorsteps |
| Zum stillen Erzählen niederkauerten, | And listen in silence to storytellers, |
| Mit kleinen, horchenden Herzen | With young and heedful hearts |
| Und neugierklugen Augen;—[18] | And widened, inquisitive eyes—[19] |

The sea is nowhere to be seen. We find ourselves on a stoop in Düsseldorf, and the only echo that remains of the sea is the story told by the neighborhood boys. Or perhaps it would be more accurate to say that the sea is an echo

---

17 Heinrich Heine, "Twilight," in Heinrich Heine, *The Complete Poems of Heinrich Heine*, trans. Hal Draper (Frankfurt: Suhrkamp/Insel, 1982), 132.
18 Heine, "Nächtliche Fahrt," 1:177/178.
19 Heine, "Twilight," 132.

of those stories, and is present only as an echo of those land-bound stories. If the sea has stories of its own, if the seaside has "uralte, liebliche Märchen" to relate, we do not hear them, or only hear them as our stories. This is how the sea ballad seems to function for Heine: like the ancient city of Vineta that he espies in the depths, like the chariot of Hertha, or the exotic island maidens, it overlays the facticity of the seashore with fanciful stories that are ultimately an index of our own anthropomorphism, solipsism, and provincialism. In the ballad "Die Nixen," a group of water spirits emerge from the waves to curiously examine and caress a knight in armor who, we are invited to infer, has been washed up dead on the shore. The final stanza reveals that the man is simply feigning sleep, content to let the nixes offer their increasingly amorous ministration.

When Heine's poems venture into the open ocean, by contrast, when they leave the shackles of the touristic gaze and of Heine's own biography behind, their language changes. Heine's late ballad "Das Sklavenschiff" (first published in the *Gedichte 1853 und 1854*), takes the materialist view of the ocean to a horrifying, if appropriate, extreme. Heine's language, deliberately stripped of nature lyricism and autobiographical touches, instead presents itself as an international business-speak. In "Das Sklavenschiff," his mercantile update of Goethe's "Totentanz" set on a slave ship on the Middle Passage, we hear about the "Superkargo Mynheer van Koek," "das Haus Gonzales Perreiro" in Rio, a "Doktor van der Smissen," and references to Aristotle, Shakespeare, and "maîtres des plaisirs."[20] In this polyglot capitalist pandemonium, the German language functions as framer and arbiter, excavating the slave trade's ghoulish ironies and dehumanizing doublespeak. When Mynheer van Koek prays for the safety of "his" slaves (or at least 300 of them, lest he not turn a profit), "Schaddey! Adonay!" are far from his lips.

But however much he manages to repress it in moments like this, Heine otherwise articulated a suspicion that haunted German sea balladry for much of the nineteenth century: *could* the sea carry universal connotations about "us" as human beings, as Germans, as moderns, or would it always reveal us as interlopers and tourists, whisper back stories that were really about us as particular biographies, about days on the beach and things spied on sea voyages? German balladry turned to the sea throughout the nineteenth century, but the number of famous sea ballads picked up at mid-century, and reached a crescendo as more and more Germans actually encountered the sea, and the area abutting it, on their own terms. These poems clearly have the same suspicion about regionalism, particularity, and the sea as Heine's, but

---

20 Heinrich Heine, "Das Sklavenschiff," in *Romanzero, Werke und Briefe in zehn Bänden* (Berlin: Aufbau, 1972), 2:201.

they, unlike Heine's, feel compelled to excavate some sort of universality in maritime stories.

This was because the sea had since been recognized as a national concern. With the Jade-treaty of 1853, Prussia purchased a tract of land along Jade Bay on the Oldenburg shore. Before long, the moors and salt marshes gave way to Prussia's first North Sea port, Wilhelmshaven. At first, the harbor was a Prussian exclave, but before long national unification, as well as the railway network and the Ems-Jade Canal (completed in 1888), made it a national naval hub. Unlike in the fleet-obsessed 1890s, the claim to the sea was still largely symbolic: the creation of a national navy was an important aspect of German unification, but it is worth noting that neither the Prussian navy, nor its successor after the Austro-Prussian War, the North German Federal Navy, played a significant role in any of the wars of unification. But the nationalization of the seashore nevertheless completed a transformation of the landscape begun earlier in the nineteenth century. All along the coast, levee systems, drainage systems, and canals brought the raging sea under control, straightened the coast line, and disrupted many of the ecosystems and annual rhythms unique to the area. The legendary submerged town across the bay from Wilhelmshaven became the site of a gun battery guarding access to the Jade Bay.[21] The landscape of moors, heaths, and marsh, so perfectly regional, so well suited to balladic exploration, gave way to the Anthropocene, and, not coincidentally, to the projection of national power.

How could sea ballads mark regional difference while acknowledging that regionalism had increasingly come under pressure in the later nineteenth century? They did it by staging a reconciliation of particular and universal in their poetry. Heine had staged their fateful mismatch—the attempt to find the universal yielded at each turn simply the unreconciled particular. The sea ballad of the later nineteenth century saw reconciliation as its prime mission. Specifically, it sought to stage a dialogue between high German and *Plattdeutsch* vernaculars. In the case of the ballad, this touched on something beyond regional pride or widespread anxieties about political unification under Prussia's banner. Given that the ballad was supposed to speak for "the people," the seaside ballads of the second half of the nineteenth century are trying to figure out who—regionally, geographically, linguistically—is part of the people the ballad speaks for.

The German nationalist and native of Schleswig Julius Langbehn (in his influential *Rembrandt als Erzieher*, 1890) could laud the ballad as "that ur-German form,"[22] but ur-German-ness presented itself as more complicated

---

21 David Blackbourn, *The Conquest of Nature: Water, Landscape, and the Making of Modern Germany* (New York: W. W. Norton, 2006), 145.
22 Julius Langbehn, *Rembrandt als Erzieher* (Leipzig: Hirschfeld, 1890), 31.

given German regionalism and local patriotism. As Eric Kurlander has pointed out, patriotic writing in Schleswig and Holstein tended to combine regional with national pride and frequently distinguished between a specifically North German "native" art and culture and broader (and more mixed) pan-German forms of art and culture. North Germans managed both to consider the ballad "ur-German" and to ascribe it to a German-ness located outside of their own linguistic area. In other words, the imaginary they brought to bear on balladry on the one hand drew on the idea that the ballad was an oral inheritance "of the people." On the other hand they presupposed that it belonged to high German, to written German, to Schiller and to Goethe, and was thus an import to their own particular pastures.

During the nineteenth century, German nationalism and regionalism were frequently in tension, and the ballad's claim to being "native" brought into conflict different modes of belonging: one identified with the emerging nation (and its unifying language) and one tethered to a more circumscribed *Heimat* (and its characteristic customs and local language). In the North, where *Plattdeutsch* was widely spoken and was poised to become a written language in its own right, it was largely linguistic particularism. In other areas it could be religiously or politically based. As Kurlander has pointed out, for North German liberals there was a pervasive (and troublingly racialized) sense that the rest of Germany was more "mixed," less "authentic"[23] than the North. The North was more purely German in terms of blood and heritage than the bastardized South, a bastardization that was often tied to linguistic borrowings. The discourse around regional dialects thus had what Samy Alim, John Rickford, and Arnetha Ball would call a raciolinguistic dimension: it was not taken to refer to geographic location so much as to concepts of race, of whiteness, of Germanness.[24] What's remarkable, if not particularly surprising, is that each region tended to ascribe greater distinctiveness to its own dialect, tended to position its own traditions and speech over and against the entire undifferentiated mass of the rest of the country. The Swiss literary historian Emil Ermatinger pointed out in 1921 that the distance between *Hochdeutsch* and *Mundart* was generally assumed to be more acute wherever the poet or theorist was from, and less so wherever they were not. *Hochdeutsch* was other people.[25]

---

23 Eric Kurlander, "The Landscapes of Liberalism: Particularism and Progressive Politics in Two Borderland Regions," in *Localism, Landscape, and the Ambiguities of Place: German-Speaking Central Europe, 1870–1930*, ed. David Blackbourn and James Retallack (Toronto: University of Toronto Press, 2007), 128.

24 H. Samy Alim, John Rickford, and Arnetha F. Ball, *Raciolinguistics: How Language Shapes Our Ideas about Race* (Oxford: Oxford University Press, 2016).

25 Emil Ermatinger, *Die deutsche Lyrik in ihrer geschichtlichen Entwicklung von Herder bis zur Gegenwart* (Leipzig: Teubner, 1921), 222.

By the mid-nineteenth century, the distinction between regional and national was by no means coterminous with that between the language of print circulation and that of orality. That was because, especially in the North, literary authors sought to bring *Plattdeutsch* into the sphere of print. Klaus Groth, born 1819 in Heide, wrote in Low German (*Niederdeutsch*) and sought to establish the language as a coequal literary language to the high variant. His seminal collection *Quickborn* contains several ballads. Unlike Fritz Reuter, who used Mecklenburg *Platt* to tell emphatically "popular," often humorous stories and relied on short, simple poetic forms, Groth was intent on using local languages to extend "high" literary genres. While the intersection of dialect with class was never made quite explicit, Groth also tended to focus less on the lives of the "common people," but instead sought to establish *Niederdeutsch* as a language that could tell stories across classes. The fraught question was thus one of inclusion and exclusion. North German regional poetry as pioneered by Groth and Reuter distinguished between an inside and outside. Reuter opened his *Läuschen* with the dialect motto "Wer't mag, de mag't; Un wer't nich mag, De mag't jo woll nich mägen"—"Whoever likes it, will like it. And whoever doesn't like it, won't be able to bear it."

At the same time, this particularistic focus was always necessarily in dialogue with an ever-expanding pan-German media landscape and its debates. When Groth published his *Briefe über Hochdeutsch und Plattdeutsch* (1858), he defended the use of *Plattdeutsch*, but did so in *Hochdeutsch*. "The High Germans wish to make us uniform," he complained, but in so doing necessarily interpellated as "us" all speakers of German. And of course his poetry found success outside of the German North, was integrated into the same circuits of circulation more generally activated by interest in the national language. He maintained friendships with Clara Schumann and with Johannes Brahms, who, as Celia Applegate has pointed out, also knew how to make his own performative homesickness for northern Germany aesthetically productive for a national audience.[26] By the end of the century, there were plenty of song-settings from *Quickborn* and other works, albeit almost exclusively in High German translation—including one by a young Friedrich Nietzsche. Particularism thus became an export item marketed to those supposedly excluded. The sole exception was Brahms's friend Julius Otto Grimm (1827–1903), whose *Ein Liederkranz aus Klaus Groth's Quickborn für Sopran, Alt, Tenor und Bass* relied on the Low German originals of the texts.

---

26 Celia Applegate, "Music in Place: Perspectives on Art Culture in Nineteenth-Century Germany," in Localism, Landscape, and the Ambiguities of Place: German-Speaking Central Europe, 1870–1930, ed. David Blackbourn and James Retallack (Toronto: University of Toronto Press, 2007), 52.

The quintessential ballad of the seashore circa 1860 or 1880 was neither fully in Platt nor a translation into the shared "high" German language on which the vast majority of publishing and music writing in the rapidly consolidating country relied. Rather, it contained carefully chosen bits of *Platt* within a broader frame of *Hochdeutsch*. Arno Holz's ballad "Een Boot is noch buten" ("One boat's still out"), which appeared in his 1886 collection *Das Buch der Zeit*, is exemplary of this tendency. From its title on, which would be hard to understand without context for any German living south of, say, Hannover, the poem not only incorporates regional accents and vocabularies, but it juxtaposes them to a universalized German idiom, specifically that of the narrator. Many of the sea ballads of the late nineteenth and early twentieth century proceed this way: collecting flotsam of dialect in a calming ocean of high German.

| | |
|---|---|
| "Ahoi! Klaas Nielsen und Peter Jehann! | "Ahoy, Klaas Nielsen and Peter Jehann! |
| Kiekt nach, ob wi noch nich to Mus sind! | Look whether we're still together! |
| Ji hewt doch gesehn dem Klabautermann? | You saw the Klabautermann at sea, did you not? |
| Gott Lob, dat wi wedder to Hus sind!" | Thank God that we're back at home!" |
| Die Fischer riefen's und stiessen ans Land | So the fishermen shouted and beached their boats, |
| Und zogen die Kiele bis hoch auf den Strand, | And pulled the keels high up on the sand, |
| Denn dumpf an rollten die Fluthen; | For the waters they roll up dully; |
| Han Jochen aber rechnete nach | Han Jochen however did the count |
| Und schüttelte finster sein Haupt und sprach: | And shook his head with dark foreboding and said |
| "Een Boot is noch buten!"[27] | "One boat is still out there!" |

It almost seems important for understanding the poem to not understand the passages in *Platt*, and in particular the word "buten"—or at least to understand it as potentially incomprehensible. Not only will most readers be ignorant of the dictionary-definition of the word, they will be unclear on the broader significance of a boat being "buten." We do not understand the discourse of these hard-bitten fishermen, but more important, we do not understand the life world, highly regional and specific, from which that discourse

---

27 Arno Holz, *Buch der Zeit* (Berlin: Fontane, 1892), 101.

emerges. And yet: this ignorance is not meant to be unsettling. The reader arrives rather quickly at a working understanding of what "buten" means and what it means to these people. The poem stages the reconcilability of regional patois and literary high language.

Through its rhymes, the rhyme of "Fluthen" and "buten," for instance, the poem effectively connects these two voices: the authorial voice that speaks in high German and offers objective narration, and the local voice that speaks in *Platt* and speaks its own subjective condition. In that context it seems important that the *Fluthen* roll implacably each time, even if they're described a bit differently in different stanzas (they roll "dumpf" in the first three and then "plätschern" placidly in the last one), but the titular statement "Een Boot is noch buten" changes semantically from stanza to stanza. In the first stanza, it is the worried remark of an old fisherman; in the second, it is intended to signal to a loving wife that her husband may be in mortal danger; in the third it is already a lament for a ship that clearly is not coming back; and in the final one it is almost a citation—a traumatic kernel brandished in memory of the moment of loss.

These kernels of unassimilated discourse are very common in art ballads that deal with the sea, in particular those of the late nineteenth and early twentieth centuries. This kernel is usually found at the end of each stanza, and almost invariably it drifts in meaning, resists meaning, or even reverses meaning. The high-German stanzas that frame it seek to pin it down, but its squirrely patois resists. In Detlev von Liliencrohn's "Trutz, blanke Hans,"[28] it is the title phrase. Unlike "Een Boot," it is actually glossed in the high German portion of the poem: "Wir trotzen dir, blanker Hans, Nordseeteich," the proud citizens of the fabled city of Rungholt say to the North Sea, and the North Sea punishes them and submerges their town in a storm surge. When we first encounter the phrase, the narrator hears it whispering from the depths in mockery of the townsfolk's pride. In Liliencrohn's "Pidder Lüng,"[29] it is the phrase "Lewwer duad üs Slaav," which likewise comes into focus only as the story progresses.

Sea ballads reward this sort of attention, in fact they are about the rewards for such attention. Many stage the difficult process of listening for stories in an environment that seems to allow for few stories. In Liliencrohn's "Trutz, blanke Hans," it is the lost city of Rungholt, invisible to the mariner but audible if one knows how to listen. Richard Dehmel's "Die Glocke im Meer" has an old mariner tell his two sons on

---

28 Detlev Liliencrohn, "Trutz, blanke Hans," in *Ausgewählte Gedichte* (Berlin: Schuster & Loeffler, 1913), 195.

29. Detlev Liliencrohn, "Pidder Lüng," in *Ausgewählte Gedichte* (Berlin: Schuster & Loeffler, 1913), 170

his deathbed that on certain nights one can hear a bell peal at the bottom of the sea. One son assumes his father is senile. But "der andre sprach wir sind noch jung, / er singt aus tiefer Erinnerung."[30] With his father's song in his ear he eventually comes to hear the same sound and finds succor in it; his brother, his ears closed to the distant ringing as to his father's song, dies embittered and disbelieving.

If the *Plattdeutsch* phrases are semantically slippery, their meaning always becomes clear in the course of the poem. The point is not to starkly contrast the two discursive systems of *Platt* and high German, but rather to guide the reader through a process by which to reconcile them. This insistence on reconciliation, and indeed the insistence that it is possible, sets balladic tales of the sea apart from many other sea stories, which insist instead that what happens at sea cannot effectively be communicated to those back on dry land. To cite an example fairly contemporary to Holz: Marlow's story in Joseph Conrad's *The Heart of Darkness* is one that cannot be told on dry land. It is a story of the sea, it is a story of colonialism, and it is a story of men. "It's queer," Marlow says, "how out of touch with truth women are. They live in a world of their own, and there has never been anything like it, and never can be."[31] News of the sea and the world overseas is impossible to relay to women, Marlow insists. When Kurtz expires saying, "The horror! The horror!," Marlow finds it impossible to translate that horror into the domestic sphere inhabited by Kurtz's fiancée. When the "intended" asks him what Kurtz's last words were, Marlow famously dissimulates: he claims Kurtz died with her name on his lips. And he insists that his dissimulation means he has "remained loyal to Kurtz to the last."[32] John Peck has made clear that maritime fiction of the nineteenth century is rife with such moments of homosocial dissimulation: sailors have to sanitize the harsh masculine world of the seafaring folk for domestic consumption, especially by women.[33] For that reason, Marlow seems to be able to tell his audience about "the horror" only on a boat and to a bunch of men—even if it is a pleasure cruise of various business types on the River Thames. Similarly, the story of Hauke Haien in Theodor Storm's classic gothic novella *Der Schimmelreiter* (*The Rider on the White Horse*, 1888) is only surrendered once the narrator has encountered the ghostly rider by coming a bit too close to the storm-whipped sea.

---

30 Richard Dehmel, "Die Glocke im Meer," in *Gesammelte Werke in drei Bänden* (Berlin: Fischer, 1920), 1:14.

31 Joseph Conrad, "Heart of Darkness," in *Youth: A Narrative and Two Other Stories* (London: Blackwood, 1902), 67.

32 Conrad, "Heart of Darkness," 171.

33 John Peck, *Maritime Fiction: Sailors and the Sea in British and American Novels, 1719–1917* (London: Palgrave Macmillan, 2001).

The sea ballad never quite matched these novellas' penchant for secrecy and self-censorship. After all, contemporaries understood the nature of the ballad to lie in wide circulation. And famous models from other literatures seemed to suggest that sea ballads needed to bring the wide world into the domestic sphere, whether "domestic" meant the home or the metropole. The most famous maritime storyteller in the ballad tradition, Coleridge's ancient mariner stages his story almost as an incursion, buttonholing the narrator just as he is about to attend a wedding and forcing him to listen to his tale. But in *The Rime of the Ancient Mariner*, too, tales of death on or near the sea are an ill fit for domestic space: the poetic "I" is desperate to rejoin the world of family, of women, of domesticity. Coleridge's ballad circulated widely in nineteenth-century Germany in the translation by Ferdinand Freiligrath, and some of this juxtaposition between the domestic (meaning also the European) and the world beyond survives in many ballads of the era.[34] Ballads carry back something of the great wide world to a homeland that is not quite ready to hear it. Asking for such ballads is a slightly demonic thing, as in the case of young Senta prying from her nursemaid Mary the tale of the Flying Dutchman.

It is noticeable, however, that in Germany the sea ballad became particularly influential among poets seeking to overcome Romanticism, not among those representative of it. This belatedness meant that maritime storytelling unfolded in the context of mass media and national publics. Storm's *Der Schimmelreiter* makes clear that by the time the sea story really found its place in the German canon, any thoroughgoing dichotomy between the "domestic" sphere of the German metropole on the one hand and the ocean on the other was no longer sustainable. Literature about the sea was about the mystery of the sea and its denizens; but it was always also about its own role in demystifying the sea. The untellability of sea stories, in Storm's hands and in those of his contemporaries, became ironically entwined with the fact that sea stories were everywhere and were indeed quite popular. Storm's novella, for instance, plays throughout with dissimulation and disclosure, but it dissimulates in exactly the opposite direction as *Heart of Darkness*. Storm's novella has two framing narratives: the narrator claims to have learned the story of the ghostly *Deichgraft* (Warden of the Levees) in "the house of my great-grandmother"—albeit not from the old lady herself, but from a story in a newspaper. This newspaper story, we are told, draws in turn on the report of a traveler who is told by an old schoolmaster the tale of Hauke Haien, who once served as a Warden of the Levees and who grew so obsessive in his quest for controlling the fury of the sea through a new dike that he allowed the old ones to rupture, killing his wife and child. The seashore in German realist

---

34 Ferdinand Freiligrath, *Gedichte* (Stuttgart: Cotta, 1863), 273.

literature has a funny way of on the one hand guarding its stories fiercely, and at the same time working constantly on their remediation. Storm's novella already marks this contradiction as deeply ironic—this oral tale of the common *Volk* comes to the storyteller pre-digested as a half-remembered newspaper account.

But the uncanny demand that balladic narration places on its listeners survived. By the time Freiligrath translated Coleridge's poem, the demand was no longer primarily metaphysical, but rather had attained a political dimension. Readers were supposed to know, hear, remember, and interpret the stories of the sea not because they spoke to them about selfhood, freedom, and fate, but because they spoke to them about fleets and colonies. What Margaret Cohen has called the "sublimation"[35] of the sea, which presents the sea as the protuberance of fateful universality into particular human pursuits, was no longer the main implicit motivation for inventing and circulating these poems. Balladry circulated to entice future officers, to inspire lobbying efforts, to sway parliamentarians. The ballad gathered its audiences for political ends, and made the audience's receptivity itself a matter of politics.

Those audiences were increasingly mass audiences and those politics were mass politics. One striking fact about the many sea ballads discussed here is that hardly any of them found remediation as *Lieder*. Other poems, other ballads by Freiligrath, Holz, Liliencrohn, and Dehmel, were quickly adapted by contemporary composers like Alma Mahler, Karl Weigl, Jean Sibelius, Max von Schillings, and Hans Pfitzner. But something about the maritime ballads made them inappropriate for the concert stage or the parlor. Even though Heine's work remained a mainstay with composers in the final decades of the nineteenth century, "Das Sklavenschiff" was not adapted until after World War II. The reason was almost certainly that the realities the poem described were too stark for a genre like the *Lied*. These were not stories meant to be brought into the domestic sphere; something about their very subject matter moved them into a more public realm. And when the maritime ballad was sung, or even simply pictured being sung, it was in a context of mass mobilization.

## "Zur See, mein Volk"—Constituting National Publics

In the ballad "Die Christnacht der Hallig," Lulu von Strauß und Torney (1873–1956) tells a conventional family tale of a prodigal son whose

---

[35] Margaret Cohen, *The Novel and the Sea* (Princeton, NJ: Princeton University Press, 2010), 117.

father refuses him readmission to his house. What sets the story apart is that it takes place in a very specific, very exotic locale—the home soil never got more circumscribed or more precarious than a *Hallig*. The *Halligen* are a set of small barrier islands that the North Sea has carved out of the northern Frisian coastline. They barely rise out of the surrounding Wadden Sea, small, desperate exclaves of human life in the midst of nature at its most primal. Too small to be protected by the dikes that increasingly dominated the North Sea coastline, they represented, by the late nineteenth century, something of a remnant of a vanishing relationship to nature. As such they emerged as a favorite motif of regionally specific poetry, including ballads. In "Die Christnacht der Hallig," a storm threatens to drown the *Hallig* and its inhabitants; the father and son (who has apparently returned from his sojourn) reconcile and decide to die together. But the sea relents, and the islanders survive the night in the *Hallig*'s church.

It's an unremarkable story, even though once again it links the sea with the theme of reconciliation. What places the poem is the son's crime: "Er lief von der Slup in die Welt hinaus"[36] ("He left the sloop for the great wide world"). The son's rejection of the province in favor of "the world" seems like a fairly negligible sin. Von Strauß und Torney is careful to locate her ballad on a *Hallig*—a province as circumscribed and claustrophobic as provinces come. The father is wrong to begrudge his son his defection, and at any rate his son is, for no reason that is ever explained, there when he is needed. The very regional specificity from which von Strauß und Torney's ballad draws as though from a reservoir of authentic German-ness, emerges in the poem as something to be transcended: forgiving his son for leaving the *Hallig* opens up a space of pan-Germanness beyond the often highly confined regional space of *Heimat*.[37]

"Die Christnacht der Hallig" partakes in a movement in German maritime poetry to make the sea less regional in the wake of German unification. Rather than make the sea a metonymy of a strong regional identity, many poems of the era worked overtime to make the sea every German's concern. When the canon boat *Iltis* sank near the Shandong peninsula in 1896, Johannes Trojan (1837–1915), famous as the editor of the satirical magazine *Kladderadatsch*, wrote an entirely serious poem called "Ein Trost im Unglück" ("Succor in Misfortune") emphasizing how the ship's "Heldenschaar" constituted a German microcosm:

36 Lulu von Strauß und Torney, *Tulipan: Balladen und Erzählungen* (Munich: Diederichs, 1966), 96.

37 On the historically dynamic ambiguities of belonging and *Heimat*, see Mack Walker, *German Home Towns* (Ithaca, NY: Cornell University Press, 2015).

| | |
|---|---|
| Der stammt aus Pommern, aus Westfalen der, | This one is from Pommerania, this one from Westphalia, |
| Der aus der Ostmark an der Memel Strand, | This one is from the Eastern Mark near the Memel's shore, |
| Der ist ein Bayer, der ein Hanseat, | This one's Bavarian, this one from the Hanseatic Cities, |
| Ein Sachse der; Thüringens Berge sandten | A Saxon this one; Thuringia's mountains sent |
| Den auf das Meer, und den die Rebenhügel | This one to sea, and this one the vineyards |
| Des schönen Rheins. So kamen sie zusammen | Of the beautiful Rhine. This is how they came together |
| Aus allen Gauen unsres Vaterlandes | From all the provinces of our Fatherland |
| Und hielten treu in Noth und Tod zusammen | And stuck together in Distress and Death |
| Fest stehend zu dem Kaiser und dem Reich.[38] | Standing true to the Kaiser and the Reich. |

Several times throughout the fleet-obsessed 1890s, the Deutscher Flotten-Verein commissioned editions of a *Flottenliederbuch*, a handbook of songs for "friends of the fleet."[39] Many of the songs contained in the anthology made the same point as Trojan's poem: the sea did not just belong to the North German, it was the destiny of every German, no matter how far from the coast they grew up. At the same time, the sea and the navy, far from de-centering German nationhood, through the power of song could reflect unitary nationhood back to the fatherland:

> Go forth, then, you little blue blazer! Bring to German men and women songs that will praise our Fatherland, our beloved *Heimat*, our heroes and our morals. Help German mothers to rear their children to German thinking and German action. . . . Be a sociable companion to German seamen, who set out to sea to protect and multiply German property.[40]

Few of the songs and poems collected in the *Flottenliederbuch* were ballads, of course. Most of them were sea shanties and patriotic songs extolling the virtues of German men, women, wine, song. What ballads

---

38 Reprinted in *Marine-Rundschau* 9, no. 6 (Berlin: Mittler, June 1898), 798.
39 Robert Gersbach, ed., *Flottenliederbuch: Lieder und Handbuch für Flottenfreunde* (Neudamm: Neumann, 1900).
40 Ibid., iii.

the *Flottenliederbuch* collects run the gamut from nautically themed songs ("Es zog ein matrose einst über das meer," also sometimes anthologized as "Gerettet"[41]), some gothic ghost-ship stories, vaguely waterlogged classics like Goethe's "Fischer," as well as a few landscape-poems from Heine's time in Norderney.

But there was more contemporary fare as well. As Trojan's balladic gathering of a "Heldenschaar" makes clear, the newfound fixation on the sea and the fleet transmitted itself into ballads. Nary a ship could sink in a storm before a homebound skald immortalized the drowned mariners with a ballad. These modern shipwreck ballads retained the old implicit link between the lone singer and a universal audience, but they did so in the vernacular of modern mass media. The sea ballads of the mid-century had often started with kernels of the particular, of the regional, of the unshareable, but the process of relating the ballad amounted to the universalization of their materials. By the end, every listener was meant to have understood the story and the particular cosmos from which it emerged. Even if parts of the ballad were hard to understand, the ballad as a whole celebrated the process of understanding.

Throughout the period, shipwreck ballads performed similar universalizing work, albeit in terms of emotion rather than language. By the end, all listeners were to feel the same way about what they'd heard, and the poems frequently spent altogether more time on this fellow-feeling than on the poor souls whose drowning gave rise to the feeling. This was a mass-market version of what we encountered earlier as balladic consciousness; in Wagner's *Flying Dutchman*, Senta seeks to remake the atmosphere of the salon in the spirit of the Dutchman's tale. Her target is not so much to provide information, but to browbeat her girlfriends into a feeling in unison. Just as in the case of Senta's ballad in Wagner's opera, balladic consciousness in these shipwreck ballads depends on hearing as *anagnorisis*: in them, the reader is not meant to encounter new stories. Rather, the reader is meant to recall something they knew already. Famous disaster ballads of the mid-nineteenth century, for instance G. M. Hopkins's "Wreck of the Deutschland," Fontane's "Brück am Tay" and "John Maynard," and Longfellow's "Wreck of the Hesperus," put a distinctively modern spin on this *anagnorisis*. The shipwreck poem is frequently predicated on our having encountered the story in a newspaper. In fact, the ballad was to thicken the dispassionate official version of events, to provide affective flesh to put on the journalistic bones: On September 22, 1897, the torpedo boat S26 sank in the Elbe delta. Soon thereafter a ballad began circulating supposedly written by a sailor of the *Reichsmarine*. His affects, his interpretation of events, were supposed to gather the home audience as a community of mourners.

---

41 Ibid., 112.

Newspapers and *Flottenvereine* made Germans stakeholders in the imperialist undertakings ("Mitglieder des Vaterlandes," "members of the Fatherland," as a famous advert of the day put it); ballads made them witnesses. Although these poems vary widely, not least in quality, they are remarkably homologous in their narrative conventions, which they draw from the longer, and remarkably transnational, tradition of shipwreck ballads. In constituting a specifically German public around supposedly shared national traumas, these poems hewed to conventions identical to ones in England or the United States. Shipwreck ballads usually operate in implicit dialogue with other texts, which they presuppose, but do not explicitly invoke. They are short on details and plot, assuming that the reader will be familiar with the events, presumably from newspaper reports, though the terms of that familiarity are never spelled out. The shipwreck ballad is careful to follow the facts as they have been reported, only filling in details where reporting falls short. Even when they present something of a witness account, these poems often tell stories that allow no witnesses. They present themselves as oral reports of events that no one survived, or tell them from perspectives no one could have occupied during the event. It is not so much that they narrate omnisciently, than that they seem to combine imaginative projection with the sourcing of reportage. The ballad tells a story an individual can no longer tell.

They often shade into the supernatural, but the supernatural is present only as a possibility, as a threat at the margins, as a subjective perception that is never vindicated. The supernatural is a matter of indifference. Are the lights and the gunfire the skipper and his daughter hear in Longfellow's "Wreck of the Hesperus" natural phenomena, or do they belong to some otherworldly realm? The poem won't say one way or the other, and, unlike in "Der Erlkönig," say, or "The Rime of the Ancient Mariner," the poem's outcome does not depend on either the reader or the characters acknowledging or discounting the supernatural elements.

Shipwreck ballads are relentlessly impressionistic; the more well-known the disaster, the greater the liberty the poet could take with its telling. This was not just an attractive sleight of hand for high litterateurs. Johannes Trojan wrote a number of poems one might call quasi-ballads: these poems have narrative features, but they are either fairly undramatic improvisations on a well-known story, or they chronicle the reaction of the poet hearing about the shipwreck, or reading about it in the papers. When the cruiser *Adler* and the gunboat *Eber* sank in the harbor of Apia, in German Samoa, Trojan wrote a poem dedicated to "Den Braven" ("The Faithful Ones"). When the canon boat *Iltis* went down near the Shandong peninsula, Trojan wrote "Ein Trost im Unglück" ("Succor in Calamity"). The poem is not rhymed, and though it starts with lines in Alexandrine meter (iambic hexameter), it quickly abandons this meter. Throughout the *Flottenliederbuch* we likewise encounter poems that appear to narrate, but ultimately turn out to simply describe—they seem forever perched on the edge of balladry, but then they hold back.

While metrically and poetically uninteresting, these quasi-ballads matter in terms of what we might call their epistemology. They leave out a whole lot of story: they interweave impressions, events that are only alluded to but never spelled out, supernatural flights, elegiac bits of memorialization. The great traditional strength of the ballad—that it transmits a story clearly and distinctly to almost anyone who happens upon it—is entirely missing in these poems. The reason, it seems, is that their address is not in fact universal: they speak to, and indeed mean to speak to, only those who already possess a certain knowledge of the incident, who have read about the shipwreck in the paper and have taken a special interest in the story. They address themselves, in other words, specifically to patriotic Germans.

The shipwreck ballad had been a staple in the Anglo-Saxon world for a long time prior. And while only some of the shipwreck poems were outright hymns (Cowper's "The Castaway" is one famous example), something hymnal attached to even the most balladic of these poems. They were impressionistic, scant on details, replete more with feeling than with plot. Feeling was at any rate the point. The nation constituted itself through the melancholic, wounded backward look via balladry.[42] As Julia Wright has pointed out, these ballads served a kind of "sentimental nationalism," through which "suffering itself becomes a catalyst by which to forge the sympathetic bonds that will unite the people into a nation.[43]" Through the sharing of the news, and more important, an affective response to the news, the ballads constructed "a range of imagined national communities of mourning."[44]

The reconciliation between local argot and national language, and between the local and the national more generally, that defined the poems of Holz and Liliencrohn is entirely absent in these shipwreck ballads. The same is true for the insistence that sea stories needed to be carefully translated for a landbound audience. The art ballads about the sea around the turn of the century push the reader toward a moment of reconciliation and understanding: we may not be entirely clear what the *Platt* phrases mean or why they matter, but the poem gradually pushes us toward a moment of

---

[42] Mark H. Gelber, *Melancholy Pride: Nation, Race, and Gender in the German Literature of Zionism* (Tübingen: Niemeyer, 2000), 95.

[43] Julia Wright, *Ireland, India and Nationalism in Nineteenth Century Literature* (Cambridge: Cambridge University Press, 2007), 37. Cited in: Kirsty Reid, "Shiwrecks on the Streets: Maritime Disaster and the Broadside Ballad Tradition in Nineteenth Century Britain and Ireland," in *The Shipwreck in Art and Literature*, ed. Carl Thompson (London: Routledge, 2014), 143..

[44] Cited in: Reid, "Shipwrecks on the Streets: Maritime Disaster and the Broadside Ballad Tradition, 143.

recognition: what appeared local and parochial is after all comprehensible universally and matters universally. The popular sea ballads that sprang up around the German fleet proceeded the opposite way: they posited that the sea had to matter to all Germans, and then withheld enough narrative detail to test the reader—did they know enough to follow along? Did they recall the horrible events? And did they feel appropriately about them?[45] As Paul Ricoeur has noted in a different context, such "obligated memory" is deeply paradoxical: the injunction to remember seems to detach the remembrance from complex interplay "among individual memory, collective memory and historical memory."[46] And it seems to deny the creaturely, autobiographical dimension that attends to any individual's relationship to lived history. The ballads collected as part of the maritime project of German nationalist politics in the late nineteenth century were presented as impinging on each listener in exactly the same way. The irony introduced by Heine's autobiographical framing, or by Storm's play with remediation, was missing entirely.

The demand for a uniformity of reception that characterizes the popular shipwreck ballads of those years eventually transmitted itself to *Kunstballaden* as well. The narrative poems of Agnes Miegel, Lulu von Strauß und Torney, and Börries Freiherr von Münchhausen draw on the same epistemology as Trojan's various epitaphs to luckless German cruisers: not only do they tell clearer tales, they also celebrate their comprehensibility by circumscribed, and that meant usually national, communities of listeners. Where the shipwreck ballads, with their reliance on mass media narratives, had still implicitly acknowledged the impossibility of bringing the local and the national into perfect coincidence, these ballads aimed, in essence, to gather the German nation around the campfire. The problematic of mediating the local and the universal had been characteristic of ballads by progressive writers— Arno Holz's "Een Boot is noch buten!" appeared in a collection subtitled *Lieder eines Modernen*, and the question of how to square balladic communication with the modern world was to them a central task of the ballad. The conservative ballad writers around Münchhausen wielded the ballad as a battering ram against the modern world, and against modernism in particular. When Münchhausen took over the newly refounded *Göttinger Musenalmanach* in 1898, he decided, in a conscious throwback to Goethe and Schiller and the Göttingen *Hainbund*, to use the format for a "renewal" of the ballad form in Germany; most of the early almanacs were handed over to balladry—and Münchhausen had gathered around it a group of balladeers, among them Miegel, von Strauß, und Torney. While poets like Richard Dehmel, Frank

---

45 Peter Milward and Raymond Schoder, eds., *Readings of the Wreck* (Chicago: Loyola University Press, 1976).

46 Paul Ricoeur, *Memory, History, Forgetting* (Chicago: University of Chicago Press, 2009), 87.

Wedekind, and the young Bertolt Brecht sought to update the kinds of stories the ballad could tell, the poets promoted by Münchhausen were extremely traditional in their choice of *sujet*. Stories of valiant knights, of the Black Plague, of great historic battles abounded—as did stories of the sea. In "Die Fischer von Svendaland" (1896), Münchhausen tells a gothic tale of divine retribution against coastal pirates; in "Die Frauen von Nidden" (1907), Agnes Miegel tells of a plague-stricken fishing village on the Curonian Spit.

In their hands, the sea becomes a token of tradition, a token of non- or even anti-modernity. "The ballad, a forceful, colorful poetic genre, has been pushed into the background far too much in the past few decades," Münchhausen writes in his preface to his second *Musenalmamach*. When Münchhausen proposed that the *Musenalmanach*'s mission would be to "once again tend to the German ballad, to give it back the space it is owed,"[47] he was writing, as Gottfried Weißert has pointed out, a mere decade after Fontane's last efforts in the form.[48] Münchhausen was not talking about a quantitative dearth of ballads being written—there were plenty. He meant to deliberately discount as less-than-authentic the many ballads that had been published in the last decades of the nineteenth century. For the new propagandists like Münchhausen, the ballad functioned as a weapon in their fight against modernism and for tradition. What made it such a perfect weapon was the epistemological structure the fleet and shipwreck ballads of the *Flottenliederbuch* and other nationalist publications had promoted. The ballad spoke to people not to impart new information, but rather to rekindle in them a sense of what they already knew. Let the modernists awaken in people hitherto unknown sensations, Münchhausen suggested; the ballad speaks to the great mass of the *Volk* on its own terms, and draws its strength from the fact that it relies on a pre-attunement between a people and its poetry.

But that attunement had from the first its demonic side, a demonic side the Göttingen-group seemed to embrace and celebrate. Many of their works expand the inherent fatalism of the sea ballad, in which human will comes to naught before the power of sublime nature, to include a pronounced cultural pessimism. Many of their heroes are, as Weißert puts it, "suffering and passive."[49] They are witnesses to history, as is, in almost every instance, the narrator of the poem. The squirrely democracy of voices in the ballad in their work has given way to unifying passive receptivity. In Miegel's "Peter Harden," a ballad of disturbing sexual frankness and raging misanthropy that appeared in the 1901 *Musenalmanach*, a Danzig merchantman finds out by letter that while he has been busy "well into the night / to put your riches

---

47 Börries, Freiherr von Münchhausen, ed., *Göttinger Musenalmanach für 1901a* (Göttingen: Lüder Horstmann, 1900), x–xi.

48 Gottfried Weißert, *Ballade* (Stuttgart: Metzler, 2016), 112.

49 Weißert, *Ballade*, 113.

in numbers,"[50] his daughter has drunk and slept her way through the port city's taverns: she has lost her virginity to "a Polish dog" named Pawel, then taken up with a Frisian captain named Gerd Nissen, a French sailor, and finally the letter-writer himself. The list of paramours in the taunting note has definite racial undertones—not only do most of the daughter's partners come from non-German lands, we are also told that "all the young lads in the Hanseatic town / who are dark of hair and eye" have since been with the merchant's "blonde, angelic" daughter.[51] But what is worse, the merchant seems to see things the same way: he grabs "a log from the fire and a ring of keys," sets his house on fire and locks it from the outside—leaving his daughter and her latest paramour to die in the flames. What Münchhausen called the "strong ballad, trembling with life"[52] seemed ever ready to align itself with violence against outsiders and perceived inferiors. When Julius Kober put out a *Vortragsbuch für Front und Heimat* (*Declamatorium for Front and Heimat*) to lend poetic support to the collapsing Eastern Front in the final years of World War II, he naturally included Miegel's poem.[53]

Well before the Nazi period, this group of ballad-writers drafted the German art ballad was into a "blood-and-soil" literature, an association that shaped how it would be framed in the *Germanistik* of the Nazi period and that likely negatively impacts its reception until today. The protagonists of the Göttingen-group all became involved in the conservative revolution of the 1920s and were early converts to National Socialism. As pillars of the cultural policy apparatus of the Nazi state (such as the *Reichsschrifttumskammer*), they came to shape how the ballad was instrumentalized in the arts, culture, and teaching fields in the 1930s. Their view of the German ballad, and above all those exemplars of the genre they sought to banish as less authentic, became *raison d'état*. Lulu von Strauß und Torney signed an oath of loyalty to Hitler in 1933 and spent the Nazi years actively trying to rid German culture of "Jewish influence." Agnes Miegel wrote glowing poems about Adolf Hitler and the invasion of Poland.[54] Börries von Münchhausen occupied an ambivalent position in the Nazi state: he became something like a poet laureate of balladry in the Third Reich, his poems set to music for use in youth groups and at party events; others, however, were censored for what the Hitler Youth

---

50 Agnes Miegel, "Peter Harden (Fragment)," in Börries von Münchhausen, *Göttinger Musenalmanach* (Göttingen: Horstmann, 1901), 41.

51 Miegel, "Peter Harden (Fragment)," 40.

52 Börries von Münchhausen, "Zur Ästhetik meiner Balladen," in *Deutsche Monatsschrift für das gesamte Leben der Gegenwart*, Vol. 11 (Berlin: Duncker, 1907), 97.

53 Julius Kober, *Vortragsbuch für Front und Heimat* (Gotha: Engelhardt-Reyer, 1942), 196.

54 Michael H. Kater, *Culture in Nazi Germany* (New Haven: Yale University Press, 2019), 228.

deemed queer subtexts.[55] He dedicated himself to denouncing literature he considered "degenerate" and "Jewish" in toxic screeds, going so far as to propose writing new lyrics for the Heine-settings by Robert Schumann.[56] But he got himself in hot water for fighting censorship of Fontane's ballad "Herr von Ribbeck auf Ribbeck im Havelland," and was accused of philosemitism for an early collection of poems in response.

Münchhausen's zig-zagging career in the Nazi state, which culminated in his suicide in March 1945 as Allied forces approached his castle, demonstrates the self-defeating nature of the attempt to yoke the aesthetic form of the ballad entirely to some form of popularity. Nevertheless, the hold this idea had on the ideology of the ballad (including Wolfgang Kayser's 1936 book *Geschichte der deutschen Ballade*, which was long a classic in ballad studies[57]) cannot be overstated. Nor can the fact that the ideology Münchhausen and his fellow travelers brought to bear on the ballad retroactively reshaped the canon. Gone were the notes of irony that characterized the German art ballad's relationship to its audience; gone was the ambiguity that surrounded its pretense at authenticity.

The unhealthy poetry of symbolism, Münchhausen had claimed in the 1898 *Musenalmanach*, could only appeal to unhealthy audiences, "for an artist can only awaken what was already in him," and "only those strings vibrate in his readers, whose keynote already thrummed inside of him."[58] The ballad speaks of a pre-stabilized harmony between the singer and his or her listeners. In Lulu von Strauß und Torney's "Schiff ahoi," a ship is lost at sea, but everyone knows what happened to it:

| | |
|---|---|
| Und die "Anne Kathrin" ist nie wiedergekommen. | And the "Anne Kathrin" never came back. |
| Aber es weiss doch ganz Westerland, Wie er sein Ende genommen. | And all of Westerland knows How he came to his end. |

This is because after presumably going down in a storm, the captain Lars Jessen appears to his younger brother at sea. When the brother rushes ashore to tell his sister-in-law the news, it turns out she knows already—Lars has appeared to her in her house to say goodbye. Knowledge in "Schiff ahoi" is not something one carries from one place to the other, it is something one

---

55 Börries von Münchhausen, Levin Ludwig Schückin, "Deine Augen über jedem Verse, den ich schrieb." *Briefwechsel 1897–1945* (Oldenburg: Igel, 2001), 17.

56 Börries von Münchhausen, "Heinrich Heine in Deutschen Tönen," in *Heine und die Nachwelt, 1907–1956*, ed. Hartmut Steinecke (Berlin: Erich Schmidt, 2008), 385–387.

57 Wolfgang Kayser, *Geschichte der Deutschen Ballade* (Berlin: Junker und Dünnhaupt, 1936).

58 Börries, Freiherr von Münchhausen, ed., *Göttinger Musenalmanach für 1899* (Göttingen: Lüder Horstmann, 1898), 2.

discovers deep in oneself, an *anagnorisis* born of instinct and a deep attunement to the sea. The poem stages this knowledge as a kind of extreme unction. The ship's owner in his faraway office never finds out what happened to his ship, and will get no closure, but the relatives of the crew know full well. And while Lars Jessen's widow laments "that he won't have a cross on his gravesite," the certainty which his double apparition, and his legend, provides to his community becomes a memorial and a final resting place of its own.

This was the sort of knowledge that Münchhausen hoped ballads inspired in their readers—or, more specifically, that German ballads inspired in their German readers. The German ballad had lived since Goethe and Schiller in the tension between print culture and supposed oral extraction, which was also to say between high German and local dialect. In drafting more modern ballads into his imagined tradition based on a near fantastical scene of balladic receptivity, Münchhausen precisely elided this crucial difference. In his 1923 edition with commentary *Meisterballaden: Ein Führer zur Freude (Master Ballads: A Guide to Their Enjoyment)*, Münchhausen presents a selection of regional and sea ballads, but reframes them as specifically and nationally German. And yet, in a self-defeating gesture, Münchhausen's hypostasis of an imagined balladic tradition can legitimate itself only by turning to emphatically modern metrics: in inveighing against the "Ewigheutigen" ("those of the eternal today") of modernism, he essentially treats the sales successes of Felix Dahn, of Agnes Miegel, and not least of all of Münchhausen himself as the direct expression of *Volksgeist*. In earlier centuries it was the survival of tales and songs that told us what mattered to the *Volk*; in the twentieth century, it seems, sales are its direct cognate.[59] Holz, Liliencrohn, Dehmel (and earlier, Fontane and Heine) had wondered what it meant to turn to a supposedly folk-based genre in an age of mass media; Münchhausen, like the sea balladeers of the *Flottenverein*, believed that mass media were simply an extension of the folk.

---

59 Thomas Schneider, "Ein 'Beitrag zur Wesenserkenntnis des deutschen Volkes': Die Instrumentalisierung der Ballade in der extremen politischen Rechten und im Nationalsozialismus," in *Die deutsche Ballade im 20. Jahrhundert*, ed. Srdan Bogosavljevic and Winfried Woesler (New York: Peter Lang, 2009), 136.

# | Epilogue

*The Ballad as Record*

The ballad is a genre of the border. Sometimes it tells stories of the borderlands, as in the British tradition, or simply of the margins of society, as was often the case in Germany. Heathen gods, vanishing landscapes, disappearing peoples and practices are its mainstays, and through the ballad receive belated vindication. The ballad genre bridges, but also articulates, the border between high and popular culture, between colony and metropole, between orality and print, between the music of language and the more formalized conventions of art music.

This border has a temporal dimension: Even outside of the self-consciously antiquarian revivals of the eighteenth century, the ballad involves a mission of recovery. But it recovers by distinctly modern means: this is why Scott's "Lay" chooses as his mouthpiece the Last Minstrel, "the last of the race, who . . . might have caught some of the refinement of modern poetry, without losing the simplicity of his original model." Susan Stewart has drawn attention to the fact that the question of the ballad's authenticity arose only "in situations where there is a self-conscious perception of mediation."[1] Stewart means a retroprojective authenticity: the concern that what we receive is in whatever way "genuine"; but the ballad includes a future-directed authenticity as well. What Scott called its "imitative harmony"—its reliance on repetition, assonance, and rhythm—is as much about how the poem got to us as it is about what will happen to the poem *once* it gets to us.

---

1 Susan Stewart, "The Scandals of the Ballad," in *Crimes of Writing* (New York: Oxford University Press, 1991), 105.

As we have seen, this projective authenticity was a preoccupation in Germany more so than in, say, the British Isles. Germany, as a country that could locate itself in the past and the future, but not in the present, was profoundly interested in establishing something authentically its own at some as-yet-undetermined point in the future. Since Bürger, the German art ballad persisted on a particular dynamic of repetition and development, and relied both on recuperation and proliferation. If the art ballad records a trace, it is not a trace left by the event, but rather a trace hoping to call forth the event. The claim German art ballads make on their listener is that without the listener that trace may well vanish; the second claim they make is that the listener become a potential future teller of the tale.

There is, in other words, an ethic to the German art ballad genre, and perhaps to the ballad genre more broadly. The way German ballad meter conforms to everyday speech, the simple rhyme scheme in most ballads, the frequent use of assonance and the strongly mimetic quality of the prosody are intended as markers of *past* oral transmission, the mnemonics of ancient minstrels; but just as much, they are intended to impress themselves upon the listener as demands of *future* oral transmission. The story tells us that it must be carried forward, and it comes in a form that is supposed to vouch for such carrying.

This leads to a paradoxical situation that several chapters in this book have outlined: the German art ballad pretended to be plucked from oral, communal circulation, even though they were of course composed by individual poets. But these poems did have a kind of oral currency after the fact. They were publicly recited and sung, memorized, parodied, and adapted. Ballad aesthetics were fixated on the point of rupture between an oral culture of the ballad and a written one, between the *Volksballade* and the *Kunstballade*. But, especially when we take seriously the broad range of aesthetic objects that went by the name of "ballad" in the nineteenth century, a different rupture comes to matter more. Namely, what happens to the ballad as it stops being a record of something and becomes a recorded something?

"Die Uhr" ("The Watch"), written by the Austrian poet Johann Gabriel Seidl (1804–1875), juxtaposes time as what Kant called a "form of intuition" and as a phenomenological entity. The poet describes a timepiece entrusted to him and the implacable beat by which it measures time. Whether he wanted it to go slow or fast, it has always accompanied his life at a steady beat. Much of the poem is given to a kind of temporal stoicism: the clock abstracts from the subjective experience and mapping of time, it keeps calm measure beyond our "unwise dreams" (*törichten Wunsche*). The poet makes clear that the watch will not be passed on to another person; like the beat of the heart it ticks only for one owner. If it ever were to stop beating, he says, he would have to return it to its maker "out there, beyond the earth / Out in eternity."

"Die Uhr" is not the most profound poem, nor is it entirely clear that it is a ballad. Seidl didn't publish it with that generic designation, but by the end of the nineteenth century it was widely considered one. The reason for this is likely that nineteenth-century Germans were poised to recognize the ballad as combining objective reportage and subjective experience—since Goethe, this had been taken to vouch for the "dramatic" content of the ballad. The experiences relayed in it do not begin and end with the subjectivity of its speakers—there is an objective narrative authority reporting, for instance, that, whatever the father and his son see in "Der Erlkönig," by the end of the poem the son is incontestably dead.

It is precisely here that "Die Uhr" becomes interesting; for it seems to feel the need to decide to which version of time its own formal operations as ballad belong. Seidl suggests that the ballad keeps objective time:

| | |
|---|---|
| Ich wollte, sie wäre rascher | I wished that it had quickened |
| Gegangen an manchem Tag; | its beat on certain days; |
| Ich wollte, sie hätte manchmal | I wished it that it would slow |
| Verzögert den raschen Schlag.[2] | Its ticking from time to time. |

Note the double enjambment signaling that, whatever the speaker wishes about time, the poem has no interest in acceding to those wishes—like the watch, the poem's lines neither slow down nor speed up. Insofar as "Die Uhr" is balladic, it fails to indulge subjective whim; it has a measured record to create. The ballad, and especially the regularity of its cadence and rhyme, which seem to emerge organically from within as a divine gift rather than being imposed from without, are small pockets of eternity within history.

Although adapted by multiple composers, it became immensely popular in a song setting by Carl Loewe (1796–1869), the most successful of Germany's "ballad composers." His version of "Die Uhr (op. 123, no. 3, written in 1830) seems to extend Seidl's understanding of the ballad form. Easy as it would have been in a temporal medium to demonstrate the hoped-for distension of time, Loewe resolutely allies music with form, with reality rather than wish. In the couplet discussed above, Loewe's metronomic markings make clear that he does not want either singer or instrument to indulge the poet's wishes for increased speed or a slowing down. No *ritardando*, no *accelerando*, neither the wish how time *might* flow, nor the perception of how it *does* flow have any bearing on the piece's own pace.

It may have been for that very reason that it is among the earliest commercial ballad recordings in the German-speaking world—a 1901 gold mold

---

[2] Johann Gabriel Seidl, *Gesammelte Schriften*, ed. Hans Max (Vienna: Braumüller, 1877), 1:25.

cylinder featuring the opera singer Franz Schumann and an unknown pianist. The limitations of this early phonographic medium actually redound to the piece's advantage; for the faithful time-keeping of the piano is joined here by another, a mechanical one. Like in all early cylinder recordings, the revolutions of the cylinder are themselves audible, which in the case of Loewe's song has the effect that the record itself seems to take over the role of the pocket watch—a mechanical time-keeper insensate to what the singer might want to express. As Jason Camlot has pointed out, early sound recordings did not offer, nor were they understood to offer, "a transparent or unmediated record" of a certain performance. Instead, they "demanded greater accommodation of the affordances of the recording technology and preservation media."[3] In this way the new technology became an extension of what in Seidl's poem had been accomplished by the enjambments. That is the impression the song gives to a modern listener: The recorded ballad seems to accept the technological parameters of the record as part of the ballad form. Schumann sings Loewe's song fast by today's standards, which gives it a more popular quality and heightens the gulf between ballad and art-*Lied*. He keeps pace carefully. The piano is given perhaps a more prominent role. Another way of putting it: when recording his interpretation of Loewe's song, Schumann seems to have retroactively accepted the ballad form as a precursor to recording technology.

At the same time, Schumann's adjustments don't do the piece much damage—other recordings from the same collection, of Wagner arias for instance, are today only funny—rushed, tinny, ravaged by the demands of the new technology. By contrast, the new technology was in some ways a natural fit for the ballad form—these were poems to be heard, after all, and audiences had listened to them in settings that resembled phonographic listening for over almost a hundred years. Programs of ballad recitation had been among the ballad's most important forms of dissemination since at least the turn of the nineteenth century, along with cheap anthologies and musical settings. An idea of emulating precise repetition, in memory or intonation, had been encoded into the form's popularization from the first.

Even the mode of reproduction expected of the reciter had come to resemble a phonographic record. As we have seen, in the nineteenth century German audiences tended to recognize a wide variety of declamatory strategies that differed in terms of their affective dimension.[4] The ballad always had a somewhat unusual position within these strategies, because in ballads the

---

3 Jason Camlot, *Phonopoetics: The Making of Early Literary Recordings* (Stanford, CA: Stanford University Press, 2019).

4 Judith Eisermann, *Josef Kainz: Zwischen Tradition und Moderne* (Munich: Utz, 2010), 284.

target of mimesis was usually not psychology, but sound.[5] And this moved balladic circulation, proliferation, and remediation close to a technology. As Shane Butler has pointed out, when Thomas Edison laid claim to the word "phonograph" in 1877, his was only the latest, and most definitive, in a long line of attempts to represent the voice in written form.[6] The ballad had long participated in these attempts.

The actor Josef Kainz (1873–1910), who successfully toured with programs of monologues and poetry, tended to musicalize recitation, pairing certain tones and vocal pitches with a particular emotional register. But when it came to ballad recitation, Alfred Kerr's description of Kainz's recitation of Uhland's ballad "Des Sängers Fluch" in 1897 suggests a far more predictable, far more transferable, and far less idiosyncratic recitation style: "One single long crescendo all the way to the curse, then a decrescendo, a trailing-off, and an almost toneless denouement."[7] There is a lot less subjectivity in this sort of performance, and a lot less variation—hearing one rendition was supposed to be rather like hearing any other. Public declamation and the persistent efforts at its systematization, pedagogical practices, and the valorization of memorizing poetry had in central respects anticipated this kind of accommodation. Reciting balladry was in its own way a form of recording.

But if factors like these tended to make ballad recitation protophonographic, in other respects the new technology disrupted the formal parameters of the ballad form. The ballad's cadence invited misremembering and misquoting—throughout nineteenth-century letters we find supposed quotations from ballads that are metrically correct, and say the right thing, but do not hew to the printed letter of the text. This was to some extent by design: the same formal features of the ballad that made it memorable were supposed to suggest (and enable) some variance within the prosody of the poem—they reminded you that these were poems to be recited from memory, with the risk of mis-reciting them always part of the equation.

After all, this was how, at least in the just-so story of ballad poetics, art ballads had come into existence in the first place: modern reconstitutions of old stories that only survived in multiple and fragmentary versions under different titles. Johann Gottfried Herder had insisted that what mattered in ballads was the spirit rather than the letter—the story "behind" the prosody, not its particular shape. Many ballads dramatized this dialectic of difference and repetition, both in Germany and outside of it. Often enough a poem presents its story as a justification for its own repetition; it knows

---

5 Irmgard Weithase, *Geschichte der deutschen Vortragskunst im 19. Jahrhunder* (Leipzig: Böhlau, 1940), 75.

6 Shane Butler, *The Ancient Phonograph* (New York: Zone Books, 2015), 12.

7 Alfred Kerr, "Singakademie: Vorlesung von Josef Kaunz" (1897), in *Wo liegt Berlin?* (Berlin: Aufbau, 1997), 265.

why it needs to be repeated by its hearers. It knows what the stakes are it is reproduced badly or unfaithfully.

Mis-recitation is a frequent topic of these poems, and one of the modes of misrecognition involved their remediation—their illustration, parody, adaptation, and song setting. Given that it brings the formal demands of the ballad (variance within repetition) into contact with the demands of the far more repetitive *Lied*-form, there will be moments when music grasps the poem, and others when it does violence to it. Like the sorcerer's apprentice, the song setting intervenes into the recitation—with all the risks that entails. This dynamic endures in the classic ballad settings of the nineteenth century. These *Lieder* are not content merely to project a certain mood or to present memorable melodies; they shape our understanding of the plot of the poems they describe, to the point that they can even distort them.

Both Loewe's and Schubert's settings of Goethe's ballad continue this journey of reinterpretation through repetition. Neither composer changes a word of Goethe's text, but each of them makes formal decisions that have enormous ramifications for our understanding of that text. Most adults who have spent any time in the German school system will have encountered the text and will remember the story. But here is the interesting part: they will most likely remember aspects of the story that are not actually in the poem. A father rides quickly through a storm, in his arms a sick child; by the time he reaches the help he seeks, the child is dead. None of this is in the poem. It has become part of the story thanks to Schubert.

Even when they rein in possible differentiations in and through balladic repetition, ballad settings add to the events *recorded* in the ballad. Things that are not printed on the page start to be transmitted, to become accepted wisdom in a way that strikingly resembles the standing reserve of *Volksgeist* that is supposed to authorize ballad writing in the first place. Even if it transforms balladic modes of transmission rather dramatically, then, the vogue of ballad settings of the early nineteenth century does not change the way the ballad creates and transmits a record.

It is clear that an Edison gold cylinder of Loewe's "Die Uhr" records and transmits quite differently—as did the ballad recitations that were soon available on the cylinders and other early phonographic media. They depend on a radically altered ideology of audience listening. Where the traditional art ballad's record-character frequently implicated its listener as a future teller of the tale, the ballad as recorded sound creates an asymmetry between listener and sound producer. In this shift, the epistemic character of balladry changes wholesale, and the community becomes a listening community, a listening public that is in principle infinite. However much of an expensive fringe hobby it may have represented, Schumann's recording of "Die Uhr" reversed the privatizing character of the old ballad, which knew inside and outside.

But here too the ballad record only activated potentialities that had been recognized well before the invention of the new medium. By the time Schumann recorded his version of Loewe's "Uhr," audiences were already primed to repress the impulse to pass on these ballads. That is because the instrumental ballad had already raised similar questions decades earlier: it was universally agreed that they told stories, were probably based on linguistic constructions, and many listeners and scholars thought they knew what those were. But that is where the rupture occurs: one cannot pass them on the way one could the actual poem.

In a famous 1837 review of Chopin's second ballade, Gottfried Wilhelm Fink observed in the *Allgemeine musikalische Zeitung* that "since we have songs without words, why not also ballads without words?" At the same time, Fink acknowledged that perhaps a wordless ballad posed problems different from those posed by Mendelssohn's "Songs without Words" of 1832. After his first listening, Fink decides that "the whole story seems utterly strange," and dutifully listens to the piece again and again, coming away with a clearer sense of what the ballad is "about." But he thinks that this sense is entirely peculiar to him, that "we are left with no other option than to give a poetic interpretation [*Auslegung*] of the poem, which, though not difficult, can only be undertaken by each person for themselves."[8]

But Mendelssohn's "Songs without Words" were largely concerned with emotions, whereas ballads tended to be concerned with action. Quite dutifully, people started parsing Chopin's ballades for action. Fink proposed right away that this meant that what story one found was largely one's own. And he seems to sense that this is a rather outrageous demand to make in a piece that partakes, in whatever fashion, of the ballad tradition, which is, after all, about shared, even communal meaning-making. Chopin's ballades transform us from listeners who may and maybe should become new purveyors of the tale to pure listeners. The structure of Chopin's op. 23 prohibits the kind of easy recall, the kind of broad accessibility that had marked the German art ballad as communal art form. Hermeneutically, Chopin's pieces treat us no different than a listener to a recording cylinder.

The ballad had become less participatory, a hermeneutic monolith. Its temporality was cast in gold, standardized and unmoored from the subjective. The only difference that could be introduced into its retellings were now of a technological nature. The comedian Karl Valentin reflects on this dynamic in a skit from 1927—one centered on another technologically challenged recording of Loewe's setting of "Die Uhr." Valentin conceived this and other sketches for distribution as records, with each side holding exactly one

---

[8] Gottfried Wilhelm Fink, "Musikalisches Album," *Allgemeine musikalische Zeitung*, no. 2 (January 1837): 25–26.

number. This is the technological stricture that supplies Valentin with his running gag, as he introduces and begins to sing Loewe's song, only to feel the need to gloss things further, clarifynig for instance that though Loewe made "Die Uhr," he is a composer rather than a watchmaker. In the end, Valentin interrupts himself one last time, saying: "Unfortunately I will not be able to sing to you the ballad, since there is no more room for it on the record. A record really should by rights be a meter wide."

In the age of the ballad as recorded sound, we might say, it is not the poet or composer who keep balladic time—Valentin's poetic reauthorization is not that of a poet, or a musician; it is that of a watchmaker. And like him, it was the parodists and the ironists who kept the ballad alive for the next hundred years in Germany. But of course the inauthenticity on which a parodist like Valentin drew was neither new nor altogether heretical when it came to the German art ballad. The form's strength had long been an ability to combine sincerity and irony.

Like Valentin's appropriation of the ballad, many twentieth-century revivers of the ballad managed to be impertinent and cavalier—but for that precise reason they were perhaps the best stewards of a genre that had always been more wayward, more playful than some of its conservative advocates had supposed. From them a lineage runs through a song like Bertolt Brecht and Kurt Weill's "Die Moritat von Mackie Messer" (made famous in the United States as "Mack the Knife"), via the modern folk ballads of the 1970s all the way to Wolf Biermann, the audience in the Cologne Sporthalle. To the unprepossessing man with his guitar and the gigantic audience, to his Prussian Icarus and the immense weight of history lightly born.

INDEX

Note: Figures are indicated by *f* following the page number

Abbaté, Carolyn, 113, 117
*Abhandlung über den Ursprung der Sprache* (Herder), 87
absolute music, 206–210
acting
  *Declamatorium* and, 80–81, 85
  Goethe on, 103
  overacting and, 80–81, 85
Addison, Joseph, 11
Adorno, Theodor, 67
*Aesthetic Theory* (Adorno), 67
Albrecht, Professor Doctor, 141–142
Albrecht, Sophie (1757-1840), 82
Albright, Daniel, 122
Alexis, Willibald, 16–17, 22, 135, 138. See also *specific works*
Alim, Samy, 245
*Allgemeine musikalische Zeitung* (newspaper), 269
Alpine Symphony (Raff), 202
"Alte Hanns, Der" (Weidmann), 99
*Altenglische und altschwäbische Balladen* (Bodmer), 220
amateurs/amateurism, 2
Anacreontic lyric poetry, 11
Anderson, Benedict, 18
"An einen auf dem Schlachtfeld ausgeackerten Schädel" (Kind), 99–101
Anschütz, Heinrich Johann, 80
antiquarianism, 7, 46–47
Applegate, Celia, 246

*'apprenti sorcier, L'* (Dukas), 200
"Archibald Douglas" (Loewe), 219
Arndt, Ernst Moritz, 98
Aristotle, 57
Arnim, Achim von, 9, 22, 47. See also *specific works*
Assmann, Jan, 33
assonance, 159–160, 201–202, 263–264
*Athenäum für Freunde der Deklamation* (Kramer), 96, 100
Atkinson, David, 33
Aubier, 126
"Auf eine Unbekannte" (Hebbel), 178
*Aufmerksame, Der* (periodical), 83
"Aus der Kindheit" (Hebbel), 177
*Ausgabe letzter Hand* (Hebbel), 177
*Aus meinem Leben* (Hanslick), 80
Austro-Prussian War, 244
*Auswahl von Gedichten zu deklamatorischen Übungen* (Klar), 94
authenticity, 264
  antiquarianism and, 46–47
  Biermann and, 1, 5
  defining, 40
  lack of, 18, 28
  modernity and, 31
  nationalism and, 28
  orality and, 46–57, 184
  of *Ossian*, 47–57
  popularity and, 104

authenticity (*cont.*)
   provenance and, 8, 13, 33, 47, 56, 82, 105, 116, 128–129, 142
   source of, 12–13
   transmission and, 57
*Autobiographische Skizze* (Wagner), 110–111

Bakhtin, Mikhail, 37, 45
Ball, Arnetha, 245
ballad. See also *Lied*; *specific type*; *specific work*
   as art, 28–29
   boom of 1780s-1970s and, 5–6, 10–11, 23–24
   defining features of, 5–32
   as hereditary sayings, 16
   intermedial nature of, 21–22, 55, 185
   market for, 27–28
   memory and, 32–39
   mobility of, 21, 23, 26
   origins of, 8–13
   as record, 263–270
   sharing of, 6–7
   temporality of, 11–12
   theories of, 8, 10–11, 15, 21, 23–24
   visual representation of, 6, 8, 9f
   year of 1797 and, 6
*Balladenjahr*, 55–65
*Ballades* (Chopin), 41
balladic charge. See charge, balladic
balladic form. See form, balladic
*Bänkelsang*, 30
*Bardenhain* (Heinsius), 44–45
*Bardenhain für Deutschlands edle Söhne und Töchter* (Heinsius), 96–97
*Barrack-Room Ballads* (Kipling), 115
Batteux, Charles, 133
Bauer, Lukas, 239
Bayer, Joseph, 17
Beauclerk, Lady Diana, 201
bedtime ritual, 154–155
Beer, Michael, 6
Beethoven, Ludwig von, 105
*beiden Grenadiere, Die* (R. Schumann), 192
Bellman, Jonathan, 185, 188–189
*Belsatzar* (R. Schumann), 192
"Belsazar" (Heine), 106–111
*Bemerkungen zur Aufführung der Oper* (Wagner), 122
Benda, Georg, 21
Benjamin, Walter, 32–33
Beresford, Benjamin, 78

Berger, Karol, 187
Berliner Ensemble, 1
"Berlioz und seine Harold Symphonie" (Liszt), 206–210
Berner, Hannah, 47
"Betrachtung und Auslegung" (Goethe), 124
"Bettler und sein Kind, Der" (Gerhardt), 99
Betz, Franz, 216
Biedermeier period, 76, 88
Biermann, Wolf, 1–7, 28–29. See also *specific works*
*Bildung*, 36, 38, 97, 225, 237
Binder, C., 184
Bingham, Ruth O., 27
Birgfeld, Johannes, 82
Blake, William, 201
Bloch, Ernst, 48
Blomberg, Hugo von, 215, 221
blood-and-soil literature, 259
Blumenberg, Hans, 18
Bodley, Lorraine Byrne, 71
Bodmer, Johann Jacob (1698-1783), 8, 10, 12, 33, 220. See also *specific works*
Boehe, Ernst, 200
Böhme, Franz Magus, 157–158
Boieldieu, François-Adrien (1775-1834), 105
"Boot is noch buten, Een" (Holz), 247–248, 257
Borges, J. L., 130
Borrow, George, 47, 234–236
Boswell, James, 50–51, 53–55. See also *specific works*
Böttiger, Carl August, 65
Boulanger, Louis, 201
Brahms, Johannes, 76, 191, 191f, 204, 246
Braun, Joseph, 95
"Braut von Korinth, Die" (Goethe), 67–70, 138–141, 153
Brecht, Bertolt, 1, 29–31, 36, 258, 270
Brentano, Clemens, 9, 22, 47, 94
*Briefe über Hochdeutsch und Plattdeutsch* (Groth), 246
"Brück' am Tay, Die" (Fontane), 237, 254
Brunow, 99
Brydon, William, 218
Buchan, David, 11
*Buch der Lieder* (Heine), 20
*Buch der Zeit, Das* (Holz), 247
Büchmann, Georg, 39

"Buchstabierende Kind, Das"
    (Langenschwarz), 99
*Buddenbrooks* (Mann), 37
Bülow, Hans von, 199–200, 205
Bulthaupt, Heinrich, 115
Bulwer-Lytton, Edward, 6
Bumm, Peter, 148–149
Bürger, Gottfried August (1747–1794), 7–10,
    14–23, 30, 200–210, 264. See also
    *specific works*
  *Declamatorium* and, 78–79
  Hegel on, 54
  Heine on, 20
  memory and, 33
  orality and, 42
"Bürgschaft, Die" (Schiller), 44, 142
Büsching, Johann Gustav Gottlieb, 9
Butler, Judith, 160–161
Butler, Shane, 267
Byron, George Gordon (Lord Byron), 234

Callimachus, 132
Camlot, Jason, 266
Carlyle, Thomas, 6
"Castaway, The" (Cowper), 256
censorship
  exile and, 2–3, 98
  Nazi Germany and, 259–260
Cervantes, Miguel de, 42
Chamisso, Adelbert von (1781-1838), 16,
    158, 192, 223, 237
charge, balladic, 130–131, 235
*Chausseestraße 132* (Biermann album), 1
"Che cos'é la poesia?" (Derrida), 37
"Chevy Chase, The Ballad of," 44
  L.A. Gottsched translation of, 11
  Klopstock version of, 11
*Chevy Chase Strophen,* 11, 83
children. *See* family
Chopin, Frédéric, 22, 41, 42, 118
  Fink on, 269
  Schumann and, 187–191, 208
choral ballad, 192–199
  nationalism and, 193–194
  setting and, 192–193
choral societies, 193–194, 226–233, 232f
"Christnacht der Hallig, Die" (Strauß und
    Torney), 251–252
Chromatopen, 12 brilliant *Tonstücke*
    (Oesten), 183
chronotope, 45

Cicero, 132
classical setting, 142
classicism, 10, 12
  Enlightenment, 17
  German, 40, 82–84
  Weimar, 61, 96
Claudius, Otto Carl, 127
Cohen, Margaret, 251
Coleridge, Samuel Taylor, 126, 158, 250–251.
    See also *specific works*
  flow and, 138
  on orality, 137
  on Romanticism, 137–138
collective memory, 184
*Comala: A Dramatic Poem* (Gade), 195
community, 22–23
compression, 49, 53, 91, 200
  epic form and, 166–167
  opera and, 113–114, 120
concealment
  education of Germans and, 148
  exile and, 147, 149–150
  homosexuality and, 146–152
  memory and, 145–153
  meter and, 146
  nationalism and, 147–148
  Romanticism and, 149–150
Conrad, Joseph, 249–250
Cornelius, Peter (1824-1874), 156–157,
    178, 231
*costumbrismo,* 7
Cotta (publisher), 58
Cowper, William, 256
cultural heritage of Germany, 7–8, 10, 32–39.
    *See also* memory
  maritime ballad and, 251–261
  projection and, 12
  transmission and, 33

Dahlhaus, Carl, 32, 189, 204, 206
Dahn, Felix, 261
"Danish Poetry and Ballad Writing"
    (Borrow), 235
Dante Alighieri, 45, 131
Daverio, John, 185, 188, 195
*Declamatorium,* 73–103
  acting and, 85
  anthologies of, 81
  balladic form and, 95, 97
  defined, 77
  Enlightenment and, 84

INDEX | 273

Declamatorium (cont.)
  family and, 97
  features of, 83
  German classicism and, 83–84
  *Lied* and, 76
  literature and, 77–78, 80, 92–103
  Napoleonic Wars and, 73–84, 87–92, 98
  nationalism and, 73–103
  opera and, 81
  orality and, 73–92
  overacting and, 80–81
  parody and, 79, 91, 103
  pedagogy and, 96–97, 101–102
  in print, 92–103
  Restoration Era and, 81, 87
  reviews of, 85–86
  Romanticism and, 81–83
  setting of, 84–92
  transmission and, 87
  Wars of Liberation and, 73, 88, 98
*Declamatorium für die Jugend* (Vogl), 95
Dehmel, Richard, 248–249, 251, 257, 261
*Deklamator, Der* (Hanisch), 90, 99–100
*Departmental Ditties and Ballads* (Kipling), 115
Derrida, Jacques, 37
Detering, Heinrich, 148
*deutsche Literatur der Gegenwart, 1848–1858, Die* (Prutz), 221
*Deutsche Literaturgeschichte* (Storck), 143
*Deutscher Musenalmanach*, 223
*Deutscher Musen-almanach für das Jahr 1852* (Gruppe), 223–224
*Deutsche Romanzen, Balladen und Erzählungen* (Braun), 95
*Deutsches Museum* (magazine), 14
*Deutschlands Balladen- und Romanzendichter* (Hub), 8
*devin du village, Le* (Rousseau), 105
Devrient, Ludwig, 40, 122
*Dichterliebe* (R. Schumann), 195
Dilthey, Wilhelm, 208
disaster ballad, 254
distressed genre, 4
*Divine Comedy* (Dante), 131
"Don Juan" (Lord Byron), 234
"Donna Clara sits in Spain" (Rudolph Wagner), 226
*Don Quixote* (Cervantes), 42
Dorn, Heinrich (1804-1892), 188

Draeseke, Felix, 186
"drei Lieder, Die" (Uhland), 198
"Drei Schwestern" (Hebbel), 175–177
*Dr. Katzenbergs Badereise* (Jean Paul), 79–80
Droste-Hülshoff, Annette von, 21, 30–31, 41, 142, 156–175, 179, 181–182
Droste-Hülshoff, Clemens August von, 168
Duff, David, 47
Dukas, Paul, 29, 200
Duparc, Henri, 210
Dupree, Mary-Helen, 97
Dvořák, Antonín, 200

Ebert, Karl Egon, 94
Echtermeyer, Ernst Theodor (1805-1844), 24
*Eclogues* (Virgil), 132
Edison, Thomas, 267
education of Germans. *See also* pedagogy
  concealment and, 148
  family and, 157–158
  memory and, 35–39, 41, 134, 141–145
"Edward" (Brahms), 191, 191f, 204
"Edward" (Herder), 191, 191f, 204
*Effi Briest* (Fontane), 27–28
Eichendorff, Joseph von, 192, 237
Eiserman, Judith, 84
Eisler, Hanns, 1
*ekphrasis*, 202
*Elements of the Philosophy of Right* (Hegel), 207
"Elverskud" (Syv), 44
enjambment, 52, 265–266
Enlightened Republic of Letters, 50, 86
Enlightenment, 51
  aesthetics of, 12
  *Declamatorium* and, 84
  philosophy of, 11
Enlightenment classicism, 17
*Entführung aus dem Serail, Die* (Mozart), 105
*envoi*, 68–69
epic form, 33
  compression and, 166–167
  transmission and, 56
epic travel. *See* wandering ballads
*Epigonen, Die* (Immermann), 92
"Erforsche mein Geheimnis nie" (Platen), 151–152
*Erlebnis und die Dichtung, Das* (Dilthey), 208–209
"Erlkönig, Der" (Goethe), 25–26, 36, 38, 45–46, 74, 155, 204, 255, 265, 268
"Erlkönigs Tochter" (Herder), 44–46, 58

Ermatinger, Emil, 245
eroticism, 149–150, 225
*erste Walpurgisnacht, Die* (Mendelssohn), 197
Ertel, Paul (1865-1933), 90
*Esclave de Camoëns, L'* (Flotow), 106
"Essay on the Imitation of the Ancient Ballad" (Scott), 201
"Es sehnt sich ewig dieser Geist ins Weite" (Platen), 150
Esser, Heinrich (1818-1872), 230
"Eugenien's Verzweiflung," 91
exile
　censorship and, 2–3, 98
　concealment and, 147, 149–150

fairy tales, 13, 18, 22, 33, 138
　Grimm Brothers, 22, 154, 239
　settings and, 142
Falk, Walter, 10
Fallersleben, Hofmann von, 98
family, 154–182
　bedtime ritual and, 154–155
　behavior and, 155–157
　*Declamatorium* and, 97
　education of Germans and, 157–158
　*Geist* and, 167
　gender and, 154–182
　inheritance and, 155, 166–175
　motherhood and, 45–46, 155–158, 161–165, 172, 177, 179
　orality and, 167
　pedagogy and, 158
　projection and, 157, 171–178
　sisterhood and, 158–166, 163f, 170–177
*Faust* (Goethe), 60, 210
*Fées du rhin, Les* (Offenbach), 106
Fermor, Patrick Leigh (1915-2011), 35–39
Ferris, David, 27
Fichte, Hubert, 148
Fichte, Johann Gottlieb, 86–87, 97
*Fingal* (Macpherson), 48–49, 166
Fink, Gottfried Wilhelm, 269
"Fischer" (Goethe), 254
"Fischer von Svendaland, Die" (Münchhausen), 258
*fliegende Holländer, Der* (Wagner), 40–41, 106–107, 110–128, 254
　memory and, 132
　narrative and, 183, 193, 195, 197–199
Flotow, Friedrich von (1812-1883), 106
*Flottenliederbuch*, 253–256, 258

flow, 132–138
　memory and, 152–153
　meter and, 133–134
Flying Dutchman. See *fliegende Holländer, Der* (Wagner)
folklore, 239–240
Fontane, Theodor, 27–28, 30, 261. See also *specific works*
　censorship and, 260
　education of Germans and, 38
　orality and, 42
　Percy and, 217–218
　*Der Tunnel über der Spree* and, 215–225
Foreit, Anton, 90
Forest Symphony (Raff), 202
form, balladic, 95, 97–98, 152, 201
　Goethe on, 124–125, 137
　memory and, 137–145
　meter and, 137–141
　narrative and, 204–210
Fouqué, Friedrich de la Motte, 220
4 ballads op. 10 (Brahms), 191, 191f
"Francesca von Rimini" (Heyse), 225
Franzel, Sean, 97
"Frauen, Den" (Strachwitz), 221
"Frauen von Nidden, Die" (Miegel), 258
Freiligrath, Ferdinand, 98, 251
*Freischütz, Der* (Weber), 99, 111
Freud, Sigmund, 110, 114, 154
　on memory, 138–140, 153
　"Ritter Toggenburg" (Schiller) and, 6
"Friedensfeyer" (Klopstock), 21
"From the Days of the Minstrels" (Rudolph Wagner), 226

Gade, Nils, 195
Gaier, Ulrich, 5–6, 44
"Gang nach dem Eisenhammer, Der" (Claudius), 127
*Gang zum Eisenhammer, Der* (Kreutzer), 105
*Gang zum Eisenhammer, Der* (Schiller), 85, 114
*Gassenhauer*, 15
*Gay Science, The* (Nietzsche), 132
gaze
　gendered, 171–174
　tourist, 239–240, 243
GDR. See German Democratic Republic
Geck, Martin, 192, 193
*Geflügelte Worte: Der Citatenschatz des deutschen Volkes* (Büchmann), 39

INDEX | 275

Geibel, Emmanuel, 216, 223
"Geisterschiff, Das" (Tausig), 191
*Geist/Volksgeist*, 16, 19–20, 40, 48, 55
    family and, 167
    Greece and, 61
    Hegel on, 53, 56
    memory and, 33
    opera and, 116, 125
"Gelebt: Gestrebt, Gelitten, Gestritten, Gestorben, Umworben" (Raff), 202
gender, 45–46
    choral societies and, 226–233, 232f
    community and, 22
    family and, 154–182
    gaze and, 171–174
    literary societies and, 214–226
    *Männerbund* and, 214–215, 222
    narrator and, 170–172
    national masculinity and, 42
    patriarchal power of orality and, 181–182
    Romanticism and, 228–229
    setting and, 211–214, 226–233
    *Der Tunnel über der Spree* and, 222–226
    women in story and, 111–112
*Genoveva* (R. Schumann), 192
George, Stefan (1868-1933), 145
"Gerechte Rache" (Platen), 133
Gerhardt, 99
German classicism, 40, 82–84
German Democratic Republic, 1–4
German Idealism, 16
German Renaissance, 34
German Romanticism, 105, 188, 220
Gernsheim, Friedrich von (1839-1916), 146, 227
*Gesangsbildungslehre für Männerchor* (Nägeli), 194
"Gesang und Krieg" (Uhland), 198
*Geschichte Deklamator, Der* (Schreiber), 98
*Geschichte der deutschen Ballade* (Kayser), 29–30, 260
Gibbs, Christopher, 25
Gillis, John, 238
Gleim, Johann Wilhelm Ludwig, 8, 10–11, 29. See also *specific works*
"Glocke im Meer, Die" (Dehmel), 248–249
"Glück von Edenhall, Das" (R. Schumann), 192
"Goblin Market" (C. Rossetti), 158–166, 163f
Goehr, Lydia, 62–63
Goerth, Albrecht, 143–144

Goethe, August, 74
Goethe, Johann Wolfgang von, 14–15, 17–21, 29, 30, 40. See also *specific works*
    on acting, 103
    on balladic form, 124–126, 137
    *Declamatorium* and, 74–75, 79, 96–98
    education of Germans and, 36–39
    Hegel on, 54
    irony and, 57–65
    Lewald on, 34
    on Macpherson, 48–51, 54
    memory and, 32, 138–140
    *Musenalmanach auf das Jahr 1798* (Schiller) and, 65–72, 71f
    narrative and, 208, 210
    nationalism and, 74–75
    opera and, 106, 118
    orality and, 42, 45–46, 48–50, 55, 58–63, 67–72, 71f
    Schiller and, 55, 57–72, 71f
    on Solbrig, 73–75
Góngora, Luis de (1561-1627), 10
"Goodwin-Sand" (Fontane), 237
"Götter Irrfahrt, Der" (Eichendorff), 237
Göttingen *Hainbund* (Sturm und Drang poets), 11, 257
*Göttinger Musenalmanach*, 257–260
Gottsched, Johann Christoph (1700-1766), 10–11, 80, 220
Gottsched, Luise Adelgunde, 11, 22
"Gott und die Bajadere, Der" (Goethe), 6, 67–72, 71f
"Grab im Busento, Das" (Platen), 29, 41
    concealment and, 145–153
    memory and, 134–137, 141–153
"Grab im Busento, Das" (Weißert), 186
*Grafen von der Esche, Die* (Heyse), 80
Grass, Günter, 30
"Grenadiere, Die" (Heine), 110
Grenby, M. O., 154
Grey, Thomas, 117, 126
Grimm, Julius Otto (1827-1903), 246
Grimm Brothers, 22, 154, 239
Groth, Klaus, 246
Grün, Anastasius, 98
Gruppe, Otto Friedrich, 223
Gundolf, Friedrich, 145, 153

Hackel, Anton (1799-1846), 90
Hafis, 141

Hagen, Friedrich Heinrich von der, 9
"Haideknabe, Der" (Hebbel), 177–179
*Hallesche Jahrbücher* (Echtermeyer), 24
Hamlin, Cyrus, 61
*Handbuch der Declamation* (Kerndörffer), 87
"Handschuh, Der" (Schiller), 57
Hanisch, G. A., 90–91, 96, 98–101
*Hans Ibeles* (Kinkel), 194
Hanslick, Eduard, 80
"Hans und 's Bäsle, Der" (Binder), 184
Hardy, Thomas, 6
Harold, Edmund de, 51
*Hausmärchen* (Brothers Grimm), 154
*Heart of Darkness, The* (Conrad), 249–250
Hebbel, Christine, 175–177
Hebbel, Friedrich, 165–167, 175–182
Hegel, Georg Wilhelm Friedrich, 24, 48, 52–57, 125–126, 207
   on *Geist*, 53, 56
   on Schiller, 53–54, 62–64
Heideck, Carl Wilhelm von, 8, 9f
Heidegger, Martin, 115
Heine, Heinrich (1797-1856), 19–21, 25, 30–31, 38, 41, 98, 106–111, 127–128, 192, 261. See also *specific works*
   on Bürger, 20
   censorship and, 260
   irony and, 257
   Norderney and, 238–244, 254
   Platen and, 110, 150
   on Schlegel, 19–20
   on Tacitus, 239–241
   on Uhland, 20
   Wagner and, 110–111
Heinsius, Theodor, 44–45, 96–99
*Heinrich von Ofterdingen* (Novalis), 220
Hensel, Fanny, 227–228
Herder, Johann Gottfried, 7, 8, 10, 13–14, 23, 26, 28, 101, 155, 204, 220, 267. See also *specific works*
   *Declamatorium* and, 75, 87
   on Macpherson, 48, 51–53
   memory and, 39
   orality and, 44–46, 52, 58, 60
hereditary sayings, 16
"Herr von Ribbeck auf Ribbeck im Havelland" (Fontane), 260
Herwegh, Georg, 98
"Herzensausguß über Volkspoesie" (Bürger), 14–15

Heym, Georg, 30
Heyse, Paul, 42, 80, 220, 223–226, 233. See also *specific works*
Hiller, Ferdinand, 183, 228
Hitler, Adolph, 259
*Hochdeutsch,* 102, 245–247
Hoffmann, E. T. A., 105, 220
Hoffmann, Heinrich, 155–156
Hofmeister, Friedrich, 90, 183, 185, 190
Holtey, Karl von, 210
Holz, Arno, 246–248, 251, 256, 261
homelessness, 150, 187
Homer, 48–49, 55–57
homesickness, 150, 224, 246
homosexuality, 146–152
Hopkins, G. M., 254
Hub, Ignaz, 8–9
Hufeland, Christoph Wilhelm, 238
Humboldt, Wilhelm von, 48

*Iliad* (Homer), 57
Imhoff, Amalie von, 31
imitative harmony, 137–138, 141, 146, 201, 263
Immermann, Karl, 92
"Im Sängersaal" (Redwitz), 230
*Indra, das Schlangenmädchen* (Flotow), 106
inheritance, 155, 166–175
innocence, 20, 30, 48, 176
*Institution Oratoria* (Quintilian), 133
instrumental ballad, 187–191, 191f
intergenerational transmission. See family
*Intermezzo, Das* (Kotzebue), 85
irony, 11, 14, 20, 29–31, 36, 40–41
   *Balladenjahr* and, 56–65
   maritime ballad and, 257
   orality and, 56–65
irregular meter, 159
"Isle of the Dead" (Rachmaninoff), 202

Jade-treaty of 1853, 244
"Jadis regnait en Normandie" (Meyerbeer), 117
Jauß, Hans-Robert, 16
Javůrek, Josef, 201
Jean Paul (Johann Paul Friedrich Richter), 79–80
"John Maynard" (Fontane), 237, 254
Johnson, Samuel, 17. See also *specific works*
   on Macpherson, 49–51, 54–55, 64–65, 236
   on orality, 49–50

*Journal of a Tour of the Hebrides with Samuel Johnson* (Boswell), 50–51
*Journey to the Western Islands of Scotland, A* (Johnson), 49
Jüllig, Franz, 183
*Jungfrau von Orleans* (Schiller), 56

Kahnt, C. F., 90
Kainz, Josef, 267
Kalbeck, Max, 28
Kalliwoda, Wilhelm, 229
*Kampf der Sänger, Der* (E. T. A. Hoffmann), 220
Kant, Immanuel, 264
Kästner, Erich, 30–31
Kayser, Wolfgang, 29–30, 260
Kerndörffer, Heinrich August, 87
Kerr, Alfred, 267
Kind, Johann Friedrich, 99–101
"Kind, Das" (Droste-Hülshoff), 156–157
"Kind am Brunnen, Das" (Hebbel), 177
*Kinderszenen* (R. Schumann), 178
Kinkel, Johanna, 194, 228
Kipling, Rudyard, 115–116
Kistner (publisher), 183
Kittler, Friedrich, 158
*Kladderadatsch* (magazine), 252
Klar, Aloys, 93–95
*Kleinepik* (Droste-Hülshoff), 167
"kleine Schiffer, Der" (Plönnies), 184
Klingemann, August, 79
Klopstock, Friedrich Gottlieb, 11, 21, 82. See also *specific works*
Klughardt, August, 201
*Knaben Wunderhorn, Des* (Arnim & Brentano), 9, 22, 47
Kober, Julius, 259
Kohler, Ernst, 217
Kommerell, Max, 67
"König Hakons letzte Meerfahrt" (Leitner), 237
"König Harald Harfager" (Heine), 237
"König in Thule, Der" (Goethe), 237
"Königssohn, Der" (R. Schumann), 193
Kopisch, August, 237
Kord, Susanne, 172
Körner, Theodor, 98
Kotzebue, August von, 85
Kramer, Friedrich, 96, 100
"Kraniche des Ibycus, Die" (Schiller), 19, 38–39, 53–54, 57, 61, 63–65, 142

Kraus, Karl, 75
Kregor, Jonathan, 201
Kreutzer, Conradin (1780-1849), 99, 105, 194. See also *specific works*
Kristeva, Julia, 160–161
Kügele, Richard, 201
Kugler, Franz, 223
"kühne Schiffer, Der" (Stiehl), 184
Kummer, Friedrich August, 183
*Kunstballade*, 30, 40, 47, 169
    characteristics of, 67
    flow and, 133
    opera and, 118, 125
    *Volksballade* and, 53–54, 138, 264
Kunzen, Friedrich Ludwig Aemilius, 23, 78
Kurlander, Eric, 245

Lachmann, Karl, 81–82
Lachner, Franz, 230
Lamport, F. J., 50
Lang, Josephine Caroline (1815-1880), 228–229
Langbehn, Julius, 14
Langenschwarz, Maximilian, 99
Langenzweig, 99
language
    *Hochdeutsch*, 102, 245–247
    nationalism and, 244–249
    *Niederdeutsch*, 246
    *Plattdeutsch*, 244–246, 249
Laun, Friedrich (Friedrich August Schulze), 85
*Läuschen* (Reuter), 246
*Lavengro* (Borrow), 234–235
"Lay of the Last Minstrel, The" (Scott), 55, 263
Le Beau, Luise Adolpha (1850-1927), 229–233, 232f
    "Im Sängersaal" (Redwitz) and, 230
    *Vätergruft, Die* (Uhland) and, 230–233, 232f
*Lebenserinnerungen einer Komponistin* (Le Beau), 230
*Lectures on Aesthetics* (Hegel), 125
*Legenden*, 6
*Lehrbuch des Naturrechts odor der Rechsphilosophie* (C. Droste-Hülshoff), 168
*Leiden des jungen Werthers, Die* (Goethe), 48–50

Leitner, Karl Gottfried von, 237
"Lenore" (Bürger), 8, 9f, 14–15, 23–24, 28, 42, 200–210
   balladic form and, 138
   flow and, 133, 138
   Reichardt's setting of, 78–79
Lepel, Bernhard von, 215, 223
*Lesegesellschaften,* 82
Lethen, Helmuth, 36
Levi-Strauss, Claude, 33
Lewald, Fanny (1811-1889), 34–35
Lichtenberg, Georg Christoph, 238
*Lied,* 25–28, 40. See also ballad; *Volkslieder*
   *Declamatorium* and, 76
   decorum of, 31
   emergence of, 23
   nationalism and, 26, 28–29
   Romanticism and, 26–27
*Lieder eines Modernen,* 257
*Liederkranz aus Klaus Groth's Quickborn für Sopran, Alt, Tenor und Bass, Ein* (J. O. Grimm), 246
*Liedertafel. See* choral societies
*Liedflugschriften,* 201
"Lied von der Glocke" (Schiller), 58
Liliencrohn, Detley von, 248, 251, 256, 261
Lisecki, Wieslaw, 187
Liszt, Franz, 31, 42, 89, 117, 201
   absolute music and, 206–210
   "Lore-Ley, Die" (Heine) and, 211–212
   New German School and, 185–186
   Raff and, 201–202
   *Symphonische Dichtung* and, 189, 204
   *Vätergruft, Die* (Uhland) and, 230–231
   on Wagner, 121
   Weißheimer and, 186
literature/literacy
   blood-and-soil, 259
   censorship and (*see* censorship)
   *Declamatorium* and, 77–78, 80, 92–103
   flow and, 132–138
   gender and, 214–226
   literary societies and, 214–226
   maritime ballad and, 237–251
   nationalism and, 244–249
   orality and, 25, 33, 46–47, 81, 109, 119, 123, 246, 263, 264
   *Sturm und Drang,* 11, 47, 55, 61, 201
Loewe, Carl, 24–26, 31, 76, 115, 183–184, 190. See also *specific works*
   birth of, 27
   domesticity and, 193
   dramatic trappings of, 192
   "Der Erlkönig" (Goethe) and, 204, 268
   "Die nächtliche Heerschau" (Zedlitz) and, 90–92
   opera and, 118
   Runze on, 28
   "Schmied auf Helgoland, Der" (W. A. Schreiber) and, 237
   *Der Tunnel über der Spree* and, 216, 220
   "Uhr, Die" (Seidl) and, 265–270
"Lohn, Der" (Brunow), 99
Longfellow, Henry Wadsworth, 130–131, 235–236, 254–255
Lord Byron, 234
"Lore-Ley, Die" (Heine), 25, 38, 211–214
Loster-Schneider, Gudrun, 217
Luckhardt (publisher), 183
*Lyrical Ballads* (Coleridge & Wordsworth), 158

*Macmillan's Magazine,* 159
Macpherson, James, 195. See also *specific works*
   Boswell on, 50–51, 53–55
   *Declamatorium* and, 76
   family and, 166
   Goethe on, 48–51
   Harold on, 51
   Herder on, 48, 51–53
   Johnson on, 49–51, 54–55, 64–65, 236
   orality and, 48–57, 60–61, 65–66
   Sturz on, 51
Mahler, Alma, 251
Mahler, Gustav, 42
Mann, Thomas, 37
"Männen, Den" (Strachwitz), 221
*Männerbund,* 214–215, 222
"Margherita Spoletina" (Heyse), 225
maritime ballad, 234–261
   cultural heritage of Germany and, 251–261
   *Flottenliederbuch* and, 253–256, 258
   irony and, 257
   literature and, 237–251
   modernity and, 257–258
   nationalism and, 244–249, 253–256
   Norderney and, 238–244, 254
   Romanticism and, 250–251
   shipwreck ballad and, 254–258

Markull, Friedrich Wilhelm, 183
Marschner, Heinrich, 40, 105, 117
May, Karl, 6
Meisl, Carl, 79
*Meister-Balladen* (Münchhausen), 29
*Meisterballaden: Ein Führer zur Freude* (Münchhausen), 261
*Memoiren des Herrn von Schnabelewopski* (Heine), 126–128
memory, 32–39, 130–153
    balladic form and, 137–145
    collective, 184
    concealment and, 145–153
    education of Germans and, 35–39, 41, 134, 141–145
    flow and, 152–153
    *Geist* and, 33
    nationalism and, 147–148
    orality and, 144
    pedagogy and, 141–145
    rhyme scheme and, 138–140
    rhythm and, 132, 135, 137–139, 146, 153
    transmission and, 134, 136–138, 144, 149
    understanding and, 142–144
Mendelssohn, Felix, 76, 197, 228, 269
Mendelssohn-Hensel, Fanny, 159
Menzel, Adolph, 216
Menzel, Wolfgang, 25
Mercadante, Saverio, 201
Merckel, Wilhelm von, 225
Merz, K., 183
*Messias* (Klopstock), 82
metanarrative, 184
meter, 10–12, 35
    balladic form and, 137–141
    concealment and, 146
    flow and, 133–134
    irregular, 159
    opera and, 107, 119
    orality and, 52, 68–72
    symphonic ballad and, 201
Metternich era, 98
Meyer, Wilhelm, 39
Meyerbeer, Giacomo, 40, 106, 117, 122, 126. See also *specific works*
Meyer-Kalkus, Reinhart, 80
*Meyers Großes Konversationslexikon*, 227
Mickiewicz, Adam, 188
Miegel, Agnes, 30, 257–259, 261

*Minnesang*, 81
*Minstrelsy of the Scottish Border* (Scott), 218
*Mittheilung an meine Freunde* (Wagner), 113
mobility, 21, 23, 26
modernity, 184
    authenticity and, 31
    maritime ballad and, 257–258
    orality and, 144
Mögele, Franz, 6
Moncrif, François Augustin Paradis de (1687-1770), 10
*Morceaux characteristiques* (Schuberth), 183
*Morceaux mignons* (Merz), 183
*Morgenblätter für gebildete Leser* (journal), 77
*Moritaten*, 29, 31–32, 153
"Moritat von Mackie Messer, Die" (Brecht & Weill), 270
Moscheles, Ignaz, 183
motherhood, 45–46, 155–158, 161–165, 172, 177, 179
Mozart, Wolfgang Amadeus, 105, 115
Müller, Heinrich von, 216–217
Müller, Wilhelm (1794-1827), 24–25, 90
Münchhausen, Börries Freiherr von, 29–30, 257–261
murder ballad, 5, 10, 19, 32, 54, 63, 132, 201
"Murderous Proprietor, The" (Rudolph Wagner), 226
*Musenalmanach auf das Jahr 1798* (Schiller), 40–41, 58–59, 61–63, 65–72, 71f, 181–182
*Musikalisches Wochenblatt*, 226
"Musik zu einem Ritterballet" (Beethoven), 105
*Mustersammlungen*, 95–103

"Nächtliche Fahrt" (Heine), 240
"nächtliche Heerschau, Die" (Zedlitz), 89–92
Nägeli, Hans Georg, 194, 227
"Naïve and Sentimental Poetry" (Schiller), 17
naïveté, 20, 30, 48, 176
Napoleonic Wars, 40, 42
    nationalism and, 73–84, 87–92, 98
    Norderney and, 238–244
    opera and, 104, 106
    Wars of Liberation and, 73, 88, 98
narrator/narrative, 3, 127, 166, 183–210
    balladic form and, 204–210
    choral ballad and, 192–199
    gender and, 170–172

instrumental ballad and, 187–191, 191f
  metanarrative and, 184
  setting and, 183–184, 190, 201
  symphonic ballad and, 199–201
  unreliable, 170–172
nationalism, 29–30, 43
  authenticity and, 28
  choral ballad and, 193–194
  concealment and, 147–148
  *Declamatorium* and, 73–103
  *Flottenliederbuch* and, 253–256, 258
  Goethe and, 74–75
  language and, 244–249
  *Lied* and, 26, 28–29
  literature and, 244–249
  maritime ballad and, 244–249, 253–256
  memory and, 147–148
  Napoleonic Wars and, 40, 42, 73–84, 87–92, 98
  Nazi Germany and, 29–30, 259–260
  orality and, 81
  Restoration Era and, 76, 81, 87
National Socialism. *See* Nazi Germany
Naumann, Emil, 231
Nazi Germany, 29–30, 259–260
"Neue Gedichte" (Strachwitz), 221
New German School, 28, 185–187, 192, 200
Newman, William, 202
New Mythology, 17
*Niederdeutsch*, 246
Nietzsche, Friedrich, 132, 220, 246
"Nixen, Die" (Heine), 243
Norderney, 238–244, 254
*Nordsee, Die* (Heine), 239–244
Norton, Caroline, 159–160, 164
nostalgia, 7
Novalis, 48, 154, 220
nursery rhyme, 36, 155–166

*Oberon, or The Elf King's Oath* (Weber), 106
"Odin's Ocean Ride" (Loewe), 237
*Odysseus* (Boehe), 200
Oesten, Theodor, 183
*Oesterreichischer Zuschauer* (periodical), 89
Offenbach, Jacques, 106
*Old English and Old Swabian Ballads* (Bodmer), 12
Ong, Walter, 23, 161
opera, 104–128. *See also specific work*
  compression and, 113–114, 120
  *Declamatorium* and, 81

  German Romantic, 105
  *Kunstballade* and, 118, 125
  meter and, 107, 119
  Napoleonic Wars and, 104, 106
  rhyme scheme and, 119
  rhythm and, 105, 119
  Romanticism and, 118
  transmission and, 120, 126
  *Volksgeist* and, 116, 125
*Opera and Drama* (Wagner), 184–185
orality
  authenticity and, 46–57, 184
  *Balladenjahr* and, 56–65
  Boswell on, 50–51
  Coleridge on, 137
  consciousness and, 111
  *Declamatorium* and, 73–92
  failure of, 181
  family and, 167
  irony and, 56–65
  Johnson on, 49–50
  literacy and, 25, 33, 46–47, 81, 109, 119, 123, 246, 263, 264
  memory and, 144
  meter and, 52, 68–72
  modernity and, 144
  musicality and, 25
  nationalism and, 81
  nature of, 167
  parody and, 62
  patriarchal power of, 181–182
  Platen on, 140
  primary *vs.* secondary, 32, 34
  process of, 55
  rhyme scheme and, 52, 67–69
  translating, 65–72, 71f
  transmission and, 39, 41, 45–46
orality effect, 119, 138
oration. *See Declamatorium*
*Orpheus und Euridice, odor So geht es im Olymp zu!* (Meisl), 79
*Ossian, The Works of* (Macpherson), 45–57, 60–61, 65–66, 76, 195
  authenticity of, 47–57
  Boswell on, 50–51, 53–55
  *Fingal*, 48–49, 166
  Goethe on, 48–51
  Herder on, 48, 51–53
  Johnson on, 49–51, 54–55, 64–65, 236
  *Temora*, 48–49, 166
Otto-Peters, Louise, 221

Palmer, Fiona, 229
*Paradies und die Peri, Das* (R. Schumann), 197
Parakilas, James, 187, 189, 200
Parker, Robert, 117
parody, 29–30, 32, 38, 41
    *Declamatorium* and, 79, 91, 103
    orality and, 62
patriarchal power of orality, 181–182
patriotism. *See* nationalism
Paul, Jean (Johann Paul Friedrich Richter), 76
pedagogy. *See also* education of Germans
    anti-methodological, 34
    *Declamatorium* and, 96–97, 101–102
    family and, 158
    memory and, 141–145
*Pièces de salon* (Kummer), 183
Percy, Thomas (1729-1811), 4, 11, 13, 20, 39, 47, 217–218. *See also specific works*
    orality and, 76
    Ritson on, 47
Pestalozzi, Johann Heinrich, 101
"Peter Harden" (Miegel), 258–259
Petzold, Dieter, 159–160
Pfitzner, Hans, 251
"Pidder Lüng" (Liliencrohn), 248
*Pierre Minard, Author of the Quixote* (Borges), 130
"Pippin der Kurze" (Streckfuß), 95
Platen, August von, 21, 29, 41, 182. *See also specific works*
    concealment and, 145–153
    flow and, 133–138
    Heine and, 110, 150
    memory and, 140–141, 144–153
    on orality, 140
*Plattdeutsch*, 244–246, 249
Plönnies, Luise von, 184
*Poetics* (Aristotle), 57
Pohl, Richard, 193, 197–199
*Preussische Kriegslieder* (Gleim), 11
*Principes de la littérature* (Batteux), 133
projection, 50
    cultural, 12
    gender and, 157, 171–178
*Prolegomena ad Homerum* (Wolf), 55–57
Proust, Marcel, 154
provenance, 8, 13, 33, 47, 56, 82, 105, 116, 128–129, 142
"Prussian Icarus, Ballad of the" (Biermann), 2–6

Prussian schools, rules and regulations, 35
Prutz, Robert Eduard, 221
*Psychopathologie des Alltagslebens* (Freud), 138
public recitation. *See Declamatorium*

*Quickborn* (Groth), 246
Quintilian, 133, 137–138, 151–152

Rachmaninoff, Sergei, 202
Raff, Joachim, 28, 42
    "Lenore" (Bürger) and, 186, 201–210
    Liszt and, 201–202
Randhartinger, Benedict (1802-1893), 89–92
Rappaport, Jill, 162–163
Raumer, Karl Georg von, 142
Realism, 217, 220
recitation. *See Declamatorium*
record, ballad as, 263–270
*Reden an die Deutsche Nation* (Fichte), 86–87, 97
Redfield, Marc, 86
Redwitz, Oscar von, 230
"Regeln für Schauspieler" (Goethe), 103
regionalism, 43
Reicha, Antonín, 201
Reichardt, Johann Friedrich (1752-1814), 26, 78–79, 201
    *Declamatorium* and, 77–79
    "Ritter Toggenburg" (Schiller) and, 6
    on Seckendorff, 83
Reichardt, Louise, 228
Reil, Johann Anton Friedrich, 105
*Reliques of Ancient English Poetry* (Percy), 11, 39, 47, 76, 217–218
"Remembering, Repeating and Working Through" (Freud), 110, 114
Republic of Letters, 50, 86
*Requiem for Mignon* (R. Schumann), 192
Restoration Era
    *Declamatorium* and, 81, 87
    nationalism and, 76, 81, 87
Reuter, Fritz, 246
revolutions of 1848, 187, 217, 221–222
*Rezitation*, 84–85
Reznicek, Emil Niklaus von, 200
Rheinberger, Josef Gabriel, 229
    "Das Thal von Espingo" (Heyse) and, 225–226
*Rheingold, Das* (Wagner), 128
rhyme
    memory and, 138–140

nursery, 36, 155–166
opera and, 119
orality and, 52, 67–69
symphonic ballad and, 201
rhythm, 16, 33–34, 201
  memory and, 132, 135, 137–139, 146, 153
  opera and, 105, 119
  symphonic ballad and, 201
  Zelter and, 72
Richter, Johann Paul Friedrich. *See* Jean Paul
Rickford, John, 245
Ricoeur, Paul, 257
"Riesenspielzeug, Das" (Chamisso), 158
Riha, Karl, 30
*Rime of the Ancient Mariner* (Coleridge), 126, 250–251
"Ring des Polykrates, Der" (Schiller), 57
Ringelnatz, Joachim, 30
Ritson, Joseph (1752-1803), 4, 47
"Ritter Toggenburg" (Schiller), 6, 186
*Robert le Diable* (Meyerbeer), 106, 117
Robinson, Henry Crabb, 48–49
Robson, Catherine, 37
Röder, Martin (1851-1895), 90
Röhrich, Lutz, 155
Romanticism, 8–9, 11, 19–20, 22–27, 31, 40
  Coleridge on, 137–138
  concealment and, 149–150
  *Declamatorium* and, 81–83
  gender and, 228–229
  German, 105, 188, 220
  instrumental ballad and, 187
  marine ballad and, 250–251
  memory and, 39
  mythology and, 17
  opera and, 118
  Realism *vs.*, 217, 220
  Scott on, 137–138
Romantic opera, 105
*romantische Schule, Die* (Heine), 19
*Romanzen*, 6, 241
*Romanzen und Balladen* (R. Schumann), 195
Rossetti, Christina, 158–166, 163*f*
Rossetti, Dante Gabriel, 153–164, 163*f*
Rotenhan, Hermann Freiherr von, 147, 150–151
Rousseau, Jean-Jacques, 101, 105
Rückert, Friedrich, 192
Rühm, Gerhard, 30
Runze, Max, 24, 28

Sacher-Masoch, Leopold von, 6
Sachs, Melchior Ernst, 229–230
"Salas y Gómez" (Chamisso), 237
*Salon, Der* (Heine), 111
*Sammlung deutscher Volkslieder* (Büsching & Hagen), 9
Samson, Jim, 190
*Sängerkrieg*, 220–222
*Sängerkrieg auf der Wartburg, Der* (Fouqué, Friedrich de la Motte), 220
*Sängerliebe* (Uhland), 198
"Sängers Fluch, Des" (Bülow), 199–200
"Sängers Fluch, Des" (R. Schumann), 184, 192–199
"Sängers Fluch, Des" (Uhland), 75, 192–199, 205, 267
Saphir, Moritz Gottlieb (1795-1858), 89–91
"Saphir's Akademie und humoristiche Vorlesung," 89–91
Sauerwald, Burkhardt, 194
"Scharfrichter, Der" (Langenzweig), 99
"Schatzgräber, The" (Goethe), 60, 68
*Schauspielerin, Die* (Laun), 85
Schebest, Agnese, 98
Schelling, F. W. J., 55–56
Scherenberg, Christian Friedrich, 216
"Schiff ahoi" (Strauß und Torney), 259–261
*Schill, oder das Deklamatorium zu Krähwinkel* (Klingemann), 79
Schiller, Friedrich von, 6, 16–21, 29–30, 35, 38–40, 85, 181. *See also specific works*
  *Declamatorium* and, 96–98
  education of Germans and, 35, 37–39
  Goethe and, 55, 57–65
  Hegel on, 53–54, 62–64
  irony and, 57–65
  Lewald on, 34
  memorial performances for, 97
  memory and, 32
  *Musenalmanach auf das Jahr 1798* and, 40–41, 58–59, 61–63, 65–72, 71f
  opera and, 118
  orality and, 44, 53–65
  on Shakespeare, 55
Schillings, Max von, 251
*Schimmelreiter, Der* (Storm), 249–250
Schlegel, August Wilhelm, 16–17, 19–20
Schlegel, Friedrich, 27, 48
Schleiermacher, Friedrich Daniel Ernst, 48
*Schlemihl* (Rezniçek), 200

"Schloss am Meere, Das" (Uhland), 237
Schmalenbach, Herbert, 215
Schmidtlein, Eduard, 146–147, 150
"Schmied auf Helgoland, Der" (W. A. Schreiber), 237
Schneider, Friedrich Hermann, 90
Schocher, Christian Gotthold, 83–84, 88
*schöne Müllerin, Die* (Müller), 90
Schopenhauer, Arthur, 126, 206, 209
Schreiber, M. L., 98–99
Schreiber, Wilhelm A., 237
Schröder, Heinrich, 39
Schubert, Franz, 24, 26, 31, 71–72, 76, 89
  birth of, 27
  domesticity and, 193
  "Der Erlkönig" (Goethe) and, 25–26, 204, 268
  "Die nächtliche Heerschau" (Zedlitz) and, 90
  opera and, 118
  "Ritter Toggenburg" (Schiller) and, 6
Schuberth, Carl, 183
Schulze, Friedrich August. *See* Laun, Friedrich (Friedrich August Schulze)
Schumann, Clara, 42, 187, 211–214, 228–229, 246
Schumann, Franz, 266, 269
Schumann, Robert, 21, 31, 42, 92, 117, 178–179, 184, 185, 192–199
  "Belsazar" (Heine) and, 168
  birth of, 27
  censorship and, 260
  Chopin and, 187–191, 208
  as conductor, 192
  as critic, 187–191
  "Die nächtliche Heerschau" (Zedlitz) and, 90–91
  New German School and, 185–186
  Pohl and, 193, 197–199
  Uhland and, 192–199
Schurtz, Heinrich, 215
Schwab, Gustav, 223
"Schwestern, Die" (Droste-Hülshoff), 170–175
Scott, Sir Walter, 55, 201, 218, 263
  imitative harmony and, 137–138, 141, 146, 201, 263
  on Romanticism, 137–138
sea ballad. *See* maritime ballad
Seckendorff, Gustav Anton von, 82–83, 88, 102

SED. *See* Socialist Unity Party
"Seegespenst" (Heine), 240
Seidl, Johann Gabriel, 264–270
semiotic mode, 160–161
Semler, Christian August, 88
setting, 21, 25. *See also specific work*
  choral ballad and, 192–193
  classical, 142
  of *Declamatorium*, 84–92
  fairy tales and, 142
  family and, 156–157, 178–179
  gender and, 211–214, 226–233
  Kalbeck on, 28
  narrative and, 183–184, 190, 201
  nationalism and, 78–79, 89–92
  opera and, 108
  orality and, 58, 69–72, 71f
Shakespeare, William, 12–13, 36, 55
sharing, 6–7
shipwreck ballad, 254–258
Sibelius, Jean, 200, 251
*Siegesfest* (Schiller), 142
Silcher, Philipp Friedrich, 25, 194, 211–212, 228
*Sing Song* (C. Rossetti), 162–165
sisterhood, 158–166, 163f, 170–177
"Skeleton in Armor, The" (Longfellow), 130–131
"Sklavenshiff, Das" (Heine), 243, 251
*Skogsrået* (Sibelius), 200
Smetana, Bedřich, 200
Socialist Unity Party, 1, 3
society, 22, 137. *See also* community
Solbrig, Christian Gottire, 73–75, 98–99
"Soldat, Der" (R. Schumann), 92
*Soll die Rede auf immer ein dunkler Gesang bleiben* (Schocher), 83–84
Sommer, Elise, 79–80
*Songs of Dawn* (R. Schumann), 192
"Songs without Words" (Mendelssohn), 269
*Spectator, The* (periodical), 11
*Spiegel, Der* (magazine), 3, 5
Spina (publisher), 183
Spohr, Louis, 105
Staël, Madame de, 45–46
"Steam Power, Horse Power, Human Power, Money Power etc., or: How Many Powers Does Man Require in Order to be Right and Truly Stuck" (Saphir), 89
Steiner, George, 86

284 | INDEX

Stewart, Susan, 4, 37, 116, 263
Stiehl, H., 184
*Stimmen der Völker in Liedern* (Herder), 7, 13–14, 52, 60, 75, 191, 191f, 204
Stone, Lauren Shizuko, 172–173
Storck, Karl, 143
Storm, Theodor, 249–250, 257
Strachwitz, Moritz von, 191, 221
Strauss, Richard, 200
Strauß und Torney, Lulu von, 251–252, 257, 259–261
Streckfuß, Karl, 95
*Studies of Oral Presentation* (Schebest), 98
*Sturm und Drang*, 11, 47, 55, 61, 201
Sturz, Helferich Peter, 51
symbolism, 160–161, 165, 260
symphonic ballad, 199–201
*Symphonische Dichtung*, 189, 204
Syv, Peder, 44, 46
Szondi, Peter, 83

Tacitus, 239–241
"tägliche Spektakel, Das," 91
Tannhäuser, 42
*Tannhäuser und der Sängerkrieg auf der Wartburg* (Wagner), 220
*Tanzlied*, 11
Tatar, Maria, 154
"Taucher, Der" (Schiller), 57–58, 85, 237
Tausig, Carl (1841-1871), 191
Taylor, Benedict, 27
Tchaikovsky, Peter Ilyich, 200
*Temora* (Macpherson), 48–49, 166
temporality, 11–12
Teniers, David, 120
"Teone" (Klopstock), 82
"Thal von Espingo, Das" (Heyse), 223–226
Thurman, Kira, 26
*Till Eulenspiegel* (Strauss), 200
Titl, Emil (1809-1882), 90
"To a Friend" (Sommer), 79–80
*Todtenschauen* (Zedlitz), 90
"Toggenburg" (Weißheimer), 199
Tönnies, Ferdinand, 22
"Totentanz, Der" (Goethe), 74–75, 89, 138, 243
tourist gaze, 239–240, 243
"Tragedy of Afghanistan, The" (Fontane), 218–219
translating orality, 65–72, 71f
transmission. *See also* literature/literacy; orality

authenticity and, 57
cultural, 33
*Declamatorium* and, 87
epic form and, 56
intergenerational (*see* family)
memory and, 134, 136–138, 144, 149
opera and, 120, 125
travel. *See* wandering ballads
Treitschke, Heinrich von, 193
Trojan, Johannes, 252–253, 255
"Trost im Unglück, Ein" (Trojan), 252–253, 255
Trumpener, Katie, 51, 75–76
"Trutz, blanke Hans" (Liliencrohn), 248
Tucholsky, Kurt, 30
*Tunnel über der Spree, Der*, 42–43, 215–225

"Über Bild, Dichtung und Fabel" (Herder), 52
"Über Deklamatoren und Deklematoria" (Semler), 88
*Überlieferungen*, 142
*Übersicht über die absolvierten Pensen* (Prof. Dr. Albrecht), 141–142
"Ueber Balladenpoesie" (Alexis), 16
"Ueber epische und dramatische Dichtung" (Goethe), 59
*Uebersicht der declamatorischen Melodiezeichnung als das einzige Mittel, Grandsätze und Regel in der Declamation herzustellan* (Schocher), 88
Uhland, Ludwig (1787-1862), 19, 21–22, 30. See also *specific works*
  *Declamatorium* and, 75
  Heine on, 20
  Pohl and, 193, 197–199
  Schumann and, 192–199
"Uhr, Die" (Seidl), 264–270
unreliable narrator, 170–172

Valentin, Karl, 269–270
*Vampyr, Der* (Marschner), 105, 111, 117
*Vätergruft, Die* (Uhland), 230–233, 232f
"Vater und Sohn" (Hebbel), 166, 177, 179–181
Vecchio, Palma, 175–177
Vedder, Ulrike, 169
*Venus in Furs* (Sacher-Masoch), 6
"Verbannte, Der" (Fontane), 219
*Vermischte Klavierstücke* (Hiller), 183
*Versuch einer critischen Dichtkunst* (Gottsched), 10
*Vertonung*, 23

"vertriebenen und zurückkehrenden Grafen, Ballade vom" (Goethe), 124
*Verzeichniss sämmtlicher in Deutschland und den agrenzenden Ländern gedruckten Misukalien* (Hofmeister), 183, 185, 190
Vesque von Püttlingen, Johann, 25
"Ritter Toggenburg" (Schiller) and, 6
Virgil, 132
Vogl, Johann Napomuk, 95
Volek, Jaroslav, 208
*Volksgeist*. See *Geist/Volksgeist*
*Volksballade*, 53–54, 138, 167, 264
*Volkslieder*, 7, 13, 25. See also *Lied*
*Volkstümlichkeit*, 22
"Vom Pagen und der Königstochter" (R. Schumann), 192–193
*Von deutscher Art und Kunst* (Herder), 13–14
"Vorgeschichte" (Droste-Hülshoff), 168–169, 172, 181
*Vorlesen*, 84–85
*Vorlesungen über Deklamation und Mimik* (Seckendorff), 82, 88
*Vorschule der Ästhetik* (Paul), 76
"Vorspiel auf dem Theater" (Goethe), 60
*Vortragsbuch für Front und Heimat* (Kober), 259
Vulpius, Christiane, 73

Wagner, Cosima, 200
Wagner, Günther, 187
Wagner, Joseph, 80
Wagner, Richard, 21, 31, 40–41, 106–108, 110–128, 184–185, 200, 220. See also *specific works*
   on ballad, 28
   Heine and, 110–111
   Liszt on, 121
   New German School and, 185–186
   Schopenhauer and, 209
Wagner, Rudolph, 226
*Wahlverwandtschaften, Die* (Goethe), 79
Walle, Taylor, 50
Wallenstein, Albrecht von, 61
"Wanda" (Heyse), 225
wandering ballads, 42, 44–56, 66, 236
Wars of Liberation, 73, 88, 98
"War Song, in Imitation of the Old Song of the Chevy Chase" (Klopstock), 11

"Wasserneck, Der" (Würst), 184
Weber, Carl Maria von, 81, 99, 105–106, 126. See also *specific works*
Weber, Max, 215
Wedekind, Frank, 30, 257–258
Weidmann, Franz Carl, 99
"Weigenlied am Lager eines kranken Kindes" (Hebbel), 178–179
Weigl, Karl, 251
Weill, Kurt, 36, 270
Weimar classicism, 61, 96
Weißert, Gottfried, 20
Weißheimer, Wendelin, 6, 186, 199
Weithase, Irmgard, 84
"Wettersäule, Die" (Kopisch), 237
White, Michael, 218
*Wilhelm Meisters Lehrjahre* (Goethe), 106
*Wilhelm Tell* (Schiller), 35
Willkür, 206–207
Winckelmann, Johann Joachim, 83
Wohlbrück, Wilhelm August, 117
Wolf, Friedrich August, 55–57
Wordsworth, William, 158
*Wreck of the Deutschland* (Hopkins), 254
"Wreck of the Hesperus, The" (Longfellow), 254–255
Wright, Julia, 256
Wright, Sylvia, 39
Würst, Richard, 184

Yates, Francis, 131

Zahn, Christoph Jacob, 58, 72
"Zauberlehrling, Der" (Goethe), 19, 29, 42, 55, 58, 62–63, 69–70, 138
Zedlitz, Johann Christian, Freiherr von, 89–92. See also *specific works*
Zelter, Carl Friedrich (1758-1832), 26, 58–59, 69–72, 71f, 193, 197
   choral ballad and, 193–194, 227
   rhythm and, 72
*Zemire und Azor* (Spohr), 105
Zerlett, Johann Baptist (1859-1935), 146
*Zukunftsmusik* (Wagner), 119
Zumsteeg, Emilie, 228
Zumsteeg, Johann Rudolf (1760-1802), 6, 21, 26, 58, 65, 69, 72, 193, 201, 212